© 2002 Algrove Publishing Limited
ALL RIGHTS RESERVED.
No part of this book may be reproduced in any for
permission in writing from the publishers, except
passages in a magazine or newspaper or on radio o

D0744796

Algrove Publishing Limited
1090 Morrison Drive
Ottawa, Ontario
Canada K2H 1C2

National Library of Canada Cataloguing in Publication Data

Downing, A. J. (Andrew Jackson), 1815-1852
    The architecture of country houses : including designs for cottages, farm-houses
and villas / by A.J. Downing.

(Classic reprint series)
Reprint. Originally published: New York : D. Appleton, 1854.
ISBN 1-894572-43-2

    1. Architecture, Domestic. 2. Cottages. 3. Farmhouses. 4. Country homes. I. Title.
II. Series: Classic reprint series (Ottawa, Ont.)

NA7561.D78 2002   728   C2002-902696-2

Printed in Canada
#21102

PUBLISHER'S NOTE

MUCH of the architecture described herein is European in origin.
The first reason is that an American style was still developing
in 1880; most architectural inspiration still drew heavily on
European experience. The second reason may be that copyright
law was not nearly as effective as it is today and it was easy to
lift drawings from other sources (Europe was the best source) to
illustrate a book like this.

Leonard G. Lee, Publisher
Ottawa
August, 2002

THE

ARCHITECTURE

OF

COUNTRY HOUSES;

INCLUDING

DESIGNS FOR COTTAGES, FARM-HOUSES, AND VILLAS,

WITH

REMARKS ON INTERIORS, FURNITURE, AND THE BEST MODES OF WARMING
AND VENTILATING.

With Three Hundred and Twenty Illustrations.

BY A. J. DOWNING,

AUTHOR OF "DESIGNS FOR COTTAGE RESIDENCES," "HINTS TO PERSONS ABOUT
BUILDING," ETC.

THIRTEENTH THOUSAND.

NEW-YORK:
D. APPLETON & CO., 346 & 348 BROADWAY.
M.DCCC.LIV.

TO

Henry Winthrop Sargent, Esq.,

OF WODENETHE, ON THE HUDSON

WITH THE SINCERE REGARD OF

The Author.

PREFACE.

THERE are three excellent reasons why my countrymen should have good houses.

The first is, because a good house (and by this I mean a fitting, tasteful, and significant dwelling) is a powerful means of civilization. A nation, whose rural population is content to live in mean huts and miserable hovels, is certain to be behind its neighbors in education, the arts, and all that makes up the external signs of progress. With the perception of proportion, symmetry, order, and beauty, awakens the desire for possession, and with them comes that refinement of manners which distinguishes a civilized from a coarse and brutal people. So long as men are forced to dwell in log huts and follow a hunter's life, we must not be surprised at lynch law and the use of the bowie knife. But, when smiling lawns and tasteful cottages begin to embellish a country, we know that order and culture are established. And, as the first incentive towards this change is awakened in the minds of most men by the perception of beauty and superiority in external objects, it must follow that the interest manifested in, the Rural Architecture of a country like this, has much to do with the progress of its civilization.

The second reason is, because the *individual home* has a great social value for a people. Whatever new systems may be needed for the regeneration of an old and enfeebled nation, we are persuaded that, in America, not only is the distinct family the best social form, but those elementary forces which give rise to the highest genius and the finest character may, for the most part, be traced back to the farm-house and the rural cottage. It is the solitude and freedom of the family home in the country which constantly preserves the purity of the nation, and invigorates its intellectual powers. The battle of life, carried on in cities, gives a sharper edge to the weapon of character, but its temper is, for the most part, fixed amid those communings with nature and the family, where individuality takes its most natural and strongest development.

The third reason is, because there is a moral influence in a country home—when, among an educated, truthful, and refined people, it is an echo of their character—which is more powerful than any mere oral teachings of virtue and morality. That family, whose religion lies away from its threshold, will show but slender results from the best teachings, compared with another where the family hearth is made a central point of the Beautiful and the Good. And much of that feverish unrest and want of balance between the desire and the fulfilment of life, is calmed and adjusted by the pursuit of tastes which result in making a little world of the family home, where truthfulness, beauty, and order have the largest dominion.

The mere sentiment of home, with its thousand associations, has, like a strong anchor, saved many a man from shipwreck in the storms of life. How much the moral influence of that sentiment may be increased, by making the home all that it should be, and how much an attachment is strengthened by every external sign of beauty that awakens love in the young, are so well understood, that they need no demonstration here. All to which the heart can attach itself in youth, and the memory linger fondly over in riper years, contributes largely to our stock of happiness, and to the elevation of the moral character. For this reason, the condition of the family home—in this country where every man may have a home—should be raised, till it shall symbolize the best character and pursuits, and the dearest affections and enjoyments of social life.

After the volumes I have previously written on this subject, it is needless for me to add more on the purpose of this work. But it is, perhaps, proper that I should say, that it is rather intended to develop the growing taste of the people, than as a scientific work on art. Rural Architecture is, indeed, so much more a sentiment, and so much less a science, than Civil Architecture, that the majority of persons will always build for themselves, and, unconsciously, throw something of their own character into their dwellings. To do this well and gracefully, and not awkwardly and clumsily, is always found more difficult than is supposed. I have, therefore, written this volume, in the hope that it may be of some little assistance to the popular taste. For the same reason, I have endeavored to explain the whole subject in so familiar a manner, as to interest all classes of readers who can find any thing interesting in the beauty, conven- ience, or fitness of a house in the country.   A. J. D.

Newburgh, on the Hudson.
    June, 1850.

CONTENTS

PART I.

SECTION I.

ON THE REAL MEANING OF ARCHITECTURE.

SECTION II.

WHAT A COTTAGE SHOULD BE.

SECTION III.

MATERIALS AND MODES OF CONSTRUCTION.

SECTION IV.

DESIGNS FOR COTTAGES.

SECTION V.

WHAT A FARM-HOUSE SHOULD BE.

SECTION VI.

DESIGNS FOR FARM-HOUSES.

SECTION VII.

MISCELLANEOUS DETAILS.

PART II.

SECTION IX.

WHAT A COUNTRY HOUSE OR VILLA SHOULD BE.

SECTION X.

DESIGNS FOR VILLAS OR COUNTRY HOUSES.

SECTION XI.

INTERIOR FINISHING OF COUNTRY HOUSES.

SECTION XII.

FURNITURE.

SECTION XIII.

WARMING AND VENTILATING.

PART I.

COTTAGES AND FARM-HOUSES.

COUNTRY HOUSES.

SECTION I.

ON THE REAL MEANING OF ARCHITECTURE.

CERTAINLY the national taste is not a matter of little moment. Whether another planet shall be discovered beyond Le Verrier's may or may not affect the happiness of a whole country; but whether a young and progressive people shall develop ideas of beauty, harmony, and moral significance in their daily lives; whether the arts shall be so understood and cultivated as to elevate and dignify the character; whether the country homes of a whole people shall embody such ideas of beauty and truth as shall elevate and purify its feelings;—these are questions of no mean or trifling importance.

Now, the real progress which a people makes in any of the fine arts, must depend on the public sensibility and the public taste. Sensibility to beauty must exist, and there must be some means afforded of developing and cultivating the taste; for, however instinctive and natural a gift the former may be, a correct taste is only the result of education: the feeling must be guided by the judgment.

While a general ignorance on the subject of architecture among us, must be admitted, we must also avow that the live-

1

liest interest in it is now strongly felt on all sides. And this very ignorance is mainly owing to the dry and barren manner in which architects have usually written on the real meaning or philosophy of their art. It would seem that men who work out beautiful thoughts in ponderous stone, seldom wield so slight an implement as a pen with grace and power. Why else should nine-tenths of even the educated, believe that the whole circle of architecture is comprised in the five Orders; or, at most, that a Greek temple and a Gothic cathedral are the Alpha and Omega of the art? Why should so many of the most intelligent persons imagine, that Domestic Architecture is only perfect when it is similar to that of public edifices; or, at least, when it borrows all its ornaments from such structures?

It is not an easy task to lay bare the principles of an art, compounded thus of the Useful and the Beautiful; to show how and why it appeals so powerfully to the whole nature of man—to his senses, his heart, and his understanding.

But it is, perhaps, this very compound nature of Architecture, this appeal which it makes to the sensation, the sentiment, and the knowledge of man, which has left it in so unsatisfactory a shape to the popular apprehension; which has caused it to be looked upon by some as the mere province of the builder; by others, as the object of enthusiastic admiration, and by the rest as a subject of scientific investigation; until half the world imagines the beauty of an edifice, like genius, to be a happy accident, to be enjoyed when found, but as difficult to seize as the rainbow itself.

It would be a boon to the age, if some gifted artist would show the world the secret sources of the influence which Architecture wields in all civilized nations. This is as far beyond our province as our ability. Still, we must be indulged in a brief analysis of the elements of interest which Architecture possesses for the human mind, and a glance at the partially concealed sources of that power which it exerts over our hearts and understandings.

Something of this kind seems to us to be demanded by the inquiring mind and the expanding taste of our people; and Domestic Architecture itself, which, amid the louder claims of civil and ecclesiastical art, has been too much neglected, seems to demand a higher consideration in a country where the ease of obtaining a house and land, and the ability of almost every industrious citizen to build his own house, constitute a distinctive feature of national prosperity.

THE USEFUL IN ARCHITECTURE.

The senses make the first demand in almost every path in human life. The necessity of shelter from the cold and heat, from sun and shower, leads man at first to *build a habitation*.

What this habitation shall be, depends partly on the habits of the man, partly on the climate in which he lives. If he is a shepherd and leads a wandering life, he pitches a tent. If he is a hunter, he builds a rude hut of logs or skins. If he is a tiller of the soil, he constructs a dwelling of timber or stones, or lodges in the caverns of the rocky hill-sides.

As a mere animal, man's first necessity is to provide shelter; and, as he is not governed by the constructive instinct of other animals, the clumsiest form which secures him against the inclemency of the seasons, often appears sufficient: there is scarcely any design apparent in its arrangement, and the smallest amount of convenience is found in its interior. This is the first, primitive, or savage idea of building. Let us look a step higher in the scale of improvement.

On the eastern borders of Europe is a tribe or nation of the Sclavonic people, called the Croats, who may be said to be only upon the verge of civilization. They lead a rude, forest, and agricultural life. They know nothing of the refinements of the rest of Europe. They live in coarse, yet strong and warm houses. But their apartments are as rude as their manners, and their cattle frequently share the same rooms with themselves.

Our third example may be found in any portion of the United States. It is nothing less common than a plain, rectangular house, built of timber from the forest saw-mill, with a roof to cover it, windows to light it, and doors to enter it. The heat is kept out by shutters, and the cold by fires burnt in chimneys. It is well and strongly built; it affords perfect protection to the physical nature of man; and it serves, so far as a house can serve, all the most imperative wants of the body. It is a warm, comfortable, convenient dwelling.

It is easy to see that in all these grades of man's life, and the dwellings which typify them, only one idea has as yet manifested itself in his architecture—viz. that of utility. In the savage, the half civilized, and the civilized states, the idea of the useful and the convenient differ, but only in degree. It is still what will best serve the body—what will best shelter, lodge, feed, and warm us—which demands the whole attention of the mere builder of houses.

It would be as false to call only this, Architecture, as to call the gamut music, or to consider rhymes poetry, and yet it is the framework or skeleton on which Architecture grows and wakens into life; without which, indeed, it can no more rise to the dignity of a fine art, than perfect language can exist without sounds.

There are also certain principles which belong to *building* (as this useful part of Architecture is properly called), which are of the utmost importance, since they may not be in the slightest degree violated without proving more or less destructive to the enjoyment of the finest work.

Many of these are mechanical principles involved in masonry, in carpentry, and other kinds of artisanship, which are sufficiently familiar in their nature to the general reader, and are subjects of technical expertness on the part of those employed in building.

But there are also other principles besides these, which govern the workmen in their labors, and which must always control even him who only aims at the useful in Architecture.

The first and most obvious of these rules of utility is, that the cost of the building shall not exceed the means of the owner or occupant. Out of a want of practical knowledge in the builder grow, not unfrequently, mistakes that are fatal to the use of a house, since, if too much is expended in the whole structure, the owner may be forced to sell it to another, rather than enjoy it himself: if too much is expended on a part, the economy necessary in the remainder, may render parts of the house uncomfortable from defects in their construction.

The second rule governs the quality of the materials and workmanship employed in the construction. That the materials should be of the soundest and best quality in the best edifices, and of ample strength and durability for the end in view, even in those of the humblest class, is a rule which may never be for a moment violated by the builder, without injury to the structure. Nature here, as always, must be constantly respected, or she punishes severely all infringements of her laws. A wall that is not perpendicular, a foundation that is not firm, a roof that is not tight, a chimney that smokes, sooner or later, but inevitably, shows the builder's want of comprehension or respect for the laws of gravitation or the atmosphere, and impairs or destroys the usefulness of all architecture.

The last and highest rule of utility is that which involves convenience. In all architecture, adaptation to the end in view is important; in domestic architecture it is a principle which, in its influence on our daily lives, our physical comfort and enjoyment, is paramount and imperative. Hence, however full of ornament or luxury a house may be, if its apartments do not afford that convenience, comfort, and adaptation to human wants, which the habits of those who are to live in it demand, it must always fail to satisfy us, or to merit the approval of the most matter-of-fact critic. Such a house may be compared to a column with well-moulded shaft and richly decorated capital, but composed of such flimsy material that it will bear no weight; or, to a person whose education has been that of accomplishments, with a total neglect of solid acquirements.

This practical part of architecture involves, more particularly, what is called the plan of a building—providing apartments for the various wants of domestic and social life; adapting the size of such apartments to their respective uses, and all other points which the progress of modern civilization has made necessary to our comfort and enjoyment within-doors.

The illustration of these points will be found, to a considerable extent, in the treatment of the various designs which follow. It may be remarked, however, that no absolute rules for guidance can be laid down here. Domestic life varies not only in different countries, but even in different portions of a territory so broad as that of the United States. Even different families have somewhat various habits, and therefore require different accommodations. The ingenuity and talents of the architect must therefore be put in full activity, even to meet the requirements of this humblest platform of his art. And we may add, that it is a proof of weakness rather than strength, to treat with the slightest neglect, this, its wholly utilitarian side. To the majority of mankind the *useful* is the largest satisfaction derived from architecture; and while an able architect will always treat the materials placed in his hands for a new design, so as to give something of the expression of beauty even to the simplest forms, he must never imagine that in his art he can largely neglect the useful for the beautiful. As in the Apollo every muscle must be found which enters into the body of the hardiest day-laborer, so in all perfect architecture no principle of utility will be found sacrificed to beauty, but only elevated and ennobled by it.

THE BEAUTIFUL IN ARCHITECTURE.

We have shown as yet, only the Useful in architecture. At least, we have endeavored to show how an edifice may combine fitness in all respects, how it may be strong, well built, warm, comfortable, and convenient, and no more. To attain this there is no need of its displaying any appreciable grace, harmony, or beauty; nay, it may be even faulty in its proportions, and unpleasing in effect. Such examples are, in fact, every day before us—buildings which completely answer the useful requirements of man, and yet give not a ray of pleasure or satisfaction to his heart or understanding. And yet there are persons who, because the Useful and the Beautiful, in some arts, may be most intimately combined, imagine that they are identical. This is the grossest error, of which, if the commonplace buildings we have just quoted are not a sufficient refutation, abundant others may be drawn every day from the works of nature or art.

A head of grain, one of the most useful of vegetable forms, is not so beautiful as a rose; an ass, one of the most useful of animals, is not so beautiful as a gazelle; a cotton-mill, one of the most useful of modern structures, is not so beautiful as the temple of Vesta; yet no one thinks of comparing them for utility.

The truth then is undeniable, that the Beautiful is, intrinsically, something quite distinct from the Useful. It appeals to a wholly different part of our nature; it requires another portion of our being to receive and enjoy it.

There are many, to whose undeveloped natures the Useful is

sufficient; but there are, also, not a few who yearn, with an instinct as strong as for life itself, for the manifestation of a higher attribute of matter—the Beautiful.

We have said that the Useful in architecture is based wholly on the physical wants of man; that it is a response to the demand of our senses.

We may also add that the Beautiful is an original instinct of the sentiment of our nature. It is a worship, by the heart, of a higher perfection manifested in material forms.

To see, or rather to feel how, in nature, matter is ennobled by being thus touched by a single thought of beauty, how it is almost deified by being made to shadow forth, even dimly, His attributes, constitutes the profound and thrilling satisfaction which we experience in contemplating the external works of God. To be keenly sensible of the power of even the imperfect reproduction of such ideas in the various fine arts—poetry, music, painting, sculpture, architecture, etc.—is to acknowledge the power of beauty over our feelings in another and a more personal form.

To desire to surround ourselves with such sources of enjoyment, rather than to be content with mere utility, is only to acknowledge the existence of a sentiment which, next to the religious one, is the purest and noblest part of our nature.

Looking at the subject before us, it must be admitted, that if it is a step forward in civilization to separate ourselves from our cattle, rather than share our apartments with them, like the Croats, it is a much higher step to evince, by the beauty of our architecture, that our hearts are alive to some of the highest emotions of which they are capable.

What is beauty in architecture? In order to rid ourselves

of the vague and indefinite meaning which hangs about this part of our subject, like a thick mist, in the minds of most persons, let us examine it somewhat closely.

All beauty in architecture seems to us to resolve itself into two kinds—*Absolute* and *Relative*.

ABSOLUTE BEAUTY lies in the expression, in material forms, of those ideas of perfection which are universal in their application. We find them in nature as well as in art. We find them in the figures of the heavenly bodies, in the orbits of planets, in drops of water, in animal forms, in the growth of trees, in the structures of crystals. This proves not only that they are divine in their origin, but that they pervade all time and space. These typical ideas of beauty are PROPORTION, SYMMETRY, VARIETY, HARMONY, and UNITY. They may be called abstract ideas of beauty of form, and apply to all the arts, as well as to every thing in nature—to a symphony of Beethoven or a statue by Powers, as well as to the sublime curve of Niagara or the varied outlines of the Alps.

In order that the uninitiated reader may be able to analyze and understand these universal ideas of Beauty, let us look at them, architecturally, a little in detail.

A fundamental idea of the Beautiful in architecture is Proportion.

PROPORTION, in material objects, is the relation of individual parts to the whole. Mr. Ruskin has cleverly defined it to be "the sensible relation of quantities." In all the arts, it is the realization of the most perfect idea of the height, breadth, outline, and form of the object aimed at, and therefore involves the highest single feeling of pure material beauty.

In architecture, proportion is shown first in the composition

of the outline or mass of the entire building. If endowed with
this quality, it will neither be too long nor too broad, too low
nor too high. It will exhibit to the eye, at a glance, that nice
relation of all the parts to each other and to the whole, which
gives to that whole the stamp of the best, most suitable, and
perfect form.

Proportion may be shown in the smallest building as well as
in the largest; in a cottage of twenty feet as well as in St.
Peter's of ten acres. In the former, however, it is much more
simple, as it involves only the height and breadth of a few
parts: in the latter, it is evolved by the skilful grouping of
many parts. Hence, in large piles of buildings, the central
mass is raised up in a dome-like or pyramidal form, not only for
the sake of making a whole, but also to give that proportion of
the whole which great extent and the multiplication of parts
render necessary. But proportion does not merely govern the
form of the whole mass in architecture; it descends into the
smallest details. It demands that the height of a room, of a
window, or a door, should accord with its breadth and length
The minutest object, the smallest details, are equally capable of
expressing it. It applies as well to the form of a cornice, a
moulding, or an ornament, as to the whole outline of the edifice
itself.

Proportion, in architecture, has been aptly likened, by a
German writer, to time in music—that measure which confers
a completeness of form on the entire melody; and though the
parallel cannot be carried so closely as to enable us strictly to
agree with Madame de Staël, who called architecture " frozen
music," the illustration is scarcely less forcible.

That proportion is one of those qualities of beauty most

universally felt, it does not require any argument of ours to prove. The immediate delight which all persons experience in a well-proportioned human figure, a statue, or a Grecian column, is well known. That this is quite independent of education, that it only requires sensibility to beauty, is equally true. Hence the want of proportion in a building is felt as a great and irremediable defect, at the first glance, by many who are totally ignorant of architecture as an art; and hence, if absent, it is a fundamental want, for which no decoration, no style, no beauty of parts, however excellent in themselves, can ever wholly compensate.

One would suppose that some definite rules would have been deduced for the production of so fundamental a quality as this, in architecture.* But no such rules exist at the present day, and its production seems to depend mainly on the genius of the artist. That education and study of the best examples will aid in the appreciation of it, is undoubtedly true; but the many blunders in proportion, which the works of modern artists exhibit, prove that it is one of the qualities of beauty less vividly felt, and less easily produced, than any other, at the present time.

SYMMETRY is that quality of beauty in material objects which may be defined, that balance of *opposite parts* necessary to form an agreeable whole. Thus, in the human figure, it is the joining of the opposite sides, each with its separate limbs, which makes the whole symmetrical: if an arm is wanting, the symmetry is destroyed. In trees, it is seen in the balance of the op-

---

* Mr. Hay, of Edinburgh, in his ingenious treatise on Beauty of Form, has endeavored to prove that the Greeks, whose architecture certainly displays the most perfect *proportions*, were possessed of a system of rules which enabled them uniformly to produce it.

posite sides of their heads: if a large limb is cut away, the balance is lost. In architecture, it is the arrangement on each side of a centre, of two parts that balance each other, and that do not make a whole without this centre. Hence the superior effect of a building which is a plain cube with a wing on each side, over a cube without wings. The wings raise the character of the form from uniformity to symmetry.

This leads us to remark here, that regularity and uniformity, two qualities common in architecture, are often classed as distinct elements of beauty in themselves. They may be such, in an artistical point of view, as denoting the presence of art, but they are, in fact, only primary steps towards symmetry, which comprehends them both. A *regular* building in architecture is one in which a given form is repeated at regular distances, such as a square house in which the same windows and doors are repeated at regular intervals, or a long row of houses in a street, in which the same general forms are regularly repeated.

A *uniform* building is one in which the same forms are repeated on all sides; as a cubical house with the same windows all round, or a block formed of two or more houses exactly alike, and placed side by side.

Symmetry involves something more. It asks for a central part, which shall connect the two other parts into a whole, and thereby make something involving a more complete idea than regularity and uniformity. Thus Design VI is a symmetrical cottage, from the front of which neither the central part nor the sides can be taken away without destroying the composition as a whole. The difference between this and a regular or a uniform building of the same length, is that the latter might be divided into several parts, each of which is equally regular and uniform, and therefore as complete in itself as the whole building.

Symmetry is one of the greatest beauties in all architecture. The author of "Modern Painters" conceives it to be the symbol of *abstract justice ;* and certainly, in material forms, when joined to proportion, it conveys at once an idea of completeness of form, which gives universal satisfaction. The Grecian temples owe to these two elements their great and lasting power over the human mind for so many ages; for it is a beauty which may be bestowed on a cottage, a villa, or indeed any kind of building; and as it is one which appeals intuitively to every mind, it is never neglected by artists who wish to impress the Beautiful upon their works.

Symmetry is quite distinct from proportion. It is only necessary to remember that it is a balance made between opposite parts, and that proportion is the relation between all the parts, to comprehend it more clearly. Thus, a statue may be perfectly symmetrical on all sides, and yet too short or too high in its proportions. The central part of a symmetrical building, like that in Design VI., might be raised or lowered several feet, without injuring the symmetry of the composition, though the proportion would be at once destroyed.

It has been justly said, that though symmetry is not the highest quality of beauty, yet no object can be perfectly beautiful without it. Hence, in many beautiful objects, where, from the nature of the structure or purposes, exact or regular symmetry is impossible, a certain balance must be found, before they can give full satisfaction. There are, then, in nature and art, two kinds of symmetry; that which is regular, and strikes us at a glance, like that of a poplar or fir tree whose limbs are equal on all sides of the head; and that which is irregular, such as we see in a spreading oak with branches unequal, but forming altogether a head which is equally symmetrical with respect to the trunk.

The strict application of the principle of a regular balance of parts, as it would be deduced from our remarks, would prevent our finding any symmetry in all irregular buildings. But in fact this is not the case. The most irregular building, if composed by an artist of genius, will always evince symmetry; that is to say, it will form an outline, in which there will be a central portion or point, which unites two sides into one symmetrical whole; two parts, which, if they do not balance each other in exact forms and proportions as in regular symmetry, do balance in the general impression which they make on the eye, in the mass and grouping of the composition. The villas in Designs XXI., XXII., are examples of irregular symmetry, and may be compared with the symmetrical villas, in some of the other designs. Any building so irregular as not to show some recognition of this principle of irregular symmetry, can never be called beautiful, though it may be strikingly odd or grotesque.

We may remark here, that buildings in an irregular style, highly expressive of irregular symmetry, are much more striking in a picturesque point of view, and are therefore preferred by many artists. They are more expressive of character and individuality (in other words, of relative beauty) than of abstract or universal beauty; and while they are, perhaps, not so agreeable to the universal mind, they are far more so to certain mental organizations. We may also add, that irregular symmetry can rarely be expressed, with much success, in a

small edifice. It requires considerable extent, and the introduction of a variety of parts, to enable one to introduce this quality,
in a manner altogether satisfactory, in a dwelling of small size.
For this reason those cottages and small villas give the greatest
pleasure, in which proportion and regular symmetry are the
prevailing elements of beauty.

VARIETY, though always a subordinate, is still an essential
quality of absolute beauty. As, in nature, it gives richness and
interest to landscape, to sky, to the vegetable and animal king-
doms, so, in art, it adds to the interest of the whole by the
diversity which it affords in the arrangement, sizes, or forms of
the different parts. In architecture, variety is of the greatest
value, often preventing simple forms from degenerating into
baldness, or plain broad surfaces from being monotonous, by its
power in the arrangement or the decoration of details; for it
is in the details of regular and symmetrical buildings, such as
the cornices, mouldings, etc., that variety is chiefly to be
introduced. In irregular buildings there may also be variety
in the various parts, projections, recesses, towers, etc. A slight
difference in the forms, sizes, or decorations of certain parts
of a building, is sufficient to give it an expression of variety,
and by the judicious employment of this quality, every architect is able to increase the beauty of his whole composition.
But it should be remembered that in architecture, even more
than in the other arts, it must be kept under the control of the
judgment, since, if carried to a great length, it leads to confusion, the result of which is always painful and destructive of all
beauty. Intricacy, which is a complex sort of variety, is therefore to be avoided in domestic architecture, as likely to become
wearisome and perplexing.

HARMONY is an element of beauty little understood, though in the highest degree necessary to our enjoyment of all complicated or elaborate productions. It may be defined, an agreement made in the midst of the variety of forms, sounds, or colors, by some one feeling which pervades the whole and brings all the varied parts into an agreeable relation with each other.

Thus, in landscapes involving the utmost variety of colors and forms, the softening effect of the atmosphere spread over them brings all into harmony: in music, changes of opposite character are brought into harmony by dominant chords: in painting, strong contrasts of colors are introduced, not only without discord, but with a most powerful and agreeable effect, by the introduction of some other tint or some pervading tone that brings the whole into harmony.

In architecture, harmony, in its highest sense, is only possible in buildings of considerable extent, where there is sufficient variety of form and outline in the parts to demand its presence. In simple and regular buildings, when the same forms are repeated with little or no variation throughout, harmony cannot exist, because there is no tendency to confusion or disagreement; and the beauty of harmony is only felt when it so presides over all, like the charm of a golden temper, or the glow of a rich sunset, as to bring every thing it touches under the influence of its magical power for unison.

As simple examples of the production of harmony, we may mention the Ionic column, in which the agreement between the circular lines of the shaft and the straight line of the entablature is brought about by the intermediate, partly straight and partly curved lines of the volutes. In Gothic architecture, the square-headed door and window heads are made to harmonize with

those of pointed form, by introducing an arched spandril
under the square-head. A rosette in the middle of a square
ceiling, is out of harmony with it; but it may be made to
harmonize, by surrounding it with a border in which the two
forms are ingeniously blended. The façade of a villa in which a
round tower is joined to the square angles of straight walls, is
destitute of harmony; but harmony is made by repeating the
same feeling of the beauty of the curve in the arched windows.
(See the Norman villa—Design XXI.) In Mr. King's villa, at
Newport (succeeding page), the architect has introduced a
variety of Italian window forms. The effect would be discordant, were it not that the arched or round-headed window
predominates over all, and brings out of this great variety a
complete harmony.

Examples of this kind might be multiplied to an endless
extent, but we have said enough to suggest how the presence
of this predominant feeling gives unity and completeness to a
whole composition, which, without it, would only show tasteless
diversity and discord.

In domestic architecture, the feeling of harmony is more demanded, and more easily evinced in the interiors than in the
exteriors of houses—because the interiors show a greater variety
of lines, forms, and colors; or in the shape and arrangement of
the rooms; or in their architectural decorations, and their furniture. Harmony is evinced in all these cases, by rejecting all
forms, outlines, and colors that do not intrinsically admit of
being brought into harmonious agreement with each other.
Harmony may pervade an entire mansion, so that all its portions
and details exhibit the most complete agreement throughout, or
it may be confined to each apartment, extending its influence

only over the various objects which enter into its composition. As regularity is the simplest quality of absolute beauty, and the first recognized, even by those of least sensibility to the beautiful, so harmony, being the most complex, is the last recognized, and usually requires some cultivation to lead us to its full perception. We see, every day, buildings in which symmetry and proportion are not wanting; but those in which we find these united to variety, and the whole pervaded by harmony, are comparatively rare.

It by no means follows, however, that SIMPLICITY is without its charms, because harmony, which can only grow out of the display of a greater variety than simple forms admit, involves a higher charm. On the contrary, the pleasure which in a small building we derive from simplicity or chasteness, is far greater than that derived from the pretension of harmony, since, in a small cottage, there is no legitimate reason for variety.

It is plain, therefore, that proportion and symmetry are the proper sources of beauty in a cottage of small size, and that we should look for variety and harmony only in private dwellings of a larger size, where there is opportunity for the production of these elements.

UNITY is the highest idea or quality of abstract beauty, for it comprehends, includes, and governs all the others. It is the predominance of one single feeling, one soul, one mind in every portion, so that, whether of the simplest or the most complicated form, the same spirit is recognized throughout the whole.

To understand the value of Unity, we may suppose a building finely proportioned, symmetrical, varied, and harmonious, and yet composed of such different and unsuitable materials as to have no unity of substance; or of different though perhaps harmonious kinds of architecture, so as to have no unity of style; or of different hues, so as to have no unity of color; or, in character, partly a cottage, partly a farm-house, and partly a villa, so as to have no unity of expression. Ideas of beauty, of various kinds, there certainly would be in such buildings, but no unity—nothing to indicate that they sprang from a single comprehensive feeling, or from one wise and consistent mind.

RELATIVE BEAUTY. Having shown the qualities of simple or absolute beauty—the sources of our pleasure in what is commonly called "beauty of form," we turn to the consideration of relative beauty—that beauty which expresses peculiar moral, social, or intellectual ideas. and which is usually termed "beauty of expression."

Relative Beauty, in architecture, is the expression of elevated and refined ideas of man's life. In this art, its first and most powerful expressions are those of his public life, or his religious and intellectual nature—in the temple, the church, or the library or gallery of art—all forms of Civil Architecture. Its secondary expression is confined to the manifestation of his social and moral feelings, in the dwellings which man inhabits; and this is Domestic Architecture.

We cannot better convey an idea of the beauty of expression of which the grander generic forms or styles of architecture are capable, than by the following brief description by another hand.*

---

* Literary World

" In the forms of the Gothic cathedral are embodied *the worshipping principle, the loving reverence for that which is highest, and the sentiment of Christian brotherhood*, or that perception of affiliation which is founded on recognizing in man goodness and truth, and reverencing them in him. This is expressed in the principal lines, which are all vertical [aspiring, tending upward]; in the whole mass falling under, or within the *pyramidal* (the fire, or symbol of love) form ; in the pointed character of all the openings, *ogive*, as the French call it, being the ideal line expressive of firmness of base, embracingness of tendency, and upward ascension, as its ultimate aim; and in the clustering and grouping of its multiple parts. Gothic architecture being thus representative rather of the Unity of Love, than of the diversities of Faith, it seems proper that it should be the style used for all ecclesiastical and other purposes having reference to religious life.

" But it is not Gothic art, alone, that has developed the form of some principle of life : all architecture is as expressive. In Roman art, we see the ideal of the *state* as fully manifested as is in the Gothic the ideal of the church. Its type-form is the *dome*—the encircling, overspreading dome, whose centre is within itself, and which is the binding of all for the perfection of the whole. Hence the propriety of using this style in state-houses, capitols, parliament-houses, town-halls, where this idea is to be expressed.

" Again, we have the pure Greek temple as another architectural type. This can also be used in a special way (having its individual expression). It is the most simple, rational, and harmoniously elegant style, that can be conceived, for simple halls, for public, oratorical, lecture, and philosophical rooms

Buildings which have but one object, and which require one expression of that object, cannot be built in a style better adapted to convey the single idea of their use, than in the Grecian-temple form. Here, with the single exception of the pediment (which distinctly, by its outline, marked the place as the abode of the gods, and the tympanum, which was always occupied by statues of the highest intelligence, and the representative arrangement of all deities expressive of the perfect subordination of all principles, human and divine, under the supremacy of Almighty Love), every thing falls under the *horizontal line*,—the level line of rationality; it is all logical, orderly, syllogistically perfect, as the wisdom of the schools."

In Domestic Architecture, though the range of expression may at first seem limited, it is not so in fact, for when complete, it ought to be significant of the whole private life of man —his intelligence, his feelings, and his enjoyments.

Indeed, it is from this complexity of feelings and habits, that Domestic Architecture is capable of a great variety of expression. This will not appear singular when we reflect that public buildings, for the most part, are intended for a single and definite use—as a church for public worship, or a town-hall for political assemblies; while man's dwelling, in its most complete form, may be regarded as the type of his whole private life. It is true, the private life of many men is simple almost to monotony, but that of others abounds with infinite diversity.

Now, all this variety, in domestic life, is capable of being expressed, and really is expressed, in Domestic Architecture, especially in Country Architecture, which is not cramped in its manifestation, but develops itself freely, as a tree expands which is not crowded by neighbors in a forest, but grows in the unrestrained liberty of the open meadow.

If we pass an ill-proportioned dwelling, where the walls and the roof are built only to defend the inmates against cold and heat; the windows intended for nothing but to admit the light and exclude the air; the chimneys constructed only to carry off the smoke; the impression which that house makes upon us at a glance, is that of mere utility.

If, on the other hand, the building is well proportioned, if there is a pleasing symmetry in its outward form, and (should it be large) if it display variety, harmony, and unity, we feel that it possesses much absolute beauty—the beauty of a fine form.

If, in addition to this, we observe that it has various marked features, indicating intelligent and cultivated life in its inhabitants; if it plainly shows by its various apartments, that it is intended not only for the physical wants of man, but for his moral, social, and intellectual existence; if hospitality smiles in ample parlors; if home virtues dwell in cosy, fireside family-rooms; if the love of the beautiful is seen in picture or statue galleries; intellectuality, in well-stocked libraries; and even a dignified love of leisure and repose, in cool and spacious verandas; we feel, at a glance, that here we have reached the highest beauty of which Domestic Architecture is capable—that of individual expression.

Hence, every thing in architecture that can suggest or be made a symbol of social or domestic virtues, adds to its beauty, and exalts its character. Every material object that becomes the type of the spiritual, moral, or intellectual nature of man, becomes at once beautiful, because it is suggestive of the beautiful in human nature.

There are, doubtless, many persons who rarely analyze their feelings, and who usually see nothing of this beauty of expression in domestic architecture—they see only the fact that a house is a house (more or less costly, and therefore to be admired), a window a window, and a door a door: these are those who pay no attention to expression in nature—a daisy-spangled meadow is to them only a "field," or the most poetical landscape, only a "prospect;"—those who never see their friends' characters in their faces, only in the *facts* of their lives. But this no more proves that the expression does not exist in all visible forms, than that the earth is not round because common observation tells us it is flat.

More than this, beauty of expression, in architecture, as in other arts, and even in nature, requires educated feeling—it is as obscure and imperceptible to the majority of those who have never sought for it, as the beauty of clouds or aerial perspective in landscapes is to the most ignorant ploughman in the fields.

We are bound to add here, that in all arts, other thoughts may be expressed besides those of beauty. Vices may be expressed in architecture as well as virtues; the worst part of our natures as well as the best. A house built only with a view to animal wants, eating and drinking, will express sensuality instead of hospitality. A residence marked by gaudy and garish apartments, intended only to dazzle and impress others with the wealth or importance of the proprietor, will express pride and vanity instead of a real love of what is beautiful for its own sake; and a dwelling in which a large and conspicuous part is kept for show, to delude others into the belief of dignity and grace on our part, while our actual life is one in mean apartments, expresses any thing but honest sincerity of character.

It requires the more judgment to guard against the effect of such vicious expression, because it is often coupled with some beauty. A house may be copied after a pure model, and thus possess absolute beauty in the fine symmetry and proportion of its leading forms, and yet be debased in certain parts by the expression of the pride, vanity, egotism, or other bad traits of its possessors.

Yet, after all, this, like all other manifestations of the individual man, while it has a tendency to degrade art, gives us the key to the character of the artist and the possessor. And we often find that the want of virtue and beauty of character in the owner of a house which is beautiful, because designed by other hands (a want which almost certainly shows itself in the details or the furniture), deadens or destroys its beauty by overlaying its fair features with a corrupt or vicious expression.

After these remarks, it will not appear singular to our readers, that we believe much of the character of every man may be read in his house. If he has moulded its leading features from the foundation, it will give a clue to a large part of his character. If he has only taken it from other hands, it will, in its internal details and use, show, at a glance, something of the daily thoughts and life of the family that inhabits it.

Admitting the truth of this, it is evident that Domestic Architecture is only perfect when it is composed so as to express the utmost beauty and truth in the life of the individual. It is not always that a proprietor can design his own house, or even that his architect knows him so completely as to make his work express the individual truly. Hence we seldom see entirely satisfactory architecture, where a beautiful house fully reflects a fine character; but as character always makes its mark, something of this kind always does happen, and in proportion to its completeness does it heighten our pleasure.*

The different *styles* of Domestic Architecture, as the Roman, the Italian, the Swiss, the Venetian, the Rural Gothic, are nothing more than expressions of national character, which have, through long use, become permanent. Thus, the gay and sunny temperament of the south of Europe is well expressed in the light balconies, the grouped windows, the open arcades, and the statue and vase bordered terraces of the Venetian and Italian villas: the homely, yet strong and quaint character of the Swiss, in their broad-roofed, half rude, and curiously constructed cottages: the domestic virtues, the love of home, rural beauty, and seclusion, cannot possibly be better expressed than in the English cottage, with its many upward-pointing gables, its intricate tracery, its spacious bay windows, and its walls covered with vines and flowering shrubs.

There are positive and human elements of beauty in these styles which appeal at once to the feelings. But there is,

---

* Hence, also, it is impossible in a series of designs, like those which follow, to make any one of them entirely satisfactory, as a residence, to any individual of taste. To do this, the architect must know the man. All that we can do, is to offer to the feelings and judgment of our readers a number of designs. If their own character is more or less typified in any one of them, that design will be at once preferred by them.

besides, another source of pleasure to most minds, which springs not from the beauty of form or expression in these styles of architecture, but from personal or historical *associations* connected with them; and which, by a process half addressed to the feelings and half to the intellect, makes them in the highest degree interesting to us. Something too of novelty and strangeness makes mere *style* in architecture, like accent in a foreign language, captivating to those whose love of novelty is stronger than their love of what is intrinsically beautiful. So far as an admiration of foreign style in architecture arises from the mere love of novelty, it is poor and contemptible; so far as it arises from an admiration of truthful beauty of form or expression, it is noble and praiseworthy. A villa in the style of a Persian palace (of which there is an example lately erected in Connecticut), with its oriental domes and minarets, equally unmeaning and unsuited to our life or climate, is an example of the former; as an English cottage, with its beautiful home-expression and its thorough comfort and utility, evinced in steep roofs to shed the snow, and varied form to accommodate modern habits, is of the latter.

Architectural style is only exhibited in its severity and perfection, in public buildings of the first class, whose dignity, grandeur, and importance demand and permit it; such as the church, the capitol, public institutions, etc. In them we see, for example, the Gothic or Greek styles, in their greatest completeness and fullest development. Domestic Architecture, on the contrary, should be less severe, less rigidly scientific, and it should exhibit more of the freedom and play of feeling of every-day life. A man may, in public halls, recite a poem

in blank verse, or deliver a studied oration with the utmost
propriety; but he would be justly the object of ridicule if at
the fireside he talked about the weather, his family, or his
friend, in the same strain. What familiar conversation,
however tasteful and well bred, is to public declamation,
Domestic is to Civil or Ecclesiastical Architecture; and we
have no more patience with those architects who give
us copies of the temple of Theseus, with its high, severe
colonnades, for dwellings, than with a friend who should
describe his wife and children to us in the lofty rhythm
of Ossian. For this reason the Italian, Venetian, Swiss,
Rural Gothic, and our Bracketed style, all modified and
subdued forms of the Gothic and Greek styles, are the
variations of those types most suitable for Domestic Architecture.

A word or two may, perhaps, not be out of place here, on
the *Picturesque*, as distinguished from the Beautiful, in architecture. Whatever critics may affirm, we look upon them as
distinct in their nature, though often blended together in Rural Architecture.

The Beautiful, in architecture, is the complete embodiment
of ideas of beauty in a given material form; an embodiment
in which the idea triumphs over the material and brings it
into perfect subjection—we might almost say, of repose; where
there is neither want of unity, proportion, harmony, nor the
right expression.

The Picturesque is seen in ideas of beauty manifested with
something of rudeness, violence, or difficulty. The effect of
the whole is spirited and pleasing, but parts are not balanced,
proportions are not perfect, and details are rude. We feel

at the first glance at a picturesque object, the idea of power exerted, rather than the idea of beauty which it involves.

As regularity and proportion are fundamental ideas of absolute beauty, the Picturesque will be found always to depend upon the opposite conditions of matter—irregularity, and a partial want of proportion and symmetry. Thus, the purest Greek architecture, or the finest examples of Palladio, are at once highly symmetrical and beautiful; the varied Italian villa, or the ruder Swiss chalet, highly irregular and picturesque.

As picturesqueness denotes power, it necessarily follows that all architecture in which beauty of expression strongly predominates over pure material beauty, must be more or less picturesque. And as force of expression should rightly spring from force of character, so Picturesque Architecture, where its picturesqueness grows out of strong character in the inhabitant, is the more interesting to most minds: though if the Beautiful, as we believe, signifies the perfect balance between a beautiful idea and the material form in which it is conveyed to the eye, a truly beautiful form, so rarely seen, and involving, of course, harmonious expression, whether it be in man, nature, or art, is more perfect and satisfactory than a picturesque one; as, in character, the beauty and symmetry of Washington is more satisfactory than the greater power and lesser balance of Napoleon; or, in nature, a " golden landscape of Arcady" is more perfect than a wild scene in the Hartz mountains; or, in architecture, a villa of the most exquisite symmetry is more permanently pleasing than one of great irregularity. But this is, perhaps, pursuing the matter further than our readers require. We have gone far enough to show the sources of the two kinds of interest. And no person can harmoniously combine rural architecture and rural scenery, unless he understands something, at least, of the nature of both.*

THE TRUE IN ARCHITECTURE.

Having considered architecture as addressing the senses and the heart, let us examine what control the knowledge, reason, or judgment of man has over it.

Architecture may be useful, it may be beautiful, and still not altogether satisfactory, unless it is also truthful or significant. The intellect must approve what the senses relish and the heart loves.

Now it by no means follows that Truth and Beauty are the same thing; though some writers have labored hard to convince themselves of the existence of such a synonym. Artificial flowers or false gems may awaken the same ideas of beauty in the ignorant beholder, as if they were real. A house built of lath and plaster may, with good proportions and fair ornaments, raise in us the same emotions of beauty as one built of marble or freestone. But the moment our reason discovers that Beauty and Truth are at variance, the pleasure is either greatly weakened, or altogether destroyed.

On the other hand, architecture may be full of Truth, and

---

* In the fourth edition of our treatise on Landscape Gardening, we have endeavored more fully to develop the nature of the Picturesque in scenery; and we refer those to that volume, who wish to aim at the production of the most harmonious effects, by adapting the house to the scenery where it is to be placed.

yet from the want of proportion, symmetry, harmony, or expression, fall entirely short of real beauty.*

But although Beauty and Truth are not synonymous in art, all beauty, to be satisfactory, must be based upon Truth. This is especially true in Architecture, which, it must never be forgotten, is not only a beautiful art, but an art, the primary condition of which is, that it must be useful.

Now, there are three most important truths which all Domestic Architecture should present, and without which, it must always be unsatisfactory. The first is, the *general truth* that the building is intended for a dwelling-house; the second, the *local truth* that it is intended for a town or country house; and the third, the *specific truth* that it is intended for a certain kind of country house—as a cottage, farm-house, or villa.

It may appear singular to one not accustomed to dwell on this subject, that it should be necessary to insist on the value of so obvious a truth as that a dwelling-house should look like a dwelling-house. But, strange to say, men who are blinded by fashion or false taste are as likely to commit this violation of architectural truth as any other. We recall a villa on the banks of the Hudson, built in the form of a Doric temple, all the chimneys of which are studiously collected together in the centre of the roof, and are hidden from even a suspicion of their existence, by a sort of mask that resembles nothing, unless it be a classic well-curb set on the top of the

---

* And in this respect, Architecture more than most other arts. A landscape painter, for instance, though he only copies the truth of nature, cannot fail in producing much beauty, because there is something of beauty in all nature's works; though he will not produce so much beauty as another artist who studies and reproduces only the finest and most beautiful ideas in nature.

house. Now, as chimneys, in a northern climate, are particularly expressive of human habitation and domestic life, any concealment of them is a violation of general truth, and one might well be puzzled to know what sort of edifice was intended, in the villa in question. So, too, in the neighborhood of some of our cities, we still occasionally see houses which are pretty close imitations of Greek temples; as these buildings have sometimes as much space devoted to porticoes and colonnades as to rooms, one may well be pardoned for doubting exactly for what purpose they were designed.

Every feature, on the other hand, which denotes domestic life becomes a valuable truth in Domestic Architecture. Windows, doors, and chimneys, are the first of these truths, though they are not the highest, as churches, factories, and out-buildings also have windows, doors, and chimneys; and therefore such windows, doors, and chimneys as particularly belong to or distinguish a dwelling-house from all other buildings, are more valuable truths that those forms that are merely useful without being truthful.

Verandas, piazzas, bay-windows, balconies, etc., are the most valuable general truths in Domestic Architecture; they express domestic habitation more strongly because they are chiefly confined to our own dwellings.*

---

* To show the difference between an idea of truth and one of beauty, we may here remark, that mere chimney-tops, windows, verandas, etc., though in the highest degree valuable as truths, do not become beauties until they are made beautiful by proportion, or grace of form, or by expressing some feeling other than that of mere utility. A chimney may be an ugly chimney, and yet give a truthful expression to a dwelling; or it may be a finely-formed chimney, and thus become a beautiful truth.

Local truth in Architecture is one which can never be neglected without greatly injuring the effect of country houses. And yet, such is the influence of fashion and false taste, and so little do the majority of citizens trouble themselves to think on this subject, that nothing is more common in some parts of the country than to see the cockneyism of three-story town houses violating the beauty and simplicity of country life. In our own neighborhood, there is a brick house standing in the midst of gardens and orchard, which has a front and rear pierced with windows, but only blank wall at the sides; looking, in fact, precisely as if lifted out of a three-story row in a well-packed city street, and suddenly dropped in the midst of a green field in the country, full of wonder and contempt, like a true cockney, at the strangeness and dulness of all around it. During a drive on Long Island, last autumn, we saw with pain and mortification, the suburban villa of a wealthy citizen, a narrow, unmistakable "six-story brick," which seemed, in its forlornness, and utter want of harmony with all about it, as if it had strayed out of town, in a fit of insanity, and had lost the power of getting back again.

To give an expression of local truth to a country house, it should always show a tendency to *spread out* and extend itself on the ground, rather than to run up in the air. There is space enough in the country; and because a citizen has lived in town, where land is sold by the square foot, and where, in consequence, he has had to mount four pair of stairs daily, is surely no reason why he should compel himself to do the same thing in the country. Indeed, economy in the first cost of a house (that is to say, the lessened expense of building two stories under the same roof and over the same foundation) is the principal reason why most country houses are not still more ample, extended, and rambling on the surface, than they usually are.

Another exhibition of the want of local truth in many large country houses, is seen in their internal arrangements. Their plan is, indeed, a hall running directly through the house, with two or four rooms on a floor, and hence the same meagerness, and want of variety and convenience, as in the cramped space of a small town house.

Specific truths, in our Rural Architecture, are perhaps less frequently neglected than the others. In the majority of cases, the amount of means to be expended, prevents builders from making cottages look like villas. Still, there is, undoubtedly a great want of perception of the value of specific truth in many cases here; but it arises, partly, from a foolish ambition in those who build cottages and wish to make them appear like villas; and, partly, from an ignorance of what the true beauty of a country cottage consists in—which is not architectural ornament so much as a good form, simplicity of details, and the rural embellishment of vines and foliage.

If all persons building in the country, knew how much the beauty and pleasure we derive from Rural Architecture is enhanced by truthfulness, we should be spared the pain of seeing so many miserable failures in country houses of small dimensions. A cottage (by which we mean a house of small size) will never succeed in an attempt to impose itself upon us as a villa. Nay, it will lose its own peculiar charm, which is as great, in its way, as that of the villa. This throwing away the peculiar beauty and simplicity of a cottage, in endeavoring to imitate the richness and variety of a villa, is as false in taste, as for a person of simple and frank character to lay aside his simplicity and frankness, to assume the cultivation and polish of a man of the world. The basis for enduring beauty is truthfulness, no less in houses than in morals; and cottages, farm-houses, and villas, which aim to be only the best and most agreeable cottages, farm-houses, and villas, will be infinitely more acceptable, to the senses, feelings, and understanding, than those which endeavor to assume a grandeur foreign to their nature and purpose. This we say, too, with the fullest desire that the cottage should contain every comfort and refinement which our happy country, above all others, places within the reach of working-men; and we say it, because, being intelligent working-men, they ought, more than the same class anywhere else, to feel the value and the dignity of labor, and the superior beauty of a cottage home which is truthful, and aims to be no more than it honestly is, over one that strives to be something which it is not.

In order to assist the reader in judging of truth in Domestic Architecture, we shall again refer to the significance of expression, form, and decoration in the cottage, farm-house, and villa in succeeding pages.

A word or two may very properly be said here, regarding truthfulness of materials.

The principle which the reason would lay down for the government of the architect, under this head, is the simple and obvious one, that the material should *appear* to be what it is. To build a house of wood so exactly in imitation of stone as to lead the spectator to suppose it stone, is a paltry artifice, at variance with all truthfulness.

When we employ stone as a building material, let it be

clearly expressed: when we employ wood, there should be no less frankness in avowing the material. There is more merit in so using wood as to give to it the utmost expression of which the substance is capable, than in endeavoring to make it look like some other material.*

There are certain architectural fictions with regard to apparent truthfulness of material, which are so well understood as not to deceive, and are not, therefore, reprehensible ones : such as painting the surface of wooden, and cementing or stuccoing the exteriors of brick and stone houses. Protection from the weather demands this, and no one fails to recognize wood or solid walls, though entirely hidden from the eye. And in the case of stuccoed walls, the expression of strength and solidity is very properly conveyed to the eye by marking it off in courses, to denote the bonds and courses of the solid wall beneath, and to take away the mere lath-and-plaster look, of a plain stuccoed wall. To mark off in courses a house actually built of lath and stucco, as we have sometimes seen done, is, on the other hand, a downright violation of architectural truth. For the same reason we would prefer to see the stuccoed exterior of a brick wall marked faintly,

---

* Perhaps an exception may be allowed in the case of wooden verandas, and such light additions to buildings of solid materials as we often see added in this country, in districts where the stone is so hard as to be very costly when wrought into small parts, so that wood is often used, but is so painted and sanded as to harmonize with the stone. In this case, we say, the apparent untruthfulness is permissible, for the sake of a principle almost equally important—unity of effect ; for nothing is more offensive to the eye than an avowed union of wood and stone in the same building. But, of course, this is a sacrifice to expediency ; and the more truthful treatment, viz. making all portions of one material, is the only entirely satisfactory one.

in small courses, so as to denote that brick is the material of the wall, rather than boldly in large courses, to signify stone. There is no reason why the stucco which only stands for stucco, should not have an agreeable color, wholly different from those of the brick and stone put beneath it (because it is only when stone or brick is not altogether satisfactory to the eye, that we cover it with stucco); but the principle of truth should lead us to point out, by the lines on the stucco, whether it covers a stone or brick wall.*

There is a glaring want of truthfulness sometimes practised in this country by ignorant builders, that deserves condemnation at all times. This is seen in the attempt to express a style of architecture, which demands massiveness, weight, and solidity, in a material that possesses none of these qualities. We could point to two or three of these imitations of Gothic castles, with towers and battlements built of wood. Nothing can well be more paltry and contemptible. The sugar castles of confectioners and pastry-cooks are far more admirable as works of art. If a man is ambitious of attracting attention by his house, and can only afford wood, let him (if he can content himself with nothing appropriate) build a gigantic wigwam of logs and bark, or even a shingle palace, but not attempt mock battle-

---

* Marking off stucco to indicate a stone wall, is the common and prevalent mode in this country; though we have never seen brick expressed as we have suggested. This might be most easily and effectually done by pressing a mould, marked with lines, upon the face of the stucco, as soon as it is put on the wall. Patterns of various kinds were thus stamped upon the walls in Moorish architecture, with beautiful effect. The lines would always express that the wall beneath was of brick; but they should be only faintly impressed, and not deeply stamped, and without the mortar lines whitened so as to *imitate* brick.

ments of pine boards, and strong towers of thin plank. The imposition attempted, is more than even the most uneducated person of native sense can possibly bear.

As we shall develope, little by little, our views on these and other points already suggested, in our remarks on the different classes of houses, and the designs themselves, in the succeeding pages, we shall not pursue these introductory remarks further at the present time.

We have, as we trust, already clearly impressed upon the reader the three principal sources of interest in all architecture, and especially in domestic architecture. We have shown how a house may be useful without being beautiful; how it may be useful and beautiful without being satisfactory to the understanding; and how it may be useful, beautiful, and significant or truthful, and thus thereby satisfy us fully and completely— satisfy all the rational desires of the senses, the affections, and the intellect.

If it fall short of this, it is not architecture in the true sense of the word—for as another writer has well observed, every fine art is the art of so treating objects as to give them a moral significance; and unless the architect can stamp both feeling and imagination, as well as utility, upon his work, he cannot truly be called an architect.

SECTION II.

WHAT A COTTAGE SHOULD BE.

NEARLY all the varieties of country houses in the United States may be considered as belonging to three classes—COT-TAGES, FARM-HOUSES, and VILLAS. As each of these kinds of dwelling demands its peculiar accommodation or arrangement, and is bounded by certain limits as to size and cost; as it has, or ought to have, its peculiar character of beauty in form and expression, and its peculiar truthfulness or adaptation to the purpose intended, it is plain that no architect can successfully design either Cottages, Farm-Houses, or Villas, unless he knows the wants and the means, the domestic life and the enjoyments, the intelligence and the tastes, of those who are to occupy these different kinds of dwellings.

Now a *cottage*, according to Dr. Johnson, is a small house. It is not, necessarily, something with low walls and steep roof; something covered with thatched roof or ornamented with many gables. It is a house of limited accommodation, and, above all, of very moderate size as compared with other houses. Hence, a cottage, in a country where the dwellings are all of very large size, would be a larger building than in another, where the majority of the dwellings are only of moderate dimensions. In England, a house is often called a cottage

which would here be called a villa, and the reverse, because
the great size of many mansions in England, leads Englishmen
to call all country houses of moderate size and cottage-like
appearance, cottages—even though they may contain fifty
apartments, with all the luxury of a first-rate villa. These are,
in fact, only villas built in cottage style.

What we mean by a cottage, in this country, is a dwelling of
small size, intended for the occupation of a family, either wholly
managing the household cares itself, or, at the most, with
the assistance of one or two servants. The majority of such
cottages in this country are occupied, not by tenants, depend-
ants, or serfs, as in many parts of Europe, but by industrious
and intelligent mechanics and working men, the bone and
sinew of the land, who own the ground upon which they stand,
build them for their own use, and arrange them to satisfy their
own peculiar wants and gratify their own tastes.

It is, therefore, as clear as noonday, that cottages of this
class should be arranged with a different view, both as regards
utility and beauty, from either farm-houses or villas. An industrious man, who earns his bread by daily exertions, and lives
in a snug and economical little home in the suburbs of a town,
has very different wants from the farmer, whose accommodation
must be plain but more spacious; or the man of easy income,
who builds a villa as much to gratify his taste, as to serve the
useful purposes of a dwelling.

We would gladly enforce this point in the outset, because it
is but too plainly demonstrated that many of the worst failures
in cottages all over the country, have arisen from a want of
appreciation of *truthfulness of character* in Rural Architecture.
Any intrinsic difference between the cottage, the farm-house, or

the villa, between a dwelling for one family of simple habits and limited means, and another, whose tastes and habits of life are as complex as their means are more abundant, seems to be entirely unrecognized. The cottage is not made to express, as much as possible, the simplicity of cottage life, joined with the greatest comfort, intelligence, and taste of which that life is capable, but to imitate as closely as cheap and flimsy materials and a few hundred dollars will permit, the style and elaborate ornament of the villa, with its expenditure of thousands.

There are two striking illustrations of this false taste to be found in various parts of the country at the present moment— what may be called the *temple cottage* and the *cocked-hat cottage.*

The *temple cottage* is an imitation of the Temples of Theseus or Minerva, in thin pine boards, with a wonderfully fine and classical portico of wooden columns in front. The dimensions of the whole building may be 20 by 30 feet. The grand portico covers, perhaps, a third of the space and the means consumed by the whole dwelling. It is not of the least utility, because it is too high for shade; nor is it in the least satisfactory, for it is entirely destitute of truthfulness: it is only a caricature of a temple—not a beautiful cottage.

The *cocked-hat cottage* is, perhaps, a little better, for it is an imitative exaggeration, not a downright caricature. This species of cottage has grown out of an admiration for the real and intrinsic beauty of the rural-Gothic cottage, of which *gables* are strongly characteristic features. But some uneducated builders, imagining that the whole secret of designing a cottage in the Gothic style, lies in providing gables, have so overdone the matter, that, turn to which side of their houses we will, nothing but gables salutes our eyes. A great many gables in the front of a Gothic villa of large size may have a good effect; but to stick them in the front of a cottage of 25 feet front, and, not content with this, to repeat them everywhere else upon the roof where a gable can possibly be perched, is only to give the cottage the appearance, as the familiar saying goes, of having been "knocked into a cocked hat." A journey among the attic sleeping-rooms of such a cottage is like that geographical exploration of the peaks of all the highest mountains, made by beginners, in the corner of a map of the world.

Another serious objection to this imitation of the elaborate architecture of villas in small cottages, is the impossibility of executing the ornamental parts in a proper manner. Take, for example, the *verge-board* of a rural-Gothic gable. As part of a well-built villa, this verge-board is carefully carved in thick and solid plank, so as to exhibit all the details of outline and tracery boldly to the eye, and so as to endure as long as the house itself. Now let this be imitated in a cheap cottage, and it is almost always sawn out of thin board, so as to have a frippery and "gingerbread" look which degrades, rather than elevates, the beauty of the cottage. It is useless to talk about carving it as well for the cottage as for the villa, because it would cost more than cottage decorations should cost, and because, if other parts of the cottage were not brought up to the same point of style and execution, the verge-boards would be inconsistent and out of keeping.*

---

* The only exceptions to these remarks, are cottages built as gate-lodges or gardeners' houses on gentlemen's estates, where every other part is in still higher style ; because in this case, the life and taste of the tenant is not so much indicated as

In each of the three classes of country houses, there is a predominant character, to which all other expressions, whether of beauty, usefulness, or truth, should be referred. In cottages, this predominant character is *simplicity*. It ought, accordingly, to pervade every portion of cottage architecture. There should be a convenient simplicity of arrangement, to facilitate the simple manner of living; an economical simplicity of construction, to suit the moderate means of the builder or owner; and a tasteful simplicity of decoration, to harmonize with the character of the dwelling and its occupants.

All ornaments which are not simple, and cannot be executed in a substantial and appropriate manner, should be at once rejected; all flimsy and meager decorations which have a pasteboard effect, are as unworthy of, and unbecoming for the house of him who understands the true beauty of a cottage life, as glass breastpins or gilt-pewter spoons would be for his personal ornaments or family service of plate.

As much taste, as much beauty, as can be combined with the comparatively simple habits of cottage life, are truly admirable and delightful in a cottage. But every thing beyond this, every thing only imitated, every thing that is false, forced or foreign to the real feelings or intelligence of the inmates, is not worthy of the least approbation in a cottage.

We do not mean by this to say that it is impossible to build a highly ornamented cottage which shall be in good taste— what novel writers delight to call " a perfect bijou of a house."

---

the life and taste of the landlord and proprietor. But even in this case, the highest taste will lead to the rejection of all elaborate ornament in cottages, as not directly truthful and expressive.

The thing is quite possible; but it must either be a cottage as a plaything for wealthy people, not for them to live in, or it must be a villa disguised in cottage form, and not a true cottage; that is to say, a small house for a simple manner of living. You may cover such a small house with very beautiful ornamental work if you please, but its beauty will not be satisfactory to the reason, because it is not expressive of the life of its inmates, and because, therefore, it is destitute of truthfulness or significance; and the human mind is so constituted, that the beautiful must overlay the true, to give permanent satisfaction.

Admitting the justness of this proposition, we may state it as the highest principle in designing or building a cottage, that it should be truthful, that is, it should clearly express the modesty and simplicity of cottage life. Hence, not only should the cottage aim to look like a cottage, but it should avoid all pretension to what it cannot honestly and faithfully be. And as its object is first utility, and then beauty, the useful should never be sacrificed to the ornamental, but the latter should more obviously be connected with, and grow out of the former, in a cottage than in a more elaborate dwelling.

Among the first principles of utility in building or designing a cottage, we may state the following:

The principal entrance or front door should never open directly into an apartment of any kind, but always into a porch, lobby, or entry of some kind. Such a passage not only protects the apartment against sudden draughts of air, but it also protects the privacy and dignity of the inmates.

The roof should always be steep enough to carry off the snow freely, and there should be means of ventilation provided, in order to secure comfort in the upper sleeping apartments.*

The level of the first floor should never be less than one foot above the level of the surrounding surface of the ground, to secure dryness.

In all small cottages the kitchen should always be on the first floor, because, in such dwellings, the kitchen must be kept under the eye of the mistress. The only exception to this would be in cases where the cost of additional service, and the inconvenience of ascending and descending stairs are of less consequence than the additional room gained at a certain first cost in building.

In all cottages constructed of brick or stone (when the walls are not built hollow), the inside (lath and plaster) walls should be "firred off," to prevent dampness.

In all cottages built of wood, in the colder portions of the country, there should either be a double weather-boarding, as is common 'in New England, or the space between the weather-boarding and the inside should be "filled in" with cheap brick, as is common in the Middle States. Or, when the latter is too expensive, unburnt bricks, of clay and straw, may be used instead. The warmth of the cottage in winter and its coolness in summer are so greatly increased by this trifling additional cost, that it should never be neglected in the Northern States. In endeavoring to give beauty to cottages, the following principles must be remembered:

First, that, as beauty of outline (absolute beauty) belongs to the simplest as well as to the most complex outlines, where

* We shall explain the best mode of ventilating in a succeeding page.

beauty of decoration or ornamental members does not agree with simplicity, the former is mainly and especially to be employed in cottage architecture. Hence regularity, uniformity, proportion, symmetry, are beauties of which every cottage is capable, because they are entirely consistent with the simple forms of the cottage, while irregularity and variety are usually possible, with good effect, in a dwelling of larger size, and consisting of a great number of parts. Small cottages can scarcely be very irregular in form and outline, unless they are built in highly picturesque situations, such as a mountain-valley, or a wooded glen, when they form part of the irregular whole about them, rather than single objects, as is usually the case.

As a cottage may have all the beauty which results from proportion and symmetry, without adding a farthing to its cost, and without detracting in the least from its simplicity and truthfulness, it is evident that these two elements should be considered before any ornaments are introduced. Not only should the general outlines be well proportioned and symmetrical, but also the forms of all the smaller portions—such as doors, windows, chimneys, etc.

When the means of the builder enable him to go beyond these simple beauties of form, his first thought, on elevating the expression of the cottage, should be to add ornament to the most important parts of the dwelling. These are the entrance door, the principal windows, the gables, and the chimneys. The front door and the principal or first floor windows should be recognized as something more than mere openings, by lintels, hoods, or borders (dressings); the gables by being very simply moulded or bracketed about the junction with the roof; the chimneys, by a pleasing form or simple ornaments, or merely by having the usual clumsy mass lightened and separated into parts.

After this, the next step is to add something to the expression of domestic enjoyment in cottage life—such as a simple porch, or veranda, or simple bay-window. A much higher character is conferred on a simple cottage by a *veranda* than by a highly ornamented gable, because one indicates the constant means of enjoyment for the inmates—something in their daily life besides ministering to the necessities—while a more ornamental verge-board shows something, the beauty of which is not so directly connected with the life of the owner of the cottage, and which is therefore less expressive, as well as less useful.

After all these elements of beauty are attained in the cottage (in any style of architecture), one ought to pause before attempting much more ornament or architectural decoration. Beyond this it is difficult to go without endangering simplicity, and it is therefore difficult to lay down any other rules than the following:

Never introduce in a cottage any elaborate or complex ornament (however beautiful intrinsically or in higher architecture) which is not entirely consistent with that simple, truthful character which is the greatest source of pleasure in Cottage Architecture.

Never attempt any ornamental portions in a cottage, which cannot be executed in a substantial and proper manner, so that the effect of beauty of design may not be weakened by imperfect execution or flimsy materials.

As the effect of Rural Architecture is never a thing to be

considered wholly by itself, but, on the contrary, as it always depends partly upon, and is associated with, rural scenery, trees, shrubbery, and vines, we should not, as many architects do, wholly overlook the aid of such accessories. Cottage Architecture, especially, borrows the most winning and captivating expression from foliage. If we analyze the charm of a large part of the rural cottages of England—the finest in the world—we shall find, that strip them of the wealth of flowing vines that adorn them, and their peculiar poetry and feeling have more than half departed. And, since no architectural decorations, however beautiful or costly, can give the same charm of truthful decoration to a cottage, as flowering vines and creepers, we shall, in another page, point out the most hardy, valuable, and beautiful species for this purpose.

SECTION III.

ON MATERIALS AND MODES OF CONSTRUCTION.

THE three materials in most common use for country houses are wood, brick, and stone.

In an architectural point of view, solid materials are so far superior to all others, that where it is not a question of cost, no one should hesitate for a moment in his decision of what material to build. The finest architecture should as certainly be of stone as the finest sculpture, because in a work of art any thing which conveys the idea of eternal duration, adds incalculably to its effects upon the reason, though the effect upon the feelings may otherwise be equal. A beautiful statue, carved in wood, is far less satisfactory than the same statue in marble, even leaving out of the question the greater triumph of art and the greater *beauty* of form in the latter material.

To say nothing, then, of the additional durability and beauty of solid materials, the mere saving of after expense and trouble should be sufficient argument to induce the proprietor of a superior villa to use brick or stone in its construction.

But, in a *cottage*, economy must be a leading consideration Hence, in many parts of a country in which timber is so abun dant as in this, a large proportion of all the cottages must be built of wood. It is, therefore, wiser for an architect to endeavor to give a tasteful and appropriate character to wooden cottages, than to leave them without the pale of architectural ingenuity. We greatly prefer a cottage of brick or rough stone (painted or colored with a wash) to one of wood; but, since the want of the majority is for plans for wooden cottages, we shall submit a variety of such plans, and must therefore say something of the best modes of constructing them.

VERTICAL BOARDING. There are two modes of constructing the exteriors of wooden houses, now generally practised. The most common mode is that of covering the frame on the outside with boards or narrow siding in horizontal strips; the other is, to cover it with boards nailed on in vertical strips (up and down). In the *horizontal boarding*, the weather is kept out of the joint by the upper board overlapping the under one; in the *vertical boarding*, it is kept out by a narrow strip, called a *batten*, about two inches wide, which is nailed over the joint formed by the meeting of the two boards.

To enable the reader to understand this mode of construction, we refer him to the profile or section, Fig. 1, A. In this, *a, b, c,* are two boards tongued and grooved, and nailed, side by side, in an upright position, to form the outside of the house; *d* represents the batten nailed directly over the joint, and completely protecting the edges of the board from the action of the weather. In A, is shown (*d*) the usual form (diminished) of those battens suitable for cheap cottages or outbuildings. B and C are other forms of battens (of the exact size), rendered somewhat more ornamental by being moulded on the edges, and are frequently used in more important wooden buildings.

If these battens are made of "good clear stuff," they will last
as long as the house does.

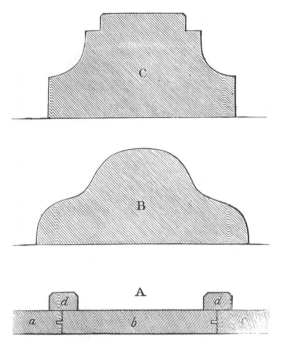

[Fig. 1.   Vertical Boarding with different forms of Battens.]

We greatly prefer the vertical to the horizontal boarding, not
only because it is more durable, but because it has an expression of strength and truthfulness which the other has not.   The
main timbers which enter into the frame of a wooden house
and support the structure, are vertical, and hence the vertical
boarding properly signifies to the eye a wooden house; in the
same manner, the main weight of a stone or brick house is
supported by walls laid in courses, and hence the truthfulness
of showing horizontal courses in brick or stone buildings.   It is

as incorrect, so far as regards truthfulness of construction, to show horizontal lines on the weather-boarding of a wooden house, as it would be to mark vertical lines on the outside of a brick or stuccoed wall.

Besides this, there is not only greater economy in vertical boarding, but, being a bolder mode of construction, it better expresses the picturesque—a kind of beauty essentially belonging to wooden houses. Thin "siding" (i. e. the small boards half an inch thick and six inches wide, known by this name) requires a great deal of labor bestowed in planing and fitting up, and it aims at a very highly finished and polished character— one which we think it fails in reaching, because that character does not legitimately belong to wood—though marble or freestone may be smoothed and polished in classical buildings with the happiest effect.

For all wooden cottages, therefore, we recommend weather-boarding of sound inch or inch and a quarter pine, tongued and grooved at the edges, nailed on in the vertical manner, and covered with neat battens. The base, or plinth of the house, upon which these battens finish at the bottom, should be formed by a horizontal plank an inch more in thickness (as is shown in all the following designs); and the boards and battens may either be continued till they meet the under side of the roof (which answers in the case of most cottages), or they may stop against a plank of the same thickness as the base which runs along under the eaves, forming a frieze or wall-plate covering.

In New England, and other parts of the country where lumber is cheaper than bricks, a wooden house is rendered warm and comfortable by a double thickness of boards. A lining of *rough boards* is first nailed upon the outside of the frame, so as to form a plain surface, and the weather-boarding or siding, which forms the outside of the house, is nailed upon this rough boarding.

In all the better houses built in this way a coat of *plaster* is also laid upon the *inside* of this rough boarding—which latter, as it is uneven on its surface, and as it does not quite meet at the edges, may be considered a sort of stout lathing—thus forming an exterior protection of two thicknesses of boards and one of plaster. As the inside wall of the house forms another separate wall of lath and plaster, there is a hollow space, of several inches, left between the two plaster walls, and the house is thus rendered a warm one.

But this mode is not so satisfactory as that adopted in the middle states, called "filling-in."

FILLING-IN. The best mode of making such wooden houses comfortable and warm is, to "fill in" a course of any cheap bricks from top to'bottom of the whole frame. This will make a wall four inches thick between the weather-boarding and the lath and plastering of the rooms. The cheapest mortar, made with a small proportion of lime, is used for this filling-in; and, as much nicety is not required, the work is very rapidly performed.

In cottages and *cheap* country houses where economy is an important consideration, it is the practice here, in filling-in, both to place the bricks *on edge*, and to build them *flush* with the inside of the timbers or studs (or rather projecting a quarter of an inch forward). This leaves a hollow space between the *weather-boarding* and the brick wall, of several inches, and it enables the plasterer to dispense with lathing.

He plasters directly on the inner face of the filling-in, and, to make the plaster adhere firmly to the timber, the plasterer "hacks" or chips the inner surface of the studs, joists, etc., so as to make them rough before plastering. We find that with timber tolerably seasoned, this makes a satisfactory interior wall for cottages, at a very moderate cost.

In the case of villas, or more thoroughly built country houses, the filling-in is executed by laying the bricks *flat*, setting back the inner face of the bricks about an inch behind the inner face of the studs, and then lathing on studs or firring for the plastered wall. This leaves a hollow space on each side of the brick filling-in, the largest vacuity being between the bricks and the weather-boarding. The result is a dry, warm, and substantial house.

Slight *wall-strips* (pieces of rough boards of the width of the brick work) are nailed across from stud to stud, every five or six courses, to strengthen the wall. Only the cheapest kind of bricks, such as are technically called "soft bricks," are used for filling-in.

In districts of country where bricks are not easily procured, the cottager may use *unburnt bricks* for filling-in, and may have them at very trifling cost by making them himself.

Any ordinary clay will answer for this purpose. It should, if dry, first be moistened and thoroughly worked by oxen, or pounded by hand till it becomes tough. Then add some straw, cut about six inches long, and mix it well with the clay by turning it over repeatedly, adding a little water, if necessary. The straw increases the tenacity, so that even common loamy soil will answer. If the clay is naturally a good brick clay, straw is not needed.

A mould is made of strong plank. The bricks may be made of any convenient size, and to save time it is well to make them considerably larger than common bricks—say six inches wide, four thick, and a foot long. The mould should have a bottom not quite air-tight, so as to allow the bricks to be turned out without sticking; and should the clay be very tenacious, the mould may be dusted with dry sand before filling in.

The mould is filled with the tempered clay just as in moulding common bricks, and the surplus clay is cut off evenly with a piece of iron hoop. With two moulds one man will mould as rapidly as two men will carry away and lay out for drying. The bricks are laid on a piece of level ground, and they are turned upon the other edge the second day. In three days of clear weather, they will be sufficiently dry to be piled up under cover; there they should lie a fortnight, when they are fit for use.

These bricks may, in filling-in, be laid on edge, and the wall of the apartments plastered directly upon their inner face, first making the face of the studs rough, as already described. In this mode, a strong and durable filling-in is obtained at a very trifling cost, and the house is as warm as one with solid brick walls.

COTTAGES OF UNBURNT BRICK. In some prairie districts where timber and stone are both scarce, the walls of cottages and farm houses are frequently built wholly of unburnt brick.

Mr. Ellsworth, the late Commissioner of Patents, paid considerable attention to the construction of these cottages, built several himself, and bears the strongest testimony to their great cheapness, warmth, and durability.

We compile the following details, comprising every thing essential, chiefly from his report. Almost every kind of clay will answer; it is tempered by treading it with cattle, and cut straw is added, at the rate of two bundles of straw to clay enough for one hundred bricks. It is then ready for moulding. This is done as we have already described, except that it is found that the most economical size for the bricks for building such cottages is the following, viz. one foot long, six inches wide, and four inches thick.

The cellar or foundation must be formed of stone or burnt brick.

In damp soils, the dampness should be prevented from rising from the soil into the unburnt wall by laying one course of slate, or of bricks laid in cement or hydraulic mortar, at the top of the foundation.

The walls of the cottage are laid up one foot in thickness, of the unburnt brick. This thickness is exactly the length of the brick, or the width of two bricks, and the strongest wall is made by laying the work with alternate courses of *leaders* and *stretchers* (i. e. one course with the bricks laid across the wall, the next course side by side). A weak mortar of lime and sand is generally used for laying the bricks, but a good brick mortar is preferable. Where lime is scarce, a mortar composed of three parts clay, one part sand, and two parts wood ashes, answers very well as a substitute for lime mortar. The division walls may be six inches thick, just the width of the brick; but, when the cottage has rooms wider than twelve feet, it is better to make the first-story partitions two bricks thick. The doors and window frames being ready to insert, the cottage is very rapidly built. These frames are made of stout plank, of the exact thickness of the walls, so that the casing inside and outside helps to strengthen the wall and covers the joints. If lintels and sills of stone are not to be had, pieces of timber three inches thick, of the same width as the wall, and a foot longer on each side than the opening, may be used instead.

The roof may be of shingles or thatch, and it is indispensable in a cottage of unburnt clay that it should project two feet all round, so as completely to guard the walls from vertical rains. The *outside* of the wall is plastered with good lime mortar mixed with hair, and then with a second coat, pebble-dashed, as in *rough-cast* walls. The inside of the wall is plastered and whitewashed in the common way.

Built in the simple way of the prairies, these cottages are erected for an incredibly small sum, costing no more than log houses, while they are far more durable and agreeable in appearance.

But we have also seen highly ornamental cottages built of this material, the bricks made entirely by the hands of the owner or occupant, and the whole erected at a cost of not more than one half of that paid for the same cottage built in an equally comfortable manner of wood or brick. When plastered or rough-cast on the exterior, this mode of construction presents to the eye the same effect as an ordinary stuccoed house, while it is warmer and far less costly in repairs than any other cheap material is.

The walls of unburnt brick absorb dampness less than those which have been burnt. As regards the durability of this material, we may add that there are instances, both in South America and on the continent of Europe, of cottages and farm houses, more than two centuries old, built of *pisé* or unburnt brick. In the neighborhood of Lyons, many of the prettier villas are constructed of pisé, where the interiors of the walls are painted in fresco.

HOLLOW WALLS. By far the best mode of building brick houses is that of constructing them with *hollow walls*.

The advantages of hollow brick walls over solid ones of the same thickness, are the following:

First, a very considerable saving in the quantity of bricks and mortar required.

Secondly, the prevention of dampness, which always strikes through a solid wall, and more or less affects the apartments within, unless the plastered walls of the rooms are *firred-off*, i. e. separated by a wooden partition, with a hollow space, from the outer solid wall.

Thirdly, the saving of all the cost of lathing and studding for the interior walls, the latter being plastered directly on the inner face of the hollow brick wall.

Lastly, and mainly, *in the great security afforded against fire*. Four-fifths of our houses are still built with hollow wooden partitions, and walls with inside firring. The inevitable consequence is, that when a fire once breaks out, it spreads with incredible rapidity through these hollow spaces lined with wood, which extend from basement to attic, and all hope of extinguishing the flames is at once abandoned. On the other hand, a house built at no more cost, with hollow brick walls and brick partitions, is nearly fire-proof. The only way in which the flames can spread rapidly from one story to the other is by means of the staircase, since this is the only wooden portion that reaches from one story to the other; and hence, in the best modern villas, the staircase is made of iron or stone, so as to be fire-proof. In a country house built in this way, nine times out of ten, a fire would never spread beyond the room where it originated; and, in almost all cases, it could be extinguished, with but little effort, by the inmates alone, since all the means of rapid communication actually provided in the usual and most careless mode of building, is wanting in a house built with hollow walls.

Hollow walls have long been the favorite mode of construction in various parts of Europe, and in some places in this country. So far as we can learn, they were first introduced here by the late Ithiel Town, Esq., Architect, and nearly all the best villas at New Haven, where he resided, are built in this mode. In the hope that our more intelligent masons and bricklayers will adopt this very superior mode of construction, in all parts of the country, we give the following simple plans, showing, at a glance, how they are constructed.

In Fig. 2, A represents a wall sixteen inches thick, with a hollow space of four inches. The double course of bricks is upon the outside, the single course upon the inside of the wall; the plastering of the room being made directly upon the latter. In this course the bricks are *stretchers* laid flat, and the inside and outside courses are tied together by the bricks marked *a*.

B represents the second course of this wall. The builder will notice here an important point, viz. that the position of the tie-brick, *a*, is changed in this course to *b*, thus breaking joints, and strengthening the wall. In laying the next course above, this tie-brick will take the same position as in the first course, *a*, and so alternately in each course, till the wall is complete.

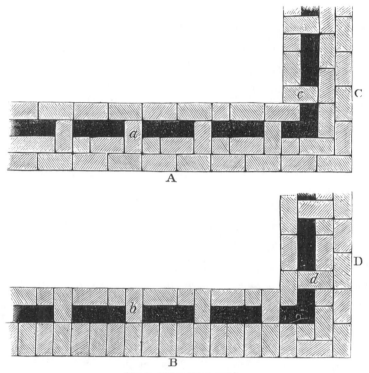

[Fig. 2. Hollow 16 inch wall.]

In B, the course of bricks in that part of the wall directly before us, is laid across the last course, forming a whole course of *headers;* and a wall built in this way (*English Bond*), is the best and strongest, when the outside is to be stuccoed or cemented. When it is to be left smooth to be colored or painted, the Flemish Bond, represented in the two courses on the other angles of the wall, C and D, are preferable, because regular courses of stretchers only are presented on the outside.

The position of the tie-bricks, *c* and *d*, it will be seen, alternates in the same way.

A very little practice will enable the mason to construct a hollow wall in this way with rapidity. As the strength of this wall is greatly increased by placing the brick *a* opposite the *side* of a brick (as shown in the plan, and not opposite a *joint* between two bricks), a little attention should be given, so as to secure this mode of construction.

A hollow wall of this thickness is amply sufficient for almost all country houses. In especial cases, when a thicker wall is thought necessary, it may easily be made by adding one brick more to the thickness of the outside of the wall, or to the inside. or to both sides, thus making it a hollow wall of twenty or twenty-four inches.

[Fig. 3. Hollow 12 inch wall.]

Fig. 3 shows a very simple and cheap mode of building a hollow wall twelve inches wide, which answers very well for low additions, or walls intended to bear but little weight. An addition of another brick to the outside would make a good sixteen-inch wall, rather more quickly built, but not so strong or so economical, as regards materials, as the mode shown in Fig. 2. The tie-bricks alternate, in the courses, as in the former mode; that is, the brick *a* is covered, in the next course, with the brick *b* (shown by the *dotted* lines); *c* by *d*, and so on, through the whole.

Fig. 4 shows a very simple and strong mode of building a hollow eight-inch wall—suitable for partitions, or even for the

[Fig. 4.   Hollow 8 inch wall.]

outside walls of small cottages to be covered with stucco or rough-cast. Two courses of stretchers, *a*, consisting of bricks *on edge*, are first laid the whole length of the wall. This leaves the hollow space *b*, between. The next course is a course of *headers*, *c*, laid flat, and reaching across the whole wall. As the mortar in this course is only placed under the ends where the headers lie on the stretchers, there is between each brick a small space left open, directly over the hollow space below, so that, in fact, the wall may be said to be partially hollow throughout, though there are no wide openings left between the *headers*, as in the other modes. This mode, when used for an outside wall for cottages, is not so dry as the construction in the former figures, because the headers go quite through the wall from one side to the other; but with a good coat of stucco or cement it makes a very good outside wall. When heavy beams are to be placed on such a wall, preparation should be made for them by carrying up a solid pier in the wall, from its base to the point of support, for the beams to rest on. This mode is the invention of Mr. Dearn, an English builder, who describes it as requiring only one-third of the bricks, and one half the mortar of a common solid wall of the same thickness.

Eight-inch hollow brick walls are sufficiently strong for cottages of small size, and as air is a better non-conductor than brick or stone, such hollow walls are warmer in winter and cooler in summer than solid walls of the same thickness. When covered with a coat of lime or cement stucco on the outside, they make excellent and durable dwellings: and as the rougher the face of the wall to be stuccoed is, the better, a wall of this kind made of hard-baked bricks may be constructed more rapidly and cheaply than any other.

In the case of villas, the walls should never be less than twelve inches thick, and this additional thickness in hollow walls of this latter construction, is gained by another course of bricks flatwise on one side of Dearn's hollow wall.

But the better mode is to build the sixteen-inch wall, as shown in Fig. 2.

The superior excellence and economy of hollow walls must, we think, bring this mode of construction into general favor in all parts of the country where bricks are abundant.

STUCCO. Stuccoed walls (i. e. those plastered externally) are in many respects superior to those of plain brick or stone. They are cheaper, warmer, and dryer than either brick or stone walls. No one would prefer a stuccoed wall, intrinsically, to a wall built of a fine stone, or of the pale cream-colored bricks which are made in some parts of the country, or to a wall built of smooth and well-faced brick, harmoniously painted, because these are not only excellent materials, but they are more truthful and genuine than stucco. But the greater warmth and protection of stucco, the ease with which it takes an agreeable tint by cheap washes, and its moderate cost, render it a most valuable material to all builders or proprietors who wish to combine beauty and comfort with moderate expenditure.

Outside plastering or stuccoing is generally so little understood in this country, and has been so badly practised by many masons, that there is an unjust prejudice against it, in many parts of the Union. Three-fourths of all the finest modern buildings of Europe are of brick and stucco, and nothing but attention to a few simple rules is necessary to insure success in stuccoing in this country.

The first of these rules is, not to use stucco except upon buildings with *projecting roofs*, in order to prevent the possibility of the wall getting saturated at the eaves.

The second is, never to use sand which has not been washed until it is perfectly clean, and no longer discolors the water that is poured upon it.

The third is, never to use " cement " or hydraulic lime, the character of which for tenacity has not been fully tested on outside walls for ten years at least.*

A strong and durable stucco for plastering the outsides of rough brick or stone walls is made in the following manner:

Take stone lime fresh from the kiln, and of the *best quality*, such as is known to make a strong and durable mortar (like the Thomaston lime). Slake it by sprinkling or pouring over it just water enough to leave it, when slaked, in the condition of a fine *dry powder*, and not a *paste*. Set up a quarter-inch wire screen at an inclined plane, and throw this powder against it. What passes through is fit for use. That which remains

---

* Several of our most popular hydraulic limes are excellent for covered work, such as cisterns, aqueducts, etc., but nearly worthless for work exposed to the atmosphere. The only one which we know to be an exception to this remark is the cement from Berlin, Conn., though there are, doubtless, others as good in various localities.

behind contains the *core*, which would spoil the stucco, and must be rejected.

Having obtained the sharpest sand to be had, and having washed it so that not a particle of the mud and dirt (which destroy the tenacity of most stuccoes) remains, and screened it, to give some uniformity to the size, mix it with the lime in powder, in the proportion of *two parts sand* to one part lime. This is the best proportion for lime stucco. More lime would make a stronger stucco, but one by no means so hard— and hardness and tenacity are both needed.

The mortar must now be made by adding water, and working it thoroughly. On the *tempering* of the mortar greatly depends its tenacity.

The wall to be stuccoed should be first prepared by clearing off all loose dirt, mortar, etc., with a stiff broom. Then apply the mortar in two coats; the first a rough coat, to cover the inequalities of the wall, the second as a finishing coat. The latter, however, should be put on *before* the former is dry, and as soon, indeed, as the first coat is sufficiently firm to receive it: the whole should then be well floated, trowelled, and marked off; and if it is to be colored in water-color, the wash should be applied, so as to *set* with the stucco.

Whoever will follow these simple directions will have a sound and lasting stucco. There are many country houses in Pennsylvania plastered with lime stucco, in this mode, eighty or one hundred years ago, the stucco of which is now as firm and sound as the stone itself.

Rough-cast is a rude species of cement, very durable and very cheap, and well adapted to farm-houses and the plainer kind of rural cottages. Examples of its introduction will be given in some of the designs which follow. It is chiefly used to cover stone houses, the walls of which are built of small stones. The mode of putting it on is as follows:

The surface of the wall being brushed off clean, lay on a coat of good lime and hair mortar. Allow this to dry, and then lay on another coat as evenly and smoothly as possible without floating. As soon as two or three yards of the second coat is finished, have ready a pail of *rough-cast*, and splash or throw it on the wall. This is usually done by another work-man, who holds the trowel with which he throws on the rough-cast in one hand, and a white-wash brush dipped constantly in the pail in the other, which follows the trowel until the whole is smooth, and evenly colored.

The rough-cast itself is made of sharp sand, washed clean, screened and mixed in a large tub with pure, newly-slaked lime and water, till the whole is in a semi-fluid state. A little yellow ochre mixed in the rough-cast gives the whole a slightly fawn-colored shade, more agreeable to the eye than white.

Wherever smooth brick walls with sandstone dressings are within the reach of a builder of a good country house, this combination should be accepted, as, next to a fine stone, produ-cing the very best effect, both as regards beauty and truthfulness. The brick should be painted to harmonize with the stone-dress-ings of the windows, doors, cornices, etc. (perhaps a few shades lighter or darker), and the effect is highly satisfactory. Mr. Van Rensselaer's manor-house at Albany, and Mr. King's villa at Newport, are excellent examples of this mode of con-struction.

Nothing, in an architectural point of view, is so satisfactory as stone. It is so permanent, enduring, and genuine in appearance, and all ornaments are so vastly increased in apparent value when executed in this material, that, were it not for its much greater cost, it should at all times have the preference over other materials for country houses.

We are here, however, compelled to admit that we have serious objections, in point of taste, to building small cottages of sombre-looking blue or gray stones. Dark limestone and granite, in a cottage, have a jail-like and severe aspect, and in all small buildings we would, if none but such dark-colored stone can be had, prefer either to color the stone or to build of rough stone or brick, covering them with stucco. Even in villas of moderate size, a sombre stone often destroys much of the cheerfulness of a pleasing exterior.

The two most satisfactory stones yet extensively used in this country for Rural Architecture are the light-brown sandstone or "freestone" of Connecticut and New Jersey (of which Trinity Church in New York is built),* and the soft, light-gray stone of Cincinnati. Both these have a mellow and harmonious effect in combination with foliage, both are easily wrought, and all ornaments executed in them are finely relieved by soft shadows. Next to these, the *light-gray* limestones afford the most agreeable and most valuable materials for building.

The objection to stone, commonly urged in this country, is, that houses built of this material are always *damp*. While this is quite true of stone houses, as they are often, and indeed usually, built in the country, it is also true that this dampness always arises from bad construction. A stone house, in a

---

* The new villa of J. S. Thayer, Esq., at Brookline, near Boston, built of brown freestone, is a fine example of the beauty of this material for country houses.

damp soil, of which the foundation walls are built of common lime mortar, will always be damp, from capillary attraction—common lime mortar offering no impediment to the absorption of the moisture from the soil, or to its gradual passage upwards into the main wall of the house. The latter, therefore, will rarely be quite dry. The remedy for this is to build the foundation walls of *hydraulic* lime mortar, which completely prevents any such foundation dampness.

A stone house, in which the walls of the apartments are plastered directly on the stone, must always be more or less damp, because all stone is more or less pervious to water; or because the plaster wall, being of the same temperature as the outer or stone wall, condenses the dampness of the apartments on its inner surface. The remedy for this is, either to *firr-off* a hollow space between the stone wall and the plaster wall, or (which is much the most solid mode) to form a *hollow* wall by a single thickness of brick built up and connected with the stone wall while constructing the latter.

In choosing stone as a material for building, not only should the size of the house be considered,—the more dignified and grave character of the *mansion* allowing, with good effect, the employment of a much darker stone than the simple and more cheerful character of the small cottage,—but the expression of the style of architecture adopted should also be considered. A light and cheerful villa, composed in the Italian or Venetian style, would almost lose its expression of cheerfulness if built in dark-blue limestone, while a Gothic villa or mansion, of large size, would have its antique character supported and developed by such a material. A little reflection will convince any observing person of taste, that the *color* of a stone building has a great deal to do with its expression and with the effect it has upon our feelings; and that the outward hue which the material employed will force the edifice forever after to represent to the eye, is a point worthy of very serious consideration.

SECTION IV.

DESIGNS FOR COTTAGES.

WE offer, in this section, a series of designs for cottages. They are by no means to be looked upon as perfect models for this kind of dwelling, and we may add that, although "model cottages" are often talked of, they are very seldom found.

The habits of life, even of persons who live in cottages, are very different in New England from those in New York, while the habits of the latter are unlike those at the south and west; it will therefore readily be seen, that what would precisely answer the demands of this class in one part of the country, would fall short of their expectations in another. One desires, above all things, snugness, and economy of space; another, as much room as possible, and as large a space as can be afforded; while all desire to get far more accommodation than is practicable for a given sum.

It is, therefore, far more difficult to design a satisfactory cottage than a satisfactory villa. In the former, the architect is bound down by rigid notions of economy, and must bring all the accommodation within very narrow limits; in the latter, the cost is not so carefully considered, and space enough is afforded to allow elegance and variety of form and arrangement.

It does not follow, however, that tasteful cottages cannot be designed. There are no buildings, however simple, to which either good forms or something of an agreeable expression may not be given.

In designing the following cottages, we have aimed rather at producing beauty by means of form and proportion, than by ornament; hence, it is not unlikely that those who have only a smattering of taste, and think a cottage cannot possess any beauty unless it is bedizened with ornaments, will be disappointed with the simplicity of most of these plans. But we trust, on the other hand, that persons of more information and more correct taste, and especially those who have followed us in our development of the true sources of interest in rural architecture, will agree with us that tasteful simplicity, not fanciful complexity, is the true character for cottages.

Besides this, we have been most anxious to give designs for *cheap cottages.* There are tens of thousands of working-men in this country, who now wish to give something of beauty and interest to the simple forms of cottage life; there are many of these who are desirous to have their home of three rooms tasteful and expressive, no less than among those whose dwellings number thirty rooms. We have, therefore, avoided unsuitable ornaments, chosen cheap materials, and, for the most part, have taken simple and symmetrical forms, so that, in some cases, not a dollar more would be expended in the execution of our designs than the same accommodation would cost in the usual plain modes of building; while in other examples, only a very trifling additional sum would be required.

FUNDAMENTAL POINTS. In all the following designs for cottages, we have assumed that the interiors shall be finished in a simple and plain manner. The walls are to be plastered with two coats, and finished with a *brown coat*, so as to receive a coat of whitewash, or some water or oil color, or to be papered.

The height of the rooms on the first floor or principal floor of these cottages is ten feet; that of the rooms on the second floor, either eight and a half, or nine feet—the former in the half-story designs, the latter in the full-story designs.

Our estimates for cottages do not include the painting of the exterior, since many cottagers will prefer to color the outside of their dwellings themselves, with one of the cheap paints or washes we shall recommend in a subsequent page, rather than incur the cost of having them painted in oil colors.

ESTIMATES. Nothing is more difficult than to give an estimate for executing any design, which shall be precise and satisfactory to the readers of a work in so broad a country as the United States. A cottage which may be built in Bangor, where wood is abundant, for a comparatively small sum, would cost a great deal more in Charleston, and considerably more here. A brick dwelling can be erected, here, at about the same price as one substantially built of wood; but in a district where wood is plentiful, and bricks scarce, a brick dwelling would, perhaps, cost nearly double. The only mode, therefore, is for our readers to compare the prices of materials at home with those of the same materials here, and let the builder make the necessary alterations. Placing good bricks, here, at four dollars per thousand, box boards at fourteen dollars per thousand feet, and good inch and a quarter matched plank at from twenty to twenty-two dollars, they will have the necessary data for comparing the cost here with the cost there.

DESIGN I.

A LABORER'S COTTAGE.

Fig. 5.

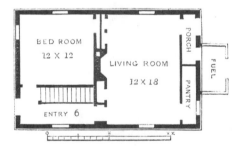

PRINCIPAL FLOOR.

Fig. 6.

DESIGN I.—*A small Cottage for a Working-man.*

THIS simple design is given to show how a very small cottage, built of wood, may be made to look well at very trifling cost. In form, it is a mere parallelogram, and while it is devoid of very strongly-marked architectural character, it combines something of picturesqueness, and something of home-like or domestic expression.

The picturesque character is partly owing to the bold shadows thrown by the projecting roof, and partly to rafter brackets and window hoods.

Let any one imagine this little cottage, with its roof cut off close to the eaves, with the rafter brackets that support the projecting eaves omitted, with the windows and door mere bare frames, and he has an example of how this same cottage would look as we commonly see it built; that is to say, without the picturesqueness of wood clearly expressed by using it *boldly* (not neatly and carefully); by a sense of something beyond mere utility, evinced in the pains taken to extend the roof more than is absolutely needful; and by raising the character of the windows and doors by placing hoods over their tops.

Accommodation. The single apartment called the *living-room* (Fig. 6), twelve by eighteen feet, is the common apartment, the kitchen, sitting-room, and parlor of this family, for it is intended for a family which "takes care of itself."

Opening the front door of this cottage, we see an entry six feet wide, which contains the stairs to the second floor.

Underneath this stairs, another flight descends to the cellar.*

On the left of the entry is a small bed-room twelve feet square. If this bed-room is used constantly, it would be better to have it communicate with the living-room by the door on the left of the chimney flue, which is now the closet door; and this arrangement, supposing this the bed-room in constant use, will give greater convenience and greater warmth in winter, since one fire will keep both rooms warm. If, on the contrary, it is only to be used occasionally, it would be better not to make it communicate. Indeed, with a little nicety of construction, there is space enough to retain a small closet for the living-room, and still have these two rooms connected.

The living-room is thirteen by eighteen feet, a convenient size for daily use. It is lighted by a window on each side, and the chimney being nearly in the centre of the house, no heat will be lost in winter. Near one corner of the opposite side of this room is a door opening into a small pantry which is lighted by a window; and at the opposite corner is another door opening into a narrow porch. We have cut off the passage, to form this small porch, in order to protect the back door, which opens into the main apartment of the family, from sudden draughts and cold blasts, a point most important in a northern climate, but too often neglected, to the serious discomfort of the inmates of small cottages. From this back porch another door will be seen opening into a small wood-house, so that fuel may be had

---

* A *scale* will be found attached to this and most of the other plans, by which any dimensions of the plans, not given in the text, may be ascertained by the reader's own measurement.

without going into the open air. This wood-house is represented of small size, but it may be extended in depth several
feet, if more room is wanted.

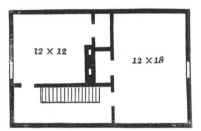

[Fig. 7. Chamber Floor.]

The second floor of this cottage, Fig. 7, contains two good
sleeping rooms and two large closets. There are no fireplaces, but openings are left for stove-pipes in the flues, so that
one or both rooms can be warmed.

There is a cellar under this cottage, and the outer cellar
door should be provided just beneath the pantry window, if no
more convenient position is found for it.

Cottages of this size usually have the stairs placed in the
living-room, while the front door opens directly into one of
the apartments. We think, in this respect, our plan has
much greater comfort and convenience to recommend it.

CONSTRUCTION. This cottage is to be built of wood, and the
weather-boarding is to be put on in the *vertical manner*, with
battens nailed over the joints, described in our last section.

In many parts of the country, where lumber planed by
machinery is not easily obtained, we would use inch boards
rough, or without planing, and put them on with square edges
(not matched). The batten completely covers the joint. This
will cheapen the cottage considerably, if planing is to be done

by hand; and for all outbuildings and cheap cottages, rough boarding, either painted and sanded, or washed over by the cottager himself with a cheap wash, which we shall give the recipe for, produces an effect even more satisfactory to the eye, because more rustic and picturesque, than planed boards.

But steam-planed boards and plank are now offered so cheaply (that is to say, at only three or four dollars per thousand feet additional cost, being at the same time matched or tongued and grooved), that they are now almost universally used for covering houses with vertical boarding.

Planed-and-matched flooring boards, one inch thick, and of good quality, can be had, here, for about seventeen dollars per thousand feet, or at Rochester or Bangor for fourteen dollars. The same boards *rough*, are worth on the Hudson fourteen dollars, and at Rochester eleven dollars;* and as this cottage would require about fourteen hundred feet of weather-boarding, the economy in either of these localities, by using rough boards, would be only about five dollars in the cost of the whole cottage; so that, under these circumstances, we should prefer the planed boards, because there is some additional warmth in the closer joints made by having the edges matched.

To make the cottage comfortable for the north, it should be *filled-in* with soft bricks, placed on edge, so as to allow the inside wall to be plastered on the brick, as described in page

---

* Inch boards are sufficient for small cottages; but for villas or country houses of a superior class, *inch and a quarter* planed and matched *floor planks* are used for weather-boarding. These are worth, here, from twenty to twenty two dollars per thousand; at Rochester they are worth from fifteen to twenty dollars, and at Bangor, fourteen to eighteen dollars.

53. In the milder parts of the Union this will not be necessary, and, if omitted, the cost of the cottage will be lessened about twenty-five dollars—counting the price of soft bricks at three dollars per thousand.

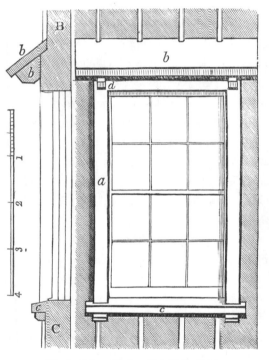

[Fig. 8. Cottage Window—Plain Rising Sash.]

Fig. 8 shows a window suitable in style and construction for this class of wooden cottages; having twelve lights, ten by twelve inches, and common rising sashes. The outside facing or dressings of this window, and especially the hood, *b*, and the sill, *c*, should be of good plank, two inches thick. The facings, *c*, should be four or five inches wide, and should project the whole thickness of the stuff beyond the face of the weather-boarding. The *hood* itself, *b*, projects eight inches beyond the face of the weather-boarding, and is supported by two plain brackets, *d*, made either of common joist, or thick plank. In this figure, B C is a *profile* section of the same window, in which the letters refer to the same parts.

We have been thus minute in describing this cottage window, because the error, into which carpenters frequently fall, is that of making wooden window dressings so meager in all that meets the eye on the outside, that they have none of that force and picturesqueness which should belong to a cottage built of wood in this manner.

The hood over the front door, as shown in Design I., is a foot wide, and is supported by brackets more ornamental than those under the windows, to denote the greater importance of the principal entrance.

The roof of this cottage projects two feet, and, like all cheap cottages in this country, is covered with shingles. On the sides, the rafters are continued out to support the eaves, and on the gables, short pieces of joist are fitted in to support the sheathing of the roof, and to give unity of effect.

Estimate. On the Hudson, this cottage, with a cellar under the whole building, and filled-in with bricks on edge, will cost $400. An estimate from an experienced builder at Rochester, places the cost there at $330.

DESIGN II.—*A small Bracketed Cottage.*

THIS little cottage, with about the same number of square feet as Design I., is more picturesque, from its irregular form.

DESIGN II.

SMALL BRACKETED COTTAGE.

Fig. 9

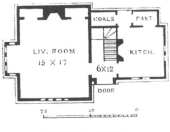

PRINCIPAL FLOOR.

Fig. 10.

It would, on this account, be selected by all those who prefer irregular to regular symmetry.

There is also a good deal more *feeling* shown in this cottage than in Design I. The features which express this are the bay window, the rustic trellises covered with vines, and the bracketed vine-canopy over the end window in the principal apartment.

Now, every cottage may not display *science* or knowledge, because science demands architectural education in its builder or designer, as well as, in many cases, some additional expense. But *feeling* may be evinced by every one possessing it, and there is no more striking or successful way of manifesting it in a cottage than by the employment of permanent vines to embellish it. Something of a love for the beautiful, in the inmates, is always suggested by a vine-covered cottage, because mere utility would never lead any person to plant flowering vines; and much of positive beauty is always conferred upon simple cottage forms by the graceful growth of vines, through the rural and domestic expression they give to the cottage. We say domestic expression, because, as vines are never planted by architects, masons, carpenters, or those who build the cottage, but always by those who live in it, and make it truly a home, and generally by the mother or daughter, whose very planting of vines is a labor of love offered up on the domestic altar, it follows, by the most direct and natural associations, that vines on a rural cottage always express domesticity and the presence of heart.

If any one wishes to know the effect, in a simple cottage, of a little feeling of this kind added to that simplest kind of architecture which rises but little above common sense, he has only to compare the view of this cottage in Fig. 9 with Fig. 11, which is precisely the same cottage (though in Fig. 9 the front and entrance side are shown; in Fig. 11, the same entrance side with the rear end).

[Fig. 11.]

In the view before us, the architecture is the same, but the end window is stripped of the bracket overhung with clustering vines, and the cottage wants the softening and humanizing expression which these accessories give to Fig. 9.

A *bay-window*, such as that seen in the living-room, Fig. 10, since it does not of necessity belong to a small cottage, raises the character of such a cottage wherever it is simply and tastefully introduced. It also adds very considerably to the agreeable effect of the apartment itself—giving an air of some dignity to even the smallest dwelling.

The little rustic arbors or covered seats on the outside of the bay-window may be supposed to answer in some measure in the place of a veranda, and convey, at the first glance, an impression of refinement and taste attained in that simple manner so appropriate to a small cottage.

Accommodation. The plan of the first floor of this cottage (Fig. 10) shows an entry, six by twelve feet, containing a flight of stairs to the chamber floor, under which are stairs to the cellar. On the left is the living-room of the family, fifteen by seventeen feet. The deep chimney-breast at the end of the room gives space for two large closets. The bay-window measures six feet in the opening (in the clear), and is three feet deep.

On the right of the entry is the kitchen, a small room, ten by twelve feet. As the living-room of the family will, in a great measure, be also the kitchen, this small kitchen will in fact be used as a *back*-kitchen for the rough-work, washing, etc., so that in summer, and indeed at any time, the living-room can be made to have the comfortable aspect of a cottage parlor, by confining the rough-work to the kitchen proper. Back of this kitchen is a small lean-to addition, containing a small pantry, four by six feet, and a place for coals. There is a small passage between this closet or pantry and the coal-hole, and opposite the door opening from the kitchen into this passage, is a door which serves as a back door to enter the kitchen without going in the front entrance.

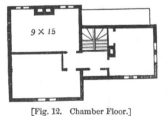

[Fig. 12. Chamber Floor.]

Fig. 12 shows the chamber floor, with two bed-rooms, each nine by fifteen feet, and one bed-room ten by twelve feet. Flues, with places for stove-pipes, are shown in two of these rooms.

Variation of the plan. This plan may be easily varied, so

as to give a more agreeable and symmetrical effect, with little additional cost. To do this, lessen the depth of the chimney-breast at the end of the room, and reject the two closets there. This would make the living-room two and a half feet longer, or fifteen by nineteen feet six inches. Next place the bay-window exactly in the centre of the wall, which would add to the external symmetry. By turning the place for coals into a closet, with a door opening into the living-room, and having a wood-house or coal-house detached, space would be gained, and the arrangement would be more pleasing, though, perhaps, not quite so convenient.

CONSTRUCTION. The construction of this cottage is the same as that of Design I. Planed-and-matched or rough boards may be used for the vertical weather-boarding; we should prefer to have them rough (if the cottage is filled-in), and painted and sanded.

We have shown in this cottage the simplest form of cottage window—that is, the casement window opening in two parts, from top to bottom. These sashes are less expensive than rising sashes with weights, but more so than those without weights. The latticed sash with diamond panes we have introduced as more significant of a cottage. Indeed, there is something in the associations connected with latticed windows so essentially rural and cottage-like, that the mere introduction of them gives an air of poetry to a house in the country.

The chimney-tops are built of brick, in a very simple, but, at the same time, more tasteful manner than the common heavy brick stacks usually seen.

The front door is merely covered with a hood on brackets. Its beauty would be enhanced by making this canopy or hood

DESIGN III.

SYMMETRICAL BRACKETED COTTAGE.

Fig. 13.

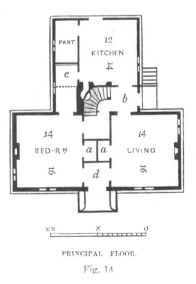

PRINCIPAL FLOOR.

Fig. 14

bolder and extending it five feet, making the sides of lattice work, and covering the whole with vines.

Estimate. The whole cost of this cottage, in this part of the country, would be $512. In the interior, where wood is cheaper, it may be built for about $400. In this, we include a cellar under the kitchen and entry, but not under the living-room. The foundation walls of the latter should be laid three and a half feet below the level of the ground.

DESIGN III.—*A Symmetrical Bracketed Cottage.*

WE trust our readers will agree with us in looking upon this as a successful example of a rural cottage. It appears to us to combine more beauty, both of form and expression, than the majority of designs of this class, and, therefore, to be worthy of a little critical examination.

In the first place, the good *proportions* of this cottage strike the eye. It is neither too high nor too low. The eaves could not be raised or lowered a foot without more or less disturbing this balance between the upper and lower portions of the building.

Perhaps the first charm which this cottage has for the eye, arises from its symmetry. There is such a direct and real pleasure in this balance of three parts made by an arrangement like this, when a leading feature, like the gabled window in the front of this cottage, is placed exactly in the centre, that the eye has something of the same satisfaction in contemplating it that the ear has in listening to the rhythm of easy and correct versification.

Though small, this cottage is not wanting in variety; and though there is not enough variety to allow of harmony, yet the whole displays an entire unity of feeling. Take away the gabled window, and the porch ornament, and substitute a straight-lined roof and a plain, common doorway, and the front loses its symmetry, and falls to the rank of plain regularity.

But the greatest charm of this cottage to our eyes, is the expression of simple but refined home-beauty which it conveys. No person would build such a quaint yet modest porch as this, no one would give this simple character of beauty to the windows, and no one would reach this exact height of tasteful simplicity in the whole exterior character, unless he had a real appreciation of the beautiful and truthful in cottage life, rather than that false ambition which leads men to make small cottages ape great villas. The owner of this cottage either lives in a climate so far north that he needs no veranda, or he feels that he cannot afford one: but the pretty little open porch, with its overhanging window and its seat, where, in the cooler hours of the day, the husband, the wife, and the children may sit and enjoy the fresh breath of morning or evening hours, convey an idea of something beyond the merely physical wants, quite as forcibly as the veranda usually does.

Altogether, this cottage evinces much of absolute and relative beauty—the universal beauty of form, and the relative beauty of refined purposes. Without recommending it as a model cottage, we should be glad to find that dwellings of this simply beautiful character become greater favorites, with those of our countrymen who build cottages, than designs of more pretension. We cannot but look upon it as greatly superior in truthful beauty of character to cottages of this class highly decorated, as we frequently see them, with overwrought verge boards on all the gables, and an excess of fanciful and flowing ornaments of a card-board character.

ACCOMMODATION. The plan of this house, Fig. 14, is that of a very simple cottage, with only a living-room, bed-room, and kitchen on one floor. The arrangement of this floor, however, shows a good deal of compactness and convenience for a small family. The porch or entry, *d*, is 5 feet wide, opening on one side into the living-room, and on the other into the bed-room—each 14 by 16 feet. Each of these rooms has a closet, *a*. The living-room has an open grate, or fire-place: the bed-room may have an open fire-place or a stove flue, as the occupant pleases.

The back entry is shown at *b*—also 5 feet wide. This back entry communicates with the living-room, the kitchen, and the bed-room—as well as with the open air by a back door opposite *b*. This door opens on a landing or platform with a railing on the left-hand side, to guard the stone steps which on that side descend to the cellar. This back entry, *b*, also contains the stairs to the chamber floor. These stairs, placed as they are in this back entry, are much more conveniently located, for all parties, than if placed in one near the front door—while they are accessible from all the rooms, without, as is often the case in small cottages, being located in any one of the rooms.

The kitchen, 12 by 14 feet, is lighted by two windows, and has a well-lighted pantry 4 by 7 feet, as well as another closet, *c*, for cooking utensils, etc. In this closet, a partition is shown by the dotted lines. This closet, *c*, may be left entire by omitting this partition, when it would make a good store-room. As it now stands, the portion nearest the bed-room would make a second closet for the latter apartment. A large brick oven is shown alongside the fire-place, the body of which runs under the stairs.

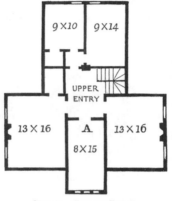

[Fig. 15. Chamber Floor.]

The second floor of this cottage, Fig. 15, gives a great deal of sleeping accommodation for a dwelling of this size—no less than five good bed-rooms.* Two of these bed-rooms are quite large cottage rooms, 13 by 16 feet, and the others sufficiently large for children. The neat little bed-room, A, with the hanging window over the porch, though only 8 by 15, would be a pretty apartment for the eldest daughter—where she would have an opportunity to arrange her little cottage boudoir to show her own taste.

---

* By an error in transposing the drawing, the position of the *stairs* in the Figs. 14 and 15 do not correspond. The stairs in Fig. 15 should occupy the space on the *left* of the upper entry, where the closet now stands, instead of being on the right of the entry.

A cellar under the kitchen wing of this cottage would be sufficient in most cases. In this case, a good stone foundation, 3 feet deep, should be laid under the main building.

Variation in plan. As there is sufficient bed-room accommodation in the second floor of this cottage for most families, the plan of the first floor might be improved by turning the bedroom into a parlor. In this case the two closets, *a*, *a* (Fig. 14), may be dispensed with, so that the two rooms might communicate by large doors—the closets being moved to the entry space between the bed-room and the back entry, *b*, which would no longer need to be left open—this would leave an open space with doors five feet wide at *a*, on one side of which would be the front entry, *d*, and on the other, the altered closets. This would give a much more spacious and agreeable, as well as more airy and cheerful character to the principal rooms of this cottage with no additional cost.

CONSTRUCTION. This is a wooden cottage, and the vertical boarding already described is the mode adopted in covering the exterior. The roof, which projects 2 feet at the eaves, is supported on plain rafter brackets.

The porch, though simple, being somewhat novel, we give a sectional working drawing (to the scale of a quarter of an inch to a foot). This drawing shows the *profile* of this porch. Now, in order to convey the proper expression of strength and solidity, the perpendicular brackets of this porch, *a*, should be made of heavy plank, not less than 4 inches thick, so that it shall not have a meager and paltry appearance when executed; *b* shows the floor of the bed-room running out in the hanging window; *c*, the projection of the roof over this window.

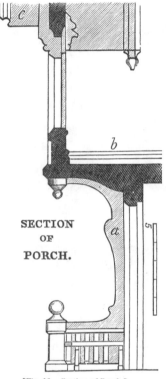

SECTION
OF
PORCH.

[Fig. 16.   Section of Porch.]

COTTAGE CASEMENT WINDOW. Having shown in Fig. 8, **a**
cottage window with rising sashes, we here give a casement
window, suitable, in size and proportion, for cottages of this
class, and adapted in construction to vertical-boarded wooden
cottages.

One of the glaring sins of our country carpentry is the
want of character in the windows of our wooden houses. To
give character to a window, the dressings should have some
boldness and weight of substance, otherwise it looks like a
mere hole in the wall. A piece of window frame an inch or

two wide, seen on the outside of the building, is not sufficient to produce any impression on the eye at the distance of fifty rods. The wooden cottage window should therefore have a dressing, not less than 3 or 4 inches wide, and in some cases they may be still bolder.

The window here shown is one designed especially for this style of building before us. The hood over the window may be adopted or not, but it adds beauty and force to the win-

[Fig. 17. Casement Cottage Window.]

dow, individually, and brings it more completely into harmony with the other features, and especially with the projecting roof.

In Fig. 17, A A, represents the elevation, C D, the profile section, and E F, the horizontal section or plan of this window, all drawn to the scale given in the figure, of half an inch to a foot. The hood *a*, sill *b*, and facings *c*, are made of good sound plank, not less than 2 inches thick (and better $2\frac{1}{2}$ inches); *c* is 5 inches wide, the mullion in the centre of the window, *d*, being of the same width. The *battens*, *e*, extend down over the top of the hood in this window, which gives it a more picturesque character than in Fig. 12.

We have shown lattice or diamond sashes in this window, and in most of our cottage windows, not because we think this form of sash indispensable, but that we think it most expressive of that simple, rustic beauty, which belongs to, and as we have already remarked, is so strongly associated with, cottage life in the country. Any one who prefers large panes, set in square sashes, may adopt them instead, but he will sacrifice something of the poetry in order to gain perhaps a little more of utility and economy.

The *mullion*, as the central division of this window, *d*, is called, is, we think, a very expressive and important feature. It is not only useful as a post, for the centre of casement sashes to shut against, but takes away from the leanness of a common window frame. Besides this, it lessens both the breadth of sash, as well as the breadth of outside blind necessary in a window of a given size and proportion. A broad mullion like this gives, also, not unfrequently an opportunity in certain parts of the house, to divide closets or rooms by abutting a partition against it, so that two closets, or two small apartments may be lighted with one window—which is something that could never be done with good effect in a common window.

Indeed, so much do we value the *mullion* in houses of this style that we would retain it even where rising sashes are used, and would make these sashes harmonize with it by having a broad *style* in the centre of the sash opposite, or behind the mullion, which would conceal the mullion from the inside and bring it into keeping on the outside of the window.

Where outside shutter blinds are to be used, as they now are almost universally in this country, the brackets, *i*, under the hood, must be kept high enough to allow the shutters to open and shut freely without touching them. Though we think windows of this kind are greatly improved by the introduction of the mullion, yet the general effect will not be injured by its omission.

The chimneys of this cottage may be taken as an example of the most simple treatment of common materials—brick and mortar, with little or no increase of expense. A common brick chimney (see DESIGN V.) gives no positive pleasure by its form, because that form is *lumpish* and unmeaning. To make a chimney form interesting, however simple it may be, it must be divided into three parts, viz. a base, a shaft, and a cap. A chimney should never spring out of the roof with no apparent preparation for it, but a base more or less wide should always be shown, upon which the part exposed may evidently rest and obtain a solid foundation to withstand high winds. After dividing a chimney top into three parts, the next point of art is to *proportion* the whole so that it may, in the first place, have the most agreeable form, and in the second place, a form in keeping with the rest of the dwelling.

The first story of this cottage is 10 feet, and the second 8½ feet high. Both stories to be furnished with brown walls, the bed-rooms to be whitewashed, and the two best rooms to be papered.

Estimate. The estimated cost of this cottage, on the Hudson, is $975.

In portions of the country where materials are much cheaper it may be erected for from $600 to $700.

DESIGN IV.—*A small Cottage of Brick and Stucco, in the Gothic Style.*

IN this design we have a much more architectural cottage than the foregoing ones, and one built in solid materials. Stone, indeed, would most perfectly express the spirit of this design, but, except in a few cases when it could be very easily and cheaply obtained, brick and stucco, or rubble stone and rough-cast, must necessarily be used to bring it within the means of the occupant.

When we say this design is more architectura. than the foregoing, we must be understood to mean that it is more expressive of architectural style. The pointed windows in the sleeping rooms, and especially the triple, lancet-shaped window in the nearest gable, as well as the finished character of the bay-window, would seem to indicate the expenditure of more *means* than is generally at the command of the occupant of a cottage of two or three rooms on a floor. The principles which we have already laid down, therefore,. would lead us either to consider this design as intended for the gardener's house or gate-lodge on a gentleman's place, where sufficient architectural style to harmonize with the general air of the estate is permissible, or to simplify it so as to render it sufficiently *truthful* to express the life and means of the occupant.

To do this it will only be necessary to substitute single square-headed windows in the attic rooms instead of those shown in the plan, and to give the bay-window a rather more simple form. The rest of the house may remain as it is at present.

As contrasted with the last plan, this little cottage is an irregular one, or its form is one of the irregularly symmetrical kind. It will, therefore, please those who prefer picturesque, to more regular beauty of form. Its little porch, bay-window, and clustered chimney-tops render it expressive of more refinement and cultivation than we generally see in a cottage—though in the design as presented in the engraving there is, as we have said, so much science combined with the expression that one does not feel at a glance, that the refinement all springs from the heart and mind of the inmates themselves, as in Design II.

ACCOMMODATION. The living-room of this dwelling, 16 feet square (see Fig. 19), is a remarkably nice apartment for a cottage, and being not only dignified with a fine bay-window, but forming, as it does, a separate portion of the cottage, it gives this floor an air of superior comfort. There is a small closet for china on the right of the fire-place in this room. The door on the left of this fire-place opens into the back entry, in which is placed the flight of stairs to the second floor, beneath which descends the flight to the cellar.

There is a sort of double porch, the first part (marked *umbrage* on the plan) being open, and the second part, being the porch proper, which is closed. By making the door between these a large one, the whole of this is turned into a cool and pleasant little shaded passage or veranda in summer.

The kitchen, 14 by 16 feet, has a square flue in the corner to admit the pipe of a kitchen cooking-stove, the peculiar convenience of American cottages. In the rear of the kitchen is a small room 8 feet square, which may be used as a large pantry, or *store-room* (with a smaller closet in the rear), or as a back kitchen or wash-room, as best suits the wants of the occupant.

There is also a closet at the back of this room, with an entrance under the stairs and near the back door, which is intended for "stove-wood."

The plan of the chamber floor, Fig. 20, shows three bedrooms—two of ample size, and the third smaller—8 by 12 feet.

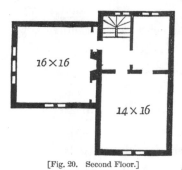

16×16

14×16

[Fig. 20. Second Floor.]

A cellar under the whole of this cottage, except the living-room, will probably be large enough for the wants of such a family as would occupy it.

CONSTRUCTION. This cottage could in many localities be built of rubble or cobble stones, and cemented externally at a very moderate cost, so as to give the effect of the perspective elevation. Or it may be built with hollow brick walls, as explained in the preceding section, and covered with stucco on the exterior. As the roof, however, does not project, it does not offer so good a protection to stucco as we desire in this climate. The best

DESIGN IV.

SMALL GOTHIC COTTAGE.

Fig. 18.

LIVING-Rᴹ
16 × 16

KITCH.
14 × 16

UMB.   PORCH

PRINCIPAL FLOOR.

Fig. 19.

DESIGN V.

WORKINGMAN'S MODEL COTTAGE.

Fig. 22.

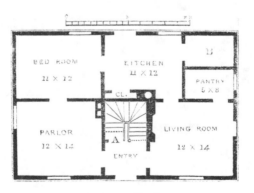

PRINCIPAL FLOOR

Fig. 23.

mode, therefore, would be to build a hollow 16 inch brick wall, with a plain stone coping to the gables, and color the whole with the wash for brick walls, described in a succeeding page. The chimney tops shown in the elevation are a pair of the Garnkirk fire-brick material, sold by Jas. Lee & Co., of New York and Boston, at $6 each—which have an excellent effect, and are durable in our climate.

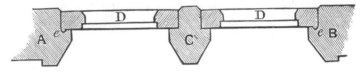

[Fig. 21. Section of Window.]

Fig. 21 shows a section of a Gothic window, suitable for this cottage; A, B, show the splayed jambs of the exterior; C, is the mullion; D, the sash. To make a casement sash like this perfectly tight, if there are no outside blinds to protect it against driving storms, it is necessary to mould the small heel, e, on the outer corner of the sash; this, shutting into a corresponding hollow, prevents the most violent storm from entering.

Estimate. If cut stone labels and coping are used for this cottage it will cost $1200. If moulded brick are used for the labels (lintels) over the windows, and common stone, hammer-dressed, for the coping, it may be built for $996.

DESIGN V.—*A Working-man's Model Cottage.*

OUR object, in this design, is to give the greatest amount of accommodation and convenience, at the smallest cost, for the dwelling of a large family who live in a very simple and economical manner. While the exterior is, therefore, very plain, the least possible ornament being used, there is still an expression of symmetrical beauty, and a certain cheerfulness of external effect. It is certainly a cottage which will convey an idea of taste in the occupants, so far as the exterior is concerned.

The interior is one which contains a great deal of room, most compactly and conveniently arranged—so arranged, in short, as to enable the inmates wholly to " do their own work," if either inclination or necessity prompts them, without any loss of convenience, or the necessity of taking any unnecessary steps.

The exterior of this cottage would be raised in character as well as comfort, by a veranda, like that in Design IX. This could easily be added; but we have preferred in this example to make the interior accommodation the first object.

ACCOMMODATION. The rooms in this cottage are none of them large, but they are all *snug*, and their number and connection compensate for the want of extra size in any one apartment.

The entry (see Fig. 23) is 7 feet wide. It contains a flight of stairs to the second floor. At A, is a door, opening which, you descend the cellar stairs, which occupy the space under the highest portion of the other flight.

The living-room, which is the common family-room, eating-room, and almost every thing else, in such a cottage, measures 12 by 14 feet. It has a well-lighted pantry opening into it. Close adjoining the living-room, and connected with it by a door, is the kitchen. The kitchen opens directly "out of doors," and this door, which is virtually the back door, may be protected by a temporary porch in winter—if desirable. B, is a small room which may be used as a store-room, if there is a wood-house near the house; or if not, it may be used for keeping stove-wood or fuel for the kitchen and living-room. There is a closet for crockery, ect., at the side of the chimney flue in the kitchen.

Out of the kitchen opens a bed-room 11 by 12 feet. This may be used as the bed-room of the master and mistress, in which case it must have a large wardrobe-closet placed in it, and in which case also, it will always be most convenient and comfortable in winter from its proximity to the kitchen, which the mistress of such a cottage as this is supposed not to be able to have too near her for her own supervision. Or it may be kept as a "spare bed-room;" when the door and the entrance to this room may be through the parlor.

We have given a parlor to this cottage, though in most cheap cottages, the living-room is virtually the parlor, because we think in a cottage with so much accommodation as this, there should be one apartment of superior character. The American cottager is no peasant, but thinks, and thinks correctly, that as soon as he can afford it, he deserves a parlor, where he can receive his guests with propriety, as well as his wealthiest neighbor. We respect this feeling entirely, and only object to the parlor when it is brought in, to the exclusion of any other apartment more necessary to the every-day comfort of the family.

As this parlor is less frequently used in winter, we have

shown only a flue for a stove, and not a chimney for an open
fire-place or grate, as in the living-room.

All of that part of this cottage required for daily use, viz.
the living-room, kitchen, bed-room, pantry, and room for stores
or fuel, are so connected together that they can, if necessary,
be warmed by one fire, and not a step need be lost in
conducting the business of the household. If B is used as a
place for fuel, it should have an outer door for receiving the
same, and there should also be an outside cellar door (with
steps) in the rear of the house, to allow vegetables, &c., to be
taken in without passing through the entry. This cellar door
may be placed under the window in the bed-room, so as to be
convenient of access to the back door of the kitchen.

The flue in the kitchen is drawn into the dining-room
chimney-breast.

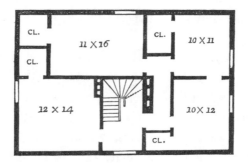

[Fig. 24. Chamber Floor.]

The chamber floor of this cottage (Fig. 24) contains four
good bed-rooms, all provided with excellent closets. The two
largest bed-rooms should have openings left in the flues for
stove-pipes, and the bed-room 10 by 12 may also be warmed

by a stove, by conveying the pipe (high enough to walk under) across the small entry into one of the stove flues from the living-room chimney stack.

CONSTRUCTION. For the construction of this cottage, we refer the reader to Design I. Vertical boarding with plain battens and the boards left rough, and colored with the cottage wash (given in a succeeding page), the whole filled in with brick on edge, would be a very satisfactory mode of building for it. In many parts of the country, it may, however, not be necessary to fill in the frame, and then, matched and planed plank may be used, and the exterior painted two coats and sanded, for about the same cost. Indeed the difference in cost between rough boards (unmatched), and matched and planed boards, when the latter can be bought machine-planed, would be only about $6 for the whole of this cottage.

For the form and construction of the windows of this cottage, we refer to Fig. 8. The windows shown by our engraver in Fig. 22, are not so well proportioned as those built after Fig. 8 would appear when executed.

Estimate. Supposing a cellar to be made under the whole of this cottage, the construction such as we have pointed out, and the exterior to be painted with our cottage paint, the cost here would be $600—a very moderate sum for the great amount of accommodation afforded. An estimate made by a builder at Rochester, N. Y., places the cost, exclusive of outside painting, at $575.*

---

* Perhaps the cost of materials and labor in the interior of the State of New York, may be taken as about a fair average for the country at large.

The following is the general estimate of labor and materials of this working-man's cottage, made at our request, by a carpenter in Rochester :

DESIGN VI.—*A Gate-Lodge in the English style.*

THE chief merit of this cottage is its picturesqueness. It is as irregular as so small a cottage can well be, and retain any thing of symmetrical beauty in its composition. Placed among fine groups of trees, with a well-wooded background, this design would have a striking and most agreeable effect, because the variety and irregularity of its outline would be

4200 ft. of framing timber, ...	$42 00
Framing and setting partitions, ...	26 00
1500 ft. of planed and matched boards, ...	22 50
420 ft. for battens, ...	6 10
Labor on weather-boarding, including nails, . . .	18 00
1152 ft. of sheathing-boards for roof, ...	11 52
Labor and nails in sheathing, ...	5 00
11¼ squares of roof, shingles, nails and labor, . . .	40 25
1600 ft. flooring, ...	24 00
Labor and nails for laying do., ...	8 00
320 ft. of base—6 inches wide, ...	12 00
11 windows glazed and finished inside and out, with plain 4-inch architraves, ...	38 50
16, 4-panel doors, with plain architraves, ...	58 00
Stairs, ...	13 00
Pantry, closets, shelves, and fixtures, ...	11 50
Chimneys, materials, and labor, ...	24 00
Lead for valley of roof, ...	1 75
343 yards of plastering, two-coat work, ...	61 74
Add, for cellar walls, work and materials, ...	100 00
And other hardware fixtures, and sundries, etc., . . .	40 00
	$573 86

DESIGN VI.

A GATE LODGE.

Fig. 25.

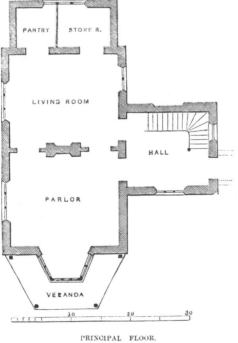

PRINCIPAL FLOOR.

Fig. 26.

supported by the varied forms of foliage and bough. Placed in an open space, bare of trees, where Design II. would look very well, this design would appear out of keeping and inharmonious.

As the most economical form for a cottage is a square, and next to that a parallelogram, it is evident that all irregular cottages are more costly than regular ones. Such a design as this, therefore, will not be chosen by any one with whom economy of first cost is a primary consideration. We offer it, however, either as an ornamental cottage for some small family who desire a snug little residence for part of the year, or as a pretty gate-lodge for the entrance to a gentleman's place.

The style of this design is the Rural Gothic, that beautiful modified form of Gothic architecture which we adopt from the English people; and which certainly expresses as large a union of domestic feeling and artistic knowledge as any other known.

The outline of this little cottage as shown in the elevation, is varied by the projecting bay in both stories, with a truncated gable over it, by the other ornamental gabled window in the roof, and the small gabled porch. The little veranda round the lower bay-window, from its small size, and its not being directly connected with any of the apartments, is evidently intended as much for ornament as for enjoyment. A veranda 8 or 9 feet broad might extend along one side of the cottage, so as to cover the two large windows of the living-room and parlor—either or both of which, extending to the floor, would give easy access to the veranda, and render it, for summer enjoyment, equal to another apartment on the same floor.

Such a veranda would be more convenient and comfortable, but not quite so harmonious and picturesque as that shown in the present elevation.

ACCOMMODATION. Taking this plan as it appears in Fig. 26, it is evidently intended for a small, genteel family. The hall or entry, 12 by 14 feet, is more spacious than most cottages of this size would require, and there is no kitchen on the first floor. The kitchen for a family of this kind, would be a basement room directly under the living-room. Its windows in this case must be lighted by areas, if the ground is so level on that side of the cottage that the slope of the surface is not sufficient to allow of lighting them without it. The inside entrance to this basement kitchen is by a flight of steps descending under the stairs in the hall. All this is based upon the supposition that the cottage is occupied by a small family, keeping servants.

If occupied by a small family without servants, or as a gate-lodge, what is called the living-room on the plan, would become the kitchen, and the parlor a bed-room or a living-room. In this case, the hall might be turned to further account by running a partition through the middle of it, the longest way— making half of it an entry, 6 feet wide, containing the stairs, and the other half a pantry or store-room. This will enable us either to dispense with the little wing containing the pantry and store-room at the end of the kitchen (living-room), or to turn it into a wash-room, or small bed-room 7½ by 15 feet.

We do not give the plan of the second floor. If not much room is wanted, it would most easily be divided into three bed-rooms—one over each of the two rooms—and a third, 10 by 12 feet, over part of the hall not wanted for the passage.

(The wing containing pantry and store-room, is only one story high.) If more bed-rooms are required, then one of the large rooms can be divided into two small ones, which would give four bed-rooms for the second floor.

CONSTRUCTION. The roof of this cottage is covered with shingles of uniform size, the lower part of which being cut to a point, they form, when laid on, a diamond pattern. (For this mode of shingling, see section on *Miscellaneous details.*) This is a very simple and effective mode of increasing the beauty of a cottage roof.

Particular attention must be paid, in all irregular cottages of this kind, to the roofing of the *valleys*, or lines where the intersecting roofs meet—because the water from the higher parts of the roof all finds its way to these valleys before reaching the eaves, and, therefore, if these valleys are not thoroughly constructed, and made perfectly tight, leaky places are certain to show themselves immediately, to the great injury of the house and inconvenience of the inmates.

To make a tight roof, these valleys should be lined or covered before shingles or slates are laid on, with broad strips of copper, lead, or galvanized iron—the former is the best, and the latter the poorest material; good thick lead is most commonly used for cottages, being less expensive than copper. This strip of metal laid down in the valleys should be not less than 8 inches wide,—extending up the roof each side, at least 4 inches. In the best villas, a still wider strip of copper is used. The shingles or slates are laid over this metal valley so as to leave 3 inches uncovered, the whole length serving as a channel or gutter from the top of the valley down to the eaves; this affords a free passage for the accumulated current of water, guards against leakage, and prevents the roof itself from decaying or rotting, and the metal from rusting in the angle of the valley.

The walls are 12-inch hollow brick walls, covered on the outside with the lime and sand stucco described in the preceding section. The porch and veranda are built of wood, painted and sanded so as to harmonize in color with the stucco. The roof projects two feet, and the ornamental verge-boards are carved out of two-inch plank. (For the pattern of this verge-board see Fig. 29.) The chimney-stack is built of brick, four separate flues in a cluster.

Estimate. The cost of this cottage, with basement kitchen, so as to fit it for a neat little establishment, would be $1360. If finished very plainly inside, and the living-room turned into a kitchen, it may be built for about $1100. The extra cost, as we have already remarked, is owing to its irregularity, and the introduction of so many decorated gables.

DESIGN VII.—*A Symmetrical Cottage.*

WHOEVER loves symmetry and the simpler kind of cottage beauty, including good proportion, tasteful forms, and chasteness of ornament, we think, cannot but like this little design, since it unites all those requisites. It is an illustration of a cottage made ornamental with a very trifling expense, and without sacrificing truthfulness to that kind of tasteful simplicity which is the true touchstone of cottage beauty.

This. cottage is designed in the rural Gothic or English manner, but much modified, so as to adapt it to almost any site. Instead of adopting a very ornate verge-board, which properly

DESIGN VII.

SYMMETRICAL COTTAGE.

Fig. 27.

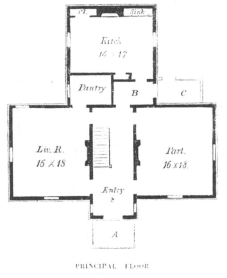

PRINCIPAL FLOOR

Fig. 28

belongs to a villa, it will be seen that the form here shown (of which Fig. 29 is a portion, to a scale of $\frac{1}{4}$ inch to a foot) is so

[Fig. 29.   Verge-Board.]

simple as to be easily executed without fear of its falling into the gingerbread character.   It should be made of two-inch plank.

The light, open porch of this cottage may be omitted without injuring the design, but it gives the front an air of so much feeling and refinement, aside from its manifest utility, that we should always hope to see it adopted by those about to execute the design.   [For the details of front windows, see section on Miscellaneous Details.]

ACCOMMODATION.   The plan of this cottage (Fig. 28), though not so simple as the foregoing, is still by no means complex. There is however, a much greater combination of the agreeable and the useful here, than in Design IV.—since the kitchen is on the same floor with the living-room.   Many families would prefer to use the room marked "parlor" in the plan, as a bed-room, and, if so used, the cottage would be a very complete one for a small family—having living-room, bed-room, pantry, etc., on the same floor.   But to others who would prefer to have no bed-room on this floor, a parlor would be looked upon as far more important.

In the plan of this floor, A is the porch, from which we enter
the hall or entry, 8 feet wide—with the two best rooms, each
16 by 18 feet, on either side of it. Connected with the living-
room, in its rear, is a good pantry. B is the back-entry
communicating with the kitchen. C is the back-porch, which
may be left open in summer and enclosed in winter, when it
will serve as a place for coal and wood. On one side of the
kitchen fireplace is a closet, and on the other a sink, into which,
if possible, a water-pipe should be brought.

The second floor of this cottage,

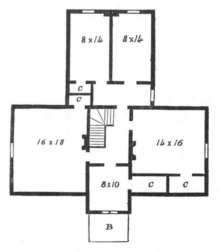

[Fig. 30. Chamber Floor.]

Fig. 30, shows 5 bed-rooms. B is the balcony on the porch;
C C are closets. The two stacks of chimneys may be drawn
over in the garret, and united to form one, as shown in Fig. 27,
or they may be carried up separately.

The effect of the two best rooms on the principal floor of this house will be simple and chaste if they are tastefully papered and painted. A variation might be made by cutting off the corners of the parlor, thus turning it into a small *octagon* room. The space in those corners, not occupied by doors, might then be finished with simple bookcases built in the walls. By not carrying these bookcases to the floor, a space would be left below them for a couch or divan, which would have a pretty effect. (See Fig. 31, a sketch of the octagonal corner.)

[Fig. 31. The Parlor finished as an Octagon.]

This parlor would of course appear larger, and would cost less, if finished with square corners as in Fig. 28, but we suggest the octagon form to those who desire a little novelty.

The first story of this cottage is supposed to be 10 feet, and the chamber story 5 feet on the sides, and 8 feet in the middle of the rooms. The pitch of the roof is a right angle.

As the entry, or hall, of this plan is wide, and the arrange-

ments both simple and convenient, we think it will be difficult
to build a more agreeable cottage, for the sum proposed, than
the present design.   Though picturesque in its exterior, it is not
so much so as to *demand* a highly rural or picturesque site, but
would look equally well either in the suburbs of a town or in
the midst of the country.

[Fig. 32. Chimney-Tops.]

The chimneys in the elevation show one of the forms made
in Garnkirk fire-clay.   Two patterns are shown in Fig. 32,
either of which is a well-proportioned and pleasing one for a
cottage of this kind—*a* is four feet nine inches high; *b*, four
feet six inches.   These are sold by the importers (Jas. Lee &
Co., New York and Boston) at from $4 to $6 each.   The base
for this chimney (of common brick-work) should be carried

DESIGN VIII.

SUBURBAN COTTAGE.

Fig. 33.

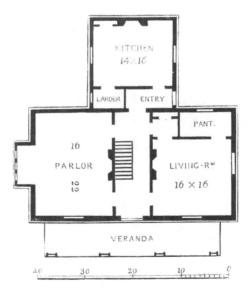

PRINCIPAL FLOOR

Fig. 34.

up a couple of feet above the level of the ridge of the roof, before the chimney-tops are set.

CONSTRUCTION. The exterior of this cottage is vertical boarding—of planed and matched floor-plank, about ten inches wide. The window frames are from three to three and a half feet, inside measure—with a centre mullion and latticed sashes. The roof of the porch is nearly flat and roofed with tin, so as to form a balcony to the bed-room window over it.

The house is, of course, filled-in with brick on edge, set flush with the outside of the frame, and the inside walls plastered on the face of the brick.

Estimate. The cost of this cottage, with the interior neatly finished and painted in oil color, and the wood of the two principal rooms grained and varnished like oak, and their walls papered with suitable paper, all the other walls being brown walls white-washed, would be $835.

DESIGN VIII.—*A suburban Cottage in the Italian style.*

THIS design is an attempt to redeem from the entire baldness of some examples and the frippery ornament of others, a class of cottages very general in the neighborhood of our larger country towns.

We have not, of course, endeavored to give this cottage much architectural style. The projection of the roof supported by cantilevers, and the simple but bold window dressings, give, however, the character of the Italian style.

The trellis-work veranda along the front of this cottage, and the bay-window in the best apartment, convey at once an expression of beauty arising from a sense of a superior comfort or refinement in the mode of living; and the whole exterior effect, without having any decided architectural merit, is one which we should be very glad to see followed in suburban houses of this class.

As a *country* cottage, strictly speaking, by which we mean a house not in the midst of streets and other suburban dwellings, but only surrounded by green trees and fields, this design might properly be objected to, as a little cockneyish in character. It is, in fact, a design for a suburban dwelling. The full second story gives it a certain air of comfort and space, which will recommend it to many who do not appreciate the more rural expression of the succeeding design.

ACCOMMODATION. This is a larger and more expensive cottage than our previous examples. Though offering only the same accommodation in the number of rooms, the rooms themselves are larger, and there is much more space devoted to passages. The front entry, Fig. 34, is eight feet wide and twenty-two feet long, containing the stairs. The back entry is five feet wide.

The parlor here is quite a handsome apartment for a cottage, being sixteen by twenty-two feet, with a bay-window, square in its opening, as all bay-windows should be, in this style. The width of this window is eight feet.

The living-room, sixteen feet square, has a well-lighted pantry, five by ten feet, and a small closet for china in the side passage leading to the closet. There is a small larder, and a closet in the kitchen.

The second-story plan, Fig. 35, is so simple, that it requires little explanation. It should be remarked, however, that the kitchen wing is not so high, in either the first or second floor, by two feet,* as that of the main building—consequently, the bed-room over the kitchen is entered from the *landing*—two-thirds of the way up the stairs—and not from the level of the floor of the main building at the top of the stairs.

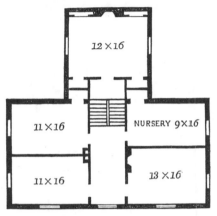

[Fig. 35. Second Floor.]

CONSTRUCTION. This cottage should be built of brick and stucco, with sixteen-inch hollow walls, or with smooth brick, painted of some pleasing neutral tint. The window dressings, where dressed stone is scarce or costly, should be built of brick and stuccoed—except the lintels and sills, which should be of dressed stone, colored like the rest, or of rough stone covered with stucco.

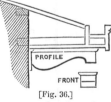

The roof of this dwelling should project twenty inches, and the shape of the bracket or cantilever and cornice is shown in Fig. 36.

[Fig. 36.]

The front door should have the two long panels glazed, so as to light the main entry.

---

* The first story of the main building of this cottage is eleven feet, the second nine.

The veranda should be seven and a half feet in width, and should not extend the entire length of the front, but stop a couple of feet short at both ends (as shown in the elevation). If extended along the whole length, a veranda has the disagreeable effect of cutting the *façade* into two halves, and destroying its character and proportion.

Estimate. Supposing a cellar under the main body of this house only, this cottage, if built in a substantial manner, would cost about $2000. Our estimate is formed upon the supposition that good hard bricks, suitable for hollow walls and outside stucco, are to be had at present prices on the Hudson, say $3 to $4 per 1000. Where the price of bricks is higher, of course that addition in price must be added in the estimate.

DESIGN IX. — *A regular, Bracketed Cottage.*

THIS cottage is designed in one of the simplest of all forms—the parallelogram. As regards beauty of form, it does not rise so high as symmetry—but it is higher than uniformity. Its beauty, considered in the mass, involves that simple idea which we call *regularity.* If every side were alike, it would exhibit uniformity, or if one front were divided into a central and two other equal portions, it would display symmetry. We make these remarks merely to assist the novice in architecture in analyzing the sources of beauty of form, for himself.

Though there is not much beauty of form in a cottage which is a simple parallelogram, yet the architect may bestow beauty of expression on such a form. In the Design before us, Fig. 37,

DESIGN IX.

REGULAR BRACKETED COTTAGE.

Fig. 37.

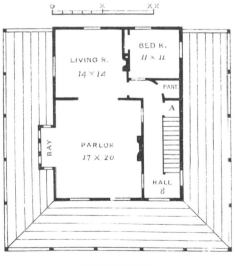

PRINCIPAL FLOOR.

Fig. 38.

there is an air of rustic or rural beauty conferred on the whole cottage by the simple or veranda-like arbor, or trellis, which runs round three sides of the building; as well as an expression of picturesqueness, by the roof supported on ornamental brackets and casting deep shadows upon the walls.

To become aware how much this beauty of expression has to do with rendering this cottage interesting, we have only to imagine it stripped of the arbor-veranda and the projecting eaves, and it becomes in appearance only the most meager and common-place building, which may be a house or a barn: at the most, it would indicate nothing more by its chimneys and windows, than that it is a human habitation, and not, as at present, that it is the dwelling of a family who have some rural taste, and some love for picturesque character in a house.

We have said nothing, as yet, of the greater value of projecting roofs in the production of that kind of beauty called the Picturesque. But in fact, this is one of the simplest, cheapest, and most effective modes of giving force and spirit to any building. The secret source of the Picturesque is the manifestation of Beauty through *power*, not, as in the Beautiful, the concealment of power under the external repose of Beauty. Hence, every thing that conveys the idea of strength or force in attaining any agreeable form, adds to the picturesqueness of that form. For this reason, in picturesque architecture, the rude timbers which support the roof, are openly shown, and in others, bold brackets support the eaves, not only for actual support, but to suggest the idea of that support directly to the eye. The more finished and polished the style of the building, the less this exhibition of power is pleasing, because the polish supposes a perfection and nicety of construction based

upon a concealed strength,—the very meaning of polish being
to please by suggesting ideas of smoothness, completeness,
perfect adjustment—in other words, Beauty.

There is another way in which projecting roofs convey the
idea of power, or heighten picturesque character in a building.
They cast broad and deep shadows. Now, the strongest
impression which the eye receives of objects in the open air
are those of light and shadow; and in the open sunshine of
so bright a climate as ours, the intensity of the light is such
that the most striking and brilliant effects are produced by
casting on the walls of a house, in broad sunshine, a dark
shadow from a roof which projects from two to four feet.

A much stronger and more definite idea is thus conveyed
to the mind of the outline and real form of such a house, and
of every detail of it which either casts a shadow or receives the
outline of that shadow, than can possibly be obtained by looking
at the mere outline of a house, the eaves and projecting
features of which are so small as to cast little or no shadow.

So much for the expression of picturesque character conveyed by a projecting roof. When we add that this character
is peculiarly suited to country houses; that it is still more
peculiarly suited to country houses built of wood; that the
projection itself keeps the whole house dryer and more
thoroughly protected from the storms, and renders the upper
story rooms cooler and more agreeable in summer; we trust
we present arguments enough to the sense of beauty and
sense of fitness of our readers, to induce them to rate at
its true value, the advantage of a projecting roof in all
suitable styles of architecture.

ACCOMMODATION. The plan of this cottage, Fig. 38, shows

that it is designed, not for general use, but for particular wants. There is a kind of half villa, half cottage-like air about the first floor, which shows very plainly that the inmates wish to give their dwelling something of the superior air of a villa, within the limits of a cottage. There is a space and simple elegance about the entry and front parlor, and a snugness and compactness about the living-room and bed-room, which show a little social ambition, and convey the idea that the house is designed for a family whose circumstances allow them to entertain, much more than those who live in most houses of this class.

When an unusual amount of " elegant entertainment" is to be put into a very limited space—when a rather large parlor for a cottage, has to be accommodated in a not very large dwelling, it generally follows that something very necessary to cottage completeness must be crowded aside. Accordingly, in this cottage, for the first time, we have been obliged to place the kitchen in the basement. Now, we entirely object to this arrangement, *unless* the mistress of this cottage has means enough to enable her to keep one more servant than any cottage of this size usually requires—or unless for the " basement kitchen," etc., is substituted a kitchen at the opposite end of the house directly beyond the living-room, and on the same floor with it.

Such a kitchen, on the same floor, would make this cottage much more truthful and satisfactory—but it would cost nearly two hundred dollars more than the present arrangement— because the same walls and roof that make the body of the house, give also the space for the kitchen, when the latter is a basement room. The disadvantages are, that a basement kitchen is neither so convenient nor so economical for the mistress of a cottage; it is not so accessible, and therefore demands more personal attention, since it is not so directly under her own eye, and, consequently, what is done there, costs her more time and money. The cottage, therefore, we repeat, should not, generally, have a basement kitchen, with the parlor and living-room up stairs, unless hospitality is more important than economy, and unless the wages of an additional servant are of no account in the items of house-keeping.

The parlor here is well proportioned, and is prettily varied by the bay-window opposite the mantel-piece. Sliding doors between this and the living-room give a good deal of available space on this floor for social purposes. The front windows in the parlor may reach to the floor—but, we think, no others. The bay-window should be furnished with a *window-seat*, all round the inside, fifteen inches high. (This window, by an error in the view, Fig. 37, is shown on the wrong side of the house.)

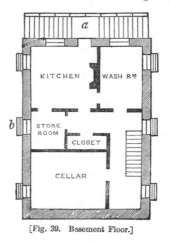

[Fig. 39. Basement Floor.]

The basement floor is shown in Fig. 39. A flight of stone steps, at the rear of the house, descends from each side to a landing, *a*, at the level of the basement floor, from which we enter the kitchen door. If the ground falls away on this side of the house, few or no steps will be needed, and the front windows of the kitchen will be entirely out of ground. If the ground is level, a large sunk area should be built, so as to give room for the steps, and light the front windows of the kitchen and wash-room.

The cellar windows, as well as all the side windows in the basement story, are below the surface of the ground, and are lighted by small sunk areas, eighteen inches wide, which are covered with wooden trellis-work or iron gratings, *b*, so as not to interfere with the walk round the house.

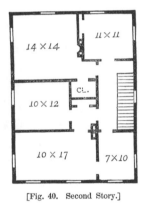

[Fig. 40. Second Story.]

The second story of this cottage, Fig. 40, contains five bed-rooms.

The *arbor-veranda* of this house is one of its most important features. To build a substantial roof with a veranda of this size round the whole cottage, or round three sides of it, would be too expensive an outlay for most occupants of such a dwelling. This arbor, which is barely the skeleton of such a veranda—

being, in fact, only an arbor with rather better posts than
usual, would cost but little, and would not only be productive
of much beauty, but a good deal of profit. We suppose it to
be covered with those two best and hardiest of our native
grapes—the Isabella and Catawba—the most luxuriant growers
in all soils—affording the finest shade, and, in the middle and
western States, giving large and regular crops of excellent
fruit—worth, in the market, from six to twelve cents a pound.
This arbor requires twenty vines, which will, in four years
after being planted, cover all the trellis overhead, and, with
the simple and proper pruning, afterwards necessary, produce
annually, at least twenty pounds of fine fruit per vine—worth,
at six cents, $20 per annum.

All the pruning required by the vines can be done in two
days, at any time during the autumn and winter when labor is
worth least, and thus the arbor will very speedily produce
enough to pay its first cost, to say nothing of the pleasure derived
from its abundant shade in the hottest days of summer.

To be sure, the leaves fall in autumn, and the veranda of
summer is only a leafless arbor, affording little or no shelter in
winter—but if the vines are neatly trained and regularly
pruned every November, it will be far from presenting an
unpleasing appearance even at that season; while in summer it
will be far more beautiful in its rich foliage and pendent
clusters of fruit than any cottage veranda.

This arbor-veranda is ten feet broad, and there should be
either a paved surface or floor, or a firm gravel walk all round
the house beneath it. A wooden floor would answer very well,
though it is not so durable or appropriate as a paved walk. In
either case, the walk or floor should be raised six or eight

DESIGN X.

BRACKETED COTTAGE, WITH VERANDA.

Fig. 42.

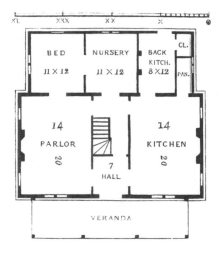

PRINCIPAL FLOOR.

Fig. 43.

inches above the level of the surrounding surface, so as to render it as dry as possible at all times.

CONSTRUCTION. This is, as the plan shows, a wooden cottage, with vertical boarding, and it is filled-in with brick. The roof projects twenty-six inches, and the brackets (the form of which is shown in

[Fig. 41.] Fig. 41) should be cut out of two-inch plank.

As the parlor chimney-stack does not come directly under the apex or ridge of the roof, and as it ought to come out there (as shown in the perspective view of the house), it will be necessary to *draw it over*, when building the stack through the garret. In doing this, it will require staying, and care must be taken that this support does not bear upon the partition between the two bed-rooms (ten by twelve and ten by seventeen) in the chamber floor; because that partition is a slight one, resting on a void below. The bricklayer should, instead, make a strong base or offset to the stack, a little above the floor-beams in the attic, and the carpenter should secure some strong pieces of timber, sufficient to carry the weight of the stack from this shoulder to the point in the rafter near the ridge where the chimney is to come out.

Estimate. The estimated cost of this cottage, well finished, is $1278.

DESIGN X.—*A Symmetrical, Bracketed Cottage, with Veranda.*

A PLEASING, symmetrical form, some picturesqueness of roof, united to considerable simplicity of construction, and an expression of more domestic enjoyment than cottages of this size usually exhibit, are the characteristics of this design.

The larger expression of domestic enjoyment is conveyed by

the veranda, or piazza.   In a cool climate, like that of England, the veranda is a feature of little importance; and the same thing is true in a considerable degree in the northern part of New England.   But over almost the whole extent of the United States, a veranda is a positive luxury in all the warmer part of the year, since in mid-summer it is the resting-place, lounging-spot, and place of social resort, of the whole family, at certain hours of the day.   It is not, however, an absolute necessity, like a kitchen or a bed-room, and, therefore, the smallest cottages, or those dwellings in which economy and utility are the leading considerations, are constructed without verandas.   But the moment the dwelling rises so far in dignity above the merely useful as to employ any considerable feature not entirely intended for use, then the veranda should find its place; or, if not an architectural veranda, then, at least, the arbor-veranda, covered with foliage, as in Design VIII., or the open porch, as in Design VI.   To decorate a cottage highly, which has no veranda-like feature, is, in this climate, as unphilosophical and false in taste, as it would be to paint a log-hut, or gild the rafters of a barn: unphilosophical, because all that relative beauty suggested by features which indicate a more refined enjoyment than what grows out of the ne-cessities of life should first have its manifestation, since it is the most significant and noble beauty of which the subject is capable; and false in taste, because it is bestowing embellish-ment on the inferior and minor details, and neglecting the more important and more characteristic features of a dwelling.

ACCOMMODATION. The interior of this cottage, though it gives a neat and pretty parlor, of 14 by 20 feet, is arranged on a principle totally opposite to that of Design VIII. The principle there, is to give a cottage with limited room on the first floor, the appearance of more space and elegance than it really possessed—it was, in some degree, a sacrifice of the convenience of daily life to the desire for the utmost good effect at certain times; the principle here, is to get as large an amount of convenience and comfort in every-day life as possible, and leave the rest to take the secondary rank.

Hence the kitchen, bed-room, nursery, and back-kitchen, the scene of a good deal of the daily life of the mistress of this cottage, are all on the first floor, and all close together. The last three of these are economically obtained by putting them in a one-story *wing* added to the rear of the cottage; and though the rooms thus afforded are not large, yet they are large enough when they are to be kept in order with very little " help."

The kitchen, in this plan, is properly the living and eating room of the family, and in order that it may always be kept neatly, there is a small back-kitchen adjoining, with its separate flue for a small range or cooking-stove, so that all the rougher work can be done there, which makes the larger kitchen, usually, a pleasant family dining-room.

There is a partition across the hall, just by the stairs, which is intended to serve as the extreme limits of nursery excursions, on all occasions when decorum in the parlor is the order of the day. The door here, as well as the front door, should have the two uppermost panels glazed, so as to light both parts of the hall when they are closed.

The second floor of this cottage is divided so as to give the utmost amount of room—five bed-rooms in all. A more simple mode would be to repeat the form of the lower hall, and divide each of the two large rooms into two bed-rooms. This

would give four bed-rooms, each $9\frac{1}{2}$ by 14 feet. The advantage
of the arrangement in Fig. 44 is, that an excellent room, 12 by
14 feet, is placed in the centre of the front, so as to have the

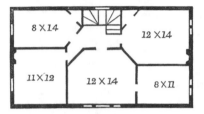

[Fig. 44. Chamber Floor.]

advantage of the large triple window in the front gable. The
smaller bed-room, 8 by 11 feet, communicating with it, might be
used as a children's bed-room.*

CONSTRUCTION. The veranda of this cottage is 8 feet wide and
32 feet long. It is one of the most pleasing forms of bracketed

[Fig. 45. Bracketed Veranda from the inside.]

* Those who prefer the more elegant arrangement of Design VIII., figs. 34 and
35, can easily adapt them to the exterior of this Design, making the rear building 2
stories high.

DESIGN XI.

A SWISS COTTAGE

Fig. 46.

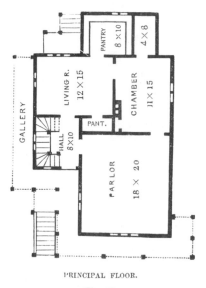

PRINCIPAL FLOOR.

Fig. 47.

piazza, and is built with but little cost. The whole is of wood; the rafter, *a* (Fig. 45), being worked fair, and beaded at the angles, as well as the narrow sheathing-boards, *b*, which cover them, and form the under side of the roof. Thus, no plaster ceiling is required. The roof itself is usually made of tin, galvanized iron, or shingles.

The materials of this cottage are outside weather-boarding, put on in the vertical mode, and filled-in with brick, so as to make a warm and dry house. There would be a cellar under the main building, but not under the back wing, unless some extra space is required. The entrance to this cellar from the interior, would be by a flight of steps under the stairs in the hall, and from the exterior by a cellar door and flight of stone steps on the kitchen side of the house. The windows would all have outside, Venetian blind shutters.

In Fig. 46 is shown the form of the gable brackets.

The first story is 10 feet, the second, 9½ feet high.

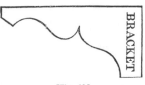

[Fig. 46.]

Estimate. The whole cost of this cottage is estimated at $1,356. Of course, in portions of the country where timber is more abundant, the cost would be from 15 to 20 per cent. less.

DESIGN XI.—*A Swiss Cottage.*

THE genuine Swiss cottage may be considered the most picturesque of all dwellings built of wood. Bold and striking in outline, and especially in its widely projecting roof, which is peculiarly adapted to a snowy country, rude in construction, and rustic and quaint in ornaments and details, it seems especially adapted to the wild and romantic scenery where it originated.

The expression of the Swiss cottage is highly domestic, as it abounds in galleries, balconies, large windows, and other features indicative of home comforts. But, as generally seen abroad, it is also significant of the most rustic kind of domestic life. There is no need, however, in our copying a Swiss chalet, that we should copy all its defects; we may retain much of the picturesqueness of the Swiss cottage without making its basement a stable for cows, or piling large stones on the roof. These local characteristics should never be transplanted out of a country where they are in keeping with the manners and customs of the people, into one where they are not.

One thing, however, should never be lost sight of in the selection of any distinct and striking architectural style. This is, to remember that its peculiarity and picturesqueness must either be greatly modified to suit a tame landscape, or, if preserved, then a scene or locality should be selected which is in harmony with the style.

The true site for a Swiss cottage is in a bold and mountainous country, on the side, or at the bottom of a wooded hill, or in a wild and picturesque valley. In such positions the architecture will have a spirit and meaning which will inspire every beholder with interest, while the same cottage built in a level country, amid smooth green fields, would only appear affected and ridiculous.

The design before us was made by G. J. Penchard, Esq., Architect, Albany, and has been exceedingly well built, under his direction, as a tenant's cottage, at the foot of a slope near the public road, at Mount Hope, the estate of E. P. Prentice, Esq., about a mile below that city.

Mr. Penchard, in designing this cottage, has apparently been guided by the first of the two principles of adaptation which we have laid down—viz. that of so modifying the character of the

Swiss style as to suit a situation much less picturesque in character than that where the Swiss cottage properly belongs. Fig. 46 shows the general effect of this cottage as seen by the visitor, the other side being backed by the hill. It is subdued and chastened in picturesqueness, and much less bold and rude than this kind of cottage might with propriety be, if built among forest or mountain scenery.

It still retains the picturesque roof, the bold brackets, and the long outside galleries—but all much more delicately made than in Swiss examples. While, therefore, it is not sufficiently bold for wild scenery, it is quite enough so for many sites where ornamental Swiss cottages are usually built.

ACCOMMODATION. Fig. 47 shows the interior of this cottage as we should prefer to distribute the rooms. In this arrangement, the kitchen, wash-room, etc., are in the basement story, Fig. 49—so that the principal floor has a comfortable living-room with a large pantry, closet, etc.; a bed-room which also has a large closet; and a handsome parlor in front.

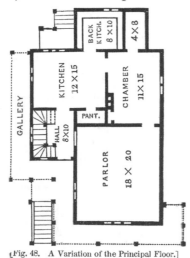

[Fig. 48. A Variation of the Principal Floor.]

Fig. 48 shows a less elegant but more convenient distribution for a cottage family—being, in fact, the way the rooms are actually used at Albany. The variation consists in using the living-room as the kitchen, and making the back-kitchen or "sink-room" of what is a pantry in Fig. 47.

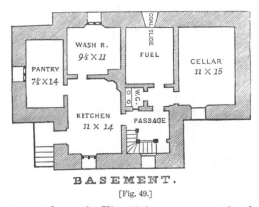

BASEMENT.

[Fig. 49.]

The basement shown in Fig. 49 is very conveniently arranged, but is intended to correspond with Fig. 47 as the plan of the principal floor. In case the kitchen is preferred up stairs, as in Fig. 48, then the basement would be chiefly cellar and store-room. There is a water-closet (W. C.) in a part of the lower passage, which gives this cottage quite a villa-like completeness.

CHAMBER FLOOR.

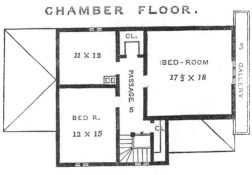

[Fig. 50. Chamber Floor.]

The arrangement of the chamber floor, Fig. 48, shows three good bed-rooms.

The plan of this cottage shows no open fire-places, but only flues for stoves, a mode of warming which we regret to see growing so popular in this country, since we think it consults economy at the cost of both health and cheerfulness. If we were building this cottage, therefore, we would have an open grate or fire-place in the living-room or parlor.

CONSTRUCTION. Fig. 51, which is an elevation of the south side of this cottage (that on which the hall and staircase are), shows the part, to a rather larger scale, and more correctly.

This is a frame house, doubly covered on the outside of the frame, i. e. with rough but jointed inch boards, so as to

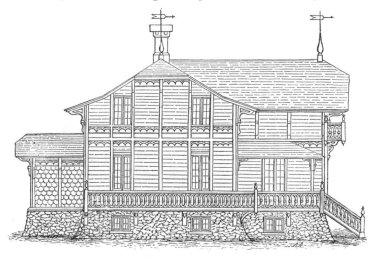

[Fig. 51. Elevation of the Side.]

form a plane surface, and then with an external coating of shingles cut in an ornamental pattern. The main body of the house, in Fig. 51, shows the building as covered with the boarding before the shingles were put on. The back wing shows the shape in which the shingles are cut, and the effect when finished.

This mode of covering wooden houses with shingles is a very durable mode, and, when the shingles are cut in ornamental patterns, it has a more tasteful and picturesque effect than common weather-boarding. It is quite as durable a material for exteriors as wood in any form, and we can point to examples of shingle-covered Dutch farm-houses in our vicinity, more than a hundred years old, and still in good preservation.

The form of the brackets which support the roof is seen at the corner of the building in Fig. 51, the same pattern being used all round the eaves. The roof of this house projects three and a half feet, and it is slightly *hipped*, which increases its picturesque character.

Altogether, this cottage, which is quite ornamental in character, is well worthy of the inspection of the admirers of the cottage ornée, and those who like the Swiss style would do well to examine it. It appears, indeed, much better in reality than it does in an engraving.

Estimate. Constructed as we have pointed out, in which case it would not require filling-in, unless in very cold sites this design may be built in a finished, simple manner, for $2600. As actually built near Albany, with a good deal of extra labor and cost, the entire expenditure was about $3000.

DESIGN XII.—*A Square Suburban Cottage.*

THIS is only an attempt to give a tolerable exterior to a species of cottage of very moderate size, common in the suburbs of all our villages.

The roof projects eighteen inches, upon rafter brackets of the plainest description, being only common joists or the small timbers of the roof.

An open porch of trellis-work for vines assists in giving an air of some taste to the exterior of this cottage.

ACCOMMODATION. In a cottage of this kind not an inch should be lost, and, therefore, a form nearly square has been adopted.

[Fig. 52. Elevation.]

An inspection of Fig. 53, which is the first floor of this cottage, will show the arrangement of the apartments of this

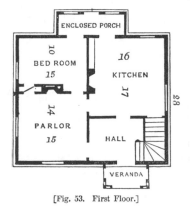

[Fig. 53. First Floor.]

story. The rooms are of good size for a dwelling of this class, and as they all communicate, and as the chimneys are all in the middle of the house, not an unnecessary step need be taken, not a particle of heat will be lost. The back-porch would be very necessary in a northern climate, but may be dispensed with in warmer portions of the Union.

Fig. 54 is the plan of the second story, which contains three good bed-rooms. This story is shown nine feet high, so that

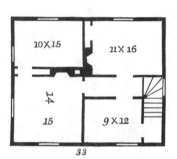

[Fig. 54. Chamber Floor.]

the upper rooms have an abundance of air; a height rendered more necessary in a cottage the roof of which has but little pitch, than in any dwelling the roof of which is steep.

The flues of the two stacks are all drawn together in one chimney in the garret of this building.

CONSTRUCTION. This design may be built of brick, stone, or wood. In the elevation (Fig. 52) it is supposed to be built of wood, and vertically boarded. Constructed in this way, and filled-in with brick, it would make a warm and very comfortable house, and the estimated cost of erecting it here, is $760— supposing it to have a cellar under the whole, and to be filled-in with brick. In portions of the country where lumber is abundant, and close economy is used in building, it may be erected at little more than $500.

This plan may be reduced in size one-fourth, and still give a snug cottage for a small family; it may then be built for $150 less than the estimate above named.

DESIGN XIII.—*A Cubical Cottage in the Tuscan Style.*

THIS design presents an elevation adapted to almost any situation, and may be built of any materials most readily obtained—though it is supposed, in Fig. 55, to be built of brick and stucco.

The style is a very simple and unpretending modification of the Tuscan or modern Italian architecture—the roof rising six feet in the centre and projecting two and a half feet at the eaves, the window-dressings simple and bold in character.

[Fig. 55. Elevation.]

An arbor-veranda, the roof of which is nothing more than open trellis bars (like that described in Design IX.), and covered with grape vines planted at the base of each post, forms the cheap and appropriate decoration, as well as the characteristic and comfortable feature of this cottage.

An arbor-veranda of this kind may, if the house is built of

wood, be constructed of rustic work at a very trifling cost.
To build a complete veranda, of the size indicated in Fig. 56
(ten feet wide), and around three sides of this cottage, would
be quite too costly to comport with the rest of the plan—
though, with slight alterations of the interior, the whole might
be raised in character so much as to become a cottage-villa,
when the veranda would very properly be constructed in the
most solid manner.

ACCOMMODATION.   A most comfortable, convenient, and

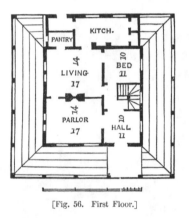

[Fig. 56. First Floor.]

compact arrangement is afforded in this design (see Fig. 56).
A hall or passage, 10 by 11 feet, opening into the parlor,
gives an impression of more space and elegance than is
generally received in dwellings of this size; and the position
of the stairs, placed by themselves in a space 8 by 11 feet, not
only enables the occupants of this design to use the front hall,
occasionally, as a little vestibule or small apartment, but gives
the staircase that privacy more commonly found in a villa than
in a cottage arrangement.

The living-room, bed-room, and kitchen have that immediate connection so desirable to families dwelling in houses of moderate size—when the main points are, to employ the least domestic assistance in household labors, and to have every thing under the personal care of the mistress.

The kitchen is a one-story *wing*, of the same height as the arbor-veranda, with the roof on the same level, so as to correspond externally with this veranda. The kitchen is 10 by 16 feet, with two closets at one end, and a back porch (behind the pantry), in which is the back door at the other end.

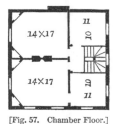

[Fig. 57. Chamber Floor.]

The second floor of this cottage, Fig. 57, shows four good bed-rooms.

Variation. By changing the position of the fire-places or flues from the partition wall between the two principal rooms to the other partition—viz. between the bed-room and living-room, and between the parlor and hall—which would only require a slight alteration in the position of the doors—the two principal rooms may be made to communicate, with large sliding or folding doors. This, retaining the rest as it is, would give more elegance, but perhaps less convenience, for the majority of those who would build this design.

Let us modify the design a little further, and besides throwing these two parlors into one, by sliding doors, let us suppose the veranda carried all round the house, and the kitchen placed in the basement, and we have an arrangement much more villa-like, but one also costing more at first, and involving a much greater annual expenditure for servants to perform the necessary labor.   It becomes, in fact, a small villa—exceeding, as it does, the limits we have defined for a cottage.

Estimate.   To execute this design according to the plans in Figs. 53, 54, 55, of brick and stucco, with a cellar under the whole, would cost about $1300.

SECTION V.

WHAT A FARM-HOUSE SHOULD BE.

In every agricultural country, the most numerous habita
tions that meet the eye of the traveller are farm-houses.

In this country, where a large proportion of the whole
population is devoted to agriculture, this is especially the
case. For every twenty persons who live in villas, suburban
cottages, or town houses, there are eighty persons who live in
farm-houses. It requires no argument, therefore, to prove that
the comfort or, convenience of farmers is of more weight and
importance, numerically considered, than that of any other
class ; or that whoever desires to see his country adorned with
tasteful dwellings, must not overlook its most frequent and
continual feature—the farm-house.

Granting the importance of this branch of Rural Architecture,
it is not a little singular that we, in America, so rarely see a
satisfactory farm-house.

Most thinking persons explain this to themselves by saying
that only those who have money to spare, can afford to build
tasteful houses, and that the farmer has no money to spare for
ornamental decoration. If, however, we have been rightly
understood in our remarks on cottages, we trust we have plainly
shown that beauty does not depend solely upon ornament, and

hence that a house may be tasteful, without any additional cost, merely by exhibiting good forms.

Setting aside, therefore, this reasoning as insufficient, we must attribute the common-place and meager character of farm-houses to two other causes—one, that architects usually consider them beneath their notice; and the other, that farmers seldom consider what the beauty of a farm-house consists in.

It is not, perhaps, remarkable that foreign architects look on the farm-house as so little worthy of their attention. In countries where the farmers are serfs, as in Russia, or even tenants from year to year, as in England; wherever, in short, the farmer has no property in the soil he cultivates, we might naturally expect that the comfort and beauty of his habitations would be a matter of trifling consequence to architects, whose profession is dependent upon the wealthier class of landlords and proprietors. But in this country, where almost every farmer is a proprietor, where a large portion of the farmers are intelligent men, and where farmers are not prevented by any thing in their condition or in the institutions of the country, from being among the wisest, the best, and the most honored of our citizens, the wants of the farming class deserve, and should receive, the attention to which their character and importance entitle them.

We have said that farmers, generally, misunderstand the true sources of truth and beauty in a farm-house. Our farmers are by no means all contented with a comfortable shelter for their heads. On the contrary, we see numberless attempts to give something of beauty to their homes. The designs continually published by agricultural journals, most of which emanate from the agricultural class, show the continual aiming after some thing better, which characterizes every class in this country. Some of these designs are appropriate and tasteful. But a large number of the better and more substantial farm-houses, especially those where some effort at taste is apparent, are decidedly failures, considered either in a tasteful or architectural point of view.

They are often failures, indeed, not because there are no evidences of comfort or beauty in their exteriors or interiors; but because they are not intrinsically farm-houses; because they are not truthful; because they do not express the life and character of the farmer; because they neglect their own true and legitimate sources of interest, and aim to attain beauty by imitating or borrowing the style or decorations of the ornamental cottage or villa.

Now, if we have clearly explained, in a previous part of this work, the great value and importance of truthfulness in domestic architecture, it cannot but be plain to our readers that a farm-house must, first of all, look like a farm-house, or it cannot give us any lasting satisfaction; and that as one of the highest sources of beauty in domestic architecture is derived from its embodying the best traits of character of the man or class of men for whom it is designed, it is equally plain that to raise the farm-house in the scale of truth and beauty, we must make it express that beauty, whatever it may be, which lies in a farmer's life.

How shall we make a farm-house truthful and significant, so that it shall look like a farm-house? Only by studying the characteristics of the farmer's life, and expressing, first of all, in the forms of his dwelling, the peculiar wants and comforts of that life.

Some of these we conceive to be the following: extended space on the ground, to afford room for all the in-door occupations of agricultural life, which will always give the farm-house breadth rather than height; a certain rustic plainness, which denotes a class more occupied with the practical and useful than the elegant arts of life; a substantial and solid construction, which denotes abundance of materials to build with, rather than money to expend in workmanship.

The genuine farmer is peculiarly the man of nature—more sincere, more earnest than men of any other class; because, dealing more with Providence than with men, he is less sophisticated either in manners or heart, and, if less cultivated, is more frank, and gives us more homely truths and less conventional insincerity than dwellers in cities.

The farm-house, to be significant, should therefore show an absence of all pretension. It should not borrow Grecian columns, or Italian balustrades, or Gothic carved work from the villa; or merely pretty ornaments from the cottage ornée. It should rely on its own honest, straightforward simplicity, and should rather aim to be frank, and genuine, and open-hearted, like its owner, than to wear the borrowed ornaments of any class of different habits and tastes. The porch or the veranda of the farm-house should not only be larger, but also simpler, and ruder, and stronger than that of the cottage, because there is more manly strength in the agriculturist's life than in that of any other class; the roof should be higher and more capacious, for it is to overshadow larger families and larger stores of nature's gifts; and, above all, the chimneys should be larger and more generous-looking, to betoken the warm-hearted hospitality of the farmer's home. Their large and simple tops should rather suggest ample hearths and good kitchens than small grates and handsome parlors.

Now, the real elements of beauty in the farm-house must be found in giving expression to the best and most beautiful traits in the farmer's life. And since the farmer's life is neither devoted to the elegant nor the ornamental arts, he should no more be expected to display a variety of architectural ornaments in the construction of his house, than he would be to wear garments made by the most fashionable tailor in Broadway, or to drive to his market town in one of Lawrence and Collis's most modish carriages.

Expecting, as we do, to find every species of domestic architecture typifying the character of the man or class of men inhabiting it, we do not desire any elaborate artistic effect or any thing like carefully studied attempts at architectural style in the farm-house. The farmer's life is not one devoted to æsthetics, and we do not look chiefly for the evidences of carefully elaborated taste and culture in his house, as in the dwelling of the scholar and the man of letters.

But we ought to find, in every farm-house, indications of those virtues which adorn the farmer's character, and which, if expressed at all in his dwelling, must give the latter something of the same beauty as the former. His dwelling ought to suggest simplicity, honesty of purpose, frankness, a hearty, genuine spirit of good-will, and a homely and modest, though manly and independent, bearing in his outward deportment. For the true farmer despises affectation; he loves a blunt and honest expression of the truth; and he shows you that he knows the value of a friend, by shaking hands with you, as if his heart acted like a magnetic machine on the chords of his fingers.

It would be false and foolish to embellish highly the dwelling of such a man with the elaborate details of the different schools of architecture. We must leave this more scientific display of art and learning to villas and public edifices, and endeavor to make the farm-house agreeable, chiefly by expressing in its leading forms the strength, simplicity, honesty, frankness, and sterling goodness of the farmer's character. Although we must recognize, first of all, the constant industry which gives so much dignity and independence to his life, in the arrangement of the interior of his house mainly for useful ends, yet we would also introduce every comfort and convenience denoting the intelligence and ease of the successful farmer's life in a country where that life is so truly intelligent and reputable as our own. But in adding the veranda, the bay-window, and other architectural features significant of social cultivation and enjoyment, we should still bear in mind that these features are to be stamped with the strength, simplicity, and downrightness of character which denote that they belong to the dwelling of a man who cannot wear fine ornaments, even upon his house, because they are foreign to his nature—however significant the same ornaments may be of the life of another man or another class of men.

The principles which we would lay down for designing farm-houses may be stated as follows—so far as the production of *beauty* is concerned.

That the form of the building should express a local fitness, and an intimate relation with the soil it stands upon—by showing breadth, and extension upon the ground, rather than height.

That its proportions should aim at ampleness, solidity, comfort, and a simple domestic feeling, rather than elegance, grace, and polished symmetry.

That its details should be simple and bold, and its ornaments, so far as they are used, should rather be rustic, strong, or picturesque, than delicate or highly finished.

That in raising the character of the farm-house, the first step above the really useful, is to add the porch, the veranda, and the bay-window, since they are not only significant of real but of refined utility.

So far as the *useful* is concerned in the farm-house, its principles are better understood, but we shall do no harm in recapitulating the most important :—

The farm-house should be built of strong and enduring materials, whether of timber or stone, so that it may need repairs very seldom.

The pitch of the roof should always be high, not only to keep the chamber-floor cooler, and to shed the snows in a northern climate, but to give sufficient garret room for storing and drying many of the smaller products of the farm.

The *living-room* of the family should be a large, and usually the largest and most comfortable apartment; it should be so placed as to be convenient to the other apartments used in the every-day occupations of the family, and its size should never be sacrificed to that of the parlor.

Every farm-house should contain a room for milk (even when the dairy is a separate building, as in most American farm-houses), as well as a room or back building for wood or other fuel.

When the means of the farmer allow him to extend his accommodation, they should first be applied to multiplying and rendering as complete as possible, all apartments, on the first floor, calculated in any way to facilitate the domestic labors of the family or farm, before he increases the size or number of his parlors.

In addition to the rules laid down in SECTION II. for the production of fitness and tasteful effect in cottages, we may also add, that though a farm-house should always be built of solid materials when economy will permit, yet there is a mental satisfaction in finding at all times, that it is constructed of materials most abundant on the farm, or at least in the district where the house is placed.

Wherever good building materials abound, their use in building the house of the owner of the land, not only enables us to understand that the abundance and cheapness of those materials have made it easy to build a large house there, but it also affords us an index of the natural products of the earth, and has therefore a local meaning, much more valuable than any novelty that we may gain by bringing our bricks from Holland, like the original settlers of New York, or importing portions of a French chateau, like some of our modern architectural virtuosi.

SECTION VI.

DESIGNS FOR FARM-HOUSES.

In the following designs for farm-houses, it must be remembered that we have been controlled by two circumstances—first, a desire to bring the cost of the buildings designed, within the means of farmers in easy circumstances throughout the country generally; and second, the necessity of adapting the designs to the materials which farmers are, for the most part, obliged to employ in the United States.

To make a farm-house realize our own conceptions, it should be especially remarkable for *simplicity* and *breadth* combined. But as there is only one farmer in ten thousand who can afford to build, at once, a farm-house as large as either the fullest convenience or the best effect would dictate, we have sought to make our designs more useful, by keeping them within very moderate limits; several of them being so arranged as to admit of additions to any extent.*

Again, the only perfectly satisfactory farm-houses are those

---

* On the other hand, many of our readers will be farmers of small means, who do not wish to expend more than $500 or $600 on a farm-house. We must refer such to our designs for cottages—some of the simplest of which, as Design IV., would make excellent farm cottages, with very trifling alteration.

built of solid materials—quarry stone, small stones and rough-cast or cement, brick, or brick and stucco. We believe it was Dr. Franklin who went into a calculation to show his farming countrymen how many *millions* were wasted by every genera-tion, in building of so perishable a material as wood. We fully agree with him, and, wherever the power of choice exists, would by all means counsel the farmer to build of lasting materials, which, unlike wood, will not need continual repairs during his own lifetime, only to be pulled down at the end of fifty or sixty years by his successors.

On the other hand, when the farmer is obliged to build of wood, he should especially avoid all fanciful and highly finished workmanship, and all slender and frail construction; but using strong timber of all kinds, he will, at the same time, give dura-bility and fitness of character to the building he erects.

In point of taste and truthful expression, a farm-house, as we have before suggested, should never be high. It should rather spread upon the ground than be piled up in the air. There is, too, an appearance of rural simplicity—an honest resting on the earth—about a low farm-house, which a dwelling of two full stories never has. And as the second-floor apartments in a farm-house are bed-rooms for those who go into them merely for the purpose of sleeping, and not, as in a villa, for the purpose of passing the time in elegant leisure, we do not find that farmers are at all luxurious in their notions of these second-floor apartments. We would always, therefore, prefer to build a farm-house of what is called the " story-and-a-half" height—as being both less expensive and more character-istic. Some of the designs which follow we have, accordingly, shown in this way—while to suit those who (not perhaps

DESIGN XIV.

SYMMETRICAL STONE FARM HOUSE.

Fig. 58.

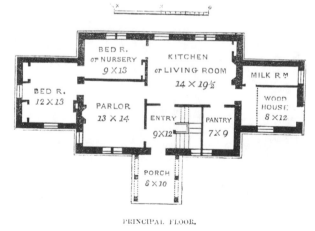

PRINCIPAL FLOOR.

Fig. 59.

wholly farmers in their habits) prefer a full chamber story, we have also given examples of the latter construction.

We have supposed in all these designs a very plain but substantial *finish* of the wood-work—with only the simplest mouldings to the doors and windows, and the interior walls to be finished by the plasterer in two coats for white-washing; the height of the first story to be 10 feet, and that of the second to vary from $8\frac{1}{2}$ to $9\frac{1}{2}$, according to the height or proportion of the building.

It would have been very easy to make these designs more architectural in style, and more attractive by external ornaments. But, in our opinion, this would have destroyed in a good degree the honesty of character and truthfulness of expression which constitute the highest beauty of a farm-house. As soon as our farmers grow wealthy enough to require larger and more architectural dwellings, architects of ability will arise to satisfy those wants.

DESIGN XIV.—*A Symmetrical Farm-House of Stone and Rough-cast.*

IF we have among our readers a single farmer who is ambitious, who loves show on the surface, who likes to dazzle passers-by with a great shingle palace stuck full of windows, he will by no means admire or approve of this design.

But, on the other hand, every reader who is a farmer at heart, who loves his farming life because it is simple and honest and unpretending, because it has no sham and no artifice, who wishes his home to be significant of this **very**

life, will certainly find something agreeable and satisfactory
in this plan of a farm-house.

A glance at the design tells us that this is a dwelling for a
northern climate—its thick walls, steep roof, and air of comfort
giving us the index to this fact immediately.

Whatever beauty our readers may find in a farm-house built
after this design, they may be sure it will not be purchased at
the expense of truthfulness. It has undeniably the merit of
" expressing the subject,"—of looking like a farm-house. And
since, as we have already remarked, we should not and ought
not to look for elaborate architecture in a farmer's dwelling,
we think the beauty which it possesses is of the most satisfactory kind—that is, it expresses the beauty of a farmer's life
—it is simple, honest, strong, and frank—so that it tells its
story at a glance. While it is humble and unambitious, it is
not mean nor meager. It looks as though you might find it
among blossoming orchards and green pastures, and no more
question its right to-be there than you would the right of the
very trees over your head or the turf under your feet.

We have purposely avoided much of scientific or ornamental
details in this design; the " springing stones" at the corners of
the eaves, and the quoins or corner-stones—roughly dressed by
the hammer of the mason—give something of strength as well
as architectural meaning beyond what we find in farm-houses
built without regard to any thing but the severest utility. But
in its truthful and sincere expression of a farmer's life, in the
symmetry of its form, and the fitness of its proportions, lie
whatever of merit may be found in this design. Its type may
be found in the farm-houses of the Middle States in a thousand
instances—we have only purified and elevated the character of

the original—and we should be glad to find so good a form as this adopted at the north, wherever stone is abundant as a building material.

ACCOMMODATION. Our aim in the plan of this house (see Fig. 59), is to accommodate the family of a farmer in comfortable circumstances—a family above want, independent through its own labor, but with little or no superfluous means. Such a family will prize convenience, snugness, and comfort more than display; and we have endeavored to meet its wishes by making the living-room or kitchen the best and largest apartment in the house—with a good pantry, a wood-house, a milk-room, and a bed-room or nursery, all communicating with it— so that as few steps as possible need be taken to perform the household labors. The parlor is placed in an appropriate and accessible position—communicating with the front entry—and opening into a bed-room, which would probably be the bed-room of the mistress of the house—in which case it could always be reached from the kitchen without going through the parlor, by passing through the nursery or children's bed-room.

The open porch, of hewn timber (either painted of a stone color, to harmonize with the outside walls, or stained and oiled, to show the grain of the wood), is a feature which we think one of the most important to the expression of this dwelling, both as regards beauty and comfort. Its size, and the seats on each side of it, point out its use—since it answers the purpose of a veranda, with much less cost. Covered by the grape-vine, such a porch is at once a beautiful and a most agreeable feature to the eye of the passer-by. It gives him, at a glance, the key-note to a refinement, quite compatible with a farmer's life—a refinement not less real than that seen in another class of country houses or ornamental cottages—but simpler and less fanciful in its manifestation.

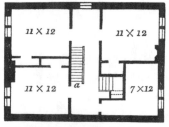

[Fig. 60. Chamber Floor.]

The second floor of this design, Fig. 60, shows four bed-rooms. At *a* is a narrow flight of stairs, leading to a garret, which is lighted by a dormer window or sky-light placed in the roof of the opposite side of the house.

Variation. This design may be cheapened by the omission of the two wings, and by placing in the rear a back porch and wood-house, about the size of the front porch—making the middle window of the rear a back door to the kitchen or living-room. This would lessen the cost considerably; but a good bed-room on the first floor would be sacrificed, and the good effect in this design, which grows out of the symmetry and the extent on the first floor, would be lost—though the house would still present a good appearance.

Another variation, which would, on the other hand, con-siderably improve this design, consists in turning the right wing into a kitchen—leaving the living-room to be strictly a living or sitting room. The wood-house may, in this case, either be a separate building, or it may be contained in the back porch just referred to in the first variation.

CONSTRUCTION. The walls of this house are 20 inches or 2

feet thick, and built of any rough rubble or cobble stones easily
and cheaply obtained on the farm—laid up, without hammering,
in what is called, random courses—and then plastered or
dashed with rough-cast, as described page 66. By laying up
the angles, and the jambs, sills, and heads of the windows, with
good building-stone, hammer dressed, and projecting a little
more than the face of the wall when covered with rough-cast,
these quoins and dressed stones will not only give architectural character to the building, but they will also protect the
rough-cast from injury at the most exposed points. The top of
the wall, at the gables, is coped with a course of flat blue-stone,
or slate laid in hydraulic cement, or in mortar to which one-
third fresh brick-dust, from the kiln, has been added.

The windows of this house are supposed to have inside
shutters, folding back in the jambs, but outside shutter blinds
may be used instead.

There is a cellar under the whole of the main building—the
stairs to which descend under the flight in the entry—and an
outside door which may be provided in any position most
convenient.

To preserve the proportions in the elevation, the first story
should be 10 feet high, in the clear, and the second story $8\frac{1}{2}$
feet.

Many persons would raise the second story of this farm-house
high enough to admit of a full second story, and of front and
rear windows to the bed-rooms. We would not do this,
partly because we think the bed-rooms in this plan could be
made as comfortable and agreeable as any farmer living in this
house would desire—for it is only for the more leisurely class
that we are obliged to provide luxurious sleeping-rooms, the

farmer's habits of industry securing him the enjoyment of a sound rest without down pillows; and, partly, because to raise this design from a story-and-a-half to a two-story house not only adds something to the cost, but takes away from that rural, lowly, contented expression which we have aimed at, and which we chiefly like in this design.

Estimate. The cost of this design, finished plainly, and with walls for white-washing, would be about $1200—supposing the farmer to deliver all the materials himself. If the stones can be procured on the farm, with only the trouble of collecting them, and if the farmer render all the necessary labor in digging the cellar and drawing the materials, this house could be built in most parts of the country for $1000— and, under very favorable circumstances, for a little less than the latter sum.

DESIGN XV.—*A Farm-house in the Swiss manner.*

THERE is something peculiarly rural and domestic in the character of the Swiss farm-houses. Their broad roofs, open galleries, and simple and bold construction are significant of strength and fitness, in a country at once picturesque and pastoral. But there are striking defects in the arrangement of these farm-houses—such as that of having the stable in the cellars or basement,—which no intelligent American farmer would tolerate in his dwelling. Our sketch in Fig. 61 therefore can scarcely be called Swiss, in a strict sense, since we have purposely made it so simple in its exterior as to lose some of those details by which we most commonly recognize the Swiss chalet. But it retains those features best adapted to our wants

DESIGN XV.

A FARM HOUSE IN THE SWISS MANNER.

Fig. 61

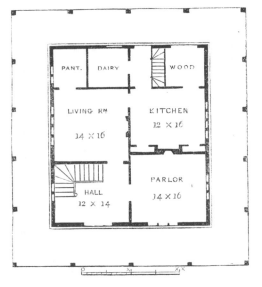

PRINCIPAL FLOOR.

Fig. 62.

and while it forms an agreeable whole, it has nothing in its construction or details which an American farmer would reject, from want of fitness or local truth.

[Fig. 63. A Picturesque Swiss Cottage.]

Though a farm-house in this simple and unpretending manner

may be placed with propriety in almost any rural landscape, yet the effect of this style is always most satisfactory in rather wild, hilly, or mountainous countries. Backed against a hill or at the side of a valley, these broad and strong roofs seem formed to protect the building against snow-slides—while the low and spreading character of the structure contrasts well with the boldness and height of the hills about it.

The true Swiss cottage is always built of wood, and often shows a great deal of ornamental work in the brackets which support the roof, as well as the borders to the doors and windows, etc. The lower story being devoted to domestic animals, the living-rooms are raised several feet above the level of the ground, and are reached by a flight of steps outside. Frequently all this outside ornamental work is done in a rude manner, with the axe alone, and the effect is more picturesque and rustic, and therefore better suited to rural buildings than highly finished carpentry. Fig. 63, which we borrow from an English journal, shows a Swiss farm cottage, built in England, in a style highly rustic and picturesque, from which some hints may be taken in the construction of this class of buildings.

The long veranda, 8 feet wide, which surrounds the whole of our Design, Fig. 61, not only forms a most comfortable and agreeable feature in this farm-house, but it affords an excellent place for drying various fruits and vegetables, under cover,—a place much prized by families in many parts of the country where these products are abundant. If to each of the posts or columns of this veranda a hardy grape-vine, such as the Isabella or Catawba, is planted, or grapes on the south side and hops on the north side, excellent and valuable crops and much beauty of effect will be combined. Whatever vines are trained on the supports to the veranda will of course be pruned and trained by the feminine inmates of such a farm-house, which, in a labor-scarce country like this, is something to be borne in mind by every farmer.

ACCOMMODATION. We offer the plan of this farm-house as one not only exceedingly convenient and comfortable, but so spacious and agreeable as to recommend it to the adoption of a large class of our agricultural population.

The entrance hall (Fig. 62) is an airy and pleasant ante-room, opening into a pleasant parlor on the front, and an equally pleasant living-room on the south side of the house.

The kitchen and living-room are here distinct, a superior arrangement to our last Design—and one which is desirable in all farm-houses, when the owner is not closely limited in his means—because it enables the family always to preserve a comfortable and orderly aspect in the living-room, superior to what necessarily belongs to the kitchen.

Among the good points of the arrangement of this floor, we may point out, that in the *back entry*, leading out from the kitchen, there is a second flight of stairs for the farm laborers to ascend to the chamber floor without the necessity of entering the front hall—a decided advantage in point of cleanliness and order. From this back entry we also enter the dairy or milk-room, 8 by 9 feet. This room is not intended for the dairy-room for a large dairy-farm, properly so called, because such a room should be in a cool basement, or cellar story, or, which is better, in a detached stone building in a suitable, shaded place; it is intended for that secondary dairy, needful in every farm-house as a room for milk wanted for daily use at all times, and for the dairy proper, at seasons when there is little space needed for milk or butter.

Adjoining the living-room is a good pantry, and adjoining the kitchen a wood-house, with two kitchen closets on either side of the fire-place.

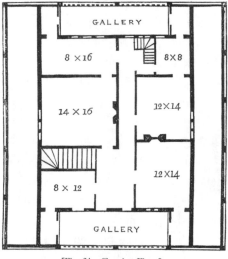

[Fig. 64.　Chamber Floor.]

The second floor, Fig. 64, contains six bed-rooms. By inclosing a small part of the gallery under the roof, on each end, four nice closets, 4 by 8 feet, are obtained. Indeed, a range of low clothes-presses, or closets, for all the rooms, may be taken out of the waste space under the roof where it extends over the veranda on each side. The two middle bed-rooms are each lighted by a dormer window in the roof, and the others by the windows in the gallery.

There is a cellar under the whole house.

CONSTRUCTION. Planed and matched floor plank for weather-boarding, put on in the vertical manner, the roof covered with shingles, the posts for the veranda of hewn oak, cedar, or chestnut, with a simple hand-rail of pine between them. The gable may be finished quite plainly, or with the simple verge-board shown more clearly in Fig. 62. The windows would scarcely need blinds, being so well protected by the veranda.*

We like the hospitable, homely, and generous look of the principal chimney in this house. Most modern chimneys have a lean and starved appearance, indicative of the scarcity of fuel to put in their throats, or rather of smoke to fill their stomachs—owing to the almost universal use of anthracite coal in our towns. But the farmer, who is supposed to have plenty of wood as well as plenty of wholesome cheer, and all of his own growth, should abjure all lank and starved chimneys, and should show by the pile of bricks in his chimney-stacks that there is room both to boil the pot and gather round the cheerful fireside under his roof.

A house built after this plan would last a long time, because the exterior, with the exception of the roof itself, is completely protected from the weather. The chimneys all being in the centre, no heat would be lost in winter, while the lower story would be very cool in summer, and the bed-rooms above would, if ventilated as we shall presently point out, be airy even in midsummer.

It will be easy to make this long veranda expensive, if the farmer allows the carpenter to seduce him into "nice work" for his posts and hand-rail—while if he keeps the whole as

---

* Some of our readers may think that rooms would be too dark with so much veranda—but in this bright atmosphere there is no fear of this—indeed, the necessity of blinds in all our houses only proves that the great desideratum here is to have our windows sufficiently screened.

severe and simple as possible, trusting to vines for decoration, he will be able to obtain it for a reasonable sum.

As the weather-boarding of this farm-house is but little exposed, instead of painting it, the farmer may produce a pleasing effect by *staining* the natural grain [see Section on *Miscellaneous Details*], so as to give the wood the color of old oak. This will have a warm, rich, and excellent effect, will preserve the wood well, and may all be done without the assistance of the painters.

Estimate. A practical builder in Rochester has estimated the cost of erecting this farm-house there at $ 1200. The estimate here for building it in a plain and substantial manner is $1,440. This supposes all the work to be done by the builder without any assistance from the farmer; but supposing the latter to be able, as most farmers are, to furnish all the stone for foundation walls, and a part of the timber for the building, the cost may be reduced to from $ 1000 to $ 1,200.

DESIGN XVI.—*A Bracketed Farm-House of Wood.*

THE proportions of this farm-house are good, the form is a simple and pleasing one, and the impression it produces upon the judgment is that of a roomy, substantial, comfortable, and sensible house. It looks essentially like a country house, and while it has rather more dignity than most farm-houses, there is neither ambition nor ostentation visible in its exterior. On the contrary, the rather low and broad chimney-stacks and the truncated gables show that there is a desire to avoid any especial affectation of elegance. It is, in short, a design which might be built in any part of the Union, and would be recognized as a country house of some importance—while it

DESIGN XVI.

BRACKETED FARM HOUSE OF WOOD.

Fig. 65.

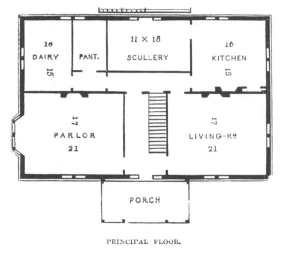

PRINCIPAL FLOOR.

Fig. 66.

has no feature cut of keeping with the position and life of a farmer in independent circumstances.

Accommodation. The exterior of this design is our own, but the arrangement of the first floor (Fig. 66) we borrow from one of Mr. Loudon's farm-houses. It is spacious and comfortable, without sacrificing too much to the parlor and living-room. The back door opens, it will be seen, into the *scullery*—which may be a wash-room or back kitchen. The passage which runs from the kitchen to the dairy should be lighted by a small sash of ground glass, placed in the partition of the scullery, exactly opposite the back door.

In many cases in this country, the dairy-room being in a separate building, persons adopting this design would prefer to turn the room devoted to this use, on this floor, into a bed-room—making the pantry a milk-room, and diminishing the size of the scullery sufficient to take a pantry out of the space occupied by it.

Indeed, the ease with which this kind of parallelogram plan may be varied to suit different wants will occur to every one of the least ingenuity ; and we therefore offer the exterior, as the most needful portion, as a guide to the mode of building to be adopted.

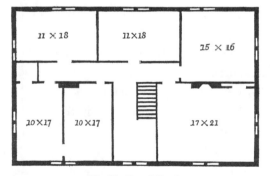

[Fig. 67. Second Story.]

The second story of this design, Fig. 67, shows six bed-rooms.

The roof of this dwelling being large and hipped, gives a spacious and convenient garret, which is of great value in any country house, and especially to the farmer. Three good bed-rooms for workmen can be finished off in this attic, or four—if a gable like that in front is formed on the rear roof.

The porch (as will be seen by trying the scale attached to Fig. 65) is 9 by 20 feet.

A cellar is intended to be built under the whole house—and there should be a back porch, which may be large enough to contain a *wood-house* (in which this plan is deficient), or, at least, to communicate with one.

CONSTRUCTION. This house may be built, with good effect, either of stone, brick, rough-cast, or wood. We suppose it, in the elevation, for the sake of economy, to be built of wood, in the vertical boarding manner.

The first story is eleven feet in tne clear, the second story nine feet. The house is to be finished with brown walls for white-washing, the windows to have rising sashes, and both these and the doors to be finished with plain architraves with simple back mouldings; the doors in the first and second story to have four panels each; the hand-rail and balusters to be of oak or black-walnut, and the whole to be executed in a very simple and plain, but substantial manner.

Estimate. To build this house here in the manner we have indicated, with planed and matched weather-boarding, and the whole filled-in with brick, would cost about $2000. At Rochester, where lumber may be taken at the average price,

DESIGN XVII.

FARM HOUSE IN THE ENGLISH RURAL STYLE.

Fig. 67.

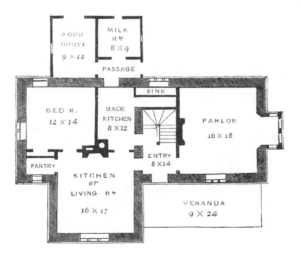

PRINCIPAL FLOOR.

Fig. 68.

it is placed as low as $1477, but this estimate is without filling-in of any kind, and without outside blinds or shutters.

DESIGN XVII.—*A Farm-House in the English Rural Style.*

To such of our readers as are looking for an expression of more beauty in a farm-house, we present this design.

We think no one can deny that it fully expresses the subject intended ; no one can accuse this dwelling of having any town-bred airs—any cockneyisms copied from streets, four stories high. It has, on the contrary, an unmistakable look of having been born and bred in the country. Its low walls, and its extension on the ground, show that neither pride, nor want of space, nor the love of imitation have been at work to destroy its honest and truthful rural character. There is an open, honest expression in its simple and broad windows, a strength and sturdiness in its low and solid walls, a look of homely, hospitable shelter in its broad overhanging roof, which altogether affect us with the feeling of beauty, because, like agreeable lines and features in the face, they are manifestations of the intrinsic goodness of the mind within.

Besides these, we must observe a feeling for the beauty of superior forms evinced in the well-moulded chimneys, the bay-window and balcony, and even the bracketed veranda-posts, which shows something more than truthfulness and beauty of purpose : they evince a love of the abstract or absolute beauty of form, and a love of it always kept subordinate to the truth-fulness of the object to be attained.

In saying that this is a farm-house in the English rural style, we do not mean that it is a copy of any building in England ;

but that in designing it we have seized upon that manifestation of rural and domestic beauty in architecture which the Anglo-Saxon race feels more powerfully and more instinctively than any other; and of which the English, who have had so much longer time than ourselves to work out these finer rural instincts, have given such admirable examples.

To a great many merely trading and delving farmers this farm-house will not be acceptable; and this for no fault of theirs, but either because it is not sufficiently matter-of-fact or not sufficiently showy to express their characters. It has too much poetry, truth, and nature in it for them. But to those who have some sentiment, and can see in material forms, even in the structure of a house, manifestations of heart and feeling, this farm-cottage will only require to be seen to be at once admired.

These *truncated* gables would be the first things objected to by an uncultivated builder, or even a pedantic architect, as unmeaning and valueless. In our eyes they are, in a farm-house, sources of beauty and picturesqueness. They give an air of rustic modesty, the very opposite to the highly finished artistic beauty of the regular pediment or the carved gables— an effect which is peculiarly expressive of honest, homely, unaffected country character. United to a broad roof of this kind, they express an easy, unrestrained, unconventional comfort, which compares with the highly-finished, architectural style of an elaborate villa, as the wide, shadowy straw-hat with which the farmer covers his head in the easiest and most comfortable manner, does with the exact and polished beaver of the man of undisputed fashion.

While, therefore, we could never use a truncated gable in a

building where architectural character, or, what we may call the science of the subject, should predominate over its *native feeling*, we think it may be used most happily in all rural dwellings, where a simple, and wholly unpretending honesty of feeling and character is to be expressed—as is particularly the case in the farmer's dwelling.

ACCOMMODATION. An examination of Fig. 68 will show that this is quite an irregular house, and that the main portion of it has been planned, not for elegance, but for utility. There is certainly a pretty parlor—with a tasteful bay-window on one side, and a veranda in front—but the rest of the house is purely for the wants of every-day life.

By placing the chimney-stack where we have, it will be seen that it serves for three apartments—the living-room, the bed-room, and the back kitchen. This back kitchen has a fixed boiler for heating water; and if a cooking stove is placed in it, all the rougher work of the household may be done here, so that the living-room will, in fact, be only a sitting and dining room. Under the broad window, in a part of this back kitchen, is a large sink, to facilitate the culinary operations; hence this apartment, though not large, will be found most convenient.

The exterior of the bay-window, in Fig. 67, shows how a villa-like feature may be adapted to a farm-house, by its modest and simple form.

The rear building, which contains the wood-house, milk-room, and covered passage to the door of the back kitchen, is only one story high, and, being in the rear, may, for economy, be built of wood, and painted, so as to correspond in color with the main building.

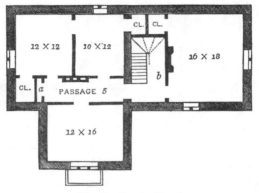

[Fig. 69. Chamber Floor.]

In the chamber floor, Fig. 69, will be found four bed-rooms, and three large closets, besides a linen closet, *a*, in the passage.

CONSTRUCTION.   This design should be built of solid materials, and would look well in stone or brick, the latter either properly colored, or stuccoed.   In our design we have shown it as it would appear built of rough stones, and covered externally with a coat of rough-cast, like Design XIII.—not only because this is the cheapest, warmest, and dryest mode of building a stone house, but also because it does not require blocks quarried of such regular forms and sizes as are usually denominated "building stone" by masons, but only such small and irregular pieces as stone fences are usually built of, and which are found in abundance on every farm in many parts of the United States, and more especially in New England and the Middle States.

The rough-cast, when put on, should be colored by the addition of sufficient yellow ochre and hydraulic lime to give it a mellow fawn, or warm gray color, and the chimneys (which are to be brick) as well as all the wood-work, should be colored or painted, to accord with the body of the building.

DESIGN XVIII.

BRACKETED AMERICAN FARM HOUSE.

Fig. 70.

PRINCIPAL FLOOR.

Fig. 71.

In the elevation of this farm-house, the appearance of the whole veranda, and especially the columns or posts which support it, are, by an error in the engraving, represented too slender and delicate to agree with the style and character of the rest of the design. They should, in construction, be made much bolder and stronger than they appear in the perspective.

The first story of this design is 10 feet, and the second story $9\frac{1}{2}$ feet high (in the centre of the room). The roof projects 2 feet 9 inches. A cellar should be constructed under the whole —with the exception of the back wing, containing the wood-house, etc.

Estimate. Built of rubble stones and rough-cast, and supposing the stones to be furnished from the farm, this design may be erected for about $1800. If constructed of good building stones, so as to show a smooth-faced wall, it would cost from $2200 to $2500, according to the value of such materials on the spot. The irregularity of this design, of course, makes it more costly than such a simple and regular form as the preceding one, although that contains a greater number of square feet of room.

DESIGN XVIII.—*A bracketed Farm-house in the American Style.*

IF we call this style American, it is only because we foresee that our climate and the cheapness of wood as a building material, in most parts of the country, will, for a long time yet, lead us to adopt this as the most pleasing manner of building rural edifices of an economical character.

If we compare this with Design XVII., we shall directly see how the character of a farm-house may be manifested in different materials and under the influence of different climates and habits. While the general expression of this elevation (Fig. 70) is not unlike that of the preceding one—which is essentially English, and while it exhibits no ostentation unbecoming an American farmer, there is, perhaps, in this house, a little more independence and a little less lowliness manifested, both being expressed in the higher stories, and the greater space from the ground to the eaves in this design. We imagine, therefore, that the majority of our farming readers will prefer the exterior of this design, not simply because it has higher ceilings in the second stories (which are indeed more necessary here than in England, because our summers are warmer), but mainly because American farmers love independence above all things, and hence instinctively and unconsciously lay hold of any thing that manifests it; and, perhaps, we should add, because, from the ambitious spirit too often begotten by the constant effort to rise in the world, they are not so likely to value that beauty which lies hidden in modesty and simplicity, as are more abstract lookers-on, like architects and artists of all kinds.

This farm-house seems to us to unite fitness and simplicity with as much architectural refinement of feature and expression as properly belong to the subject. There is not an objectionable ornament, and though the bay-window and veranda are dignified features of domestic architecture, they are, in this simple and tasteful form, both suitable and expressive features of our farm-houses. We have endeavored, by truncating one of the gables, and by giving one of the simplest and most domestic forms of rural chimneys to this building, to keep it within the bounds of truthful farm-house character.

ACCOMMODATION. The interior of this design is planned for the domestic use of a large family—with but little regard to any thing but comfort. It is quite probable, therefore, that many of our readers who are looking for handsome parlors will not be satisfied with the living-room in this house, which is all we have offered them for such an apartment. If so, they can easily satisfy themselves by turning the bed-room and nursery into a single room, 14 by 24 feet, or else by re-arranging this wing to suit themselves.

The plan, as we have given it, will, however, be found much more suitable for the majority of farmers' families in circumstances demanding a house of this class. The bed-room and nursery on the first floor, and the abundance of closet room connected with them, will especially be prized by farmers' wives, who prefer to have their own daily comfort considered, before that of guests whom they only see on a few great occasions.

On either side of the passage, 7 feet wide, leading from the entry into the kitchen, are good store and china closets, and there is a pantry connected with the living-room and a milk pantry (5 by 6) opening near the back door.

We have not shown a wood-house in this plan, but it may easily be added as a low wing in the rear.

The second-story plan, Fig. 72, gives five bed-rooms of various sizes. The narrow flight of stairs in this story leads to the attic, which, in this house, besides a good deal of " garret room," contains three apartments, each lighted by a window in the gable where it is placed.

The bed-rooms in the second story of this house are 9 feet high, and 6 feet high at the eaves, so as, in fact, to be nearly

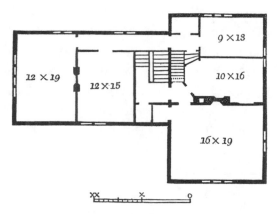

[Fig. 72. Chamber Floor.]

full height in all parts.   The first-floor rooms are 10 feet high.
The roof projects 2 feet.

We greatly prefer broad windows of three compartments
(like that shown on the bay-window in Fig. 70) to two
windows in such a position—because a few large windows give
more breadth and simplicity to the exterior of a country
house than a great number of small and narrow ones.   In
hanging shutter-blinds on such a window, however, the blind
on the central portion may be fixed, as the two other sides of
the window will, in our bright climate, give an abundance of
light.

CONSTRUCTION.   The construction is of sound, planed and
matched, inch and a quarter plank, put on in the vertical
manner, with battens to cover the joint—already so often
described in this work—the frame to be filled-in with cheap
bricks, and the whole to be constructed in a plain and very
simple, but fitting style, to correspond with the character of the
exterior.   The plastering, of course, to be brown walls, finished

DESIGN XIX.

A NORTHERN FARM HOUSE.

Fig. 73.

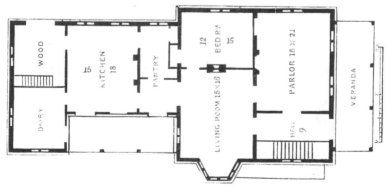

PRINCIPAL FLOOR.

Fig. 74.

in two coats. Only a simple back-moulding is to be put on the casings of the doors and windows in either story.

Estimate. The estimated cost at Rochester, taking lumber at the average price there, which, perhaps, best represents a large part of the farming district of the Northern States, is $1676. On the Hudson it would cost about $2000.

DESIGN XIX.—*A Northern Farm-House, for a large Farm.*

WE call this a *northern* Farm-house, because its high and steep roof, made to shed the snow rapidly, and its compact and solid exterior, indicate that it grows out of the wants of farming life in a country with cold winters, though its verandas indicate the luxury or comfort of shade in the American summer, even of the Northern States.

Those who have only studied the architecture of the Greeks, imagine a roof to be an ugly feature, and think any roof-pitch higher than that of a classic pediment, has no beauty. If, however, they will study the examples of the best architects in Germany and Northern Europe, they will speedily modify their opinions, for they will then find that, in all northern climates, a steep roof has a meaning in it which gives it great truthfulness, and which, rightly treated, is also a source of beauty.

Architecturally, this design aims only at being a country dwelling manifesting the strength, comfort, and substantial character of the agricultural life. But the introduction of the verandas, and the completeness and orderly expression of the composition, indicate the relative beauty of country life intelligently and rightly understood, and quite far from all pretension or affectation.

We have introduced the *curb roof*, in order to give more space in the attic or garret of the main body of the farm-house. It may be pierced with dormer windows on two or four sides to suit the wants of the owner,—and it has always a more picturesque effect than a large plain roof.

As to the *plan* of this farm-house, Fig. 74, we may safely recommend it as one which cannot fail to give satisfaction, as a farm-house, in almost any situation. The first floor not only furnishes all the accommodation which the farmer actually needs, but it gives it in a most agreeable and convenient shape. The living-room and parlor are both of good size; the former, which is the hospitable room in a farmer's house, is handsomely and well lighted by a bay-window. The front hall, 9 feet wide, opens out of this room on one side, and a back entry or lobby, 7 by 8 feet, connects it with the kitchen and pantry, as well as the kitchen veranda on the other side; while a convenient bed-room, 12 by 15 feet, connects with it directly in the rear.

A large pantry, 8 by 11 feet, a dairy (with a separate door, on the kitchen veranda or "stoop," for convenient entrance without coming into the kitchen), and wood-house,* both of ample size, complete the accommodation of this floor, and we scarcely know how it could be materially improved either for convenience or comfort.

The second floor of this farm-house is as spacious in its capacity as that of many villas, having no less than 8 bed-rooms. A large family would therefore be fully accommodated

---

* The small flight of stairs, *a* (Fig. 74), leads up to two small bed-rooms (7 by 11 feet each) over the wood-house and dairy (see Fig. 75), intended for workmen on the farm.

at all times in this dwelling. Besides these, the main building has a garret over the bed-rooms, to which access is had by means of the flight of stairs in the entry which adjoins the bed-room of 12 by 15 feet.

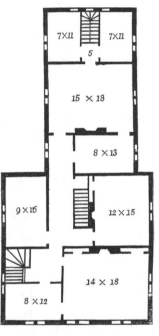

[Fig. 75. Second Story.]

CONSTRUCTION. The elevation of this design shows that it is intended for solid materials; the roof projects $1\frac{1}{2}$ feet, and is supported on plain rafter-brackets. Either quarried stone, rubble stone and rough-cast, brick, or brick and stucco may be employed in the construction of the walls. The ceilings of the first story are all 10 feet high. Those of the bed-rooms in the main building are 9 feet in the wing, ($3\frac{1}{2}$ feet in the centre, and 6 feet at the sides.) A cellar should, for a large farm, be built under the whole house, but we have, in estimating the cost, only supposed it to extend under the main building.

Variation. A glance at Fig. 74 will show how easily the arrangement of the rear building can be diminished or varied, as regards the kitchen accommodation, to suit different families. Farmers who cannot afford a large and complete dwelling at first, but still desire to commence what may finally be made such, may adopt the body of this design—using the living-room as kitchen (with a mere shed in the rear for back kitchen, wood-house, ect.), until able to erect the wing in the rear in a complete form.

Estimate. In many well-timbered parts of the country, this house may be erected in an excellent and substantial manner for $2500. Here, it would cost about three thousand. Of course, in cases where the farmer could diminish the cost by supplying a large portion of the materials and labor himself, its cost would be greatly lessened—so that, in many instances, the actual money to be paid out would not exceed $1800 or $2000. But for this sum he must not allow the carpenter or mason to seduce him into any finery—any stylish architraves, town-house mouldings, or "hard finish." These are by no means essential, either to the comfort or beauty of the design, while they add an unexpectedly large sum to the whole bill of costs.

DESIGN XX.—*A Villa Farm-House in the Bracketed Style.*

THIS dwelling is intended for the country house of a farmer

DESIGN XX

VILLA FARM HOUSE.

Fig. 76.

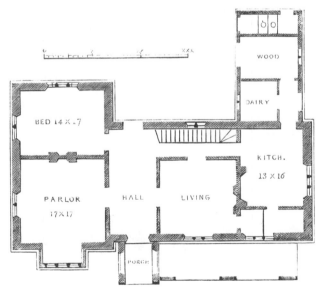

PRINCIPAL FLOOR.

Fig. 77.

of wealth, who wishes to give his dwelling a dignified and superior character, without indulging in too much ornament.

The exterior, as shown in the elevation, Fig. 76, is varied and picturesque, expressive of solidity, convenience, comfort, and a considerable degree of elegance. The bay-window and veranda, taken in connection with the construction, bestow a villa-like character on the design, while the large kitchen chimney and the absence of all tracery to the gables, indicate a country house of less pretension than the highly ornamental cottage or villa.

ACCOMMODATION. The plan of the first floor, Fig. 77, shows an entrance hall, 10 feet wide. On either side of these are the two principal apartments—the living-room and the parlor. By connecting these two rooms and the hall with large sliding doors, the whole can be thrown into one handsome suite on any occasion, and the arrangement will always add to the coolness and airiness of the rooms in summer.

At the end of the entrance hall is a staircase passage $6\frac{1}{2}$ feet wide, leading to the kitchen, dairy or milk-room, wood-house, etc.

The kitchen has a large pantry, and the living-room a small one, both lighted by one of the front windows.

There is a comfortable bed-room 14 by 17 feet on this floor. This room could easily be finished as a library, if that change of purpose is preferred; in which case it could be connected with the parlor, by opening a door on one or both sides of the fireplace.

The plan of the second floor, Fig. 78, affords six good bed-rooms. The front bed-room, 15 by 16 feet, with the nursery attached, is intended for the sleeping apartment of the master and mistress of the house.

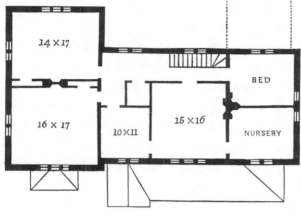

[Fig. 78. Second Floor.]

CONSTRUCTION. The superior character given in this design is largely due to the solid and substantial expression of the stone walls, shown in Fig. 76. The bold and simple details shown in the doors, windows, etc., harmonize well with the subject, and with the materials of the dwelling.

The first story of this house is 12 feet high, and the second story 10½ feet.

The roof projects 2¼ feet at the eaves. The wood-house, dairy, etc., are contained in a one-story wing in the rear, built in a corresponding manner, with projecting eaves.

The porch and veranda are built of wood, painted in stone color.

Variation. The exterior of this design might perhaps be improved, by omitting the two small gables in the front, and increasing the size of the middle gable sufficiently to allow of a small attic window. This would give more simplicity and less picturesqueness. If the building were to be erected in a bare site, the omission of the two gables would be a decided

improvement; but if in a well-wooded site, where the picturesque irregularity of the roof line would be partly concealed
and aided by the intricacy of foliage, and the lights and
shadows afforded by it, then the effect of the design would be
much better as it is at present.

Estimate. The cost of this house would vary from $4000 to
$5000, supposing it to be finished in a substantial, though
rather plain, manner. If built by a farmer who could furnish
the stone and deliver them at the site, performing all the
necessary carriage of other materials with his own horses, the
necessary outlay would not exceed the former sum.

SECTION VII.

MISCELLANEOUS DETAILS.

CONSTRUCTION OF CHIMNEYS AND FIREPLACES. Of all the minor evils which flesh is heir to, there are few which so certainly bring tears into every one's eyes as smoky chimneys. A man of nerve may steel his breast against a great misfortune, he may make no outward signs at the recital of griefs which would rouse a stoic; but take him into a room where the chimney does not draw well, and though he may be, like Othello,

"Unused to the melting mood,"

he will find himself exhibiting all its outward signs, while his heart, strange to say, is growing harder every moment.

That both country and town houses are more or less afflicted with this nuisance, is abundantly proved by the chimney-pots, ventilators, tall boys, and all other unsightly contrivances—odious in the eyes of architects—which deform the tops of so many chimneys everywhere; and there can be no doubt that the multiplication of stoves in parlors and sitting-rooms, of late years, is also owing, in no small degree, to the apparently unavoidable evil of smoky chimneys.

Granting, then, that smoky chimneys abound, and that they are a great evil, is there any certain remedy?

We answer to this, yes. The difficulty arises, in almost every instance, solely from want of knowledge of the first principles of construction, in the bricklayer who builds the chimney. We have conversed with dozens of mechanics, and have found but two who knew any thing of principles in the matter, or whose practical knowledge did not actually lead them to build chimneys that must inevitably smoke, in every situation exposed to downward currents of air.

We shall offer, therefore, a few remarks, as plain as we can make them, in the hope that every builder, into whose hands this work may fall, will directly make himself master of them, so that the practical art of building chimneys that will draw well, shall be everywhere known among brick-layers.

In the first place, then, the reason why chimneys draw at all is owing to the natural tendency of heated air to rise ; smoke being much lighter than common air. Hence, the warmer the flue, and the smoke which it contains, the better the draught. For this reason, a fire, lighted in a cold chimney, does not draw so well as after the chimney is heated, and a chimney in an interior wall of a house is more likely to draw well than one built in the exterior wall—the cold of the open air robbing the chimney of part of its heat.

The great cause of smoky chimneys, however, is their imperfect construction at the throat and the top. If a flue, as is most commonly the case, is built of uniform size, from the throat where the smoke enters, to the top where it escapes, it is evident that there is a column of heated air in the flue of uniform size from top to bottom. Whatever offers resistance to this column at the top acts equally upon the whole, because the size of the column of smoke at the top is precisely that at the bottom.

Now, the resistance is that of a current of wind upon the top of the chimney. Every time this current of wind strikes, in a direction more or less downward, upon the top of the chimney, a quantity of smoke is driven out of the throat below.

Let us now suppose that, with a flue of the same diameter, both the top and the throat are contracted. The effect of this, in the first place, is to break the force of the adverse current of wind; and in the second place, to divide the shock between the size of the opening at the top and that of the whole column of heated smoke in the flue. The effect this will have may be illustrated by supposing a canal, with a gate or opening at the end. Raise this gate across the whole width of the canal— the water flows out. Stop the gate suddenly, and we give a backward motion to the water in the *whole* breadth of the canal many feet distant; but stop it by a gate only half of the width of the opening, and we diminish this shock greatly. Now make another narrow passage the width of the small gate, fifty feet behind the gate, and we will find that the shock of shutting the gate *divides* itself in a great degree among the particles of surplus water, which make the difference between the mouth of the gate and the width of the canal behind it. Let the first gate represent the contraction at the top of the chimney, and we have the parallel.

The *principle*, then, of building chimneys to draw well, is to contract the openings both at the throat and the top, so as to break the force with which the wind (or even the air itself, in some states of the atmosphere) opposes the ascent of the smoke.

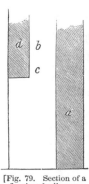

[Fig. 79. Section of a fireplace badly constructed.]

The practical mode of doing this is very simple. In Fig. 79, *a* is the back of the fireplace, *b* the flue, *c* the throat, *d* the breast of the chimney. The flue here is of equal diameter all the way up. It is plain, therefore, from what we have already said, that though such a chimney may draw well in some favorable situations, it must inevitably smoke in any exposed or unfavorable ones—because there is only a simple column of heated air, of uniform size, all the way up.

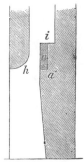

[Fig. 80. Form for a good draught.]

Fig. 80 shows a section of a chimney as it should be constructed, so far as regards the opening at the lower part. The principal difference here is, that the opening at the throat is diminished in depth (not in length) to about one third that of the flue, by building a wider back, *a*, in the fireplace, suddenly contracting by this means the throat of the chimney. This both increases the draught, by allowing less cold air to enter the throat from the room, and prevents the downward action of currents of wind, by opposing a direct check in the abrupt shoulder or offset, *i*, of this improved back to the fireplace.

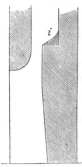

[Fig. 81. Defective shoulder.]

Experience has proved that two points must receive strict attention to insure success. The first is, that the top of the shoulder, *i*, should rise at least 6 inches above the line of the bottom of the breast, *h*; the second is, that it should end abruptly, as shown in Fig. 80. In cases where the masons have filled up the angle with mortar, as in *i*, Fig. 81, the chimney was caused to smoke—the slope modifying the check which the wind receives in its downward movement, and throwing the smoke out into the room.

On the other hand, the under side of the mantel, *h*, or breast, should always be gently rounded, as in Fig. 80, *h*, and not left square, as in Fig. 79, *c*,—the former promoting a good draught, by causing the current of cold air which enters from the room to mix *gradually* with the current of smoke, so as not to check it and force it out into the room.

This rounded form may be given, when a stone lintel is used for the soffit, by cutting the inner angle of the stone. If bricks are used they may be cut on the edge, and the curve filled out with plaster. A better mode, however, when the soffit is built of brick, is to have a broad cast-iron bar, with a rounded inner slope, so as to give the form of the mantel.

As the amount of heat radiated into the room is greatly increased by having the back of the fireplace *a* slope forward, as in Fig. 80, no intelligent bricklayer will make it straight, as in Fig. 79.

For all chimneys of moderate size it has been found that 4 inches in depth (from the inner face of *h* to *a*) is the best size for the throat of the chimney; and, as a general rule, the superficial area of the throat of the chimney should not be greater than that of the body of the flue above it. Thus, if the flue is 12 by 12 (superficial area 144 in.), then the throat should not be greater than 4 by 36, which gives the same area (144 inches). The throat can occasionally be made wider, in cleaning the chimney, by having a movable piece of soapstone or fire-brick, *n*, at the top of the back.

Having contracted the flue at the throat, let us now go to the top of the chimney.

The rule, in very windy or exposed situations, is to contract the chimney to a third less than the area of the flue. Thus, if the flue is 12 by 14 inches at the bottom (12 by 14 = 168 in.), it should be narrowed to the size of 10 by 11 inches (10 × 11 = 110 in.) at the top.

We have found, however, that in ordinary situations it is sufficient to contract a chimney at the top, so as to make the opening about two inches less in diameter than the flue below. And in situations where there is no likelihood of downward currents of air, the contraction at the throat alone proves sufficient.

A very simple and easy mode of contracting the top of an ordinary brick chimney, by drawing in the courses, is shown in Fig. 13, Design III., and another, still better calculated for a very smoky site, in the Farm-house, Design XIV.

When separate ornamental chimney-tops are used, the flue may be drawn in at its junction with the chimney-top.

Where wood is abundant, and large fireplaces are used, as is still the case in many parts of this country, large flues are required, from 12 inches to 24 inches square. In this case, the throat should be narrowed in the same proportion, but the back of the chimney should retire more at the base. But no ordinary flue for a coal fire need be over 9 by 14 inches, and the throat not more than 4 by 14 inches. For anthracite grates the flues in any country house need not exceed 8 by 12 inches.*

---

* For many excellent details on this subject see *Bernan's History of Warming and Ventilating.* To Count Rumford, who devoted his life to the improvement of

An admirable mode of building flues, which we have practised with entire satisfaction in our own residence, is that of giving them a circular form. This is done more rapidly and cheaply than in the common way, by using a cylinder of tin, easily made for the purpose by any tin-smith, like that shown in Fig. 82. It is closed at the top and bottom, and has at the top a stout handle, by which the bricklayer holds it. This cylinder is placed in the flue (which is first carried up about three feet above the opening of the fireplace, in the manner just pointed out); the mason then builds his chimney round it, always putting plaster, and not brick, *next* the cylinder.

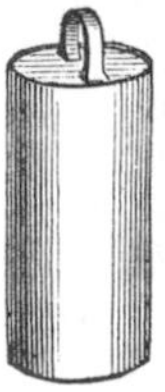

[Fig. 82. Cylinder for Flues.]

Every second or third course, he turns the cylinder round and raises it up a little; he then builds two or three courses more, and turns and raises it again, till he reaches the top of the chimney. In this way the inside of the flue is left perfectly smooth and even, from top to bottom. The bricklayer should have several of these cylinders, so as to carry up a stack with three or four flues (having one cylinder in each) without entirely removing the cylinders until the whole is completed.

We find that a circular flue, eight inches in diameter, is sufficiently large far anthracite grates, or for stove flues. Ten-inch cylinders give flues large enough for any cottage or villa when coal is the fuel used.

ORNAMENTING THE ROOF. Country houses, in a northern climate, are mostly built with steep roofs, and it is often desirable to break up the plainness of this roof, either to take

---

the domestic comforts of man, the world owes by far the largest part of all its scientific knowledge on the subject of chimneys.

away from its common-place appearance, or to bring it into keeping with the rest of the building.

Nine-tenths of all our country houses, as yet, are covered with shingles, and a very easy and efficient mode of giving a good effect to such roofs is that of cutting the shingles in certain patterns before laying them. When this is to be done, shingles of good quality and of uniform width and thickness should be chosen.

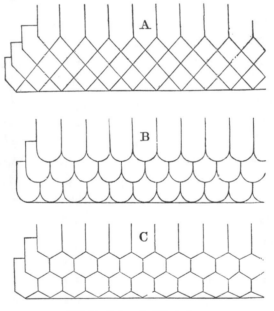

[Fig. 83. Patterns for Shingles.]

Fig. 83 shows various patterns of shingle work as they appear when overlaying the roof. One of the simplest forms, A, is made by cutting the lower end of the shingles to a point, so as to form a diamond pattern when the roof is covered with them. In B, the end of each shingle is rounded; in C, the shingles are cut somewhat as in A, but laid differently, so as to form an octagon pattern.

A very pleasing effect is produced, at little extra cost, by introducing three or four courses of these ornamental shingles between several courses of plain shingles—an example of which is shown in Design VI. A very little additional labor in this way bestows an air of taste on a common roof.

An exceedingly pretty effect in wooden cottages is produced by using these ornamental shingles for an outside covering, instead of boards, as in the case of the Swiss cottage, Design XI. A shingled cottage, properly built, is warmer than one weather-boarded in the common way, and is at least fully as durable.

In country houses of the first class, where slates are used for roofing, they may be cut in the same patterns as shingles. *Tiles* of these and various other fancy patterns are largely used in England, being afforded there at a cost not exceeding shingles ; and as they form the most ornamental and useful of all roofs, we trust some of our enterprising manufacturers will import one of the patent tile machines, and undertake their manufacture in this country.

MORTAR FLOORS. A solid and impenetrable floor in cellars and basement apartments is very desirable in many localities. In such places mortar floors are not only the most durable, —in some situations wooden floors rotting away in half a dozen years—but, if well laid, they entirely prevent the entrance of rats into the basement story, except through the doors and windows.

To make a good mortar floor, it is advisable, when the bottom is not itself a rock, to fill it six inches deep with small stones, closely and evenly laid. Over these put a layer, two inches thick, of mortar composed of gravel and newly slaked lime. The mortar should be tempered rather thinly, so as to partially settle among the loose stones, and bind them all together. When this coat has become firm, plaster it over with a coat of mortar composed of one part fresh lime to two parts sand. This coat should be made as level and smooth as possible, and, if an agreeable color is desired, the surface should be colored with the whitewash brush, as soon as it is made smooth, and before the mortar is set. The tint will then last nearly as long as the floor. For a cream color add a little yellow ochre to the whitewash; for a fawn color, or pale drab, use umber, with the addition of a little Indian red and black.

When the basement story is in a damp soil, proper drainage should be made before the mortar floor is laid down. Hydraulic lime or cement, as it is generally called, when mixed with two parts sand, always makes a harder and better floor than lime itself, and should therefore be used in preference when it can be readily obtained.

To STAIN INSIDE WOOD-WORK OR WAINSCOT. Instead of painting and graining wood to imitate oak, black walnut, or other dark woods used in the wainscoting or joinery of country houses, a very simple and excellent substitute, for cheap cottages and villas, is that of so staining the wood as to give the color of a darker wood, and yet retain all the real appearance of the grain of the wood itself. Pine, treated in this way, when the wood is clear and of good quality, is so strikingly like the plainer portions of oak or black walnut, as to produce the same general effect at first sight, while a closer examination shows only the real grain and texture—unlike a painted and grained surface, which is only an imitation. This mode of staining is, in fact, only toning down, or giving the effect of time to the actual grain of the wood, and is therefore a more truthful mode than painting it.

There are various modes of staining pine or other plain woods so as to resemble oak or black walnut: the following is one of the simplest and best.

First, prepare the wood by washing it with a solution of sulphuric acid, made by mixing it in the proportion of one ounce of sulphuric acid to a pint of warm water. It should be mixed when wanted, and put on while warm, washing it evenly over every part to be stained.

Second, stain the wood so prepared by rubbing it lightly with tobacco stain, using a piece of flannel or sponge for this purpose. By merely coating it, evenly, in this way, the natural grain of the wood will assume a dark tone, so as to resemble black walnut or oak; the effect of certain parts may be heightened by a little skill in mottling or slightly graining the wood, by repeating the coat, and allowing it to settle in places.

When the stained wood is entirely dry, brush it over, in order to preserve it, with the following mixture: $\frac{1}{2}$ lb. beeswax, $\frac{1}{2}$ pint linseed oil, and 1 pint boiled linseed oil.

It may, if desired, afterwards be varnished and polished. To make the above tobacco stain, take 6 lbs. of common shag or "negro head" tobacco; boil it in as many quarts of water as will cover the tobacco, letting it simmer away slowly till it is of the consistence of syrup. Strain it, and it is ready for use.

We may add, that when it is desired to give the wood the tone of light oak or maple, the solution of sulphuric acid should be much weaker, and only a light coat of the stain should be used. Where a dark tone is preferred, two coats of the stain should be put on.

Of course, the beauty of the wood, so stained, depends on its smoothness and the variety of its natural grain. Good " clear pine stuff," when stained in this way, and varnished, has an effect inferior only to real oak or black walnut. When sappy and knotty wood is used, though it will all take a rich dark tone, the defects in the wood will not be hidden by the staining as when covered with several coats of paint.

There is something warm and comfortable in the aspect of a room stained in this way, and when there is any scantiness of furniture it helps to give the apartment a *furnished* appearance.

In short, its advantages are, that the wood-work or wainscot of a cottage, ready for the painter, may be stained and varnished throughout in two or three days by almost any one, while painting it would require a fortnight; that it has immediately that mellow effect of old dark wood, so harmonious in some kinds of architecture; and that from its dark color and varnished surface it is far more easily kept clean than wainscot painted white or any other oil color.

For the wood-work of bed-rooms this is especially adapted, being a very cheap and excellent substitute for paint. *Seed-lac* dissolved in alcohol (at the rate of 1 pound to 1 quart) is a most excellent cheap varnish for covering the surface of the stained wood. This is also especially adapted for varnishing outside work, like the open porch of the Farm-house, Design XIV., made of hewn oak.

STAINING OUTSIDE WOOD-WORK. We are indebted, for the

following recipe for staining outside wood-work and the coarser portions of internal work, to Gervase Wheeler, Esq., an English architect of experience, who has recently settled in this country.

"Take best rosin tar, or pitch, in the proportion of 1 gallon to every 4 gallons of the following:

"Turpentine, $1\frac{1}{2}$ gallon, seed-lac dissolved in alcohol (in the proportion of 1 lb. to 1 quart), 2 quarts; cold linseed oil, $\frac{1}{2}$ gallon; boiled oil, $\frac{1}{4}$ gallon; beeswax, 6 lbs.; ox-gall, 1 lb.

"Mix all these together, and add the rosin tar first named. Lay it on with a large flat brush.

"This is a very beautiful and richly colored stain, and I have seen it frequently used in the timber-work of the simple country churches in England. Some persons use a larger proportion of the tar, and for work much exposed to the weather it would, perhaps, be better to do so."

CHEAP WASH FOR COTTAGES OF WOOD. For the outside of wooden cottages, barns, outbuildings, fences, etc., where economy is important, the following wash is recommended:

Take a clean barrel that will hold water. Put in it half a bushel of fresh quicklime, and slake it by pouring over it boiling water sufficient to cover it 4 or 5 inches deep, and stirring it till slaked.

When quite slaked, dissolve in water, and add 2 lbs. of sulphate of zinc (white vitriol), which may be had of any of the druggists, and which, in a few weeks, will cause the white-wash to harden on the wood-work. Add sufficient water to bring it to the consistence of thick whitewash. This wash is of course white, and as *white* is a color which we think should never be used except upon buildings a good deal surrounded by trees, so as to prevent its glare, we would make it a fawn or drab color before using it.

To make the above wash a pleasing cream color, add 4 lbs. yellow ochre.

For a fawn color, take 4 lbs. umber, 1 lb. Indian red, and ½ lb. lampblack.*

To make the wash gray or stone color, add 1 lb. raw umber and 2 lbs. lampblack.

The color may be put on with a common white-wash brush, and will be found much more durable than common white-wash, as the sulphate of zinc sets or hardens the wash.

CHEAP WASH FOR COTTAGES OF BRICK, STONE, STUCCO, OR ROUGH-CAST. Take a barrel, and slake half a bushel of fresh lime as before mentioned; then fill the barrel two-thirds full of water and add 1 bushel of hydraulic cement or water lime. Dissolve in water and add 3 lbs. sulphate of zinc. The whole should be of the thickness of paint, ready for use with the brush. This wash is improved by the addition of a peck of white sand stirred in just before using it. The color is a pale stone-color, nearly white.

To make it fawn color, add 1 lb. yellow ochre, 2 lbs. raw umber, 2 lbs. Indian red.

To make it a drab, add 1 lb. Indian red, 1 lb. umber, 1 lb. lampblack.

This wash, which we have tested thoroughly, sets and adheres very firmly to brick-work or stucco, is very durable, and produces a very agreeable effect.

---

* *Lampblack*, when mixed with water colors, should first be thoroughly dissolved in alcohol. Yellow ochre, Indian red, etc., are sold, in dry powders, at a few cents per lb.

CHEAP COTTAGE PAINT. The following is a very cheap and excellent paint for cottages, forming a hard surface, and is far more durable than paint; as its hardness increases by time, it will be found preferable to common paint for picturesque country edifices of all kinds.

Take freshly burned unslaked lime and reduce it to powder. To one peck or one bushel of this add the same quantity of fine white sand or fine coal-ashes, and twice as much fresh wood-ashes, all these being sifted through a fine sieve. They should then be thoroughly mixed together, while dry. Afterwards mix them with as much common linseed oil as will make the whole thin enough to work freely with a painter's brush.

This will make a paint of a light-gray stone-color, nearly white.

To make it fawn or drab, add yellow ochre and Indian red; if drab is desired, add burnt umber, Indian red, and a little black; if dark stone-color, add lampblack; or if brown stone, then add Spanish brown. All these colors should of course be first mixed in oil and then added.

This paint is very much cheaper than common oil paint. It is equally well suited to wood, brick, or stone. It is better to apply it in two coats; the first thin, the second thick.

DURABLE OIL PAINT. Mr. Wheeler uses the following paint, which he recommends strongly to us for outside work.

"Take 50 lbs. best white-lead, ten quarts linseed oil, $\frac{1}{2}$ lb. Dryers'; 50 lbs. finely sifted sharp, clean sand, 2 lbs. raw umber. Thoroughly mix and dilute the whole with the oil, adding a very little (say half a pint) of turpentine. Lay it on with a *large* brush. I use a *wire* brush, which does not cut through with the sand.

"Two coats should be used; the second coat thinner than the first. I can, from experience, recommend this paint as standing from 15 to 20 years."

CEMENT FOR STOPPING JOINTS. A cement that hardens in a short time, and more effectually resists the weather than any other, is made by mixing fine white sand with white paint (white-lead ground in oil, and made rather thicker than for common use). Sufficient sand should be used to make a stiff paste that will not run.

If there are, from faulty construction, any joints about chimney-tops, places in the roof, or elsewhere, which are not easily made weather-proof, they may be made perfectly tight by filling and covering them with this cement. It grows harder by exposure to the weather, and resists alike the action of wet and cold.

Pieces of stone that have been broken may be united with this cement so as to become as strong as at first. If the stone is of dark sandstone, red-lead may be substituted for white-lead, or white-lead may be brought to the color of the stone, by adding the necessary oil colors before mixing the sand.

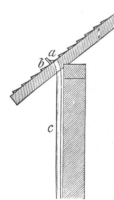

GUTTERS AT THE EAVES. For all cheap cottages, barns, and outbuildings with projecting roofs, much the simplest and best gutter is formed by introducing a piece of copper, tin, or galvanized iron, *a*, Fig. 84, in the roof, directly over the perpendicular line of the outer wall, and turning up this piece of metal against a strip of board nailed at a right angle to the roof, *b*. This board should be laid

[Fig 84. Raised Metal Gutter.] with one end a little lower on the roof than the other, so as to afford a sufficient descent in its length to carry off the water freely. It is not only the simplest and cheapest mode of forming a gutter, but it also permits the leader water-pipe, *c*, to be carried down in a straight line, without any of those awkward joints and angles which putting the gutter at the outer edge of the eaves renders necessary. This kind of gutter is well suited to all roofs where the rafters and sheathing of the roof are shown, as in Designs I., II., etc. If tin is used for gutters of this kind, it should always have a couple of coats of red-lead (the best weather-proof color) as soon as finished.

A neater and more complete mode, in well-built cottages, is

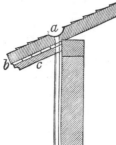

that of cutting the gutter out of the rafter itself, as at *a*, Fig. 85. The under side of the rafter, *b*, is sealed over, and short brackets, *c*, are inserted for real and apparent support. This is ·the kind of gutter supposed in Designs VI., VIII., etc.

[Fig. 85. Sunken Metal Gutter.]

VENTILATING COTTAGES. It is only very lately that any attention has been paid in this country to the important subject of ventilating houses.

At the present moment this matter is better understood in Boston, than in any other part of the Union; and indeed, it is only in the neighborhood of that city that we notice any attention generally paid to the ventilation of country houses.

The mode of ventilation adopted there is a very simple one, which has been brought into use by Frederick Emerson, of Boston, who has invented a cheap and efficient apparatus for this purpose which is already extensively adopted.

Mr. Emerson's method, in its complete form, is calculated to ventilate perfectly all the apartments, or any particular apartment in a house. For this purpose it is necessary that it should

be connected with a furnace or ventilating stove, which, in cold weather, furnishes a sufficient supply of fresh, warm air to supply the place of that carried off. In a house ventilated throughout, Mr. Emerson employs two ventilators; one, the Injecting Ventilator, Fig.

[Fig. 86. The Injecting Ventilator.]

86, which furnishes a sufficient supply of fresh cold air to the furnace, and the other the Ejecting Ventilator,

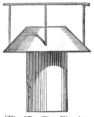

Fig. 87, which, placed on the top of the house, allows all the impure air to escape.

By means of these, a constant current of fresh warm air is brought to the house, or its principal passages and apartments; so that with an equal and agreeable temperature, a

[Fig 87. The Ejecting Ventilator.]

pure and healthy atmosphere is at all times maintained.

In the majority of cheap cottages and farm-houses, the principal necessity, as regards ventilation, is to keep the upper story or the attic cool in summer; and this can only be done by preventing the accumulation of heated air under the roof.

For this purpose Emerson's *Ejecting Ventilator*, Fig. 87, is the simplest and most effective apparatus we have yet seen. It consists of a tube, usually made of zinc, galvanized iron, or tin, open throughout, with a frustum of a cone at the end, and a fender, supported on rods over the opening, at the top. The fender keeps out the rain, and, together with the cone, acts so as to direct a blast of wind upon the structure, so that in whatever direction it falls, the effect of causing a strong upward draft will be very uniform and constant.

This ventilator top has the advantage of being stationary, so that it can be permanently fixed to the roof of a house, like a chimney; and when the house is a large one, requiring two or three ventilators, they can be brought together in a stack, like ornamental chimney-tops.*

As the effect of these ventilators, when small, is rather unarchitectural, they should be used of large size, and painted of the same color as the chimneys.

Where it is only desired to ventilate the garret, over the full height bed-rooms of a two-story cottage, it is sufficient to place one of Emerson's Ejecting Ventilators at or near the ridge or highest part of the roof, and provide for the entrance of a sufficient supply of fresh air near the floor of the garret. This

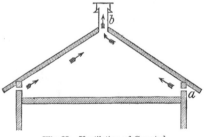

[Fig 88. Ventilation of Garrets.]

may be done by placing the garret windows near the floor, or by providing small openings close under the eaves, *a*, Fig. 88.

---

* These ventilators are patented, and may be had in Boston or New York. They are usually made of four sizes, viz. 14 inches, 18 inches, 24 or 32 inches in the diameter of the tube. For the roof ventilation of most cottages, a single Ejector, 24 inches in diameter, will be sufficient. They are for sale in Boston by Chilson and Dunkler, and in New York by Chilson, Allen, Walker & Co., 351 Broadway.

The cool air enters these openings, and immediately rises and passes out of the ventilator, *b*, thus maintaining a constant circulation of fresh air in the direction shown by the arrows.

In the case of half-story bed-rooms, when, as in all low cottages, part of the height of the bed-room is taken out of the garret, another mode must be adopted.

To understand this, let Fig. 89 be a section of such cottage,

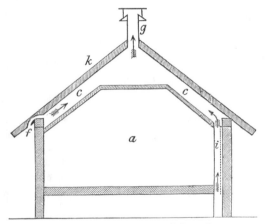

[Fig. 89.   Ventilation of Attic Bed-room.]

in which *a* is the bed-room. Instead of lathing and plastering the ceiling on the under side of the rafters, a hollow space, *c*, of six inches or more, should be left between the roof and the ceiling of the cottage, *e*. By providing apertures for the admission of fresh air at *f*, under the eaves, and placing a ventilator, *g*, on the top of the roof, a constant circulation will take place, so as to render the garret cool.

The builder or architect must exercise his ingenuity so to introduce the openings for fresh air as not to be seen, or, if seen, so as not to be unsightly.

A very easy mode of doing this, in a projecting roof, is to form apertures in the ceiling of the under side of the overhanging eaves.

Another very efficient mode, which should be adopted in all houses where it would be unsightly to pierce the attic with openings of any kind, is to carry down from the vacuity, c, a tube or box, i, of the diameter of the ventilator at the top. Space for this tube or box may, in building the house, be found in closets, or even between partitions that lead from the cellar to the garret. The bottom of this tube should communicate with the open air, either through one of the cellar windows, or by an opening especially made for it, and the top of the tube should open somewhere in the floor of the garret. This tube (which may be square or round or oblong, as is most convenient) will supply the garret with fresh air, as fast as the hot air rises and passes out of the ventilator.

In many cases a narrow window at each end of the garret will be sufficient to supply fresh air as fast as the ventilator carries off that which has become heated; but the great advantage of permanent ventilating apertures is, that they can remain open day and night both in stormy and fair weather.

It is not necessary that the ventilator top should be placed on the ridge or highest part of the roof, as we have shown it in Fig. 89, since in many cases this would detract from the good effect of the architecture. It may be placed a few feet down the slope of the roof, on the rear, or less visible side of the building, as at k, Fig. 89. In this case, however, the tube will require to be lengthened after a given proportion, which is stated in the pamphlet written by Mr. Emerson, and sent out with the ventilators.

For details respecting the warming and ventilating of rooms, we refer our readers to the close of the second part of this work.

ECONOMY IN PRACTICAL BUILDING. We extract the following hints from a letter received from a sagacious friend at Rochester, N. Y., who is much interested in the improvement of our rural architecture—and writes understandingly. It contains useful information for those who wish to build well and cheaply.

"——My own experience in building has been considerable, and I have found in every 'job' that estimates vary at least 12 per cent., while, for some particular portions of a building, the variation will be at least 25 per cent. This arises from the fact that, at the time the proposal is made, one builder may be out of work, and very anxious to do something, while another has enough to do, and therefore puts in a proposal at such a price as would compensate him for extra labor on his own part, and enable him to employ additional journeymen.

" Allow me to make one suggestion, to be embodied in your work. *Never build in a hurry.* This is well understood by those who have built as much as I have, but is overlooked by beginners. I do not mention this with reference to the durability of the work, although that is one of the most important considerations, but with reference to the expense— for the latter is usually the great thing which enters into the calculation of persons about to build in this country.

" I can illustrate this better by telling my own experience— as I am now engaged in building a dwelling-house. My plans were settled last summer. I then made application to a few *good* joiners—who had small shops—asking their lowest terms for the inside work and window frames—to be delivered at any time between this (February) and the 1st of July next. My lowest proposals came from two mechanics, who have divided the work, and who do it at such times as they have little else to do; and the prices are 20 per cent. lower than any good joiner here would contract to perform the same work next summer.

"I get my brick laid in an 8-inch wall at $2 per 1000—I furnishing the sand. The specifications are, that they shall all be laid *wet*, that all the joints shall be thoroughly filled with mortar, and the whole rubbed down every six or eight courses, so as to make a smooth surface for paint. None of our contractors would think of doing the same work at less than $2.50, and it would not be half as well done. Yet my mason will make a good profit upon it. He is a first-rate workman, employs two or three hands, and has his own time—during all next summer—to complete the work.

"After you have matured your plans, and decided to build, keep a memorandum book, and write down every thing as you hear it from those who have preceded you. Every person who has built a house can give you some new ideas, and warn you of some error he has committed. Take for example the following :—

"*Best mode of firring a brick wall.* Strips of sawn lath, laid in the courses of brick-work, make much better holds for nails than the ordinary firring bricks or wall strips *built* in the wall. The latter are never perfectly solid in the walls, and if the wood of which they are made has not been thoroughly seasoned they will become loose; while laths are split by the nails, rendering them more firm, and the firring strengthens the wall very much. An 8-inch wall, when the bricks are laid wet, in thin mortar, to which firring is nailed in this manner, is stronger than a foot-wall laid in the ordinary way, and the firring nailed to wooden blocks.

"In the *corners* of the wall the two upright firring strips should be strongly nailed together before they are nailed to the wall, and, when a partition joins a wall, the studding should be nailed very firmly to the firring strip. This will prevent any plaster cracks in the corners.

" *To prevent rats from entering walls.* I have another suggestion, which I consider a good one, and which has been carried into practice here for years with complete success. In laying the foundation wall, dig a trench to the depth of six inches below the bottom of the cellar, and a foot wider on both sides than the thickness of the cellar wall. In this trench lay the foundation first course of stone, which will project from 4 to 6 inches on each side. Be careful that these stones are well matched together. Have this course of solid flags or foundation stones covered 2 or 3 inches with earth below the cellar floor on the inside, and vermin will be effectually prevented from burrowing in the cellar.

"Rats and other like animals invariably burrow close to the wall, in the direction BA, and when they reach the angle of the stones at B, they always turn back and try in some other place, and with like success. They never go back from the base of the wall, and of course never get under.

"I may add another hint—always carry cellar walls to the top of the first course of beams or floor joists. This shuts up one of the most common harbors of rats and mice in country houses, and prevents them from working up through the floor,

as they have no resting place where they can stand and
gnaw."—*J. W. B.*

EXTERIOR COLOR OF COUNTRY HOUSES. The color of the
outside of a house in the country is of more importance than is
usually supposed, since, next to the form itself, the color is the
first impression which the eye receives in approaching it; and,
in some cases, the color makes its impression, even before we
fully comprehend the form of the building.

The greater number of all country houses in the United
States have been hitherto painted white—partly because white-
lead is supposed to be a better preservative than other colors
(though the white paint generally used is one of the worst in
this respect), and partly from its giving an appearance of
especial *newness* to a house, which, with many persons, is in
itself a recommendation.

No person of taste, who gives the subject the least
consideration, is, however, guilty of the mistake of painting or
coloring country houses white. And yet there are so many
who have never given the subject a moment's thought, that we
must urge upon them a few arguments against so great a
breach of good taste.*

Our first objection to *white* is, that it is too glaring and
conspicuous. We scarcely know any thing more uncomfortable to the eye, than to approach the sunny side of a house in
one of our brilliant midsummer days, when it revels in the
fashionable purity of its color. It is absolutely painful.
Nature, full of kindness for man, has covered most of the
surface that meets his eye in the country, with a soft green

---

* We have already published some of the following remarks in the *Horticulturist.*

hue—at once the most refreshing and most grateful to the eye. Many of our country houses appear to be colored on the very opposite principle, and one needs, in broad sunshine, to turn his eyes away from them, to relieve them by a glimpse of the soft and refreshing shades that everywhere pervade the trees, the grass, and the surface of the earth.

Our second objection to white is, that it does not harmonize with the country, and thereby mars the effect of rural landscapes. Much of the beauty of landscapes depends on what painters call *breadth of tone*—which is caused by broad masses of colors that harmonize and blend agreeably together. Nothing tends to destroy breadth of tone so much as any object of considerable size, and of a brilliant white. It stands harshly apart from all the soft shades of the scene. Hence, landscape painters always studiously avoid the introduction of white in their buildings, and give them, instead, some neutral tint—a tint which unites or contrasts agreeably with the color of trees and grass, and which seems to blend into other parts of natural landscape, instead of being a discordant note in the general harmony.

There is always, perhaps, something not quite agreeable in objects of a dazzling whiteness, when brought into contrast with other colors. Mr. Price, in his Essays on the Beautiful and Picturesque, conceived that very white teeth gave a silly expression to the countenance—and brings forward in illustration of it, the well-known *sobriquet* which Horace Walpole bestowed on one of his acquaintances—" the gentleman with the foolish teeth."

No one is successful in rural improvements, who does not study nature, and take her for the basis of his practice. Now, in natural landscape, any thing like strong and bright colors is seldom seen, except in very minute portions, and least of all pure white—chiefly appearing in small objects like flowers. The practical rule which should be deduced from this is, to avoid all those colors which nature avoids. In buildings, we should copy those that she offers chiefly to the eye—such as those of the soil, rocks, wood, and the bark of trees,—the materials of which houses are built. These materials offer us the best and most natural study from which harmonious colors for the houses themselves should be taken.

Wordsworth, in a little volume on the Scenery of the Lakes, remarks that the objections to white as a color, in large spots or masses, in landscapes, are insurmountable. He says it destroys the *gradations* of distances, haunts the eye, and disturbs the repose of nature. To leave some little consolation to the lovers of white-lead, we will add that there is one position in which their favorite color may not only be tolerated, but often has a happy effect. We mean in the case of a country house or cottage, deeply embowered in trees. Surrounded by such a mass of foliage as Spenser describes,

> In whose *inclosed shadow* there was set,
> A fair pavilion, *scarcely to be seen,*

a white building often has a magical effect. But a landscape painter would quickly answer, if he were asked the reason of this exception to the rule, " it is because the building does not appear white." In other words, in the shadow of the foliage by which it is half concealed, it loses all the harshness and offensiveness of a white house in an open site. We have, indeed, often felt, in looking at examples of the latter, set upon a bald hill, that the building itself would, if possible, cry out,

"Hide me from day's *garish eye.*"

We may also add, that while few objects are more disagreeable than *bare* and tame villages—so there are, on the other hand, few which give more pleasure to the eye than the contrast of a few white cottages surrounded by foliage, and set in a wide landscape, where only the universal green of woods and meadows is to be seen.

Having entered our protest against the general use of white in country edifices, we are bound to point out what we consider suitable shades of color.

We have said that one should look to nature for hints in color. This gives us, apparently, a wide choice of shades; but as we ought properly to employ modified shades, taken from the colors of the materials of which houses are constructed, the number of objects is brought within a moderate compass. Houses are not built of grass or leaves, and there is, therefore, not much propriety in painting a dwelling green. Earth, stone, bricks, and wood, are the substances that enter mostly into the structure of our houses, and from these we would accordingly take suggestions for painting them.

Sir Joshua Reynolds, who was full of artistic feeling for the union of a house with its surrounding scenery, once said, "If you would fix upon the best color for your house, turn up a stone, or pluck up a handful of grass by the roots, and see what is the color of the soil where the house is to stand, and let that be your choice." This rule was not probably intended to be exactly carried into general practice, but the feeling that

prompted it was the same that we are endeavoring to illustrate
—the necessity of a unity of color in the house and the
country about it.

We think, in the beginning, that the color of all buildings
in the country, should be of those *soft and quiet shades* called
neutral tints, such as fawn, drab, gray, brown, etc., and that
all positive colors, such as white, yellow, red, blue, black, etc.,
should always be avoided; neutral tints being those drawn
from nature, and harmonizing best with her, and positive colors
being most discordant when introduced into rural scenery.

In the second place, we would adapt the shade of color, as
far as possible, to the expression, style, or character of the
house itself. Thus, a large mansion may very properly receive
a somewhat sober hue, expressive of dignity; while a country
house of moderate size demands a lighter and more pleasant,
but still quiet tone; and a small cottage should, we think,
always have a cheerful and lively tint. Country houses, thickly
surrounded by trees, should always be painted of a lighter
shade than those standing exposed. And a new house, entirely
unrelieved by foliage, as it is rendered conspicuous by the very
nakedness of its position, should be painted several shades
darker than the same building, if placed in a well-wooded site.
*In proportion as a house is exposed to view, let its hue be
darker, and where it is much concealed by foliage, a very light
shade of color is to be preferred.*

Wordsworth remarks, in speaking of houses in the Lake
country, that many persons who have heard white condemned,
have erred by adopting a *cold slaty* color. The dulness and
dimness of hue in some dark stones produces an effect quite at
variance with the cheerful expression which small houses

should wear. "The flaring yellow," he adds, "runs into the opposite extreme, and is still more censurable. Upon the whole, the safest color, for general use, is something between a cream and a dust color."

This color, which Wordsworth recommends for general use, is the hue of the English freestone, called *Portland stone* —a *quiet fawn* color, to which we are strongly partial, and which harmonizes perhaps more completely with all situations in the country than any other that can be named. Next to this, we like a *warm gray*, that is, a gray mixed with a very little red, and some yellow. *Browns* and *dark grays* are suitable for barns, stables, and outbuildings, which it is desirable to render inconspicuous—but for dwellings, unless very light shades of these latter colors are used, they are apt to give a dull and heavy effect in the country.*

---

* The following hints for mixing shades for outside painting, may be of service to persons in the country who have to depend on their own wits. The colors are supposed to be first finely ground in oil, and then mixed in small quantities with white-lead and boiled linseed oil. A few trials will enable the novice to mix agreeable neutral shades—especially if he will be content to add a very *little* of the darker shades at a time, and try the effect with the brush. After the proper shade is obtained, enough should be mixed at once to go over the whole surface.

Fawn color. White, yellow ochre, and Spanish brown.

Drab. White, Venetian red, burnt umber, with a little black.

Gray stone. White, lampblack, and a little Venetian red.

Brown stone. Spanish brown, chrome yellow, with a little white and lampblack.

French gray. White, ivory black, with a little Indian red and Chinese blue.

Slate color. White, lampblack, and a little Indian red.

Sage color. White, raw umber, Prussian blue, and Venetian red.

Straw color. White, yellow ochre, and orange chrome.

Chocolate. Spanish brown and black—or, for a lighter shade, Venetian red and black.

A very slight admixture of a darker color is sufficient to remove the objections to white paint, by destroying the *glare of white*, the only color which reflects *all* the sun's rays. We would advise the use of soft shades, not much removed from white, for small cottages, which should not be painted of too dark a shade, since that would give them an aspect of *gloom*, rather worse than *glare*. It is the more necessary to make this suggestion, since we have lately observed that some persons newly awakened to the bad effects of white, have rushed into the opposite extreme, and colored their country houses of such a sombre hue, that they give a melancholy character to the whole neighborhood around them.

A species of monotony is also produced by using the same neutral tint for every part of the exterior of a country house. Now there are features, such as window facings, blinds, cornices, etc., which confer the same kind of expression on a house that the eyes, eyebrows, lips, etc., of a face, do upon the human countenance. To paint the whole house plain drab, gives it very much the same dull and insipid effect that color-less features (white hair, pale eye-brows, lips, etc., etc.) do the face. A certain sprightliness is therefore always bestowed on a dwelling in a neutral tint, by painting the bolder projecting features of a different shade. The simplest practical rule that we can suggest for effecting this, in the most satisfactory and agreeable manner, is the following: Choose paint of some neutral tint that is quite satisfactory, and, if the tint is a *light* one, let the facings of the windows, cornices, etc., be painted several *shades* darker, of the same color. The blinds may either be a still darker shade than the facings, or else the darkest green.* This variety of shades will give a building a cheerful effect, when, if but one of the shades were employed, there would be a dulness and heaviness in the appearance of its exterior.

If, on the other hand, the tint chosen is a dark one, then let the window dressings, etc., be painted of a much lighter shade of the same color.

Any one who will follow the principles we have suggested cannot, at least, fail to avoid the gross blunders in taste which we have so long been in the habit of committing in the practice of painting country houses.

Uvedale Price justly remarked, that many people have a sort of *callus* over their organs of sight, as others over those of hearing; and as the callous hearers feel nothing in music but kettle-drums and trombones, so the callous seers can only be moved by strong opposition of black and white, or by fiery reds. There are, we may add, some few house painters who appear to be equally benumbed to any delicate sensations in *shades* of color. They judge of the beauty of colors upon houses as they do in the raw pigment, and, we verily believe, would be more gratified to paint every thing chrome yellow, indigo blue, pure white, vermillion red, and the like, than with the most fitting and delicate mingling of shades to be found

---

* Thus, if the color of the house be that of Portland stone (a fawn shade), let the window casings, cornices, etc., be painted a light brown, the color of our common red freestone—and make the latter shade by mixing the requisite quantity of Spanish brown with the color used in the body of the house. Very *dark* green is quite unobjectionable as a color for the Venetian blinds, so much used in our country, as it is quite unobtrusive. Bright green is offensive to the eye, and vulgar and flashy in effect.

under the wide canopy of heaven. Fortunately *fashion*, a more powerful teacher of the multitude than the press or the schools, is now setting in the right direction. A few men of taste and judgment, in city and country, have set the example by casting off all connection with harsh colors. What a few leaders do at the first, from a nice sense of harmony in colors, the many will do afterwards, when they see the superior beauty of neutral tints supported and enforced by the example of those who build and inhabit the most attractive and agreeable houses; and we trust, at no very distant time, one may have the pleasure of travelling over our whole country, without meeting with a single habitation of glaring and offensive color, but see everywhere something of harmony and beauty.

VINES FOR THE DECORATION OF COTTAGES. Our readers must be well aware that there are two kinds of expression of which architecture in the country is capable : one, the expression of the art itself in various forms of stone or wood, and which depends wholly upon the skill of him who designs or builds the house; the other, the expression which the building derives from the aid of external objects, and especially from the trees, shrubs, and vines that immediately surround it.

It is upon these latter objects that the true *rurality* of almost all simple cottages depends; and nine-tenths of all the cottages that have endeared themselves, through their local and living beauty, to the hearts of true poets and genuine lovers of nature, have owed most of their charms rather to this rurality —this wealth of bower, and vine, and creeper, than to any carved or sculptured gables, window heads, or other features bestowed by the careful hand of the architect.

Take almost any of those exquisite cottages in an English

landscape, which charm every beholder by a wonderful beauty, found in no other land in the same perfection, and subject it to the dissecting knife of the searcher after the secrets of that beauty, and what does he find? That not one of these cottages is faultless, in a strictly architectural sense—nay, that they abound with all sorts of whimsical and picturesque violations of architectural rules and proportions, and are often quite destitute of grace of form or outline.

But, on the other hand, they are so bewitchingly rural! Partly, to be sure, by their thatched roofs and latticed windows and low stone walls, all of which seem to grow out of the ground, and to be rather a production of nature than of art (proving incontestibly how genuine is the love of rural life in those who build and inhabit such cottages), but mainly through the beautiful vines and shrubs that embower them, which, by partly concealing and partly adorning their walls, give them that expressive beauty of rural and home feeling which makes them so captivating to every passer-by.

This *drapery* of cottages—the vines that climb, or trail, or creep over them and around their porches and windows—deserves, then, something more than a passing glance from all who would understand the secret of making a simple country house beautiful at little cost. For it must be remembered, also, that while chiselling ornaments in stone, or carving them in wood, soon makes a figure in one's account-book, a few roots of those vines which will soon grow into forms of graceful and perennial beauty, may be had for a trifle, or will be gladly given by some friend whose garden overflows with its wealth of shrubs and climbers.

But, though all vines are beautiful in their appropriate

places, they are not all fitted for the decoration of rural cottages. Some are only at home when trailing over rocky precipices, others when climbing high trees, and others, again, are so delicate as to need the support of slender trellises in the flower-garden.

A vine fitted by nature for the drapery of rural cottages should unite fine foliage, which holds its verdure for a long time, and is not often the prey of insects, with a good *massy* habit of growth. If its flowers are also beautiful or fragrant, so much the better, but by no means should fine flowers, which last for a fortnight, lead us to forget fine habit of growth and good foliage, which are constant sources of pleasure.

Besides these requisites, we must add, that popular vines for a cottage must be such as are perfectly hardy, and need no protection, and which have a way, for the most part, of taking care of themselves—in other words, which will grow into pleasing or picturesque forms with only an hour or two's pruning and tying up once a year.

For cottages, at the north, one of the best hardy vines is the Virginia creeper (better known as the American Ivy, or five-leaved Ampelopsis), a wild plant, which grows with wonderful luxuriance, and attaches itself without any assistance to wood or stone by the fibres it throws out from its stem. Its leaves, glossy green in summer, but turning to the finest crimson before they fall in autumn, the rapidity of its growth, and the absolutely no-care-at-all which it requires, will commend it as perhaps the best of all plants, when the effect of foliage is desired in as short a time as possible, as well as for concealing or adding to the beauty of any gart of a *blank* wall of a cottage.

The Chinese Wistaria, now perfectly naturalized in the Middle States, is one of the finest vines for the pillars of the cottage porch or veranda. It will extend its shoots to 40 or 50 feet, if allowed, while it may be kept within the limits of a small column, if desired. Its long pendent clusters of delicate pearly lilac flowers have a strikingly elegant appearance when properly scattered over the shoots in May, and its abundant light green foliage has a pleasing effect. whether for trellis, wall, or veranda.

Climbing roses are also great favorites for pillars and porch trellises. The most deservedly popular, for the cottage, are the Boursault and the Double Prairie roses—because they have fine foliage, grow very rapidly and luxuriantly, blossom profusely, and are perfectly hardy in all parts of the Union. The *Amadis* is the best variety of the Boursault, and the Queen of Prairies and Baltimore Belle the best Double Prairies for cottage decoration. Amateurs who wish to add a still further charm, and are, willing to bestow a little more care on them, may, by budding the long shoots with Bourbon roses, have a succession of fine flowers every day during the whole growing season.

In the Southern States, the fine Noisette roses, such as Cloth of Gold and Solfaterre, take the place of the Prairie roses of the north.

Among the honeysuckles—the "lush woodbine" of the poets —there are two admirably adapted to cottage adornment, viz. the Japan or Evergreen Honeysuckle (*Lonicera japonica**) and the Trumpet Honeysuckle (both scarlet and straw color).

---

* Chinese twining Honeysuckle of some.

The former is deliciously fragrant, and blooms all summer, holding its masses of rich, dark green foliage till mid-winter; and the latter, though not fragrant, grows in fine masses, and flowers most abundantly at all times. Neither of these honey-suckles is infested with the insects which deform some of the other species, and render them unfit to be planted near a cottage window.

For cottages of stone, brick, or rough-cast, there is no climbing plant in the whole world equal to the Ivy—the evergreen Ivy of Europe. Its dark green foliage forms at all seasons of the year the richest drapery that ever festooned or wreathed either castle or cottage; and we need say nothing of the associations without number, which the mere sight of this plant always brings to the mind.

The ivy does not thrive very well in New England, except in sheltered places, for the winters are rather too severe for it; but in all other parts of the Union, it grows easily and rapidly. It likes a dry and loose soil, and should, at the north, while young, be a little protected, for a winter or two, with boughs of evergreens, till it gets established. It will often thrive in cold sites, on the north sides of houses, or under the shade of trees, when it fails in sunnier sites, because it is the sunshine, in mid-winter, and not the frost which injures it in the latter situations. The Giant Ivy (now quite common about Phila-delphia) is a larger leaved, richer looking, and more vigorous variety than the old species.

In New England, the American Ivy or Virginia Creeper may be used as a substitute for the European Ivy; both bearing a resemblance only in attaching themselves firmly (by the little rootlets sent out from their branches) to the wall, however hard it may be, and neither of them injuring it. Indeed, the European Ivy preserves a stone wall from decay.

There are many farmers and inmates of cottages, who would prefer to employ such vines to decorate their houses, as unite both beauty and usefulness.

There are two vines of this kind which are scarcely surpassed by any others, for picturesque effect, and which, at the same time, may also be turned to profitable account. We mean the Grape and the Hop.

Every painter that has studied landscape, will agree with us, that no vine in the world, take it altogether, is so grandly picturesque in growth, foliage, and fruit, as the grape—and, certainly, none harmonizes better with architecture than this, which has so often been copied both in marble and bronze by all manner of artists.

Our native grapes—the Catawba and Isabella, which grow with even greater luxuriance than the European vines, thrive well in all parts of the Union, and feast our senses with the delicious odors of their blossoms in spring, and the pleasant flavor of their fruit in autumn.

Very few persons know how graceful and pretty an effect is produced by the Hop vine, when hanging over the wing of a cottage, or wreathing some rustic trellis of the farm-house. This most rustic of all climbing beauties, whose rounded masses of green foliage and flowers fall into clusters as pretty as snow-wreaths, is usually condemned to a pole in the kitchen garden or the hop-field. There are few things, in its way, which deserve a better place in the affections of those who live in the rural cottage or farm-house, than the hop, which is ornamental and useful in the highest degree.

We must add a word or two here, regarding the *position* of vines. In all houses with projecting eaves, they should be planted as far out from the walls as the roof projects, so that the roots may be exposed to the kindly influences of the rain—which would be mainly lost to them, if planted close to the house. In wooden cottages, very nicely constructed, and which are to be painted frequently, a trellis may be placed a foot from the building, on which to train the vines, so that the latter need not be removed when the paint is to be renewed.

Some of our readers may desire to know whether it is generally in good taste to plant vines around villas and country houses of larger size, as around cottages and farm-houses. Our own feeling on this subject is briefly this : that the more rustic and rural the cottage—the less pretension it makes to architectural style, the more entirely does it demand the adornment of vines and climbing plants. They are its most becoming ornaments, and make, at little cost, its best compensation for all lack of elaborate architectural effect.

On the other hand, in proportion to the perfection of design and execution of the villa, its architecture should stand by itself. The architect does not design the spandrils of his arches and the tracery of his windows to be hidden by foliage ; they were made to invite the eye, and not to be concealed from it. The more simple and rustic villa may, however, be very properly adorned by vines, and some of the cheapest and most picturesque of country houses may be attained by laying up the roughest exterior walls to be covered with ivy and other creepers, leaving all the expense of outside finish to be applied to the comfort and convenience of the interior.

SECTION VIII.

HINTS FOR COTTAGE AND FARM STABLES.

WE do not propose to enter into details on the subject of outbuildings, which, if properly treated, might fill a volume; but merely to give a few hints, to serve those who have given it but little thought, and who desire some outlines, to enable them the better to put their own ideas in a more definite shape.

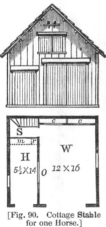

[Fig. 90.　Cottage Stable for one Horse.]

Fig. 90 shows the elevation and ground plan of a stable, measuring 18 by 20 feet outside, for a single horse and wagon. In the plan, W is the space for a wagon or chaise, 12 by 16 feet, having closets for harness, *c, c,* at one end. H is the stall for one horse, $5\frac{1}{2}$ by 14 feet (including the rack for hay, *r,* and the manger, *m,* at one end). This stall, besides its separate door, has a sliding door, *o,* 4 feet wide, which will allow the horse to pass to and from the vehicle standing in W, before and after harnessing. S, is a small passage, in which the stairs to the hay-loft above are placed. It is a common practice, even in stables of large size, to place the flight of steps to the hay-loft in the carriage-house, or space where the vehicles are kept; but as this always effectually prevents the possibility of keeping either wagon, carriage, or harness clean, since the dust of the hay will find its way down the opening of the stairway, we would always place the access to the hay-loft, if it be only by a ladder, in a passage by itself, separated by a door from the room where vehicles are kept.

The elevation of this little stable shows a broad window for receiving the hay, and over it a small space, with openings, devoted to pigeons.

This stable is in the simplest bracketed mode, and is intended to be built of wood, when it would accord with any of the cheap bracketed designs in the foregoing pages. The cost here would be about $190—and in many parts of the country, where lumber is cheap, it may be built for less than two-thirds this sum. A stable of this kind would look sufficiently well, in all cases, if built of rough $1\frac{1}{4}$ inch plank, battened at the joints, and the whole painted or colored with some cheap wash.

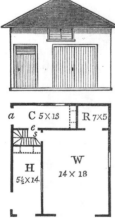

[Fig. 91. Cottage Stable for a Horse and Cow.]

Fig. 91 is the plan and elevation of a stable, measuring 20 by 24 feet, in the clear, inside. It contains accommodations for a horse at H, and for a cow at C. The space for wagon and small carriage is shown at W. The harness-room or closet at R; the stairs to the hay-loft at S. There is a separate door, a, to the cow's stall, and the stall may also, for convenience of feeding, be entered from the passage where the flight of stairs is, through a small doorway shown at e.

This design is in a simple mode, which would harmonize

with cottages in the Italian or any classical style. The walls are 14 feet high, and the roof rises 6 feet in the centre, and projects two feet at the eaves. Built of wood, in a rough manner, battened, this stable would cost about $325. It would look still better if built of hard brick, and the cost, here, would not exceed $350.

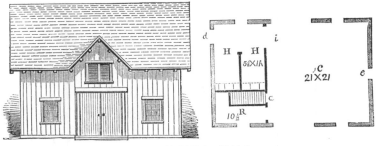

[Fig. 92. Model Cottage Stable.]

Fig. 92 is a model plan for a carriage-house, stable, and barn, calculated for two horses and three vehicles. In the plan (21 feet by 32 feet inside), c is the carriage-house, 21 feet square. The entrance to this is by two doors, so that the carriage may, if the locality will allow it, drive in at one door and out at the other; but if not, then, instead, one doorway only, may be placed in the end, where the window, e, now is. H H are the stalls for horses, each 5½ by 14 feet, with a sliding door, i, communicating with the carriage-house; a is the space partitioned off for the stairs to the hay-loft, and there is a door at the bottom to keep out dust. R is the harness-room; d the back door to the stable, through which litter is also swept out into the stable-yard. The posts of this stable are 15 feet long, and the roof rises about 12 feet (the pitch being a square or right angle ⋀). Those who prefer it may omit the small

gable, and receive the hay through windows in the large end
gables.

The elevation shown in Fig. 92 is in the simplest bracketed
style, to be built of wood. The cost here would be about
$400; at Rochester, about $320.

[Fig. 93. Cottage Stables.]

Fig. 93 shows two elevations, drawn to half the scale, but
adapted to the same ground plan as Fig. 92. The elevation to
the left, *a*, is one in a simple gothic or pointed style, showing
how easily, by the alteration of a few lines, the style of the
stable may be made to harmonize with that of the dwelling.
Another, in a more classical style, is shown at *b*.

In arranging stable accommodations, there are a few leading
points which must be borne in mind, even in the smallest
buildings, when convenience and comfort are aimed at.

In the first place, the stalls should be $5\frac{1}{2}$ feet wide,* and not
less than 14 feet deep, including the whole space behind the
horse. The partition between the stalls should extend back
not less than 8 feet, and the floor of the stall, upon which the
horse stands, should incline about $1\frac{1}{2}$ inches, till it reaches the
end of this partition, behind which should be a depression or
gutter, to carry off all the moisture. In all cases where the

---

* We know that many stables afford scarcely 5 feet—but only a *small* horse can
lie down comfortably in such a stall—and shame to him who builds a stall in which
his horse is forced to sleep standing.

hay is kept in a loft above the stable, we would make an opening through the floor, over the manger of each stall, thus supplying the hay-rack to that stall from the hay-loft above, without carrying or pitching it down. This is not only a great saving of both labor and hay, but it insures cleanliness, a

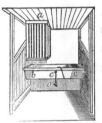

great virtue in a stable. Fig. 94, which is a sketch of the interior of a stall, shows such a hay-rack at *a*, directly under which is the manger, *b*, to catch any hay that may fall, and at the end is a box, *c*, partitioned off the manger, for corn or oats. At *e*, is a hole in

[Fig. 94. Horse Stall.] the manger rim, through which the halter-strap is passed, at the end of which is a wooden sinker, *o*, just heavy enough to keep the loose end of the halter down. This allows the halter sufficient play to give the horse room to eat or lie down, without allowing it to fall in such a position that he may get his legs over it.

The large door in the room or house for carriages should not be less than 8 feet wide, and, if a full-top carriage is used, not less than 9 feet high. The carriage-house and stables should have 9½ feet clear between the beams.

FARM BARNS AND OUTBUILDINGS. For a farm of moderate size, or one where the means of the owner are limited, the most economical mode of accommodating the stock and produce of the farm is in a barn and stable combined. This building should be placed in a situation where, either naturally or artificially, the ground slopes, so that on one side, the *barn* is entered on the level of the ground, and on the other the *stable*, which is one story lower. This latter, or basement story, opens on the cattle-yard, and contains accommodation for cows and horses, root-cellar, etc.—thus the same roof and walls cover and inclose at once the live stock below and the hay and grain above.

As one of the best and most complete examples of this kind of barn and stable within our observation, we may instance that of our neighbor, Mr. Wm. Sayer, 8 miles from Newburg. Mr. Sayer's farm lies in a grazing district, and, of course, his outbuildings are different from those required in a strictly grain-growing district. We have never seen, however, in any part of the country, a single farm building in which economy of space, excellence of arrangement, and nicety of construction were more completely combined than in this barn. We may add, that the plan is entirely Mr. S.'s, and, for a farm of this kind, is not easily improved.

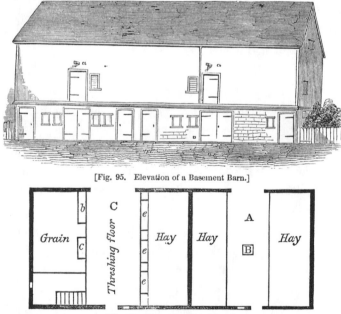

[Fig. 95. Elevation of a Basement Barn.]

[Fig. 96. Plan of the Main Floor.]

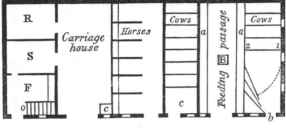

[Fig. 97. Plan of the Basement Floor.]

The elevation, Fig. 95, shows the stable or basement side, with both stories. The posts are 16 feet long, from the basement walls to the eaves. The opposite side, one story high, shows two pairs of double doors for driving in loads of hay and grain. The whole building is 30 by 72 feet, outside—30 feet square being a hay-barn, under which is the stable for cows, and the remaining 43 feet being a grain and hay barn, with horse-stalls, carriage-house, etc., below. At *a a* are shown tackle beams, with hooks, to which a block can be attached, for lowering or drawing any thing up to the main floor.

In Fig. 96, which is the plan of the barn floor, A is the main floor, 12 feet wide, with a hay-mow on each side. At B is a hay-well, or hole in the floor, with a curb round it, through which the hay is thrown into the feeding passage in the cow-stable below. This curb is removed, and a trap door put in its place in summer.

C is the threshing floor, 14 feet wide, with a hay-mow on one side, and grain on the other. On one side of this floor is a space *c*, through which straw is thrown into the straw-room, and another, *b*, through which roots are thrown into the root-cellar, both being in the basement; while on the other side are openings, *e, e*, through which hay is placed in the racks of the horses, in the stable beneath.

[Fig. 98. Threshing Floor.]

Fig. 98, which is a view of the mow on one side of the threshing floor, will show how cleverly these openings are managed, in order to occupy no space wanted for other uses. In this, *a* is the side of the mow, boarded up about $3\frac{1}{2}$ feet—in which are doors, *b*, that shut out all dust, etc. These doors are hinged on the lower side, and when thrown down, or opened, *c*, give ample space for filling the racks below in the easiest manner.

Let us now examine the basement or stable story of this barn, Fig. 97. The first feature that demands our attention is the cow-stable, occupying about 30 feet square, being that portion on the left hand of the plan, Fig. 97. Here is a large "feeding passage," 11 feet wide, including the mangers, *a a*, on a level with the floor.* This passage is supplied with hay, it will be remembered, through the hole, B, in the ceiling (which is in the floor of the barn above). This well-hole acts also as a ventilator, whenever one is necessary, for the whole cow-stable.

The cow-stable accommodates 18 cows, and the manner of placing the cows in the stalls is both original and excellent. The stalls measure 3 feet 2 inches from centre to centre

---

* This feeding passage (including the mangers) has a mortar floor, made of lime and sand, over small stones, perfectly hard and smooth, so that no hay-seed is lost, while the whole can be kept as clean as a parlor ; as indeed it is, under Mr. Sayer's excellent management.

(a width scarcely enough, in our judgment, but which Mr. S.
declares, from long experience, to be amply sufficient in this
mode). These stalls are formed of a series of light *gates*, or
rather each side of the stall is a single gate, swinging—not
upon hinges likely to be broken—but upon a wooden pivot,
made on the upper and lower end of the frame post at one end,
2, of the gate. Supposing the cows entering the door *b*, Fig.
97, to be stalled for the night—the gates being all swung open
(as the three first are represented), the first cow enters—the
gate is shut behind her, and thus forms her stall—then another,
and the gate is shut, and another, until all the gates are closed,
and the cows stalled for the night, as represented on the other
side, *c*. These gates are made of oak, framed so as to be
light and strong ; and as the pivot post, at the end on which
the gate swings, rests in a hole or socket at the bottom, by
raising it a couple of inches the gate can be unshipped and
taken out in a moment. In this way a double stall can readily

[Fig. 99. Gate Stall.]

be made for a cow about to calve.
Fig. 99 will give a better idea of
these gate stalls : *a* being the gate
turning on the wooden pivot post,
b, and being fastened, when shut,
by an oak pin, put in the strip, *c*,
which is prevented from being
lost by being fastened to the gate
by a leather strap ; the cow, on entering the stall, puts her
head through the opening at *d*, and thus, when the stable is
full, the cows all stand with their heads on a line over the
manger, *e*.

Next, on the right, see Fig. 97, is the stable, 14 feet wide, with stalls (5 feet wide) for six horses. To the left of this is the carriage-house, also 14 feet wide. At the side of the door, on entering this apartment, is the pump, *c*, a large cistern, which takes all the water from this side of the roof, being built under the floor here. There is a spout running through the wall and another through the stable, to convey water both into the cattle-yard and the stables.

The space of 14 feet wide, to the right of the carriage-house, is occupied by a small root-cellar, R; a place for straw used for litter, S; and a spare stall, F, for the occasional use of a pair of horses or oxen. Here, also, is a broad flight of stairs, *o*, which ascends to a store-room for grain, etc., on the barn floor above.

Our plans and description will convey a general notion of the arrangement of this very compact barn and stable; but nothing short of a personal examination can give a just idea of the exact adaptation of every part, and the complete manner in which the whole has been executed. Even the fastenings to the doors, all of which are made of hard wood, are so simply and ingeniously contrived, as to be superior to any of metal, both for fitness and durability; and there are few American farmers who cannot learn an excellent lesson by examining this and all the other buildings on Mr. Sayer's farm.

PLAN OF A FARMERY. Few of our farmers require much larger accommodation than such a barn and stable as the foregoing, with an additional cattle shed or two. But in the richer agricultural districts, where the farms are large, and a good deal of capital is accumulated by the proprietors, a more complete *farmery* or arrangement of farm buildings is requisite, both for greater convenience of performing the labor, and greater satisfaction in seeing a spirit of order and method reigning in the whole establishment.

The farmery, generally, surrounds a square, that being not only the most compact form, but also giving well-sheltered yards for the cattle. It is also usually placed directly in the rear of the house, or, at least, on that side of it nearest the kitchen, and should face a southern aspect.

The annexed plan of a farmery is based upon those seen in Western New York, where the farms are large grain farms, and where a considerable number of sheep are kept.

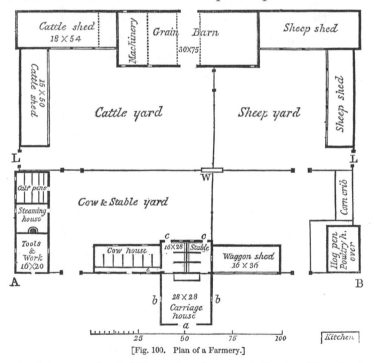

[Fig. 100. Plan of a Farmery.]

In this plan, the building placed nearest the dwelling is the *carriage-house* and stable, a building 28 by 44 feet. Instead of having the door for carriages only at the end, *a*, as shown in the plan, it would be more convenient, in many localities, to have two doors at *b b*, so as to drive through the carriage-house.

[Fig. 101. Elevation of the First Range.]

In the rear of the carriage-house is a stable for six horses, which can be made deeper on the side next the stable-yard, for any number of work-horses. As the stalls on the right communicate with the wagon and cart shed, the work-horses most constantly in use for draught should be kept there, so as to allow them to pass into their stalls after leaving the wagon or cart in the shed. The doors at *c, c*, open into the stable-yard, to allow the litter to be swept out. The hay-racks extend to the ceiling, and are supplied from above, the whole second story of this building being a hay-loft.

To the left of this stable is a cow-stable. The feeding passage, *e*, communicates by a door with the horse-stable, for convenience of feeding. Over this stable is a loft for hay, as well as over the wagon shed; both communicate with the main hay-barn over the carriage-house and horse-stable.

On the left side of the stable-yard is a range of low buildings, 16 feet wide and 55 feet long, divided into three parts, that nearest the dwelling being a tool-room and work-shop—adjoining it a steaming-house, for cooking the food, steaming chaff, etc., for cattle (with a chimney and one of Mott's boilers fixed for use), and beyond this a calf-house, with pens for keeping young calves. Under the whole of this is the *cellar for roots*, which should be dry, warm, and well ventilated.

On the opposite side of the farmery (balancing the tool-house) is the hog-pen. Over this is the poultry-house, the sides of which are filled-in, the floor covered three inches deep with sand, and the south side of the building glazed with a broad window, so as to keep the apartment warm in winter. In the rear of this is a large corn-crib.

In the centre of the rear range of the farmery is the grain barn, 30 by 75 feet, and two stories high, with doors on both sides, so as to drive a loaded grain wagon on the main floor. In the basement of this barn should be a space for horse power, connected with fanning-mill, threshing-machine, and straw-cutter on the floor above.

On the left of the grain barn are two large sheds, the lower part being open for shelter for cattle, and the upper part being filled with hay. On the right are similar sheds for sheep, with hay-lofts over them.

For greater convenience and cleanliness, the yard of the farmery has been divided into 4 parts, all opening into one, however, by gates, and the two main yards for cattle and sheep opening into farm lanes by the gates at L L. In the centre is a large trough or reservoir, W, kept full by a hydraulic ram, which gives a constant supply of water to all the yards, without any labor for the farmer.*

---

* About Philadelphia, and in many parts of this state, the *Hydraulic ram*—the most perfect little water engine known—is used to supply barn-yards and farmeries with water. Wherever there is a perpetual spring or stream, within a few hundred feet of the barns, the overflow of which will fill a pipe of 1½ inches bore, a hydraulic

Fig. 101, which is the elevation of the front range of the farmery, on the line A B, will give an idea of the exterior appearance of a part of the buildings. They are here supposed to be built of wood, with roof projecting 20 inches, weather-boarding vertical, with plain battens, 2 inches wide.

This plan, and, indeed, all others made without knowing the special wants of the farm for which they are intended, must only be regarded as affording *suggestions* to the proprietor about to build. The details, both of plan and construction, must depend partly on the character and extent of the farm, and partly on the means which can be judiciously expended for this purpose.

STABLES AND FARM BUILDINGS FOR THE WEST. We are indebted to Professor J. W. Turner, of Illinois, for the following exceedingly practical and judicious hints for farm buildings in the West. The difference between the older states on the sea-coast and those more newly settled in the valley of the Missis-sippi, is so great, that while many of his remarks will be of little value in our part of the Union, they will be invaluable there. Professor Turner's suggestions are all based upon thorough experimental knowledge of western life and western farming, in districts where the amount which the farmer, newly established, can afford to spend upon buildings, bears no proportion to the fertility of the land or the amount of his crops.

STABLES FOR THE WEST. "Throughout the vast regions devoted to stock raising in the West, especially in Illinois and Missouri, and all the states south of these, stables are used, not

---

ram may be set up, at about the cost of digging a well of moderate depth, which will convey a constant supply of water to the house or farm-yard, or both.

for sheltering common stock or their fodder, but merely for the few horses and milch cows which are kept for family use. Many farmers in these states annually fatten some one or two hundred head of oxen, and some few, even a thousand or more for the market, and still a very moderate-sized stable, or rather no stable at all, answers all their purposes.

Great numbers of these stables are now, however, being annually erected, and some hints from writers on the subject cannot but be in the highest degree entertaining and useful to all classes, and especially to agriculturists in the South and West. I say the South and West, for in the older states, models of all sorts abound, while in these warmer latitudes a man might travel for weeks together without seeing even one, of tolerable convenience.

It is proper, first, to consider what ends the great majority of those who are intending to build in these regions wish to reach, and, second, to suggest some convenient and economical mode of reaching those ends.

1. All wish to economize in lumber and labor as much as possible in all their outbuildings, because both are exceedingly scarce and relatively dear in the West. This end will, of course, be best reached by throwing as many conveniences as possible *under one roof, and in a square form,* or one as nearly square as possible.

The same plan also best economizes the foundation, which in most cases must be made of bricks or stones, transported at much cost. The people in these states are also in their period of social infancy, and both their means and their tastes lead them generally to desire to reach all their ends in the most simple and direct way. Still they love to see all their improvements present a neat, convenient, firm, and substantial appearance, and multitudes are now ready to incur all the necessary expense for such improvements, could they only see clearly how they can reach the end.

2.   Another end to be reached, which is peculiar to these states, is to have free access to and from their outbuildings without passing through the terrible mud and water which, in prairie countries, always exists on all the flat lands where cattle and swine are yarded or allowed to run in small lots. Those who are accustomed only to a rocky or gravelly soil, can form no adequate conception of the inconvenience of the prairie mud throughout all the rainy seasons of the year.

3.   Water is not found in brooks and springs, but must generally be obtained from wells of from 12 to 100 feet deep. Hence the location of the well becomes of far more importance than it otherwise would, especially when we consider that the master of the establishment, whatever his profession, or however wealthy he may be, will, in the West, often be compelled to draw the water himself, and many times when he feels quite unable to stand in the cold searching winds long enough to do it.

4.   The things to be provided for in the stable, are stalls for from one to four horses, and from one to four milch cows, though sheds are generally used for the latter—a place for pigs and fowls—and room for storing, temporarily, hay and provender for their food.   I say temporarily, for most of the hay is stacked, and the corn "cribbed," in the fields, and it is important that the stable should only hold enough of each for present use, as the housing of all the provender of a western farm is, for the present at least, out of the question.

5. A place for carriage, wagon, tools, etc., is also generally desired under the same roof, when convenient.

We apprehend these several ends may be well attained in the following manner, so far as small stables are wanted, and for larger establishments the same principles may easily be extended. Other little conveniences may also be added to the general plan here suggested, to suit individual interest or taste.

II. *Plan of procedure.* 1. Select a location for the stable as dry and convenient as possible, and so situated as to admit of a yard for stock on the east side, and a green grass surface or lawn on the south side of both the stable and stock-yard, so that the owner may pass to either on the green grass; and into which grass-yard no cattle or hogs should be allowed to enter, except the former in the harness, or the latter to pick up fallen fruit.

If the ground is level, take a shovel, scraper, and plough, and scrape the dirt from some remote point towards the intended location for the barn, making the ground highest near the barn or stable, and lowest in that corner of the yard most remote from it, so that all water will at once settle into that corner of the yard. This will cost some little labor, in locations where the ground is perfectly level, but it will be found easier than to wade in the mud half-leg deep, for half a century, after horses and cows, equally incommoded.

2. Dig a well as indicated at *g*, on the ground plan, Fig. 103, and level the earth taken from the well, about the stable ground; and if this is like most of the earth 10 and 20 feet below the surface in the West, if raised above the general level, it will readily be trodden down so hard, that no other floor will be needed for the carriage and wagon house.

3. The foundation of the stable should then be laid of brick or stone, omitting it entirely in the spaces for the wagon and

[Fig. 102. Elevation of Stable.]

carriage way. The building can then be most conveniently erected by forming studs of oak, 3 inches by 4, perpendicularly from the sill to the plate or the girder, two feet apart, from centre to centre.

A covering of any kind of clapboards can then be laid on, to suit the taste of the owner; and, on the north and west sides, at least, of all the stalls for cattle and horses, the inside of the studs should be boarded up, and the space filled with sawdust or tan-bark, or even pounded loam or clay, packed close around the studs between the clapboards without, and the boards on the inside. This will add to the strength and security of the wall, especially where horses are kept, and will, moreover, more than pay all costs, in the comfort of the stable, summer and winter, and the saving of food needful for the animals in cold weather. As it is well known now that the

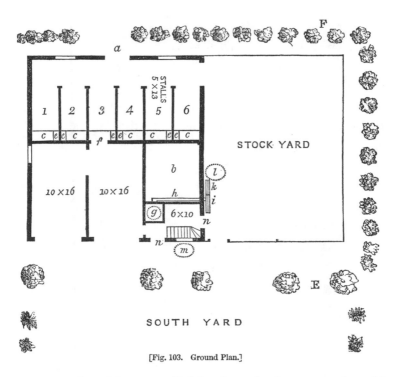

[Fig. 103. Ground Plan.]

extra supply of heat needful in the animal economy in cold weather, if not supplied by warm housing, must be supplied by an extra consumption of food, with no increase of flesh or strength, but a great loss of comfort to the exposed animal, this extra consumption of food, in a few months, even where food is cheap, will more than balance all that can be saved by withholding a few feet of boards, and a few hours' labor.

A door, *a*, should be left in the rear of the stalls, on the north, both for ventilation in summer, and for casting out the manure and litter of the stable.

The doors of the wagon-house should also be made in four parts, for the same purpose—so that the upper parts, 1, 2, Fig.

102, may be left open for ventilation, while the lower parts, 3, 4, may be closed to keep out fowls, etc.

The floor of the corn-crib, *b*, Fig. 103, and the feeding cribs, *c*, should be on the same level, about 2^1 or 3 feet from the ground, so that the pigs may at all times have free access under the whole. This is necessary, not only to give them a convenient shelter, and also to enable them to pick up all corn that may be scattered, but, above all, to prevent rats from accumulating at these points, which the pigs will, in a great measure, if not wholly, prevent, by constantly disturbing their operations, and depriving them of their food.

The feeding crib itself may be constructed to suit the taste of the occupant; but a simple long box of good width, with small raised boxes (*e, e*, in the ground plan), for feeding grain, on one side of each stall, will be found convenient.

The posts of the frame should not be less than 16, nor more than 20 feet high. The three windows in the second floor, shown in Fig. 102, are in the hen-room, and the single window above is in the dove-cote.

In one corner of this grain-box, salt and ashes, half and half, wet, and mixed into a clay, should always be kept standing for the use of the animal, especially the horse; and where contagious or epidemic diseases are about, a small quantity of assafœtida, pounded fine, should be added. I know this to be so virtually important to the health of the horse, especially where fed freely on corn, that my readers will pardon this and all similar irrelevant allusions, since I am more intent on being truly useful to them, than on the exhibition of strict method in the arrangement of my remarks.

The front of one stall should be left open, so as to admit of a passage, *f*, through from the carriage and wagon house into the stalls. In some respects, it will be more convenient to have stall No. 1 open as a passage; in other respects, No. 3 or 4 would be preferable. These stalls and feeding cribs will occupy somewhat less than one half of the area of a stable 30 feet square, according to the taste of the proprietor—some desiring stalls only 4 feet by 10 deep, others desiring 5 or 6 feet by from 12 to 15 feet, crib included. 4 feet by 13, crib included, is, at the West, a common size for a single horse.

The partitions between the stalls should extend back from the front of the crib, at least 6 feet, to the rear of the crib, and should be formed of stout plank, at least one inch thick, placed at each end, between two upright pieces of timber about 1½ inches by 5 inches, and reaching from the floor below to the floor above, to both of which they should be firmly secured, and pins or strong nails inserted throughout their whole length, so as to bind the whole partition firmly together. The corners of these upright timbers, and of all others around which horses ever pass, should be smoothly rounded off.

The corn-cribs should be elevated, as above described, and should be inclosed tightly on all sides with strong oak boards, so as to exclude all rats and mice. It may, of course, be divided into apartments or boxes for various kinds of grain, to suit the proprietor. But in the South and West the greater part of it will necessarily be devoted to the reception of Indian corn in the ear.

The well, *w*, should be located in a recess at some convenient point, where the proprietor can in all weathers draw the water comfortably, and carry it in buckets to the stalls, or into the front yard, or let it run through a spout, as at *h*, into the trough in the yard, *i*. It is indispensable, in the West, to allow a few pigs to follow the larger stock in the yard, and hence it becomes equally indispensable to provide them with water by themselves. This is accomplished by placing the first trough, *i*, for the cattle, so high that the pigs cannot reach into it. Beyond this is another trough, *k*, down on the ground, so that the water from the former will readily run into the latter when full.

Still further on, at the lower end of the pigs' trough, *n*, a large round hole, *l*, should be excavated in the ground, into which all the water from all the troughs should ultimately settle. The bottom of this hole should be paved with brickbats set on end, and the sides curbed with oak plank or flat flag-stones. In this hole the pigs will wallow, the ducks and geese will swim, and it will, in most soils in the West, soon become almost as water-tight, by the action of these animals upon the soil, as an iron kettle.

South of the stable, -also, at *m*, another similar and smaller pool may be prepared for the young ducklings and goslings before they are large enough to encounter the danger of the common stock-yard; and this pool can also be supplied from a spout leading from the well.

Temporary pens, for the few calves that ever are stabled in the West and South, can be easily made from some one of the empty stalls, as cows never need to be kept in the stable after the time of calving, in the South, except in rare instances. The same provision can also be made for young pigs, if needful.

A shed, Fig. 104, may also be extended from either of the northern corners of the stable, and also across the east side of it, over the watering trough, if necessary, with racks, etc., for foddering "out-doors stock."

If it is desirable to feed any considerable number of cattle out of doors, from stacks of fodder adjacent to the stable, the following plan will be found convenient:—Extend an upright rack, *a*, the whole length, attached to the frame of the shed, on the rear side.   Place a crib, *b*, inside, below the rack, to catch the scattering hay and fodder.   On the outside, project the roof

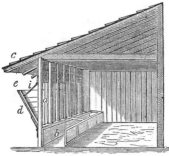

of the shed, *c*, over the back plate, into which the upright rack is framed, some 3 or 4 feet, in the form of the bracketed roof.   Bring a slanting shelf, *d*, from the bottom of the rack, rear side, backwards and upwards, to within two feet of the eaves of the bracketed

[Fig. 104. Feeding Shed.]

roof.   A transverse section of the shed or end view, will then present the appearance of Fig. 104.   The hay is put in the rack from the outside, at *e*.

This slanting shelf should be hung on hinges at the bottom, and divided into short sections, so that it may be swung down and cleared when necessary, and fastened up with long iron hasps, *i*.   The stacks of hay or fodder should of course be arranged along the back part of this feeding shed, at a convenient distance; and the sheds may be of any length, even extending hundreds of feet, if need be, entirely around the yard.   This mode of feeding accomplishes two or three desirable objects.   1. It is economical and convenient; 2. It affords a comfortable shelter for the stock in a mild climate;

3. It keeps the fodder dry in wet weather, while the cattle are eating it. And with a good supply of such feeding sheds, even constructed on the rudest plan, with straw coverings, a small stable will be found sufficient for the largest farms.

Another convenient mode of out-door feeding is, to build a square frame in the middle of the yard, with a rack all around the outside, at the bottom, coarse enough to allow the cattle to put their heads through, between every round, framed into the upright sides of the building, with a crib outside below, to catch the scattering hay, and a narrow shed roof, covering the crib, projecting from the sides of the building, just above the rack. The upper part of the frame is covered and shingled like a barn—suppose it to be ten feet square. It is then entirely filled with hay; and the cattle, reaching in about 4 feet on all sides, can eat the hay out without any feeding. The central parts will then fall over within their reach, so that several tons of hay are thus consumed without trouble, and with comparatively little waste *for the West;* and then the whole crib is replenished again from the stacks in the field.

These hints, it is hoped, will suggest modes of disposing of all the needful stock of the larger kind about any ordinary country house, even in the West, except the hogs—and they are in some regions so numerous, and so peculiarly "*sui generis,*" that, aside from the few smaller ones around the farm-yard, I must devote a section exclusively to their benefit.

I am well aware that in many districts of the United States large barns are built, furnishing every convenience for housing and feeding all kinds of stock. But, perhaps my readers are not equally well aware, that over vastly larger portions, this is not true, and never can be true, in our day; and the operations of stock raising are conducted on so large a scale, that even the cheap and rough expedients to which I have adverted cannot, in practice, at present, be universally applied. In other places they can be, and have been, and if known, would be, to a still greater extent; and as it is my desire to be useful to all classes, I hope these hints may prove serviceable to many beginners in the new country.

I pass, then, to the provision for the smaller animals in the above plan for a stable. Every householder knows the value of good fresh eggs, and an abundance of good fat poultry, the year round. But few know how to obtain them without having them cost twice as much as they are worth. A hen is much like a firebrand—a fine thing in the right place, but the worst of all things in the wrong place. Like the harpies of old, they are sure to defile all they do not destroy. But with proper conveniences for managing them, they are among the most agreeable, profitable, and useful objects in country life. To children, especially, fowls are objects of exceeding interest, and form an almost necessary part of the means of developing the moral and industrial energies of a country household. See that little fellow toppling along with his cap full of eggs for "Mamma," or patting his favorite chicken on the back. There is a whole "California" in that little fellow's heart— shining out through his eyes, and evinced in every motion of his little body. He who will educate a boy in the country without a "chicken," is already a semi-barbarian; and he who leaves his chickens to make a hen-roost of all things sacred and profane, visible and invisible, is still worse; to say nothing of the good housewife's flower-patch in the garden, the very mention of which excites no small fear of a shower of oven-brooms and brickbats, while the whole welkin rings again with the discordant "shew-there! shew-there!"

How, then, shall we dispose of companions at once so vexatious and so indispensable?

We will make an entrance from both yards at *n n*, Fig. 103, into an area, partitioned off from the corn-crib and the well, about 6 feet by 10. Let a part of this be occupied with stairs, ascending into the loft above, from the west towards the east. Under these stairs, and about this entrance-way, should be boxes, in which quite young chickens may be brooded over night, secure from rats and other vermin. The stairway should open into a space in the second-story loft, Fig. 105, about 8 feet wide, as in the entry below stairs. Into this room

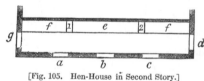

[Fig. 105. Hen-House in Second Story.]

three large glass windows, *a*, *b*, *c*, should open, facing the south, and two doors at either end, 3 feet by 6, *g*, *d*, should, on the prairies, open outward, so as to be fastened half way open to catch the southern prairie breeze in hot weather, at which time the glass windows should also be opened, or taken wholly out and laid by. The outside studs should here be boarded up, inside and out, and filled with saw-dust or tan-bark, or clay, as in the case of the stables, and the rear partition made impervious to rats or mice. At each corner a partition of lath should inclose cages, into which hens inclined to set at improper times, may be thrown and fed. Near these, on one side, a box always filled with sand, lime, and ashes, for the fowls to wallow in, and on the other side, a box filled with grain, both shielded with a cover from the droppings of the

roost above.   Between these, boxes should be made for the
hens to lay in, *e*, and set in, *f*, with the entrance for the hen on
the rear side, and a place to take the eggs from the front.
Plenty of gravel and pounded bones (with an occasional meal
of meat in winter) should be given them at all times, and a
supply of the former should be kept in the boxes 1, 2.   Overhead, the roosts should be constructed of rough poles, 1 or 2
inches in diameter, *with the bark on*.   A few movable covers,
made of lath, under which a hen can occasionally be put, will
be found convenient.   Wire gratings at windows and doors
should be applied, as far as is found necessary, to prevent
damage to the glass, or to keep out intruders when the whole
is open; and a proper railing to keep children from falling
from the side windows, from one of which the litter of the
coop can be thrown directly into the stock-yard below.

Thus provided, the hens should never be allowed to enter
any other part of the stable, and they will soon find their
quarters cool in summer; and as the hay-mow is at their backs
in winter (the rest of this story being filled with hay), and the
warm sun shines into their apartment in front, they will
continue to lay (if supplied with meat occasionally) all winter.
Indeed, they will be so thoroughly protected by the hay from
the cold, that they will hardly know when winter comes.

And with good *hedges*, which may be grown in from 3 to 5
years, they can be restrained entirely either to the front or
back yard, at the option of the proprietor, by opening the door
leading from the one or the other to the hen-loft.

In the garret loft, over the hens, there should be a place for
doves.   Some two or three or more holes may be cut, as at *e*
(see elevation, Fig. 102), through which the doves enter a

room of the same size with the hen-loft. On the rear side of their room, boxes or shelves, more or less in number, should be fitted up for the doves to lay in; and an inside blind should close the window, and shut out the light, whenever it is desirable, as doves are fond of a dark place for brooding. I once saw nearly 200 doves in such a room, with no boxes whatever for laying, but each dove selected a place for herself on the bare floor, and it was difficult and inconvenient passing over the floor without treading upon the young or the eggs— hence shelves would be preferable.

Of course, the hay is put into all such small stables by means of windows, opening from the outside, on one or more of the sides of the stable.

A small stable, about 20 by 22 feet, would furnish all these conveniences (Fig. 106), so far as necessary, to professional men and gentlemen near towns; while one 30 feet square, with proper sheds for out-door feeding, would accommodate the great majority of small farms—at least, far better than they are now accommodated—with such variations as will readily occur to all, as respects locality,* division of stalls, etc., etc.

In Fig. 106, the pigs should be allowed to pass under the hen loft, feeding-crib, and corn-crib at the same time.

The cost of my stable, 30 feet square, would not, in Illinois, be more than from $100 to $300, built in the plainest manner; and not more than from $300 to $600, built in the best mode, and painted white or any other color preferred.

One word in regard to the trees and evergreens. In some

---

* It may not be needless to remark, that where more convenient, the stable may be made to front the east, with the stock-yard on the north or south side, or both.

places in the Western States, the latter cannot be had. Wherever it is possible, they should be set, at once, along the north side of the stable-yard. Elms, the finest of shade trees,

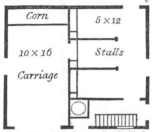

[Fig. 106. Plan of a smaller Stable.]

may be procured anywhere, and a row, ten feet apart, should be set, at once, on the south side, as they will, in a few years, add immensely to the comfort, and beauty, and value of the premises. The plums and other *smooth-skinned fruits* should also be set in the front yard, as it is the only place where they can be saved from the curculio; and, probably, if the ground is suitable, the pear-trees would be better here than anywhere else.

A *fence* of evergreen trees, placed from 4 to 6 feet apart, should be planted to form a screen, S, on the north, or outside the yard fence; and Norway spruces or hemlocks should be planted round the south yard. This should, to make it complete, be hedged round with the Osage orange, so that the fowls may be confined within the bounds of the south yard. This yard should contain an acre or more, and here the plums, peaches, and other stone fruits should be planted, to secure them against the attacks of insects.

If the yard is a large one, it will be proper to commence the ploughing and scraping the dirt from the centre, scraping each way, so as to have the outside of the yard, all around, higher than the centre. But, in many places, where the ground is undulating, and where the manure is not wanted on the soil, a location can be easily selected, in which the water will naturally run from the barn, without any grading, and carry a great portion of the manure with it. Doubtless, these sugges-

tions will appear singular and needless to two classes of readers
—those who know nothing of western mud, and those who are
already so accustomed to it, that they scarcely regard it as an
inconvenience.

A singular and characteristic hyperbole may aid the
conceptions of the former class.—A stage-driver across one of
these flat prairies once told a friend of the writer, that he had
driven a pair of mules seven years on that route, "and never
saw any thing of them but their ears." This stage-driver
would probably feel no necessity of *grading* around a stable on
any tolerably dry ground whatever. It is true, that an
undrained puddle of water in the centre of a yard is objectionable; but it is also true, that it is better than the same puddle
spread over the whole of it—and farmers, as well as voters, are
often compelled to "a choice of evils."

We have now suggested modes of disposing of all the
animals commonly retained about a country residence, except
"His Majesty, Monsieur Sus," whom a quaint old writer
pronounces "the only gentleman in England, because he does
nothing but eat, drink, and sleep."

But in the West, where from one hundred to one thousand
hogs are frequently seen about a single farm-house, they form
an aristocracy of the most exacting and relentless order; and
to meet their exorbitant demands is not so easy as at first might
be imagined—for, like many other aristocracies, they are at
once prodigal, wasteful, insolent, and intolerable—while, unlike
some others, they are averse to wearing jewels, and it is difficult, where great numbers are kept, either to get them into their
noses, or to keep them there. When they are allowed, however,
to "follow cattle," as it is called, they can be easily disposed of

with economy and profit; but where they are allowed the "fee simple" of the soil, and fattened by themselves for their own sake, to provide for them without waste of food or labor, or of both, is not so easy; as it would be found quite a losing business to build a plank or flagstone pen for each of these gentry, and feed him with boiled mush and milk, in a clean trough, three times per day, for two cents per pound, neat weight; and it is scarcely better to throw cart-loads of corn in the ear, into a yard where the mud is two feet deep, and leave them to pick it out if they can—as is now often done.

In the hope of providing a practical remedy for these difficulties, we will suggest a plan for a "self-feeding corn-crib," which we trust will be found a great saving of labor, at the same time that it will greatly diminish the expense of fattening this kind of stock, and proportionally increase the comfort of the proprietor, and the general neatness of his premises.

We will suppose two yards of suitable size, one for lean and the other for fat hogs, side by side. On the dividing line of these yards erect the corn-crib, in the following manner:

We will suppose the crib to be 16 feet square and 10 feet high; this will hold over one thousand bushels of corn in the ear, which will be sufficient for the smallest class of farmers, and others can enlarge the plan at their pleasure.

In the first place, erect the foundations of the building of stone, brick, or upon a strong wooden frame, so high that the largest swine can pass freely under it at all points, thus making a lower story of the crib, some 3 feet high, into which the hogs, at all times, have free access. It would be well to have the northwest and east sides of this lower story closed tight, and

the south side alone left open; and, perhaps, a swing door on
the north side, also, for the purpose of raking out cobs, litter,
etc., as here the hogs eat all *their corn*—for we are now
speaking of those vast regions of country where they are
fattened on nothing but corn. Let a floor be made, either of
oak plank or of hard clay, under this feeding-room;—and in the
centre, at least, it should be of plank—for reasons to be
explained. This foundation, then, being made sufficiently
high, and strong enough to bear the weight of the corn in the
crib above, erect a plain building thereon, of scantling and
boards, in the common way, 16 feet square and ten feet high.
Let it be partitioned in the centre into two equal parts with
studs, lathed up on each side, coarsely, with common lath.
This is for two reasons—first, to enable the air to circulate
more freely through the centre of the corn, and prevent it from
heating, as it sometimes will do, when in piles more than 10 or
12 feet square; and, second, to enable the proprietor at all times
to keep his old corn, if he pleases, separate from his new crop.

Lay a tight, *strong* floor under this second story, covering
the whole area, except a space 8 feet long and two feet wide in
the centre, that is, 1 foot each side of the centre partition, and
8 feet long. From the outside of this hole, on either side, a
common feeding-rack, with the rounds or standards four inches
apart, is extended downwards the whole length of the story
below, and meeting at the bottom in the same timber laid on
that floor for the purpose.

In the accompanying plan, Fig. 107 represents the plan of
the upper surface of the second floor, or floor under the corn,
with the orifices, *a a*, each side of the lathed partition, *b b*,
each 1 foot by 8 feet.

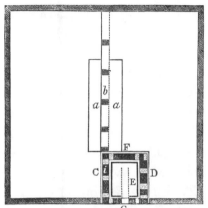

[Fig. 107. Plan of the Corn-Crib Floor.]

Fig. 108 represents an end view of the racks, extending downwards from the orifice in the floor each side, and the whole length of the same to the floor or partial floor beneath where the swine feed.

In this, *a*, *b*, is the upper floor, with the sleepers or joists, *c*, *c*, *c*, beneath; and *d*, *d*, slanting racks, 8 feet long and about three wide, extending from floor to floor.

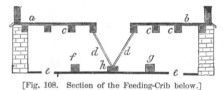

[Fig. 108. Section of the Feeding-Crib below.]

The lower floor is shown at *e*, *e*; the scantling pinned upon the upper side, to form a sort of trough for the corn that falls through the rack, at *f*, *g*; *h*, is the centre-piece, firmly secured, in which the posts of the rack or the standards are framed, or inserted in auger-holes.

Now, when the corn is thrown into the crib above, in the common way, in the West, it settles through the hole, *a*, *a*, Fig. 107, in the floor, and fills the rack, *d*, *d*, Fig. 108, beneath, and the swine, with their noses, pull it down upon the floor, *e*, *e*, and then eat it as they want it, according to the custom of the country, of keeping corn at all times before them.

When the corn is thrown into a crib, a board,* sliding

---

* A still better plan is suggested on the next page.

upon rollers, should cover each orifice, *a, a*, which may be drawn out, and the corn let down from either side, whenever it is wanted.

Slide-boards, 8 feet long and 6 inches wide, should also be laid on the outside of the racks below, so as to cover the whole surface of the same, and so that any one of them can be slipped out and removed at pleasure, without disturbing the rest. These should all be closed at the outset, and when the swine are first let into the feeder, in a lean and hungry state, only the bottom board should be removed. This will leave a row of orifices 4 inches by 6, along the whole bottom of the rack, each side, out of which *lean* hogs will readily pick all the corn they will need; and as they become more fat and lazy, a second slide-board should be removed, leaving the orifices 4 inches by 12; and, finally, if need be, a third, and a fourth, and so on, until at last the corn runs freely down into the feeding-trough with little or no effort of the swine. In one corner, also, of this lower story, a strong box should at all times stand open, containing a mixture of salt and ashes, half and half, wet into a paste, and one pound of brimstone to each half peck of salt, to which the hogs should always have free access; and in another corner a similar box should always be kept full of common charcoal, or, if that is not to be had, stone coal, as free access to these articles is as necessary to the sound health of these gentry, when fed on corn, as pills and cordials are to other epicures. And if kept constantly by them, they will make you no further charges for physician's fees, as a hog always prefers to doctor himself rather than trouble his friends to do it for him, *provided always* he can get at the medicine; and his whole Materia Medica is exhibited above—except a teaspoonful of arsenic, in rare instances, as a tonic, and the occasional use of a cob about the fore legs, as a flesh-brush, for the necessity of each of which, the above are preventives, if not substitutes.

This building is supposed to stand on the division line, between the fat and lean swine, for this purpose. Whenever the fat swine become dainty, and do not eat all the corn up clean which they pull down, it will be needful to shut them off from the rack for a day or two with the slide-boards, and then to shut them out of the feeding-room altogether, and let the lean hogs in to clean up the litter after them, when all which they leave may, without waste, be raked into the yard; and thus the feeding-room is cleared out for a new start with the fat hogs again.

The cost of such a crib, holding about one thousand bushels of corn, would in most places be only from 50 to 100 dollars, built in a firm, substantial manner. It will be found sufficient for the annual feeding of from fifty to one hundred hogs, and any practical judge will at once see that it will save at least three-fourths of the labor, and one-fourth of the feed utterly wasted in the more common modes of feeding, especially in wet seasons.

But there is another part of this crib which may easily be attached at small expense, and will make a still greater saving of food wherever it can be. I refer to the apparatus, C, D, Fig. 107, for steaming the corn in the ear.

First run a strong stud partition around an area of the crib, 4 feet square, C, D, Fig. 107, and let this stud partition extend to the top of the crib, 10 feet or more. Nail strong boards, well fitted, upon each side of this stud partition, from top to bottom, and fill the interstices, *i*, between the boards and the studs with dry clay pounded tight, as the boards are laid on from bottom to top. This is the STEAM-VAT for the corn.

At the bottom of this steam-vat place a large barrel or hogshead, or a water-tight box, E, and insert into this barrel or box a sheet-iron or copper pipe, or tube, 8 inches in diameter (water-tight), closed at the further end, and opening outwards through the box or barrel, and also through the wall of the building at G. This pipe lies in the barrel or box in the same way that a fire-flue lies in a steam-boiler, so that the water wholly surrounds it inside of the box or barrel, while it opens outwardly, so that at c, the fuel and fire can be placed in the tube or fire-flue. The interstice between this barrel or box (which is the boiler) and the sides of the steam-vat described above should be filled up also with pounded clay to the level of the top of the boiler, over which there should be a cover with holes to admit the free passage of the steam upwards, and still to keep all the ears of corn from falling into the water vessel, which is open at the top. A pipe should also run from the further end of the fire-flue upwards ($3\frac{1}{2}$ inches in diameter) to carry off the smoke and create a brisk draught within, and a tight sheet-iron cover should also be made to stop the orifice of the fire-flue at G, in whole or in part, as may be needed; and a spout or pipe should lead from some convenient place to pour water into the boiler when empty.

On the level of the board or cover over the boiler on the inside of the building at F, there should be a hole left in the wall of the steam-vat, sufficiently large when open to allow all the corn to slide out of the steam-vat, either upon the floor of the crib, or down into the feeding-racks, at the option of the proprietor, and the top of the steam-vat should be covered tight, except an orifice for shovelling in the corn, to which also a tight stopper should be fitted.

Thus prepared, the operator drives a load of corn alongside of the crib, and shovels it into the steam-vat through the orifice at top ; or, if he pleases, shovels in dry corn in the same way from the adjoining crib. A vat of this size will steam about 30 bushels in the ear at once. The boiler below has been previously filled with water, and the hopper above, through which the corn is shovelled in, is now made tight with a stopper, old clothes, straw, &c., so that no steam can pass out at any point whatever.

The fire is now kindled in the sheet-iron or copper (I use copper) fire-flue below. As this is entirely surrounded by the water, the whole heat goes directly into the water, and no part of it is lost; and, as the water is in a wooden vessel which is itself surrounded by dried clay some one or two feet thick in most places, no part of the heat escapes by radiation. The steam rises from the water, passes through the holes in the board or cover over the boiler, ascends through the whole mass of ears of corn above, condenses upon them, and runs back into the boiler, or is absorbed by the grain : the corn swells, rises, and the steam-vat, which at first was not more than two-thirds or half full, becomes filled with the swollen corn.

When it is sufficiently steamed, the operator opens the orifice, inside the building, just above the boiler, and lets the whole mass slide down upon the floor of the crib, or into the rack, as he chooses.

It will generally be best to let it slide upon the floor, and lie three or four days (before shovelling it into the rack), and get sour, as it is found that soured food will make more pork than sweet food.

The labor of steaming on this plan is small, even much less than the labor of feeding dry corn in the common way. The expense of fuel is but a mere trifle, as any one will be surprised to see how small a quantity of dry wood will keep two or three barrels of water boiling twenty-four hours, when all the heat is thus forced to pass through the water: a barrel of water will answer all purposes, if care is taken to keep it filled from time to time, as it boils away. In cold weather it may be expedient to leave the corn in the steamer, and heat it up every morning before feeding, in which case, a follower (covered with old rags or straw) to settle down on the corn, as fast as the corn sinks, would be advisable,* so as to prevent the steam from rising higher than the surface of the corn.

It may also be desirable to feed occasionally with dry, old corn, and then again with dry, new corn, as a change. To render this more convenient, it would be best to spread the dividing partition outwards, by setting two rows of studs outside of the orifice, a, a, on each side thereof—instead of one row in the centre—and then laying loose boards against the outside of the studs as the corn is thrown in, so that when full, the boards could be pulled out from the top, and allow the corn to slide in from either side; or since, in this case, the orifice, a, a, would be extended upwards to the top of the crib in the form of an open spout, one foot or more wide, by 8 feet long, the corn could be shovelled into the racks from either side at

---

* By placing followers between, 5 or 10 bushels of corn may be let out every morning at the bottom, and as much more put in dry at the top, and partially cooked each morning. But in this case, of course, the followers must be made of strips of board which can be taken out at the orifice over the boiler.

option, and the swine fed with new or old corn, wet or dry, at the will of the proprietor; while the *self-feeding* capacity of the crib would be fully restored by the removal of the boards on either side, outside of the studs as above named, with the advantage of being able to stop the current again at pleasure, which, in the first arrangement, could not be so easily done. The extra expense of thus continuing the orifice upward in the form of a spout would be but a trifle, the diminution of the capacity of the crib but small, and all purposes of ventilation would be equally well, if not better answered.

But these hints, it is supposed, will be sufficient to enable any man to construct a crib, either with or without a boiler and steamer, with such variations as the taste and interest of each may induce him to adopt.

We will now make a few remarks about the sleeping apartments of swine, and we have done.

It is well known that thousands of these animals perish in the West, by " piling-on-to-one-another," as it is called, in their nests in cold weather. The writer knew one farmer who lost fifty in a single night in this way ; and, during this past cold winter, thousands have perished in all parts of the country. Now, however commodious and elegant a gentleman's house may be, if he is a humane man, he cannot feel very comfortably, if compelled night after night to listen to the hideous and mournful complaints of his own or his neighbor's domestic animals, which he knows are perishing by scores, either by cold from without, or by suffocation and strangulation beneath the dense, struggling masses of living flesh piled upon them. A single pig in the fence on a warm summer day is bad enough, but several hundred hogs, of all ages and sizes, struggling and squealing, and growling on a cold winter night for heat and life, in one solid mass of commingled life and death, is truly abominable: a most unendurable nuisance to a whole neighborhood, to say nothing of the cruelty or the loss incurred. This needless suffering and waste may easily be prevented.

Let the farmer construct a rough shed of boards, or rails and straw, or whatever is at hand, of sufficient size to contain all his swine lying side by side; let this be divided into apartments, side and side, not to exceed 10 feet square.

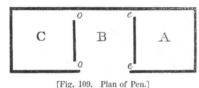

[Fig. 109. Plan of Pen.]

Leave the entrance shed, B, open to the south, and close up A and C. Make A the tightest and warmest place, and leave openings at *e, e,* only large enough for the *smallest size of hogs* to pass through. Then leave the openings *o, o,* into C, large enough for the *middle-sized hogs* to pass through.

Call all the smallest into A, and then feed them until they become wonted to it, and give them a good warm place, and at first a warm bed. Call the next size into pen C, as many as can get in, and make these quite as tolerable, but not as good nor as warm as those of A. They will soon become wonted to their place, so that when all are out in the yard together, the smallest will seek the pen A, because it is the warmest, and they can get into it. The next size will seek their pen, C, because it is the best place they know: and swine will always make themselves at home in the best place they can get. The largest size will remain in B, of necessity, where they, from age and hardihood, will be sufficiently comfortable.

In this way a hundred and fifty hogs may be kept in one

yard with perfect safety, and of all sizes, since the older cannot overlay and crush the younger and feebler, as would happen, if even fifty of all sizes were allowed to run together. To those who have, or who can afford more expensive provisions than the above, no suggestions as regards their structure will be needed. To others, we trust the above hints and outline of a "*sifting shed*" may prove useful, through which their hogs can be daily "riddled" according to size, every cold night.

PART II.

VILLAS,

INTERIORS, AND FURNITURE

SECTION IX.

WHAT A COUNTRY HOUSE OR VILLA SHOULD BE.

In our republic there are neither the castles of feudal barons nor the palaces of princes. The President's dwelling is only called "the White House." That home in the country which is something beyond a cottage or a farm-house, rises but to the dignity of a villa or mansion. And this word *villa*—the same in Latin, Italian, Spanish, and English, signifies only "a country house or abode;" or, according to others, "a rural or country seat"—as *village* means a small collection of houses in the country.

More strictly speaking, what we mean by a villa, in the United States, is the country house of a person of competence or wealth sufficient to build and maintain it with some taste and elegance. Having already defined a cottage to be a dwelling so small that the household duties may all be performed by the family, or with the assistance of not more than one or two domestics, we may add, that a villa is a country house of larger accommodation, requiring the care of at least three or more servants. This homely scale of determining the rank of country houses is one that will, more readily than any other, settle the question as regards the mere size and importance of the dwelling.

The villa, or country house proper, then, is the most refined home of America—the home of its most leisurely and educated class of citizens. Nature and art both lend it their happiest influence. Amid the serenity and peace of sylvan scenes, surrounded by the perennial freshness of nature, enriched without and within by objects of universal beauty and interest—objects that touch the heart and awaken the understanding—it is in such houses that we should look for the happiest social and moral development of our people.

Like the farm-house, the villa is, too, the more *individual* home. It is there that the social virtues are more honestly practised, that the duties and graces of life have more meaning, that the character has more room to develop its best and finest traits than within the walls of cities.

In this most cultivated country life, every thing lends its aid to awaken the finer sentiments of our nature. The occupations of the country are full of health for both soul and body, and for the most refined as well as the most rustic taste. The heart has there, always within its reach, something on which to bestow its affections. We beget a partiality for every copse that we have planted, every tree which has for years given us a welcome under its shady boughs. Every winding path throughout the woods, every secluded resting-place in the valley, every dell where the brook lives and sings, becomes part of our affections, friendship, joy, and sorrows. Happy is he who lives this life of a cultivated mind in the country!

And what should the villa be, architecturally? Those who have followed us in our first section will surely see that our answer to this will be, that it should, firstly, be the most convenient; secondly, the most truthful or significant; and thirdly, the most tasteful or beautiful of dwellings.

The villa should indeed be a private house, where beauty, taste, and moral culture are at home. In the fine outlines of the whole edifice, either dignified, graceful or picturesque, in the spacious or varied verandas, arcades, and windows, in the select forms of windows, chimney-tops, cornices, the artistic knowledge and feeling has full play; while in the arrangement of spacious apartments, especially in the devotion of a part to a library or cabinet sacred to books, and in that elevated order and system of the whole plan, indicative of the inner domestic life, we find the development of the intellectual and moral nature which characterizes the most cultivated families in their country houses.

It is therefore in our villas that we must hope in this country to give the best and most complete manifestation of domestic architecture. The cottage is too limited in size, the farm-house too simply useful in its character, to admit of that indulgence of beauty of form and decoration which belongs properly to the villa.

The villa, indeed, may be as simple and chaste as a cottage, and often, with a more satisfactory effect than if inlaid with sculpture; but its larger size, and the greater means devoted to its creation, will justify an embellishment that would be out of keeping, in all respects, with the cottage. The greater extent of the villa allows, for example, more intricacy of form and outline, as the greater completeness of the arrangement permits a luxury of space and decoration.

Larger scope as the villa gives for the architect to indulge his love for the beautiful, there are yet limits beyond which he may not wisely go. He must not, for example, forget that it is domestic architecture which occupies him, and therefore that beauty must be united to convenience and comfort, or at least must never be opposed to it. Instead of following the example of those who are always striving to make dwellings resemble temples and cathedrals, he will bestow on windows and doors, roofs and chimneys, porches and verandas—those truly domestic features—that loving, artistic treatment which alone raises material forms from the useful to the beautiful.

Both the architect and the amateur must recollect that proportion is the primary law of beauty. It should therefore be the first thing in the mere composition of the villa, as it is the universal chord which, once struck, moves all beholders to instinctive admiration. After proportion comes *decoration*, or the enrichment of beautiful parts and details; which, however important, is still as much inferior to *proportion* as the shapes and colors of the clouds are to the grandeur and beauty of the arch-form of the heaven in which they float.*

And higher and deeper than either proportion or decoration is that beauty of expression which indicates the spirit that lives within the country house. You may never have investigated it, but you have nevertheless tacitly recognized, that a spirit of frankness or reserve, a spirit of miserly care or kind hospitality, a spirit of meanness or generosity, a spirit of system or disorder, a spirit of peace or discord, may be found in the expression of every house, as well as every face in the country. Whatever gives to the villa its best and truest expression of

---

* Most especially do we recommend this fact to the notice of proprietors who are novices in architecture. It is an economical fact, as well as a principle. A perfectly proportioned building, with little or no decoration, being far more beautiful and satisfactory than one of equal bulk and cost, ill-proportioned, and with thousands lavished on the embellishment of its details.

human sympathy and affection confers on it its highest and most lasting character of beauty.

We have said the *truest* expression, and this leads us to the most difficult question that arises in the mind of the artist in designing villas in this country. To unite the beautiful and the true, to make the outward form of all about us express our best ideal of life, to mould it so that it shall evince, not merely the borrowed and accepted forms of the books and schools of art, but the deeper essence of the life, and character, and manners of the people, and even the families that inhabit it—that should be the ambition and the goal of the domestic architect of any country. It is a result which can only be fully reached here, when the habits of the people have firmly crystallized, and when our people themselves understand the true meaning and the true beauty of Architecture.

The significance or truthfulness of a man's house, especially if that house be a villa, is a matter which *he* also should well consider, for in it lies the whole philosophy of both its beauty and its utility. He may easily build, or cause to be built, a pretty villa, in any one of a dozen styles—convenient and comfortable in its accommodation; and yet, if there is no real fitness in the form and expression of the thing chosen, if it is foreign to the habits, education, tastes, and manners—in short, the life of the proprietor, he will, if he is a simple, unaffected man, sit as foolishly in it, as he would in the church or town hall, wearing the court costume of some foreign ambassador. There is, for instance, something wonderfully captivating in the idea of a battlemented castle, even to an apparently modest man, who thus shows to the world his unsuspected vein of personal ambition, by trying to make a castle of his country house. But, *unless there is something of the castle in the man,* it is very likely, if it be like a real castle, to dwarf him to the stature of a mouse.*

Shall we then have no variety, no latitude in the character and forms of our best country houses? Must all be bound with the common-sense outline of a square or parallelogram?

Far from it. The villa—the country house, should, above all things, manifest individuality. It should say something of the character of the family within—as much as possible of their life and history, their tastes and associations, should mould and fashion themselves upon its walls.

If we look into all the forms of architecture applicable to domestic life, we shall find but two elementary ideas—the rational, logical, sensible idea, bounded by the regular horizontal line of classical architecture, and the more poetic, aspiring, imaginative idea embodied in the upward lines of pointed architecture. The man of common-sense views only, if he is true to himself, will have nothing to do, in the choice or construction of his country house, with picturesque and irregular outlines. He will naturally prefer a symmetrical, regular house, with few angles, but with order, and method, and distinctness stamped upon its unbroken lines of cornice and regular rows of windows. He will do nothing without reason;

---

* Almost all imitations of castles must, as private dwellings, be petty in this country. There is one lately erected, of gray stone, on the lower part of the Hudson. We had the pleasure of welcoming to the Hudson that accomplished daughter of Sweden, Fredrika Bremer, and as we were sailing past this spot, some one near her remarked—" Do you see—a castle." : Ah !" she replied, " but it is a *very young* castle !"

he will have no caprices and no whims, either in his life or his house.

The man of sentiment or feeling will seek for that house in whose aspect there is something to love. It must nestle in, or grow out of, the soil. It must not look all new and sunny, but show secluded shadowy corners. There must be nooks about it, where one would love to linger; windows, where one can enjoy the quiet landscape leisurely; cosy rooms, where all domestic fireside joys are invited to dwell. It must, in short, have something in its aspect which the heart can fasten upon and become attached to, as naturally as the ivy attaches itself to the antique wall, preserving its memories from decay.

And, lastly, there are the men of imagination—men whose aspirations never leave them at rest—men whose ambition and energy will give them no peace within the mere bounds of rationality. These are the men for picturesque villas—country houses with high roofs, steep gables, unsymmetrical and capricious forms. It is for such that the architect may safely introduce the tower and the campanile—any and every feature that indicates originality, boldness,* energy, and variety of character. To find a really original man living in an original and characteristic house, is as satisfactory as to find an eagle's nest built on the top of a mountain crag—while to find a pretentious, shallow man in such a habitation, is no better than to find the jackdaw in the eagle's nest.

Another view of this matter of significance, and a great and leading aspect it is, leads us to consider the *nationality* of the

---

* Shall we not say, always excepting *battlements*—which have no meaning in the domestic architecture of this age?

house we build. There is no reason why the architect of this country and age should not adopt the ideas of other countries, as manifested in the styles of art begotten in those countries. But he should do this understandingly, and with some purpose in it. There is little to be said in defence of those who copy foreign houses and imitate foreign manners, *for the mere sake of the imitation,* in a country so full of good and noble suggestions for social and domestic life as our own. One would suppose that a cultivated American would exult and thank God for the great Future which dawns on him here, rather than sigh and fondle over the great Past which remains to Europe. One would rather wish that cultivated minds should find a truer and loftier pleasure in striving to form a free and manly school of republican tastes and manners, than in wasting time in the vain effort to transplant the meaningless conventionalities of the realms of foreign caste.

Far different from this is the spirit of the artist or the lover of art who gathers from the Old World—from its architecture and its domestic life, those really good and beautiful forms and ideas which are truthful and significant everywhere—rejecting all that is foreign to our life and manners. Our own soil is the right platform upon which a genuine national architecture must grow, though it will be aided in its growth by all foreign thoughts that mingle harmoniously with its simple and free spirit.

The highest merit of a villa or country house, after utility and beauty of form and expression, is, that it be, as much as possible, characteristic of the country in which it is built. In the Eastern and Northern States, high roofs, thick walls, warm rooms, fine stacks of chimneys—in the Middle and Southern, broad roofs, wide verandas, cool and airy apartments.

But everywhere, and in all parts of the country, in planning a
country house, let the habits, and wants, and mode of life
(assuming them to be good and truthful ones) stamp themselves
on the main features of the house. It is thus that our domestic
architecture will always be growing better, more truthful, more
individual, and therefore more rational and sincere, rather than
more foreign and affected.*

Placing a national feeling and national taste above all others,
we will not, however, shut our eyes to the fact which no
observer of men will dispute, that in every age and country
are born some persons who belong rather to the past than the
present—men to whom memory is dearer than hope—the by-
gone ages fuller of meaning than those in the future. These are
the natural conservatives whom Providence has wisely distributed, even in the most democratic governments, to steady the
otherwise too impetuous and unsteady onward movements of
those who, in their love for progress, would obliterate the past,
even in its hold on the feelings and imaginations of our race.

It is not for these men, who love the past, rather with instinctive than educated affection, to understand and appreciate the
value of an architecture significant of the present time. And it is,
therefore, for such as they to build houses in styles that recall
the past, and to surround themselves with the same forms and
symbols that, having been used in some former age which

---

* Foreign architects are finding their way to this country very plentifully. Some
among them who follow rules and not principles, do us great harm by building
expensive and unmeaning copies of foreign houses—as for instance, English villas,
with narrow passages, disconnected rooms, and no verandas for the warm climate of
the Middle States. Others do us service, by studying the peculiarities of climate and
mode of life, and adapting their designs to meet the peculiarities.

they most love and venerate, have therefore a power for good over their minds, which nothing else in art has. If we see such men copying in their dwellings the forms and ornaments of old English or Italian architecture, because they really live more (internally speaking) in Saxon thought or Italian art than in our own age and time, we must own that, inasmuch as the architecture expresses the life, it is fitting and good for them, however unmeaning for the many, and especially for all those who more truly belong to our own time and country.

There is, indeed, both history and poetry in the use of such foreign styles of architecture as may be adapted to our life, when they are thus lovingly and fittingly used by those to whom they are fraught with beautiful memories and associations. It is for this reason that we often see with pleasure, our adopted citizens, from various parts of Europe, who are still strongly attached to the land of their birth, seeking to awaken again something of the tenderness of early associations, by surrounding themselves, even here, with the forms and symbols of that old-world architecture, which has to them as grand and powerful a meaning as the stars themselves.

Leaving this point, is there not something also to be said in answer to the question, what a villa should be, in order that in its cost and duration, it may be true to its own time and country? It seems to us, indeed, that this is a point from which our wealthy builders of country-seats are about to go far astray. We see signs showing themselves, with the growing wealth of the country, of expenditure in domestic architecture quite unmeaning and unwise in a republic. Fortunes are rapidly accumulated in the United States, and the indulgence of one's taste and pride in the erection of a country-seat of great size and cost, is becoming a favorite mode of expending wealth. And yet these attempts at great establishments are always and inevitably failures in America.

And why? Plainly, because they are contrary to the spirit of republican institutions; because the feelings upon which they are based can never take root, except in a government of hereditary rights; because they are wholly in contradiction to the spirit of our time and people.

In a country of hereditary rights, where the custom prevails of leaving the family home and estate to the eldest son, or to a single representative of the family, there is a meaning and purpose in the erection of great manorial halls and magnificent country-seats. The proprietor feels assured that it is always for his own family, generation after generation, that this expenditure is made—that this great establishment, upon which such sums have been lavished, is to be the home of that family, and will bear its name, and stand as a monument of its wealth and power for ages. And this, in an aristocracy, consoles him for the enormous injustice of causing all his other descendants in each generation, to revolve as pale satellites round the eldest son, who represents all the wealth and power of the family.

In our republic, there is no law of primogeniture, there are no hereditary rights. The man of large wealth dies to-morrow, and his million, divided among all his children, leaves them each but a few thousands. If he has been tempted to indulge in the luxury or pride of a great establishment, no one of his children is rich enough to hold it. Public opinion—the salutary operation of our institutions, frowns upon the attempt to continue the wealth and family estates in the hands of the family, by making one descendant rich at the expense of the rest. And this home—this fine establishment which has been built in defiance of the spirit of the time and nation, must needs be abandoned by the family who built it; it must become the property of strangers, who, in their turn, will hold it but for one lifetime.

We will not urge the difficulty, with our social habits, of maintaining an overgrown establishment, the personal drudgery it involves, the care and solicitude it requires, let the immediate fortune be what it may. It is only in an old country, where there is a large surplusage of domestic service, that domestic establishments of large size can be conducted with pleasure and ease to the proprietor. Here, it is quite the contrary. A country house, where the conveniences are such that the establishment may be moderate, the living-rooms compact and well arranged, the facility of performing all household labors increased as much as possible, is the perfect villa for America.

But the main argument against the creation of large establishments is, that the whole theory is a mistake; that it is impossible, except for a day; that our laws render the attempt folly; and our institutions finally grind it to powder.

There is something beautiful and touching in the associations that grow up in a home held sacred in the same family for generations. A wealth of affection is kept alive in those old manor-houses and country halls of England, where, age after age, the descendants of one family have lived, and loved, and suffered, and died—perhaps nobly and bravely too—sheltered by the same trees and guarded by the same walls. It is quite natural that we, largely descended from this Anglo-Saxon stock, when we have fortunes to spend, should fondly delude ourselves with the idea of realizing this old and pleasing idyl of beautiful country life. But it is only an idyl, or only a delusion to us. It belongs to the past, so far as we are concerned. It is no more to be reanimated in the republic of the new world than the simple faith in the Virgin, which built the mighty cathedrals of the middle ages. It could only be reanimated at the sacrifice of the happiness of millions of free citizens.

But the true home still remains to us. Not, indeed, the feudal castle, not the baronial hall, but the home of the individual man—the home of that family of equal rights, which continually separates and continually reforms itself in the new world—the republican home, built by no robbery of the property of another class, maintained by no infringement of a brother's rights; the beautiful, rural, unostentatious, moderate home of the country gentleman, large enough to minister to all the wants, necessities, and luxuries of a republican, and not too large or too luxurious to warp the life or manners of his children.*

---

* Perhaps the true standard of the means to be expended in a country home is to be found with us by the inquiry—Can the proprietor afford to leave it to one of his children?—or, at the most, is it an expenditure that will not prove a serious loss, should they be compelled to part with it?

As a significant illustration of the folly of lavish expenditure in country houses, we recall at this moment the passing history of three villas, all built by men of fortunes large for America. Two of them, costing from $100,000 to $200,000 each, though finished hardly ten years, have already crippled or ruined their owners. The third, built in Massachusetts, with a taste and completeness that have rendered it the object of general admiration, and at a cost of, perhaps, $20,000, has just passed into the hands of one of the children of the late proprietor; and he, with that truer under-

The just pride of a true American is not in a great hereditary home, but in greater hereditary institutions. It is more to him that all his children will be born under wise, and just, and equal laws, than that one of them should come into the world with a great family estate. It is better, in his eyes, that it should be possible for the humblest laborer to look forward to the possession of a future country house and home like his own, than to feel that a wide and impassable gulf of misery separates him, the lord of the soil, from a large class of his fellow-beings born beneath him. Yes, the love of home is one of the deepest feelings in our nature, and we believe the happiness and virtue of a vast rural population to be centred in it; but it must be a home built and loved upon new world, and not the old world ideas and principles; a home in which humanity and republicanism are stronger than family pride and aristocratic feeling; a home of the virtuous citizen, rather than of the mighty owner of houses and lands.

---

standing of the right uses of wealth, not unusual in Massachusetts, was able to close his life of useful benevolence with the most noble and admirable bequests to educational institutions—bequests amounting to the whole of the difference between the cost of his beautiful villa, which he wisely enjoyed, and bequeathed to one of his children, and those which we have just quoted as having, by their great first cost and subsequent expense of maintenance, nearly ruined those for whose children's homes they were erected.

SECTION X.

DESIGNS FOR VILLAS OR COUNTRY HOUSES.

As a villa is a house surrounded by more or less land, it is impossible rightly to understand how to design such a dwelling for a given site, without knowing something of the locality where it is to be placed. The scenery, amid which it is to stand, if it is of a strongly marked character, will often help to suggest or modify the character of the architecture. A building which would appear awkwardly and out of place on a smooth plain, may be strikingly harmonious and picturesque in the midst of wild landscape.

The first point that both the proprietor and the architect will examine, in choosing the site, will be to select the best locality with regard to these three points—view, shelter, and position for kitchen offices and outbuildings. It is far better to select a view of moderate extent, which also combines the other two requisites, than to have a wide prospect on every side at their sacrifice. Especially should attention be paid to disposing the plan so that the kitchen and its offices should be placed upon a screened or blind side, or one that can be easily concealed by planting. There should be room for a kitchen yard or court, connected with a passage or a short path to the stable, and all quite turned away from the lawn or entrance side of the house.

In country houses or villas, there are never less than three or four apartments of good size (besides the kitchen, etc.) on the principal floor. In every villa of moderate size, we expect to find a separate apartment, devoted to meals, entitled the dining-room; another devoted to social intercourse, or the drawing-room; and a third devoted to intellectual culture, or the library; besides halls, passages, stairways, pantries, and bed-rooms. In what we should call a complete villa, there will be found, in addition to this, a bed-room, or dressing-room, or a lady's boudoir, an office or private room for the master of the house, on the first floor; and bathing-rooms, water-closet, and dressing-rooms, on the second floor. A flight of back stairs, for servants, is indispensable in villas of large size, and, when space can be found for it, adds greatly to the comfort and privacy of even small villas.

Though the kitchen is sometimes placed in the basement, in the Middle States, yet the practice is giving way to the more rational and convenient mode of putting it on the first floor; and it is generally provided for in a wing, of less height than the main building, divided into two stories, with sleeping-rooms on the second floor. In the Southern States, the kitchen is always a detached building, at some distance from the house.

In the arrangement of the interior of a villa, and especially of its principal floor, the greatest variety of taste will find room for manifesting itself. It is here that every family has an opportunity especially to show its prevailing character, and, indeed, always does manifest it, when about to plan, or even to suggest to another, the plan of the house. So many circumstances are to be considered, so much difference of habits is there, that no country house ever satisfied two families equally well. The family taste, character, individuality, should always, therefore, appear in its house, and not changed, only elevated by the hands of the architect.* On this subject, we will say more, in discussing various plans, which we offer as examples.

Except in the extreme northern part of the Union, all villas or country houses of the first class, demand one essential, in order that elegance of proportion and the utmost comfort may be realized—which is, a good height of the stories. Our climate demands a large supply of fresh air in the best apartment, either in summer, when large, airy space is wanted (and verandas are indispensable), or in winter, when the air of the whole house is warmed to a mild temperature, by warm air from the furnace or hot-water pipes.

The apartments on the principal floor should, therefore, in ordinary cases, not be less than 12 feet high, nor (except in very large apartments) more than 14 feet. The second story should always be a full story of 9 to 10, or 12 feet, with the space above it, hollow, and thoroughly ventilated, so as to insure its coolness in summer.

Two points should always be well considered by the proprietor, before fixing the site and commencing to build. The first, is a thorough drainage, by which, if the subsoil is wet at any season, all moisture, or, at any rate, all sewerage of the water-closets and kitchen wash, will be immediately carried away by a substantial and capacious drain, built of brick and cement. The second, is the mode of supplying the house with water. Cisterns and wells, and their location, must be arranged

---

* Indeed, wherever there is *character* in the family, it will be found that the architect is, in spite of his own taste, obliged to manifest that character, in the house designed under their direction.

so as to serve the convenience of the house as completely as possible.*

In the internal finish of villas, we always incline to the simple and chaste. Even in more decorated styles, we would adopt a modest and quiet variation, rather than one remarkable for ornamental display. The simple and more chaste forms are in better keeping with the more simple habits which prevail in country life—leaving the complex intricacy and richness of ornamental details to the more elaborate and showy life of those who live in fine town houses. We have therefore made our plans and estimates, with the view of having them carried out in a chaste and fitting manner, characteristic of the style, but neither rich nor showy in detail.

As regards the *style* to be given to the exterior, if we are to choose among foreign architecture, our preference will be given to modifications of the Rural Gothic, common in England and Germany, with high gables wrought with tracery, bay-windows, and other features full of domestic expression; or the modern Italian, with bold, overhanging cornices and irregular outlines. The former, generally speaking, is best suited to our Northern, broken country; the latter, to the plain and valley surface of the Middle and Southern States—though sites may be found for each style in all portions of the Union.

After these, there are rich materials for study in the purer Romanesque, or round arch style, and in all the domestic,

---

* Most of the new villas lately erected are supplied with water (through a tank in the roof) by that most perfect and simple of all little machines—the Hydraulic ram. By the aid of this, a small stream or overflowing spring, within 1000 feet of the site of the house, may be made to supply all the bed-rooms, water-closets, and kitchen offices with water, at any point where it is needed.

pointed architecture of Germany. It has been the fashion of
architects to decry as corrupt, all but strictly scientific architecture—the architecture of the Greek temple and the Gothic
cathedral. Their attempts to follow these prototypes in
country residences have always been utter failures, as might
have been predicted, and we are glad to see that our people,
generally, begin to perceive the impossibility of making a
dwelling-house of reduced copies of the Parthenon. The
truth is, that while Domestic Architecture allows of great
variety and great beauty and purity of form and detail, it does
not allow that severe and abstract proportion and expression
which have such grand and fitting manifestations in religious
or civil architecture. The architect, therefore, who studies
the authorities, only to copy faultless pediments and marvellous
window tracery of temple or cathedral, in his designs for
dwelling-houses, will always fail; while he who studies how to
combine beauty of form, the expression of domestic feeling, and
unity of style or composition in his designs, will always both
delight and satisfy us in the houses which he produces. It is
for this reason that, in studying the past, we should rather pore
over the merits of those quaint and home-like middle-age
edifices, where the roof is boldly shown, and rendered ornamental, the windows suitably introduced and enriched, and the
comfort and pleasure of climate and home understood, than
examples of that architecture which is more perfect and
complete in a purely artistic sense, but which is not characteristic of the social and domestic life of man.

And, lastly, we have only to repeat, that the architect will
be most successful, who, after mastering that which has been
done in other countries and in past time, works freshly from

the inspiration of his own country—its manners, institutions, and climate. Such an artist will absorb the past as Raphael and Shakspeare absorbed it, not to reproduce it in feebler forms, but to give greater meaning and stronger vitality to productions that belong wholly to the present.

DESIGN XX.—*A small Bracketed Country House.*

BOTH the elevation and plan of this dwelling express something between a farm-house and a villa; the broad, overhanging roof and the truncated gables, giving the exterior a somewhat more rustic expression than we usually find in the latter. In the ornamental veranda, stretching along the whole front, there are evidences of villa-like comfort, and the broad, shady balcony over the porch (10 feet square), not only gives character and depth of shadow to the effect of the building, but affords a somewhat retired place of rest, where views more extensive than those from the principal floor may be had, and where the ladies of the family will find it agreeable to pass their summer mornings in *demi-toilette*.

The arrangement of accommodation, Fig. 111, unites compactness, convenience, and comfort. The entrance hall, 12 by 15 feet, opens into the three principal apartments, which are drawing-room, living or dining-room, and study.

It will be noticed that the drawing-room in this country house is large in proportion to the other apartments. Many architects would have divided this space into two rooms, connected by large sliding doors. But we greatly prefer, wherever it is in accordance with the rest of the plan, one large drawing-room to two small parlors, thus connected. The

DESIGN XX.

BRACKETED COUNTRY HOUSE.

Fig. 110.

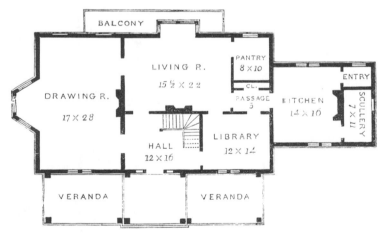

PRINCIPAL FLOOR.

Fig. 111.

large room not only has greater unity of effect, being simpler
and nobler in the impression it makes of space and breadth,
but it is more essentially country-like than rooms with folding
doors, however excellent the latter contrivance to increase effect
in a limited space. We must also add to this, the increased
coolness of single large apartments in summer, when, chiefly,
they are in daily use in the country.

The remainder of this plan is as convenient as the drawing-
room is spacious. The living-room, 16 by 22 feet (with a
handsome bay-window, 8 feet wide, on the side), has connected
with it a store-room or larder, and a passage, 5 feet wide (on
the side of which is a china closet), leading to the kitchen
The latter, with a scullery adjoining it, and a separate back
entrance or porch, is very conveniently placed, with respect to
the house itself—a villa or country house of this moderate size
being intended for a family where the mistress expects to
superintend the domestic economy of the household, and
therefore desires the kitchen as near as it can be to the living-
room, and yet exclude all disagreeable smells and noises from
the latter. In order that these latter points may be fully
accomplished, a fly-door, opening easily both ways, covered
with baize, to stifle the sound, and furnished with a spring, to
keep it closed, should be provided, as the inner or kitchen door
of this passage, leading from the living-room to the kitchen.

The arrangement of this country house shows that it is
intended for a family whose social, preponderates over their
intellectual taste—as the drawing and dining rooms are
much larger than the library—which, indeed, is here only a
" study," or small room for books, 12 feet square. In some
families, even this space will be given up for a bed-room, and

the books will find places in bookcases, in the other apartments.

In order to be well situated for external effect, this house should be so placed, that the wing containing the kitchen may be on that side not usually approached, and it should be partially concealed by plantations. If built where there is an existing shelter of trees and shrubs, this kitchen wing may be extended 20 or 30 feet more, to give a laundry, store-room, shed for fuel, etc. By making the height of the kitchen 8 feet, a half story, containing sleeping apartments for domestics, may be made over it—the posts of the wing, in this case, being 13 feet high.

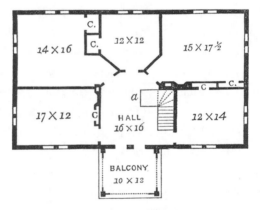

[Fig. 112. Second Floor.]

The second story of this house gives 5 comfortable sleeping rooms, with closets, etc., Fig. 112.

CONSTRUCTION. The style of this house is one well adapted for wood, though it would appear equally well if built of more solid materials. In our elevation, it is supposed to be covered with vertical plank, battened, as described in PART I. The first story is 13 feet high, the second 9 feet, the projecting eaves drooping, so as to make the upper story appear lower. The roof projects 3 feet, so as to give bold and picturesque shadows, and is supported by plain, but rather strong rafter brackets, and covered with shingles, partly plain, and partly ornamental. The posts supporting the front gable, and forming the porch and balcony, should be of sound timber, 10 inches or a foot square—of oak, or painted with the durable and richly colored stain given at p. 187. In this case, the same stain should be used for the whole veranda and all the window dressings, outside.

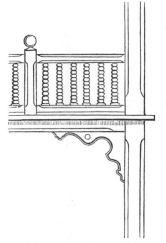

[Fig. 113. Part of the Porch.]

Fig. 113 shows the construction of a part of the porch, together with the shape and size of the brackets, to the scale of half an inch to a foot. The railing to the balcony above is turned either in the knotted or twisted pattern, which agrees best with the rustic expression of this exterior. The windows are casement windows— or, if hung with weights, are made with a broad style in the centre, to have the same effect, and should, to harmonize with the style adopted, be broader than usual. With outside Venetian shutters, and the garret ventilated as we have pointed out in a former page, this would be a particularly comfortable country house for the Middle and Western States.

Estimate. Supposing this house to be constructed of wood, filled-in with brick, with a mere cellar under the whole, the walls of the first and second story hard-finished with plaster of Paris, the kitchen with brown walls, and the joinery to be done in a simple but characteristic style, the estimated cost here (exclusive of painting) would be $4300; in Maine, $3025; in Rochester, N. Y., $3340.

DESIGN XXI.—*A Villa in the Norman Style.*

THOUGH the style called Norman in England is only Romanesque architecture, introduced into that country as early as the 14th century, the Anglo-Norman has some features peculiar to itself, that make it worthy of the study of the architectural student.

This design is one by W. Russell West, Esq., Architect, of Cincinnati. It is highly picturesque, and, in a suitable locality, would have a very striking and spirited effect. Such a locality, of course, would hardly be found in a flat country, but amid wild scenery and hills, whose pointed tops are in harmony with the strength of the heavenward-pointing round tower.

Of course, this is not a house to please a practical, common-sense man. It is not a *rational* house, in the same manner that the classical villa, full of logical, straight lines, is rational; for there is here hardly a single continuous, unbroken line—every opening is arched, and all tendency is towards the pyramid or the curve. Hence, it is clear, that only those who expect to find in a country house something that rises into the romantic and ideal, will prefer this villa.

In composing it, the architect has evidently sought to preserve a strong expression of unity throughout, for he has only introduced the simple arched window, decorated with the

DESIGN XXI.

VILLA IN THE NORMAN STYLE.

Fig. 114.

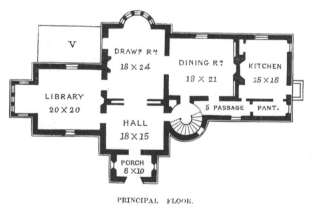

PRINCIPAL FLOOR.

Fig. 115.

zigzag or chevron moulding—and this gives an agreeable simplicity to the exterior, notwithstanding its irregularity.

There is much more of beauty in the arched windows than in square-headed ones of common form; there is much more of strength and picturesqueness in the broken outlines of tower and roof than in the unvaried horizontal lines of square houses; and there is something of historical and poetic interest in a style which was common in the early times of the Anglo-Saxons.

To a person uneducated in domestic architecture, the impression conveyed by this bold and simple elevation would be, that it looks *un*-domestic, and belongs to something else than a dwelling; but this is only ignorance of the use of that prominent feature, the tower, which here, as in olden time, contains the stair, and has a gallery at the top, lighted by a row of circular windows, affording a fine opportunity for views of the surrounding landscape by day, or the starry heavens by night. There is something of practical fitness, too, in placing the means of mounting upwards, in the tower itself; and though winding stairs are not quite so broad and pleasant as those with full tread and ample landings, yet they are sufficiently so to satisfy those who prefer a little relish of antiquity to the last result of modern convenience.

As a marked defect in this design was the absence of all veranda, arcade, or covered walk—without which no country house is tolerable in the United States—we have added a veranda in the angle between the library and drawing-room. This will be seen in the elevation of that end of the house, Fig. 116. The roof is supported on round arches, resting on rather heavy columns, common in this style, and the whole may be constructed of wood—boldly wrought, and painted and sanded.

[Fig. 116. Elevation of the End.]

ACCOMMODATION. The accommodation of this villa is both handsome and convenient. A fine effect will be produced, on entering the hall, by the vista through to the bow-window at the end of the drawing-room, especially if the latter be filled with stained glass of mellow and harmonious colors. The library is agreeably placed, and might be rendered still more secluded, by omitting the window looking on the veranda, V. The tower, which is on the right of the entrance hall, is 9 feet in the clear, inside, and communicates with a passage 5 feet wide, opening into both dining-room and kitchen. At the end of this passage is the pantry. There is evidently a want here of a scullery or back-kitchen, as well as a store-room, both of which might be easily added, if this side of the house were screened by plantations.

The veranda, V, is 11 by 20 feet, and the drawing-room opens upon it by a glazed door or window opening to the floor.

The plan of the second floor, Fig. 117, we have added. The bed-rooms, as shown in the elevation, are not of full height (as,

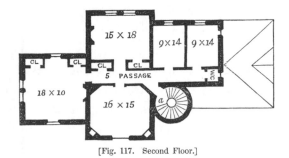

[Fig. 117. Second Floor.]

perhaps, they should be, in a villa of this size, but are about 5 feet at the sides, and 10 feet in the centre—the garret over them being well ventilated. There are three large bed-rooms and two small ones, and a water-closet (W. C.) at the end of passage. In the bed-room over the porch there are two small closets for shoes, etc., in the angles.

[Fig. 118. Norman Doorway.]

CONSTRUCTION. The whole aspect of this design shows that it is to be built of stone, or something that will give equally

solid walls. Any person who understands its character would
no more attempt to copy it in wood than to make a steam-
engine of sugar candy. It does not, however, demand smooth
ashlar, but will look better if laid in common quarry-stone—and
even if laid in random courses, it will add to the quaintness of
effect. If a soft freestone is at hand, the zigzag moulding
which runs round the window dressings may be easily worked
in it. The character of this moulding will be better understood
by the elevation of the doorway, Fig. 118. The sashes should
be made with diagonal frames, and should be hung with weights
in the ordinary manner, and they should be fitted with inside
shutter blinds, folding into boxes on each side. The upper part
of the blind, at the head or arch of the window, may be
stationary. The most complete mode, however, which is now
in use, is to *slide* the shutters or blinds (parting in the middle),
with a space between the solid wall and the plaster wall of the
apartment. This puts them completely out of the way, while
they are brought into use, when required, more readily than in
any other mode.

The roof of this villa is represented as covered with the
handsome, architectural tiles now manufactured for this purpose.
The same effect may be produced by cutting large cedar
shingles in diagonal patterns, as shown in page 181. The roof
projects 6 inches at the eaves, with a gutter, supported on
small blocks or brackets of stone. The partitions may all be
of brick, which will economize room in the plan—where they
are shown as if built of stone.

The first story should be 13 feet high, to give a proper
proportion to the rooms. In the angle where the tower joins
the roof, the junction should be made sound and weather-tight,

DESIGN XXII.

VILLA IN THE ITALIAN STYLE.

Fig. 119.

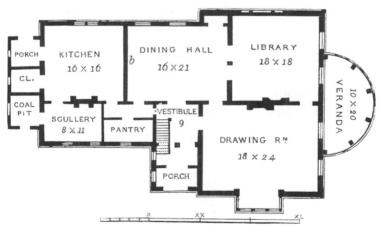

PRINCIPAL FLOOR.

Fig. 120.

by having a broad strip of copper built into the wall of the
tower, and turned up the roof, so as to form a valley of sufficiently
rapid descent to shed storms at all seasons.

All the rooms in the interior of this house should be
finished with oak wainscot, or wood grained to resemble it,
and the effect aimed at should be something between modern
luxury and the quaintness of the antique Norman architecture.
Hints for interiors in this manner, will be found in a succeeding
page. But only simple and characteristic ornaments and
mouldings should be introduced in the interior of this villa, as
its exterior indicates simplicity rather than variety of detail.

Estimate. The estimate for building this house of stone,
when a good quarry, easily worked, is upon the premises, is
$7500.

DESIGN XXII.—*A Villa in the Italian Style.*

THERE is a strong and growing partiality among us for the
Italian style. Originally adapted to the manifestation of social
life, in a climate almost the counterpart of that of the Middle
and Southern portions of our country—at least so far as relates
to eight months of the year, it is made to conform exactly to
our tastes and habits, with, perhaps, less alteration than any
other style. Its broad roofs, ample verandas and arcades, are
especially agreeable in our summers of dazzling sunshine, and
though not so truly Northern as other modes that permit a high
roof, still it has much to render it a favorite in the Middle and
Western sections of our Union.

As a rural style, expressing country life, the Italian is inferior
to pointed and high-roofed modes. If it is not so essentially
country-like in character, it is however remarkable for expressing

the elegant culture and variety of accomplishment of the retired citizen or man of the world, and as it is capable of the most varied and irregular as well as very simple outlines, it is also very significant of the multiform tastes, habits, and wants of modern civilization. On the whole, then, we should say that the Italian style is one that expresses not wholly the spirit of country life nor of town life, but something between both, and which is a mingling of both.

The leading features of this style are familiar to most of our readers. Roofs rather flat, and projecting upon brackets or cantilevers; windows of various forms, but with massive dressings, frequently running into the round arch, when the opening is an important one (and always permitting the use of the outside Venetian blinds); arcades supported on arches or verandas with simple columns, and chimney-tops of characteristic and tasteful forms. Above all, when the composition is irregular, rises the *campanile* or Italian tower, bringing all into unity, and giving picturesqueness, or an expression of power and elevation, to the whole composition.

In designing this small villa in the Italian style, our object was to show as much of the force and spirit of this style as possible, within a very moderate space, and for a very moderate cost. It would have been far easier to have increased the effect by adding more apartments—for it is one of the merits of this style that it permits additions, wings, etc., with the greatest facility, and always with increasing effect.

We must call the attention of the reader to the semicircular arcade or veranda thrown out on the drawing-room or lawn side of the house, which combines elegance with comfort, and is an agreeable variation of the common veranda. The windows of the drawing-room and library reach the floor, so as to afford an easy access to this arcade.

ACCOMMODATION. The arrangement of this villa exhibits a little contrivance to get the utmost from a limited space. It will, therefore, need some explanation.

Entering the large door in the tower or campanile which forms the porch (9 feet square), see Fig. 119, we come to the vestibule, 9 by 9 feet. The stair, which is placed here, commences at *a*, and, as it rises, enters the tower (as shown in the second-floor plan). On the right side of the vestibule is a door opening into a handsome parlor or drawing-room, 18 by 24 feet, with a bay-window in characteristic style.

Directly beyond the vestibule is a pretty dining-hall, 16 by 21 feet. This back hall will be a very airy and agreeable dining apartment in summer,* and it may be rendered essentially private, by closing the door in the vestibule, at *a*, when persons chancing to arrive during dinner can be shown into the dining-room, or library, or to the second story, without passing through the hall. A china-closet and a pantry are connected with this dining-room. We have purposely cut off the direct communication with the kitchen, in order that the passage, *c*, should stop sounds and smells. But a large closet, resembling a sideboard, might be built at *b*, with a door at the back, opening into the kitchen, through which the dishes might, to save trouble, be passed into the dining-hall.

The library is 18 feet square, and communicates with both dining-hall and drawing-room.

---

* It is supposed to be heated by a furnace in winter, or a flue can be introduced in the wall between it and the kitchen, at *b*.

The kitchen is 14 by 16 feet, with a scullery for rough work adjoining it, and back porch and closet, and pit for coals in the rear.

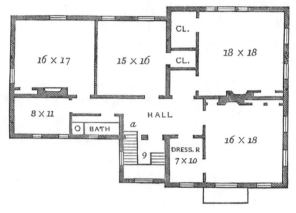

[Fig. 121. Second Floor.]

In the second-story plan, Fig. 121, we find four bed-rooms of good size, with two small ones, one of them used as a dressing-room. There is also a bath-room, with space for a water-closet at the end of the entry. At *a*, a narrow flight of stairs ascends to the apartment, 9 by 9 feet, in the top of the tower—which may be a museum or a prospect gallery.

It would be sufficient for most families, if there were a cellar constructed under all but the main part of the building. The latter would then only require foundation walls.

CONSTRUCTION. We have designed this villa for wood, to enable those who wish to build a tasteful and picturesque dwelling at an economical price to do so, in parts of the country where other materials are dear. But it may be built with still better effect of stone, or brick colored, or of brick cemented. In the latter case, however, it will require a

variation of the size of the dining-room, so that there shall be
no interruption of the wall of the main body of the house,
where it juts into the library.

The first story will be 12 feet high, throughout the whole of
the first floor, including the kitchen, since the projection of the
dining-hall partly into the wings requires it. But while the
chamber story in the main building is 11 feet high, in the
secondary building it is only 8 feet. The bed-room over the
dining-room only runs to the main platform. The bed-rooms
over the kitchen wings therefore are 8 feet high.

The window-dressings of a villa like this may be quite plain,
especially if outside shutter blinds are used. But the simple

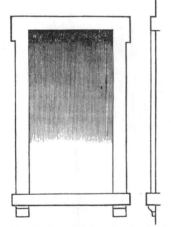

and massive dressings often employed in this style, of which Fig.
122 will convey a more accurate
idea, are in much better keeping
with the character of the architecture. An enriched Italian win-
dow-dressing is shown in Fig.
123.* If built of wood, the exterior should be of clear stuff, hori-
zontal-boarded, and finished in the
best manner.

The roofs of Italian buildings,

[Fig. 122. Italian Window—dressing plain.] having but little pitch, are usually

---

* The proportions observed in designing windows by Palladio, and the best of the
earlier Italian architects, are as follows :—The height of the opening double that
of the width, and the breadth of the architrave or dressing one sixth of the width.
Windows on the second floor have the same breadth, but less height.

covered with tiles or metal. If heavy ribs of wood **are** introduced before laying on the galvanized iron or zinc, the picturesqueness will be increased, and the effect produced which is shown in the elevation.

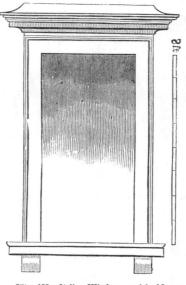

[Fig. 123. Italian Window—enriched.]

Estimate. Supposing three rooms on the first, and two on the second floor to have the walls "hard finished," and the rest to be finished for white-washing or papering, this house may be built, here, of brick and stucco—the arcade, bay-windows, etc., of wood painted and sanded—for $4600. In the cheap lumber districts, it may be substantially built of wood for about $3800.

As furnishing materials for study of simple and effective Italian composition, we give a view (from Loudon's Magazine), Fig. 124, of the villa of Mr. Nesfield, a landscape-painter. It is situated in the suburbs of London, is built of brick and stucco, and though there is a little baldness in the details, the general effect is good.

[Fig. 124. Anglo-Italian Villa.]

DESIGN XXIII.—*A small Villa in the Classical Manner.*

As a specimen of a cheap country house, producing a good effect, we give this design, which partakes of the Tuscan manner. It has been built at Rahway, New Jersey, for L. B. Brown, Esq., from the designs of Alex. Davis, Esq., Architect, New York.

The exterior of this design is characterized by symmetry, good proportion, and a certain chasteness and simplicity of detail which we like in a country house; while the whole mass obtains dignity from the height given to the central portion of the composition. The chimneys are, perhaps, a little too Tuscan or classical, and not sufficiently domestic for our own taste.

In judging of the arrangement of the interior, it must be borne in mind that the object of the person for whom this was designed, was to obtain a villa-like effect at the cost of a cottage only. Hence, while a- handsome appearance is produced by the spacious hall, and the parlor and dining-room connected with it, the absence of any apartment for books, and the close proximity of the kitchen to the dining-room, indicate the domestic life and conveniences of the cottage, rather than the villa.

The hall is entered by the large glazed doors which open upon the veranda; and this airy and open hall may be considered as a principal apartment in summer In winter, these glazed doors may be kept closed, and the side entry, A, will serve as an inclosed porch to the main hall.

In the parlor, a bay-window, 10 feet in the opening and 5 feet in depth, projects boldly. The external effect of this

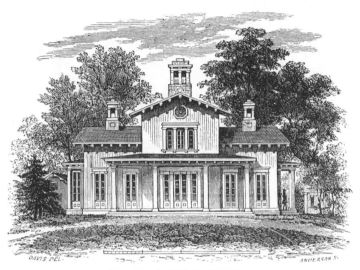

[Fig. 125. Small Classical Villa.]

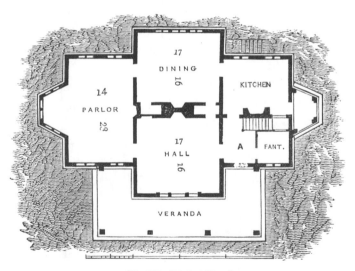

[Fig. 126. Principal Floor.]

window is balanced by the kitchen-porch, which is open. The
kitchen itself is about 12 by 14 feet, the pantry 7 feet square,
and the veranda 9 feet broad. The roof of the house projects
3 feet, and is supported by the extended rafters.

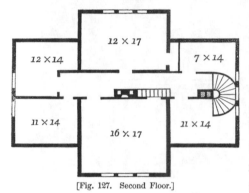

[Fig. 127.　Second Floor.]

The second story
of this design, Fig.
127, is so divided as to
accommodate a family
of considerable size,
as not an inch has
been lost. There are,
it will be seen, six bed-
rooms—though some of
them are only large
enough for the sleeping-rooms of children. The front bed-room,
16 by 17 feet, has an open fireplace, and two of the other bed-
rooms have openings in the flues for stoves.* The narrow flight
of stairs in the entry in this story leads to two rooms in the
attic, each lighted by an octagonal window in the central
gable.

CONSTRUCTION. This design is one equally well suited for
wood, or more solid materials. It has actually been built at
Rahway, of wood, and finished in a consistent manner, for
$2300—an unusually small sum for a dwelling of this extent of
accommodation. The first story is 12 feet high, and the posts
of the wings about 18 feet long.

---

* The flue of the drawing-room chimney is drawn over (in the closet behind it) to
the central stack.　The apparent chimney-top (see elevation) over that wing being
only a ventilator in chimney form.

DESIGN XXIV.—*A Cottage - Villa in the Rural Gothic Style.*

THIS design shows the front elevation and plans of the residence of Wm. J. Rotch, Esq., of New Bedford, Mass., built from the plans of Mr. Davis.

The body of the house is nearly square, and the elevation is a successful illustration of the manner in which a form usually uninteresting, can be so treated as to be highly picturesque. There is, indeed, a combination of the aspiring lines of the roof with the horizontal lines of the veranda, which expresses picturesqueness and domesticity very successfully. The high pointed gable of the central and highest part of this design has a bold and spirited effect, which would be out of keeping with the cottage-like modesty of the drooping, hipped roof, were it not for the equally bold manner in which the chimney-tops spring upwards.* Altogether, then, we should say that the character expressed by the exterior of this design is that of a man or family of domestic tastes, but with strong aspirations after something higher than social pleasures.

An inspection of Fig. 129 will show the accommodation of this house. The drawing-room and dining-room are each 18 by 20 feet, and communicate with the front hall, 14 by 18 feet, by double or sliding doors, so that these three apartments may all be thrown into one. The large and deep bay-windows at the ends of these apartments give them a light and spacious effect, when thus thrown *en suite*. The front windows have casement sashes, opening down to the floor of the veranda.

---

* The parapet of this villa surrounds a narrow walk on the roof—entered from the side of the central ridge—which commands a view of the harbor of New Bedford.

[Fig. 128. Cottage-Villa in the Rural Gothic style.

In the rear hall is the principal staircase, and in a smaller entry, between this hall and the kitchen, is the back stair.

The library is a pleasant and retired apartment, 20 by 21 feet, exclusive of the deep alcove, about 10 feet square. The kitchen is 14 by 20 feet, with a corresponding recess, 10 feet square (which might be partitioned off for a scullery). In the

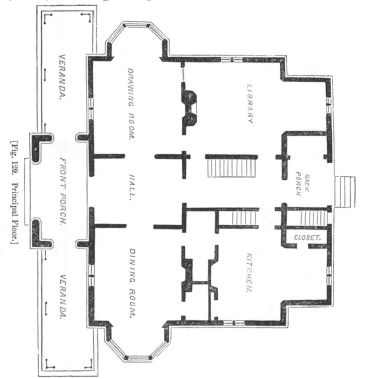

[Fig. 129. Principal Floor.]

dining-room is a china-closet. Between the kitchen and dining-room is a pantry. In the kitchen itself are two closets. In a space partitioned off from the back porch is the cellar stair.

CONSTRUCTION. This cottage should be built with hollow

brick walls, plastered on the inside, and covered with hydraulic cement on the outside. The ceilings of the bed-rooms may run partly into the roof, and are well ventilated by registers or valves, near the highest part of the ceiling, opening into a space in the apex of the garret above—the garret itself being provided with openings or ventilators, to permit the escape of warm air. Large gables, 10 feet broad, on the *sides* of the roof, light these bed-rooms abundantly. The verge-board of the front gable is boldly carved in three-inch plank. The chimney-tops—square, but set diagonally on the base—are built of common brick. The roof projects three feet at the eaves.

Estimate. The cost of this residence in New Bedford, where building is dearer than here, was about $6000.

DESIGN XXV.—*A Plain Timber Cottage - Villa.*

FOR this design, giving a very convenient and agreeable residence, which has been built in Maine, in a substantial manner, at a very economical cost, we are indebted to Gervase Wheeler, Esq., architect, Philadelphia, who has accompanied it by the following remarks.

" In this country, and especially in some districts, wood must for many years be relied upon as the material for building. It is the existence of this necessity which has, in fact, given birth to a style of erection which may be considered as almost national; for nowhere in Europe will be found the class of houses that abounds (and more especially in the New England states) in every part of the Union.

And, whilst this material seems, from causes apparent to every one, to be thus imperatively demanded, it becomes the duty of the architect to meet the emergencies of the case, and, like a true artist, to endeavor to extract beauty from the elements given to him,—beauty, too, the result, as all true architectural beauty must be, of *fitness* and harmony.

Attempts to imitate in wood, effects that can only legitimately be produced in stone or other material, may, for a time, please the vulgar eye, but they cannot ultimately fail to be as unsparingly condemned as they deserve; and were there not some consolation in the thought, that the paltry imitations and ridiculous pretences disfiguring so many of our beautiful sites, cannot, in their frailty, last long enough to outlive the attacks that the increase of a purer taste and riper experience is preparing for them, some comments might seem necessary upon the entire unfitness of the material, and the failures, necessarily the result, which many recently erected wooden structures exhibit.

The material is, itself, a beautiful and a manageable one, and examples are not wanting to show how desirable and how pleasing may be the manner in which a true artist can use it.

There are time-honored buildings in England and in Flanders, that have stood, and seem likely to stand, for centuries; and, though from local causes, these are not examples that I would advocate introducing here, still they show what may be done with the right spirit in *any* place, and are valuable as lessons in the use of the material to the architect, who may learn from them how the mighty men of old conquered *their* difficulties, and so gain encouragement how to overcome *his*.

It seems difficult to assign any particular style which, in this country, affords the best medium for the use of wood, because the character of the building must so much depend upon the scenery, the requirements of the builder, and upon other local causes.

Where a high pitched roof is admissible, the style that the accompanying design exhibits will, I think, be found suitable.

[Fig. 130. Plain Timber Cottage-Villa.]

This is essentially *real*. Its character is given by simplicity and fitness of construction, and no attempt is made with inch

board finery, to dress up and *make* Gothic what would otherwise appear a very plain house.

The building is slightly modified from one erected by the
writer at Brunswick, in Maine, at a cost not exceeding $2800.
The size and arrangement of the rooms, the spacious hall,
and the picturesque exterior, point it out as the residence of a
gentleman; and simple and inexpensive as it is, it really better
meets the requirements of those who wish to build *well*, than
many buildings that have cost more than twice the money.

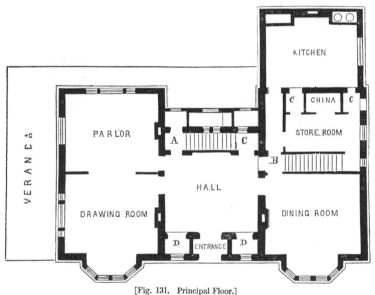

[Fig. 131. Principal Floor.]

The construction itself, though simple, is somewhat peculiar.
It is *framed*, but in such a manner as that on the exterior the
construction shows, and gives additional richness and character
to the composition.

At the corners are heavy posts, roughly dressed and champfered, and into them are mortised horizontal ties, immediately under the springing of the roof; these, with the posts, and the studs and framing of the roof, showing externally.

Internally, are nailed horizontal braces, at equal distances apart, stopping on the posts and studs of the frame; and across these, the firring and lathing cross diagonally in different directions, thus preventing the liability of injury to the inside plastering by shrinking or starting of the timbers.

On these horizontal braces the sheathing, composed of plank placed in a perpendicular direction, is supported and retained in its place by battens 2½ inches thick, and made with a broad shoulder. These battens are pinned to the horizontal braces, confining the planks, but leaving spaces for shrinking or swelling, and thus preventing the necessity of *a single nail being driven through the planks*, thereby rendering their *splitting* impossible.

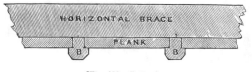

[Fig. 132. Batten.]

A representation of the batten and mode of framing is given in the accompanying section—B being the batten.

The outside is painted with a mixture of paint and fine smooth sand, laid on with a wire brush (see p. 188); a method of painting the writer has had an opportunity of personally testing during a period of twelve years, and has found it to be the most durable and economical covering for outbuildings that he has ever tried.

The windows, doors, and ornamental gables are simple and

real. The windows being made of solid frames, four inches by five, and champfered, and the doors framed and champfered.

The inside finish is of the same real and simple character. In the hall, the joists, carrying the floor above, are permitted to show; and as they are made in yellow pine, planed, and the edges champfered and stopped,—the plastering between being colored a rich blue, and the joists, cornice, and other woodwork being oiled and varnished, a rich and substantial effect is obtained, and at a very moderate cost.

The exigencies of the proprietor required the two rooms on the left of the hall to be divided by sliding doors; otherwise, the writer wished to have had them as one large room. But the severity of the winter's cold required an arrangement by which the space to be constantly warmed could be reduced.

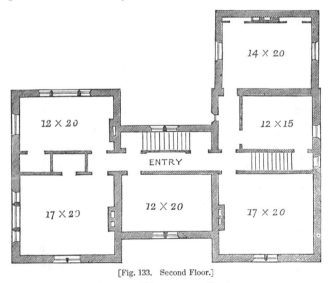

[Fig. 133. Second Floor.]

The plan of this house, Fig. 131, affords a roomy entrance-hall, 16 by 20 feet, so large as to serve for a room; an

inclosed porch, produced by a simple arrangement, which gives
ample recesses, D, D, for hat-stand and coat-stands, on either
side of the entrance door; a handsome staircase, inclosed, but
opening into the hall, whilst an outer door opens on a terrace
communicating with the garden.

The rooms are large, 17 by 20 feet, and conveniently arranged. There is a back stair at B—with ample store-room,
china-closet, etc., between the dining-room and kitchen. In
the second floor, Fig. 132, are six excellent chambers, with
suitable closet accommodation. In the roof is a space so roomy
and well ventilated, as to admit of being divided into servants'
or occasional sleeping-rooms, with great ease.

The chimneys are inside the house; and every precaution
has been taken by the arrangement of doors, etc., to make the
inside as warm as possible.

DESIGN XXVI.—*A Country-House in the Pointed Style.*

A SENSIBLE, solid, unpretending country house, with an air
of substantial comfort and refinement, not overpowered by
architectural style, but indicating intelligent, domestic life in
the country,—such is the character we have endeavored to
express in the exterior and interior of this design. The *symmetry* and *proportion* which characterize the exterior express
the love of balance, while the solidity of all the ornamental
parts denotes the love of the substantial, etc., which belong to
the sensible mind.

It will be seen at a glance, by the connoisseur, that though
this design is in the domestic Gothic or pointed manner, yet it
is no copy of any foreign cottage in this style. On the
contrary, every feature is suggested by the country life of

DESIGN XXVI.

A COUNTRY HOUSE IN THE POINTED STYLE

Fig. 133.

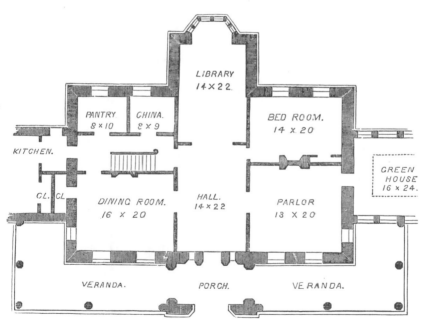

PRINCIPAL FLOOR.

Fig. 134.

those who live in residences of this size in the Middle United States. The broad and massive veranda—the full second story, overshadowed by the overhanging eaves—the steep roof, to shed the snow and afford a well-ventilated attic, and the tasteful or convenient appendages of conservatory for plants on one side and kitchen offices on the other,—these are all expressive of the comparatively modest but cultivated tastes and life of substantial country residents in the older parts of the Northern States.

In a cottage or villa of this style in England, the veranda would be useless, for the damp climate, so unlike ours, demands sun and air rather than shelter and shade. The front, therefore, would be filled with broad and large windows, and the roof with small picturesque gables, lighting bed-rooms immediately under the roof. The building would take a more irregular and picturesque form, but would lose the simple, earnest, and local expression which this has, as a country house for the Northern States.

In the Gothic villa abroad, the window is made wholly to court the sunshine. Hence, its exterior is ornamented with tracery, and made beautiful with carving. In this country house, the windows, in accordance with the acquirements of our climate, are plain box-frames, with rising sashes and outside blind shutters, as the latter give us the power of regulating the light and coolness of our apartments in summer more perfectly than any other contrivance. To put shutter-blinds on the outside of windows with Gothic tracery would be quite inappropriate, since they would hide precisely that which the architect labors to render attractive. Hence, in a simple country house in the pointed style, we prefer to adapt the window openings at once to the climate, by making them plain, and covering them with shutter-blinds. We would, however, take away the ordinary *Venetian* expression of common shutter-blinds, by making the slats much wider and bolder than usual, and staining or painting the entire shutter of a rich brown or dark oak-color.

ACCOMMODATION. The arrangement of this house, Fig. 134, suggests the occupancy of a family, in which the intellectual and social nature are equally cultivated, and where there is also a love of beauty, but where all is kept under the dominion of strong common sense. Instead of very large apartments, devoted to any special purpose of display or social enjoyment, the rooms are well apportioned for the enjoyment of all the faculties—with a certain order and symmetry pervading the whole. There is, for example, ample accommodation for the master and mistress of the house without going above the first story, since their bed-room is on the principal floor, where also are placed the kitchen offices, pantry, dining-room, etc.

Though mainly arranged for comfort, this plan is not without elegance. Thus, the entrance-hall being unoccupied by stairs, becomes a fine apartment, and being connected with a library, of equal size, by large sliding doors, the effect of this suite of 44 feet, when thrown into one, will be very agreeable on entering the house. This will be heightened by the position of the large bay-window at the end of the library. By this window the library will be lighted more agreeably than if the walls on each side were pierced with two smaller windows, while the walls themselves, being left entire, an unbroken space is afforded on both sides for books.*

---

* We have supposed this house to be heated by one of Chilson's excellent furnaces,

If it were desired to add still more to the effect of the rooms on this first floor, it could be easily done by making sliding doors between the hall and the two rooms (parlor and dining-room) on each side of it; these, when thrown open, would connect these three apartments, so that a person standing in the centre of the hall would look down the hall and library, 44 feet, and across the parlor and dining-room, 48 feet. But most families would prefer to connect the hall with these two rooms by doors of the ordinary size, as it would give the rooms the more entirely domestic and quiet expression of every-day life.

The staircase in this house is placed in a side hall or entry, 7 feet wide, which connects with the kitchen, etc.; a very good mode where there is but one staircase in a country house, as, by shutting the door between the main hall and the entry, the stairs are rendered private, or are put out of sight. This entry is lighted by an end window on the second floor.

The green-house communicates directly with the parlor, and is supposed to have a south aspect—though an east or west exposure is found to answer perfectly well in this climate. It will be easily heated by the same furnace which heats the house—a 10 inch hot-air pipe and a large register, running through the basement, and entering by the floor or side of the green-house. There should be a large door at the outer end of the green-house, for taking in the plants, and a cistern beneath it, to collect water from the roof for watering them.

As the other wing, we have the kitchen, with its closets, and back-kitchen or scullery, etc. This may be extended more

---

placed in the centre of the basement, under the hall, and have not therefore placed any chimneys in the hall or library.

than 24 feet (the length of the green-house), if desirable—and, indeed, to twice that size, if necessary,—with an inclosed kitchen yard, clothes drying-ground, etc., concealed by trees.

The porch of this house, which projects 12 feet, breaks up (see elevation) the otherwise too long horizontal line of the veranda roof—and the novice will bear in mind, that as the spirit of the Gothic or pointed style lies in the prevalence of vertical or upward lines, so all long, unbroken, horizontal lines of roof should be avoided.

This porch, being pierced with arches on each side, opens on a continuous veranda, 10 feet wide and 80 feet long, which affords a fine promenade at all seasons—terminating on one side with the green-house; and there are few greater luxuries in a country house in an American summer, such as it is in this latitude, than such a cool and airy veranda—especially if it looks out upon our fine river or lake scenery.*

The second floor of this house, Fig. 135, gives five excellent bed-rooms, with closets (marked C). The bed-room over the library, 14 by 18 feet, has attached to it a dressing-room, 8 by 10 feet, which communicates with a bath-room, A, containing a water-closet. This bath-room is also entered by the door *a*, from the landing or the stair, and can therefore be also used by any of the occupants of the second story. The bed-room over the hall is lighted by a fine oriel-window, projecting over the front door. Both this and the bed-room over the library are heated by registers and hot-air pipes from the furnace in the

---

* Any one living on the Hudson inevitably gets to look upon river scenery as an indispensable part of country landscape. This will account for the manner in which glimpses of river scenery creep into so many of these sketches of houses—often, as in this design, on the wrong side of the house.

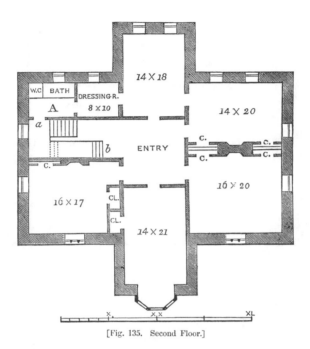

[Fig. 135. Second Floor.]

basement; and if registers are also provided for the other bed-rooms in this story, the expense of building fireplaces may be avoided.

At *b*, in the entry, is a flight of stairs, leading to servants' rooms in the attic.

CONSTRUCTION. This design demands solid walls, either of stone, brick afterwards colored, or brick and cement. It could be built as cheaply here of good hard brick (at $4 to $5 per 1000), laid up in hollow walls (see page 60), as of wood, and if colored with the durable cement-wash described in page 187, it would have a very satisfactory appearance. The projection of the eaves (2½ feet), sheltering the walls so completely, renders this also one of the most suitable houses for

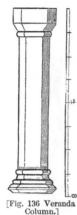

[Fig. 136 Veranda Column.]

outside stucco, as the walls will be preserved from all the perpendicular drip or leakage so injurious to cemented walls.

The veranda should be constructed in a heavy and solid manner, either of cut-stone, brick, or of solid wood, painted and sanded, to agree with the walls of the house. The columns should be 16 inches in diameter, and formed in the simple manner represented in the elevation, belonging to the early pointed style, or with the octagonal shafts shown in Fig. 136.

There should be no labels over the windows or doors, except as shown over the front door—but the window frames should have plain, splayed jambs, and should be set back a couple of inches from the outside face of the wall, with outside shutter-blinds made to fit them.

[Fig. 137. Verge-Board.]

Fig. 137 shows part of the verge-board of the gable over the porch, $\frac{1}{4}$ inch to a foot. This should be carved out of well-seasoned 3-inch plank.

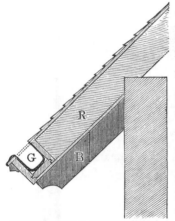

[Fig 138. Gutter in Projecting Eaves.]

The roof of this house, in the elevation, is supposed to be covered with diamond tiles, a row of *crest-tiles* running along the ridge of the roof; but prime cut shingles or slate would be equally suitable. The chimney-tops in octagonal shafts, are built of brick. The gutter is formed at the outside of the projecting eaves, as shown in the section, Fig. 138, in which R is the rafter, G, the gutter, lined with copper, and B, the rafter bracket.

The height of the rooms in the first story is 13 feet, and that in the second story 9 feet. The partitions are 8-inch brick walls, and the floors are all deafened. If built with hollow walls, the house will need no firring, and thus, if the roof is tile or slate, will be in a great measure fire-proof—that is, if a fire breaks out in one apartment, it will not easily spread to another, as there are no wooden partitions and no hollow firring to extend the combustion rapidly from one part of the building to another.

Estimate. The cost of this house, finished in a simple and appropriate manner, would be between $6000 and $7000.

DESIGN XXVII.—*A small Country House for the Southern States.*

A SIMPLE, rational, convenient, and economical dwelling for the southern part of the Union, is all that we have aimed at in

[Fig. 130. Small Southern Country House.]

this design. A modification of the Venetian mode has been chosen for the exterior, because it affords, in its broadly projecting roof and long extended veranda, that ample shade, so indispensable to all dwellings in a southern climate.

There is a double value at the South, in these wide-spreading roofs; first, in the greater coolness of the walls or sides of a building, protected by their shade from the direct rays of the sun, all the hottest part of the day; and second, in the good effect, architecturally, produced by the strong contrasts of light and shadow made by such projections.

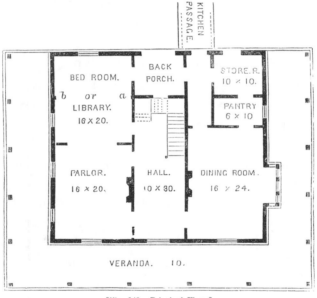

[Fig. 140. Principal Floor.]

ACCOMMODATION. A peculiar feature in all Southern country houses is the position of the kitchen—which does not form part of the dwelling, but stands detached at a distance of 20, 30, or more yards. This kitchen contains servants' bed-rooms on its second floor,—only such servants sleeping in the dwelling as are personal attendants on the family. For this reason there is not so much room required for servants in the Southern country house itself—but, as many more servants are kept there than at the North, a good deal more accommodation is provided in the detached kitchen or other negro houses.

In the plan of the first floor of this house, Fig. 140, we have practised a very simple contrivance, by which the size of this floor is considerably increased, so that a villa-like accommodation is obtained in a house only about 30 by 42 feet in the clear measurement. This is done by building the veranda of the same height as the principal story (about 12 feet), and *inclosing* the portion in the rear.

By this means we get a library 16 by 20 feet (which would otherwise be but 16 by 10 feet). The letters *a*, *b*, show the line between the main body of the house and the veranda, and a strong piece of timber should cover the opening in the wall over the void space here.

In the rear of the hall is a back porch—which is a part of the veranda—that may be left open. Adjoining it is an entry or passage-way, five feet wide, for the servants to pass from the dining-room to the detached kitchen, without the necessity of entering the back porch or hall. Alongside of this entry is a large store-room (which is also part of the inclosed veranda), 10 by 10 feet. This is the larder and pastry-room, under the care of the mistress of the house; and adjoining it and the dining-room is a pantry or china-closet.

The dining-room is a spacious and airy apartment, 16 by 24 feet, with a bay-window on the side, opening down to the veranda. The hall is 10 feet wide; and the parlor and library, on the opposite side, may communicate with it by a large sliding door, if preferred. A single fireplace would be sufficient for both these rooms at the South. In some families, it might be desirable to make the back apartment a bed-room, instead of a library.

We have shown the covered passage to the kitchen, and part of the kitchen itself, in our sketch of the *front* elevation, merely to convey an idea of their effect; though the position of those on the plan is in the rear, and not on the side of the house.   This, however, is a mere matter of locality, as the kitchen and other outbuildings will, of course, be placed on the side offering the greatest facilities for their uses, and, at the same time, keeping them most in the background.

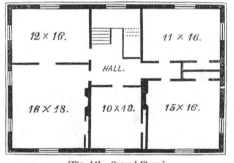

[Fig. 141. Second Floor.]

The second floor, Fig. 141, shows five good bed-rooms.

Every house at the South should have a ventilator on the roof, connected with air-ducts leading to the cellar.   This would maintain a circulation from the lowest to the highest part of the dwelling, and prevent the accumulation of hot air under the roof.   A reference to our remarks on ventilation will show how this can be most effectually accomplished.

CONSTRUCTION.   As this is especially designed as an economical country house, the material used in most parts of the South would be wood. The roof should project 3 feet, the windows should all be casement windows, with outside Venetian shutter-blinds, and the veranda should be 10 or 12 feet wide.*

[Fig. 142. Exterior of Southern Country House.]

The first story is intended to be 12 and the second 9 feet in the clear. The chimney-stacks are drawn over in the garret, so as to come out on the ridge of the roof.

---

* The floors of verandas, in this climate, should always, if possible, be made of southern pine, *oiled*, and not painted. The effect is excellent, and the floor is much more durable and satisfactory than if made of white pine, painted.

DESIGN XXVIII.

VILLA IN THE ITALIAN STYLE.

Fig. 143.

Estimate. The cost of this house would vary from $2500 to $3000, depending upon the locality where it is built, the price of lumber, labor, etc., which varies largely at the South.

VARIATION. If we suppose the body of this house increased in depth, so that it is between 40 and 50 feet from the front to the rear, Fig. 142 will give a hint of a simple variation in the bracketed mode, which would have a good effect for a very moderate expenditure.

DESIGN XXVIII.—*A Villa in the Italian Style.*

This beautiful villa, the residence of Edward King, Esq., of Newport, Rhode Island, was constructed in 1845, from the designs of Mr. Upjohn, of New York.

It is one of the most successful specimens of the Italian style in the United States, and unites beauty of form and expression with spacious accommodation, in a manner not often seen, and which is very creditable to Mr. Upjohn.

The first impression which this villa makes on the mind is, that of its being a gentleman's residence. There is dignity, refinement, and elegance, about all its leading features. It next indicates varied enjoyments, and a life of refined leisure—especially abounding, as it does, with evidences of love of social pleasures.

In a more strictly architectural sense, the exterior of this villa is worthy of note, for the *harmony* which pervades it. Notwithstanding the great variety of forms in the windows introduced—a variety which denotes different uses in various apartments—the predominance of the round arch in the majority of the leading apertures, whether in windows, doors, or verandas, restores harmony throughout the whole—while it produces an effect, as regards the details, quite different from that which results from the simplicity of most *façades*. Both are pleasing, but, to a highly cultivated taste, the satisfaction

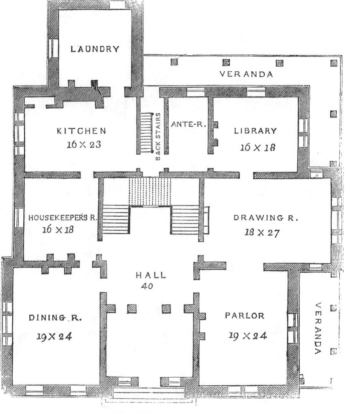

[Fig. 144. Principal Floor.]

derived from harmony growing out of variety, is as much greater than that arising from uniformity and simplicity, in architecture, as in music, where the first may be illustrated by one of Beethoven's symphonies, and the last by the simple melody of a ballad

The sky outline of this villa has the characteristic irregularity of the Italian school of design, and the grouping of the whole is a good study for a young architect who is embarrassed how to treat a large square mass of building,—for the ground plan is nearly square. The chimney-tops and heavy cornice,

[Fig. 145. Balcony Window.]

all of stone, are in excellent taste, and the arcades and verandas have been introduced subordinately, and yet so as to greatly increase the effect.

ACCOMMODATION. An inspection of the plan of the principal

floor will show that this is a villa of the first class. On entering the hall, an arcade, supported by four columns, separates the vestibule or entrance-hall from the main hall. In the latter, which is spacious, and lighted by a sky-light of colored glass, one is struck by the fine effect of the ample staircase, rising by easy flights, with broad landings. On the right of the hall is a fine suite of rooms—parlor, drawing-room and library; on the left

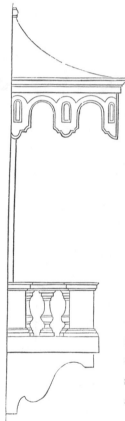

are the dining-room, housekeeper's room (with pantries), kitchen, laundry, etc.

In an entry, at the rear of the main hall, is placed the servants' staircase.

We have not given the plan of the second floor, but, it will be readily imagined, there is an abundance of sleeping apartments, with rooms for domestics on the third story of the higher portions of the building.

CONSTRUCTION. This villa is built, throughout, in a very solid and excellent manner. The walls are of brick, painted externally of a light freestone color, and the window-dressings, string-courses, cornices, brackets, etc., are all freestone. The effect is more real and satisfactory than that of any other mode of building, except it be of solid stone—and that stone one of an agreeable tone of color.

Fig. 145 (to the scale of $\frac{1}{4}$ of an inch to a foot) shows the elevation, and Fig.

[Fig. 146. Balcony—Profile.]

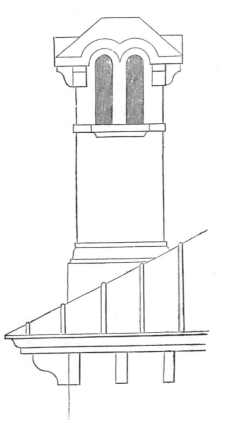

[Fig. 147. Chimney-Top and Cornice.]

146 the profile, of the handsome balcony-window in the front of the house; Fig. 147 is the chimney-top, with a portion of the roof, giving the cornice and heavy stone brackets.

DESIGN XXIX.—*A Villa in the Rural Gothic Style.*

We have designed this villa to express the life of a family of refined and cultivated taste, full of home feeling, love for the country, and enjoyment of the rural and beautiful in nature—

and withal, a truly American home, in which all is adapted to
the wants and habits of life of a family in independent
circumstances.

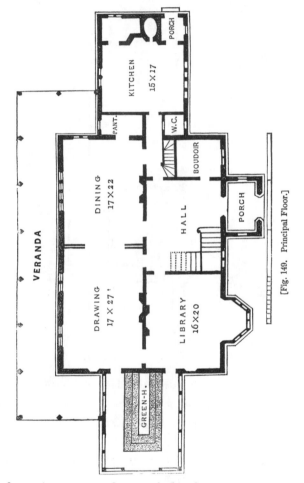

[Fig. 149. Principal Floor.]

We leave it to our readers to judge how much or how little
we have succeeded in our attempt. They will first observe
that the roof is not so abstractly pointed and aspiring as that in

DESIGN XXIX

RURAL GOTHIC VILLA.

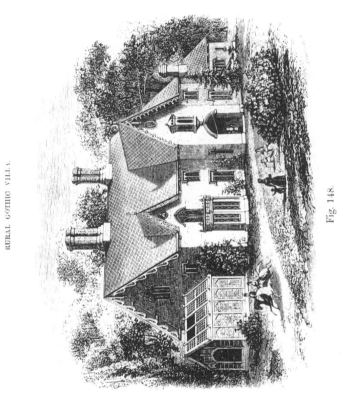

Fig. 148.

Design XXIII., neither is it so flat and reasonably sufficient as in Design XXII., but moderately high, to manifest the Northern climate, and broad, as if to cover, overshadow, and protect all beneath it. The enriched windows, of different forms, yet of the same style—the ornamented gables and chimney-tops—all indicate a love of refined and artistic forms; while their variety and position show the various uses and enjoyments pertaining to the apartments within. When we notice, also, the conservatory, extending itself on one side, and the kitchen on the other with a long veranda in the rear; it is easy to see that this design indicates the residence of a family thoroughly at home in the country, and understanding how best to enjoy it

By comparing this Design with Design XXII., our readers will, perhaps, better understand what we mean by the expression of domestic feeling in a house. However well the latter Design may satisfy our judgment, and impress us with so much of beauty as lies in abstract symmetry and proportion, it stops there. The dwelling before us, on the contrary, manifests in every part the presence of cultivated and deep domestic sympathies; in that lies its chiefest charm,—and we should add that in that, also, lies the great beauty of this style for country residences.

It will be seen, by comparing the elevation and plan, that this villa is intended for one of those sites, very common in this part of the country, where the entrance is on one side, while the most agreeable landscape view is on the other. Hence, the two finest apartments and the veranda (which pleasantly overshadows them) are on the side of the house opposite to the porch—exactly the reverse of the arrangement in Design XXV. The elevation of the opposite side of the house may show two small gables, or a single large one, breaking the otherwise horizontal line of the eaves. The veranda may resemble that in Design XXX., omitting the Tudor-flower ornament on the top of the cornice.

When window frames are decorated with tracery and labels, as in the present case, it should be remembered that the shutters or shutter-blinds must be placed on the *inside*, or the beauty of detail, which has cost so much labor, will be thrown away.

ACCOMMODATION. The plan of this house is very simple, and almost explains itself, by a reference to Fig. 149. In the entrance-hall (16 by 18 feet), a good effect may be produced, by building the staircase of oak, rather massively wrought. On the right is a pretty little boudoir, or ladies' morning-room, which should be fitted up in a delicate and tasteful manner, with chintz furniture, the walls papered with chaste Gothic or Elizabethan patterns, or ornamented with small and appropriate pictures or prints. Or, if the ladies decline this apartment, we shall offer it as the office or sanctum of the master of the house, into which strangers, coming on business with him, may be shown. In this case, it will be fitted up in a very different and much plainer manner—with a secretary, writing-table, bookcase, and iron safe built in the wall.

The drawing-room and dining-room, both spacious apartments, are arranged, *en suite*, with sliding doors. The dining-room is advantageously placed, with respect to the pantry, and the entry separated from the main hall which leads to the kitchen. In this entry is the servants' staircase, and a water-closet, (W. C.) The kitchen has a back porch and scullery, and may be extended to suit the wants of the family.

The library, which will be the most cosy and home-like

room, and which will probably be the sitting-room of the family, is an apartment of agreeable size and proportion; its beauty being enhanced by the large bay-window which lights it. The green-house (supposed to have a southern exposure) communicates both with this and the drawing-room—a walk being continued all round it. If the house is heated by a furnace, a large register will also heat the green-house; but if not, then a small furnace should be placed in a cellar made under the green-house, the flue of which may be carried (with a rise of a couple of feet only, if needful) into the bottom of the chimney-stack belonging to the library. By placing such a furnace—or one of the Boston ventilating stoves*—in a large air-chamber (about 8 feet square), built of brick, under the floor of the green-house, bringing in cold air to the bottom of this chamber, and allowing it to escape, when heated, into the green-house above, this wing could be heated all winter with a couple of tons of anthracite.

Let us now ascend to the second floor, Fig. 150. Here we have five bed-rooms. Two of these have well-lighted dressing-rooms attached, either of which may have a couch or divan, capable of being turned into a bed, whenever the hospitable inmates of the house find it needful to stretch a point to accommodate more than the usual number of guests. The bed-room (11 by 16) over the porch, containing the handsome oriel-window (which may be called the "oriel room"), would make a charming boudoir, if the gentleman takes it into his head to appropriate the apartment down stairs as an office.

---

* To be had at Chilson & Co.'s, 351 Broadway, New York, and 31 Blackstone-street, Boston.

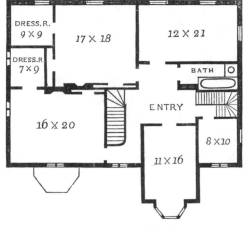

[Fig. 150. Second Floor.]

The bed-room, 12 by 21 feet, has beside it a bath and water-closet, communicating with the main entry, for general access. The waste and supply pipes for the bath-room are carried through the wall of this story, and descend through the pantry of the story below.

Over the back stairs is another flight leading to three or four good servants' rooms, finished in the garret, and lighted by windows in the gables.

There may be a cellar under the whole house—reached from the first story by a descending flight of steps under the back stairs.

CONSTRUCTION. A villa as much enriched in the details as this, and of this style of architecture, should always be built of solid materials. The most harmonious effect, when expense is but little regarded, would be produced by constructing it of the light brown sand-stone, now so much used in New York. The exterior effect would be as good, and, though not so real, yet the warmth and comfort would be even greater, if built of rough brick covered with cement or stucco on the outside, and colored of a mellow, warm drab or light freestone hue. But the cheapest mode, and one very satisfactory, would be to build the walls of good hard brick, and color them externally of an agreeable shade. The walls of the main building should be hollow walls (or solid walls, a foot thick), firred off for plastering on the inside. The kitchen walls need not be more than 8 inches thick.

The windows have *labels* or lintels of cut stone over the top of the frames.

[Fig. 151. Section of Label.]

The section of these labels is shown in Fig. 151, to the scale of half an inch to the foot.

[Fig. 152. Elevation and Plan of Window.]

The elevation of one of the windows, to the scale of $\frac{1}{4}$ inch to the foot, is shown in 152 ; below it is the plan or section through the wall, A, B. This is intended for a casement window—but if inside shutter-blinds are preferred, then rising sashes may be used. In this case, there should be a broad stile left in the centre, a little wider than the mullion which shows in the middle of the window frame.

Fig. 153 is the elevation of the bay-window, with balcony over it, to the scale of $\frac{1}{4}$ of an inch to the foot. The verge-

[Fig. 153. The Bay-Window.]

[Fig. 154. Verge-Board.]

board of the small gable over this balcony is the same as that shown in page 311.   A part of the verge-board of the gable over the porch, may be seen more in detail in Fig. 154.   All these verge-boards should be carved out of sound $2\frac{1}{2}$ or 3 inch pine plank, so as to have a real and solid appearance, very different from the thin-board imitations of them frequently seen in flimsy ornamental cottages.   The roof should project

2 feet, and the gutter should be formed at the eaves, as shown on page 311.

The chimney-tops of this design should be formed of moulded brick, if such can be obtained. If not, chimney-tops of the

[Fig. 155. Chimney-Tops.]

Garnkirk fire-clay, of the patterns shown in Fig. 155, may be had of Jas. Lee & Co., New York or Boston.

Estimate. Built in brick, or brick and cement, in a substantial manner, with labels of cut stone, this villa would cost about $7,500. The cost of the green-house, which is included, would be about $300.

DESIGN XXX.—*An American Country House of the first class.*

THIS design has been prepared for this work by Gervase

Wheeler, Esq., of Philadelphia, an architect of reputation. Mr. Wheeler's compositions show artistic ability, combined with an excellent knowledge of all that belongs to domestic life in its best development. The plan of this Design is worthy of careful study, as combining much dignity and breadth upon the ground, with that simplicity and convenience which should always characterize the best country house.

The complete arrangement of the kitchen offices shows Mr. Wheeler's English education—for this, one of the strongest points in English domestic architecture, is one of the weakest and least understood, because perhaps, as yet, least appreciated in the United States.

The following are Mr. Wheeler's remarks, explanatory of this design.

"In this country, there is no lack of examples of houses, either of an ornate and expensive character, or partaking of the nature of the smaller cottage residence; but I do not remember to have seen in actual execution or in published American books any satisfactory specimen of a *simple* country house of the first class;—a house suitable as the abode of a gentleman, and adequate, in its domestic accommodation, for the purposes of a gentleman's notions of hospitality, and for the comforts essential to the gratification of a gentleman's taste.

Those houses in which any pretension has been made to meet these demands have usually been on so expensive a scale (from $15,000 to $30,000), as to place their erection beyond the reach of that class which every day is becoming the one for which an architect's energies and skill will be most constantly called into play.

It seems to me that these next ten years will witness so

increasing a demand for a species of house not yet, I think, attained, that it is quite worth while for the profession to study how to meet it, and as an endeavor on my part to comply with the request of Mr. Downing to give the result of my own attempts to supply this demand, I present the accompanying design to the consideration of those who are in quest of a house suited in its arrangements, economical construction, and picturesque exterior, to the wants of the present day.

Without occupying space by further preliminary remarks, I will at once proceed to explain the design in the order in which the cuts representing its features naturally present themselves.

1st. The ground plan, Fig. 157. This plan represents so simple an arrangement of the rooms and passages, as to seem to need but little explanation.

A carriage-porch at the end of the main portion of the front, gives convenient entrance to the principal hall, which is 12 feet wide, and terminates in an octagonal bay containing the grand stairway.

On the right of this entrance-hall is an inner hall or gallery, leading to the various family rooms, consisting of a dining-room 23 feet by 18, a boudoir or lady's room, 18 by 12, a drawing-room, 18 by 32, and a library, 18 by 16. This last room is so situated as to be retired, and yet easy of access, and might, if necessary, be enlarged ; but as the gallery or inner hall would afford ample accommodation for bookcases, cabinets, and pictures, its dimensions, as here given, will, in most cases, be found sufficient for its owner.

On the left of the hall is the passage leading from the kitchen and offices, forming means of access for the servants to the front door, whilst across the end of the hall, and under the staircase is an open screen, *a*, filled with tracery and stained glass, behind which is the passage from the pantry or waiter's

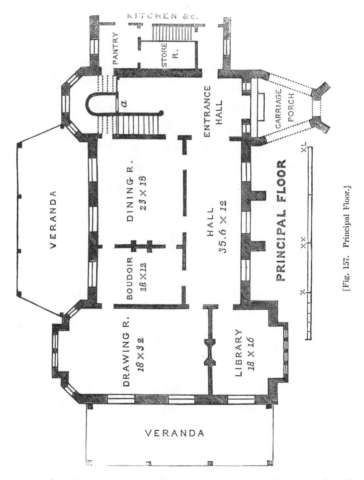

[Fig. 157. Principal Floor.]

room to the dining-room, and connected with which would also be the hat and coat closets, etc., for the family and for visitors.

The grand staircase is of a heavy massive character that would be very effective, and is thoroughly lighted and venti

DESIGN XXX.

LARGE COUNTRY HOUSE

Fig. 156.

lated : the latter object being secured by a large open lantern or cupola on the roof (see elevation), in which would be placed one of 'Emerson's ventilators,' now a *sine qua non* in all well-constructed residences.

The rooms are all well proportioned and conveniently disposed. The dining-room and boudoir open on a large veranda, which projects 15 feet east, and a similar veranda, 14 feet wide, is provided on the south for the drawing-room and library.

The domestic arrangements,—kitchen offices, etc., will be seen, by reference to the plan, which is given separately.

These must necessarily be somewhat modified by peculiarities of site, convenience of access from public roads, etc ; but

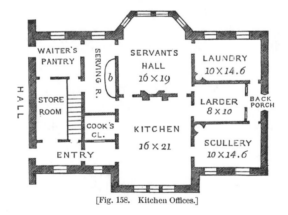

[Fig. 158. Kitchen Offices.]

the plan here shown, Fig. 158, which is supposed to form a separate wing, joined to the extreme hall, Fig. 157, is one which has some advantages, which I will proceed to explain. A waiter's pantry communicates, by means of the passage under the stairs, before described, with the dining-room. This pantry should be filled with shelves, closets, and other conveniences for the keeping of the glass and china in daily use, whilst a fire-proof safe could be built into the wall for the safe deposit of plate and such articles of value as were only occasionally required.

A large store-room communicates also with the pantry, and adjoining it is a serving-room, a long apartment, containing a dresser or table, *b*, upon which the various dishes would be deposited, previous to being brought into the dining-room.

The kitchen, which is large, has in its rear the servants' hall, a pleasant and airy apartment; and on one side is a large closet, for the use of the cook, a back and cellar staircase, and the passage to the entrance-hall, whilst on the other are a laundry, a larder, and a scullery, and for each of which an outer door affords means of communication through a porch to the yard.

These domestic arrangements, usually, are not sufficiently considered in country houses; but I have always found an architect is repaid for trouble expended in conveniently disposing their very essential accommodation.

The chamber plan presents, in all, seven large chambers on the principal floor, two of which might be used, however, exclusively as dressing-rooms; and the closets adjoining the chambers over the porch and library are each so large and well lighted as to permit of their also being occupied as dressing-rooms for the bed-rooms with which they connect. In the floor over the offices are five servants' chambers, bath-rooms, water-closets, etc.; and on the attic floor, by retaining the partition as below, and making another in the centre of the house, so as to form a passage 3 or 4 feet wide, no less than *ten* additional chambers, each well lighted and ventilated, can be obtained, thus making in all, the large number of twenty-two

chambers, a liberality of accommodation which the simplicity
and economy of the arrangements would at first sight hardly
seem capable of affording.

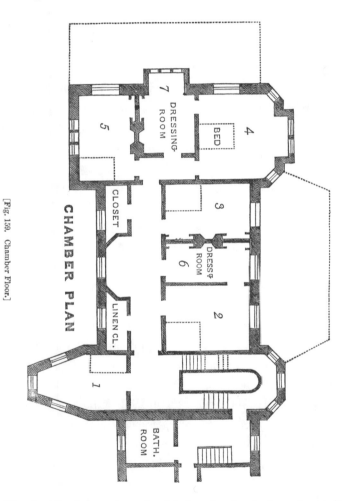

[Fig. 159. Chamber Floor.]

The inside decoration should be simple, but real; stained
glass, of that quiet tone of color which true artists are just

beginning to find suitable to domestic purposes, and of simple
design, should fill the windows,—if not all, certainly those of
the halls, staircase, and library; and the painting should also
be toned down to those quiet tender hues that never tire and
always please.

The ceiling of the hall or gallery should be panelled, with
heavy cross-beams and corbelled supports, and decorated with
shields and other appropriate ornaments; and the walls, filled
with bookcases and cabinets, with recesses here and there for
family pictures or honored busts, would easily afford opportunities for the exercise of correct taste and refined judgment in
decoration.

The other rooms might be decorated in various manners,
and I would suggest a method I have had opportunities of
trying, and always with satisfaction.

It consists in using a paper of *one* uniform color upon the
walls, which, by means of strips of other harmonious or
contrasted colors thereon, cut in such forms as the design
requires, will produce an effect equal to that which any
Polychromatic artist can secure, and at one-fifth the cost. This
material, called decorative paper, is prepared in such a manner
as to permit of cleansing, and can readily be procured. A
room 24 by 18 feet has just been finished in the manner
suggested, by Howell and Co., of Philadelphia, for $16, and
for brilliancy of color, novelty, and cheerfulness of effect, is
equal to any painting I have ever seen.

This is so superior a method of finishing a room to the cold,
white, 'hard-finish' usually seen, that, though I do not pretend to
recommend it as a substitute for decorative wall painting, I think
it a very desirable embellishment in an inexpensive house.

The exterior is of the simplest possible character, depending for its effect entirely upon the harmony and congruity of its parts, and its breadth and simplicity of outline.

No ornamental decoration is attempted that is not essential to the expression of the design, and the whole is of that subdued, unpretending, but substantial character which I think a country house should generally possess.

The material might vary in accordance with the various circumstances affecting its location; and there is no part of it which would prevent the use of any building material which the country affords.

It might be entirely of stone or of brick, with or without stone dressings; and the masonry, if of stone, will be far more effective and artistic, if treated in the simplest and most natural manner.

Stone, laid in its natural bed, as it comes from the quarry, with rough, hammer-dressed blocks of somewhat more regular form and size at the angles of the building and round the apertures for doors and windows, would produce a far more pleasing effect than expensively cut work and regular masonry, and would be far more in accordance with the spirit of the style.

The style chosen is one which, without assuming it to be solely adapted to the American country house, or, indeed, suitable in every instance, I conceive to be so economical, and possessing so many advantages over the Italian or other usually recognized types of modern buildings, that I do not hesitate to recommend its adoption in every case where economy and simplicity have to be mainly consulted.

The high roof, simple, ornamental construction, and reality

of its nature, render it peculiarly suitable for adoption by the generality of those who build; and I very much question whether any other internal arrangement or expression of style could be found which would afford the same ample accommodation at so small a cost as this.

There are other styles possessing elements of great beauty, and which may be used with equal or greater advantage in some cases; but as affording the most characteristic expression at the least possible cost, simplicity of arrangement of parts without sameness, and freedom from decoration without poverty, I think that which this design exhibits, and which, without being a copy of any one of the well-known Tudor or Elizabethan types, has as distinct a character as they have, is one which may be adopted with propriety in the domestic architecture of this country. I therefore offer to the consideration of those interested in its examination this study of an ' American family country house.' "

Estimate. Mr. Wheeler's estimate for this design is $13,000.

DESIGN XXXI.—*A Villa in the Pointed Style.*

THIS design, which is an excellent example of the adaptation of the latest or perpendicular Gothic to the wants of our villa life, we owe to the kindness of Alexander J. Davis, Esq., of New York, whose works are so well known in all parts of the country as to require no commendation at our hands.

The elevation shown in Design XXXI. unites, in no ordinary degree, symmetry and fine proportion with an expression of dignity and elegance. The greater height to which the roof of

DESIGN XXXI.

VILLA IN THE POINTED STYLE.

Fig. 160.

the central part of the building is carried, gives boldness and picturesqueness to the design, which would appear more fully in a perspective view than in an elevation.

The exterior is strongly marked in style, and is therefore likely to please those who value accurate and elaborate artistic

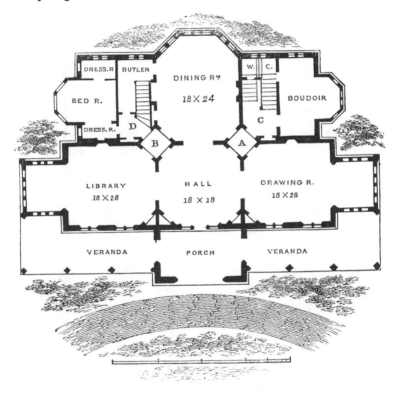

[Fig. 161. Principal Floor.]

effect. Thus, the cornice is decorated with battlements (imperfectly shown in the engraving), the small gables with crockets, and the parapet of the veranda with the Tudor-flower.

In this veranda, and in the arrangement of the principal

floor, the architect has wisely departed from all foreign examples, and has adapted the style to our climate, which requires shade and abundant ventilation, rather than apartments seeking to catch every ray of sun by their wide windows and externally uncovered walls.

A villa like this should have no common-place, contracted, or mean site. It should stand on a commanding locality, backed by fine wood, and overlooking a fine reach of picturesque but cultivated landscape. We say cultivated—for the highly architectural character of the exterior would be in better keeping with well-kept park or pleasure-ground scenery than with wild and rude landscape.

Accommodation. The interior of this villa, looking at the plan of the principal floor, Fig. 161, is not less remarkable for elegance of effect than the exterior. Indeed, standing in the middle of the hall, almost the whole of this floor may be seen at a glance, by throwing open the large sliding doors which connect it with the three principal apartments—an arrangement as agreeable and satisfactory to those who entertain much and are fond of society in their country homes, as it would be displeasing and unsatisfactory to those who prefer a retired and quiet life.

No one, however, can deny that a spacious and striking effect is produced by the arrangement of the rooms. The large and deep bays at the end of the library and drawing-room would, perhaps, give too powerful a light, were it not that the front windows are wholly, and the bays in part, shaded by the veranda.

The little spaces, A, B, between the rooms, are small passages, serving as private communications from one apart ment to the other. They should be finished with arched openings or doorways, which may be hung with heavy curtains instead of doors, and would have a very pretty effect.

In the dining-room there is a recess opposite the fireplace, for the sideboard. D, is the passage for the back stair, behind which is the butler's pantry. C, is the principal staircase. Adjoining this is a boudoir. A water-closet is placed in the space at the rear of the stairs, marked W. C.

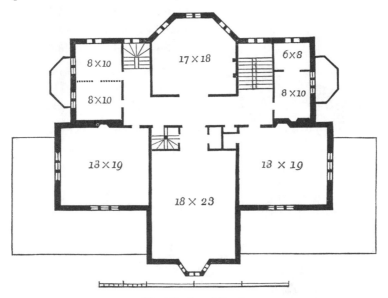

[Fig. 162. Second Floor.]

The small bed-room on the left of D has two dressing-rooms attached to it; the fireplace being placed in the dressing-room instead of the bed-room, which is by far the better place for it —since it leaves the air of the bed-room cool and fresh, and the servant who lights the fire in the morning is not obliged to enter the bed-room.

The kitchen and its offices are all placed in the basement story of this villa—a mode which, perhaps, adds to its elegance and economy, but detracts from its comfort and conven ience.

The second-story arrangement, Fig. 162, is shown in the annexed plan.

There is space for four servants' rooms in the attic.

CONSTRUCTION. This villa would have the best effect, if built of the light-colored sand-stone of New Jersey. Next to this, we should prefer brick, with sand-stone dressings, and next to this, brick and stucco. The veranda and oriel window over the front door may be con-structed of wood, colored, to harmonize with the walls. The roof may be covered with zinc, laid on a ribbed sheath-ing, without soldering, so as to allow it to expand and con-tract without detriment.

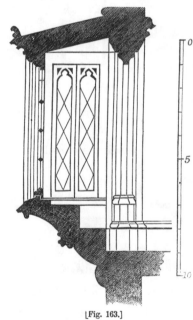

[Fig. 163.]

Fig. 163 is a section of the oriel window over the front door.

To build this design satis-factorily, working drawings would, of course, be required from the architect for all its most important details.

Estimate. The cost of this villa, on the Hudson, built of brick, with red sand-stone dressings, and finished throughout in a consistent manner, would be about $10,000.

DESIGN XXXII.

A LAKE OR RIVER VILLA.

Fig. 164.

DESIGN XXXII.—*A Lake or River Villa for a Picturesque Site.*

To a person of common sense views, whose life has been passed in a tame and prosaic district of country where the eye catches nothing on the earth's plane more elevating than unbroken levels of meadow or corn-field, this villa will almost

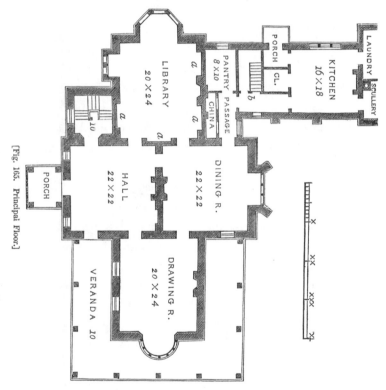

[Fig. 165. Principal Floor.]

appear an impossible necessity—if it does not seem wholly out of keeping with nature and life as he understands them.

But let another person, gifted not only with common sense but imagination, live amid such scenery as meets his eye daily on the Hudson Highlands, and he will often feel that a common-

place, matter-of-fact, square house is an insult to the spirit of all
that surrounds him.   In such bold scenery, nature overpowers
all and suggests all.   Even cultivated fields would almost appear
an impertinence in the sight of the broad river and lofty hills,
were it not that they serve, by contrast, to heighten the grandeur
of that which man can never subdue, but which always stands
ready to awe and subdue him.

It is in such picturesque scenery as this—scenery which
exists in many spots in America besides the banks of the
Hudson—wherever, indeed, the wildness or grandeur of nature
triumphs strongly over cultivated landscape—but especially
where river or lake and hill country are combined—it is there
that the highly picturesque country house or villa is instinctively felt to harmonize with and belong to the landscape.   It
is there that the high tower, the steep roof, and the boldly
varied outline, seem wholly in keeping with the landscape,
because these forms in the building harmonize, either by
contrast or assimilation, with the pervading spirit of mysterious
power and beauty in romantic scenery.

Every one with a lively perception of beauty has felt the
pleasure of that contrast which occurs in nature, where tall
pyramidal hills rise directly from the water's edge ; or something
of the same effect in smaller bits of landscape, where a single
tall poplar rises by some river bank, to contrast strongly with
the level of the shores.   It is in this mental delight awakened
by the contrast of symbols, of repose and action, of beauty and
power, in the lake that slumbers peacefully, and the hills that
lift themselves boldly or grandly above it, that we find the
explanation of part of the peculiar charm which belongs to
those picturesque towers and campaniles of the edifices and

villas of the Rhine and the Italian lakes. The same good effect
will follow from the introduction of buildings composed upon
similar principles, and placed on our picturesque river-banks.

Living on the shores of the Hudson, we are naturally
partial to picturesque architecture, and have studied its effects
with lively interest. In composing this design, we frankly
own our indebtedness to the architecture of the Rhine towns
for two features which distinguish it—the simple, square, high-
roofed tower and the twisted column. The general composition
of the design and the arrangement of the plan, of course,
belong wholly to our own habits in domestic life, and have
nothing to do with houses abroad.

We must call the attention of the reader to the combination
of power and domestic feeling in this villa—power in the high
roofs and gables, and especially in the lofty heavenward-
pointing tower, and domesticity in the peculiarly homelike look
of the wing on the right, with its twisted pillars, as well as in
the repetition of this latter expression in the porch and two
projecting windows.

There is something more than caprice in the "delicious
curve" of the roof which belongs to many of the Rhine
buildings, and which we have reproduced in this design. It
is, in fact, a repetition of the grand hollow or mountain curve
formed by the sides of almost all great hills rising from the
water's edge, and it forms the connecting link that unites
and brings into harmony the opposite lines, perpendicular and
horizontal, which are found, the one in the tower and the other
in the water or landscape level at its base. Hence, this
curved line of roof, seldom or never seen elsewhere, is always
satisfactory as well as beautiful in mountain architecture.

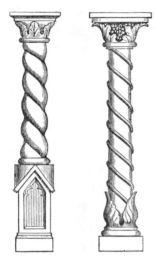

[Fig. 166. Twisted Pillars.]

A word, also, in behalf of the twist ed pillar, a feature common in the buildings of the middle ages, which classical architects have affected to despise, and which we are by no means willing to leave wholly to the other side of the Atlantic, or to be classed among barbarous things.

The twisted pillar, considered as a part of severe architecture—that is, the architecture of public buildings, is, we grant, wanting in strength and dignity. It has neither the grandeur nor the simplicity of the Greek column. But, as a part of domestic architecture, it has, rightly employed, a fitness and beauty peculiar to itself. It is not the fitness and beauty of the Greek column—as the beauty of the swan sailing on the peaceful lake is not that of the eagle poised in mid-air—though as undeniably and absolutely beautiful. Every outward material form is a symbol or expression of some-thing which is *not* matter, and which, rightly understood, gives us the key to the power with which that form, immediately and without reflection, acts upon the sense of beauty. Now, the twisted or wreathed column is the natural symbol or emblem of affectionate embrace—its type, almost pure and exact, may be found in every forest, in every thick dell or wooded valley. Wherever there is a twining vine or climber, that, obeying the law of its vital force, ascends in spiral lines around a naked stem or branch of a tree, there you have the twisted column.*

* Whoever has wandered in American woods must have seen in the spiral

It is the delicate, clinging for support to the strong—the frail, upheld by the powerful—in short, the poet's own type of affectionate, loving, trusting womanhood.

With this explanation of the meaning of the twisted pillar (which, so far as we know, has long waited for a champion), it will easily be seen that we are not among those who place it among the relics of a debased age in art. On the contrary, as we believe, it was first used by architects who worked with a fresher and more vital hold upon nature than most artists of the nineteenth century; we accept and adopt it as one of those recognitions of natural beauty rendered artistic, which will last as long as the sense of beauty lasts.

We have avoided, in the composition of this villa, all that difficult and elaborate detail which might have been introduced in a building in this style. The general spirit of the composition is pointed, without being strictly Gothic, and we have sought to produce effect by light and shade rather than intricate details. Hence, the windows (with the exception of a few in the upper portions, to preserve the spirit of the style) are simple recesses in the walls, deeply sunk, to give depth of shadow, and covered externally by the Venetian shutter-blinds, so essentially useful in this climate.

Not to be wearisome regarding our river villa, we would add that we hope the reader will find in it the expression of variety, independence and force of character, strong aspirations, and equally strong attachment to home and domestic life. As the residence of a man or family to whom such a character belongs, and built in a fittingly picturesque site, this villa would have

growth of the Bitter-sweet (*Celastrus scandens*) nature's own suggestion for the twisted or wreathed column.

a charm quite beyond the belief of those who know nothing of the effect of harmonious and spirited architecture.

ACCOMMODATION. The accommodation of this residence is spacious, handsome, and economical. The hall, 22 feet square, is itself a fine apartment, and communicates with the three other principal rooms in a very satisfactory manner. It is quite sufficiently lighted (for a hall should always be rather dark and low in tone, as compared with other rooms) by two narrow windows on either side of the porch. From this hall a door opens on the left into the *tower*, which contains a fine staircase, ascending with landings. On the right, another door opens upon a fine veranda, 10 feet wide and over 80 feet long, which entirely surrounds the north portion of the house containing the drawing-room.

We should prefer to light this drawing-room from two sides only, so as not to have cross lights—and for this reason we leave a blank wall, to be hung with pictures on one side. The semicircular or bow-window, 8 feet wide, is well-placed at the end of the room.

The library, 20 by 24 feet, is lighted by a large bay-window, which would have a good effect, if filled with stained glass of a quiet tone of color. There is a smaller bay-window on the side, in which should be a reading or window seat. The wood work in this room should be oak or black-walnut, and the bookcases should be recessed in the walls, as at *a, a,* and designed to accord in character with the style of the apartment.

The dining-room, 22 feet square, is chiefly lighted by a large transom window at the extremity. This room occupies the rear of the house, as there is less demand for a fine view in a dining room than in the other principal apartments. It is well situated with respect to the kitchen offices in the rear—being directly connected with them by a passage, which also communicates with pantry, china-closet, etc.

The arrangement of these four rooms (counting the hall as one) is somewhat similar to that in our own residence, and we have found it both convenient and beautiful. All the apartments may be thrown *en suite* by the connecting doors, or each may be rendered quite separate and distinct by closing these doors. The entrance-hall, if paved with marble or encaustic tiles, would be a most agreeable saloon in summer, opening as it does upon the porch and veranda, so that a circulation of air would always keep it cool in temperature.

To suit those who prefer disconnection and privacy in each of the different apartments, the plan may be varied by cutting off the communication between the dining-room and library on one side, and the dining-room and drawing-room on the other. This would make each room a more secluded and private apartment.

It will be seen by inspecting the plan, that the kitchen offices are conveniently situated, with respect to the dining-room. There is on the left of the dining-room a passage leading to the kitchen, and containing a back stair, at *b*. Alongside this passage are placed the pantry and china-closet. The kitchen is lighted on one side only, so as not to overlook the library window. Connected with it are the scullery and laundry, and there is also a separate porch alongside the kitchen.

This range of offices (which we have left indefinite) might be extended, so as to include carriage-house, barn, stable, etc., thus adding to the effect of the whole mass, and at the same time being more economical and convenient than having all the outbuildings detached, as is usually the case.

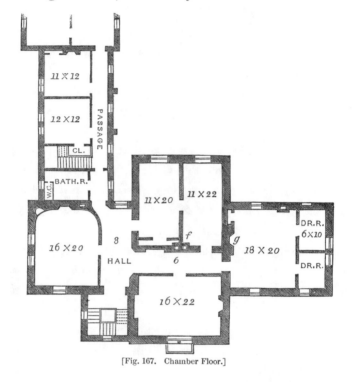

[Fig. 167. Chamber Floor.]

The accommodation of the chamber floor is shown in Fig. 167. There are here nine bed-rooms, one of which—the principal guest-chamber—has two dressing-rooms of large size. There is a bath-room, with water-closet attached. There are also servants' rooms in the attic, reached by the flight of stairs placed in the hall, 6 feet wide. The walls of the *main* partition being of stone, there is no difficulty in starting a flue at *g*, for that bed-room, or in carrying over (in the garret) all the flues of the principal rooms into two stacks, as shown in

the elevation. A smaller and lighter flight of stairs ascends in
the tower, from the chamber floor to the top, where there is an
apartment, 10 feet square, which may be the private *sanctum*
of the master of the house, or a general belvedere or "look-out"
for visitors, as the taste of the proprietor may lead him to
appropriate it.

CONSTRUCTION. To suit the picturesque character of this
design, it should be built of stone, in a manner exactly the
opposite to that shown in Design XXXI. The intention, there,
is to express artistic style and scientific nicety of construction;
here, it is to express character and picturesqueness. Common
quarry stone, that may be found in any hilly country, will best
answer for the walls of such a residence as this; and the effect
will be better, if only roughly dressed by the mason's hammer,
and even laid in random courses, than if cut with the chisel, and

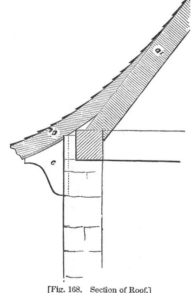

laid in smooth ashlar. The
walls should be 2 feet thick, the
foundations laid in hydraulic
lime, and the interior walls
firred off, so as effectually to
prevent all dampness.

To give the roof the curved
line shown in the elevation is
very easily done, as will be
seen by examining the section,
Fig. 168. In this, *a* is the
straight rafter, forming the
main roof; *b*, a curved piece,
spliced to the main rafter, and
projecting 2 feet beyond the

[Fig. 168. Section of Roof.]

wall; *c*, the bracket, supporting the projecting eaves. As the curved piece of false rafter is entirely covered by shingles above, and sealed on the under side, it may be cut out of good thick plank. The brackets, however, should either be of stone or of pieces of durable timber, six inches thick, built into the wall, so as to have the apparent strength and solidity of stone. The roof should be covered with best cedar shingles of large size.

The verge-board of the front gable, as well as that over the drawing-room, should be bold and heavy, so as to produce a rich and picturesque effect. It should be of carved plank, at least 2½ inches thick.

The first story of this house may be 13 feet between floors, the second 9 feet.

Estimate. If built in a district where the stone could be found on the site, and with the interior finished in a picturesque, but comparatively economical and effective manner, to correspond with the exterior, this villa might be erected for about $10,000. In the majority of hands, however, it would vary little in cost from $12,000.

DESIGN XXXIII.—*A Villa in the Romanesque Style, for the Middle or Southern States.*

THIS design is intended for the country-seat of a man of ample fortune, and for a site in the midst of highly-cultivated and beautiful scenery. It demands for " accessories," pleasure-grounds, lawns, and all that constitutes the embellished landscape of the finest country residences in America. Without costing a third of the sum expended at the present time in

Fig. 168

DESIGN XXXIII.

SOUTHERN VILLA.—ROMANESQUE STYLE.

several villas lately built upon the Hudson, it would give an abundant accommodation for all the requirements of our most refined social life.

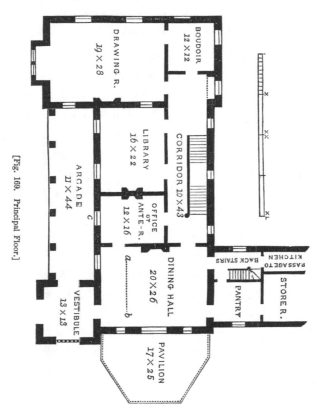

[Fig. 169. Principal Floor.]

Looking at the exterior of this design, the student of expression will find it marked by dignity, variety, and harmony; dignity in the solid entrance tower, and breadth of the façade; variety in the different outlines of pediment, horizontal cornice, and loftier campanile; and harmony in the predominance of the round arch and other features of the style chosen.

To analyze the expression more æsthetically, we would say that the composition of the exterior of this building equally denoted conservatism and *culture*—by which we mean a life in which the importance and preservation of the family name is largely valued ; in which the taste, the intellect, and the feelings are all developed ; in which intellectual accomplishments, and love of literature and the fine arts form a large part of the life and enjoyment of the inmates. We see refined culture symbolized in the round arch, with its continually recurring curves of beauty, in the spacious and elegant arcades, inviting to leisurely conversations, in all those outlines and details, suggestive of restrained and orderly action, as contrasted with the upward, aspiring, imaginative feeling indicated in the pointed or Gothic styles of architecture.

In calling this villa *Romanesque*, we only wish to be understood that we have gleaned from that style certain ideas of composition, which, appearing to us well suited for our purpose, we have adopted them in designing a country house suited to a first-class residence here. There are no Romanesque villas, properly so called, in southern Europe ; but the architecture which bears this name, and which flourished before the origin of Gothic architecture, which includes the Lombard, the Saxon, the Norman, and much of the Saracenic or Eastern modes of building, offers, as we think, a rich field of study for the architect who would work out of the materials of the past a new construction suited to the present. The prevalence of the round arch, of arcades, of intersecting arches, and of roofs higher than in the Grecian, but lower than in the Gothic styles, characterizes this architecture. Among the many fine examples from the fifth to the fifteenth century, there is, it is true, much

that is clumsy, debased, and unworthy of serious attention;
but there are also, especially in the beautiful details of door and
window decoration, and all that relates to interior embellishment, numerous examples of the most refined and artistic
treatment of forms and lines, in which the taste of some of the
Italian masters stands forth conspicuously by the side of later
Gothic art.   In short, without actually copying a single
example of Romanesque architecture, we think a student of
genius might, from a judicious study of it, elicit ideas that could
be more easily and harmoniously wrought into a new domestic
architecture of a classical character than those from any other
transatlantic source.

The Romanesque, as we would adopt the spirit of that style,
has, when contrasted with the modern Italian, more of that
quaintness, solidity, and rusticity which belong, properly, to
rural architecture.   While, therefore, we are well content with
Italian architecture, as scarcely capable of improvement, for
town houses or suburban villas, we think we see in Romanesque architecture good hints for a style of country residences,
that would be extremely well suited to the middle and southern
states.   The large, arched openings are well adapted to a
climate where every breath of air is needed in summer, and
the spacious veranda, added with some difficulty in other styles,
is here, in the shape of the arcade, a natural and appropriate
part of the edifice, as well as the most characteristic ornament
of both the Romanesque and Italian style.

Besides this, the Romanesque style is one particularly suited
to a material that will probably, ere long, come into more
general use than any other for country houses—brick.   All its
round arches, all its peculiar features, are so easily and so well

constructed of brick. Over the southern part of Europe, and
as far north as Berlin, the richest effects are produced by the
use of ornamental bricks, moulded so as to form beautiful
designs. These serve for the construction of cornices, window-
dressings, string-courses, etc. The manufacture of these ornamental bricks is just being commenced in New York, as well as
the beautiful *terra-cotta* ornaments which are so extensively
employed for the decoration of architectural façades in Italy
and Germany. With such materials, the most striking and
excellent effects may be produced in villas in the style of this
design—the entire walls being built of brick, at very moderate
cost, and being as durable, and, when properly colored, as
satisfactory to the eye as stone itself.

ACCOMMODATION. Before we examine the plan in detail, let
us remark that, in order to make a complete *Southern* house,
the kitchen should be detached 20 or 30 yards. In that case,
the plan would otherwise remain as it is; that is, it would retain
the store-room and pantry, but the *kitchen* would be placed at a
suitable distance, directly in the rear of the store-room.

If intended for the Middle States, the kitchen, etc., would
adjoin the store-room, much in the manner of Design XXXII.

Entering the vestibule of this villa (Fig. 169), it will be
seen that coolness and ventilation have been considered in
connection with spaciousness and breadth of effect. Standing
in the middle of the vestibule, the arcade extends to the
drawing-room, affording a broad and airy promenade, nearly
60 feet long, sheltered from sun and rain.

From the vestibule we enter the dining-hall, a handsome
apartment, 20 by 26 feet. If this hall were the only means of
access to the main staircase, the drawing-room, or other parts

of the house, we should object to its being used as a dining-room. But it is not. On the contrary, persons waiting in the vestibule for admittance, during meals, would be shown along the arcade into the office, or ante-room, if upon business ; or into the drawing-room or boudoir, if paying visits—as the windows, *c*, communicating with this arcade, are casement windows opening to the floor, like doors. Or, in winter, a handsome *movable screen* placed, as at *a.....b*, in the dining-hall, during meals, would shut off the table temporarily, and allow a passage for the visitor into the ante-room.

We like the custom of dining in an ample hall like this, in a large country house, for it enables us to give to the hall itself a character of spaciousness (by thus uniting the uses of two apartments), which dining-rooms rarely have, and it allows a certain breadth of effect and simple grandeur of treatment which makes such a hall the most expressive feature of a country house—characteristically decorated, as it should be, with antlers, with fine specimens of the growth of the fields and forests, and magnificent nosegays of fresh flowers. The floor of such a hall should by all means be bare (or only covered in the centre under the dining-table), and paved or inlaid with ornamental tiles, or native woods of different colors.

On the right of this hall is a noble veranda, which, for want of a better name, we call the *pavilion*. To a Southern house, this would be the greatest necessity, besides adding much to the architectural beauty of the house ; for, in fact, such a pavilion would be the lounging place, *conversazione*, and often dining-room itself, since it would be the coolest, airiest, and most agreeable part of the house during a certain part of the day. In summer, this pavilion, or its shadow,

would give a softened light to the dining-hall, while the large
windows, thrown open to the floor, between the two, would make
the dining-room fresh and pleasant in the most sultry days.
To vary the uses of the pavilion, we will only suggest that, the
dinner being over, the dessert might be served there, and the
dessert being concluded, gentlemen addicted to the soothing
indulgence of a fragrant "Havana," would find the pavilion
the best of smoking apartments, after the ladies had retired to
the drawing-room.

Even in the Middle States, the enjoyment of a large pavilion
of this kind is very great during four months of the year. The
only example that we have seen of such an appendage to the
house is at Montgomery Place—one of the finest seats on the
Hudson, where it is placed on the drawing-room side of the
house, and at once impresses every visitor by its combination
of beauty, dignity, and utility. In short, although this feature
may be omitted, without materially diminishing the beauty or
convenience of this design, its adoption would give a completeness and significance to a first-rate country house like this;
completeness, since it affords something more than a veranda
viz. a *room in the open air*, the greatest luxury in a warm sum
mer; significance, since it tells the story of a desideratum grow
ing out of our climate, architecturally and fittingly supplied.

From the dining-hall, on the side opposite the pavilion, we
enter the *corridor*—a long hall, containing the principal
staircase, and opening into all the other apartments. This
corridor being 10 feet wide, with a broad and massive stair,
would have a handsome and spacious appearance; and if the
walls were thrown into panels by the intersecting arches,
characteristic of the Romanesque style, it would, from its length

and relative position to the rooms, be one of the most striking parts of the house.

The first room on the left of this corridor is the *office*, ante-room, or gentleman's own room—a very necessary and useful apartment, especially in country houses upon large estates, or those belonging to professional men in the habit of receiving business calls at their residences. Indeed, there are few large country houses where the want of some such an apartment, into which all persons who call upon business may be shown, is not sensibly felt. Devoting this room to such a purpose, we would have an iron safe for valuable papers, built into the wall, on one side of the fireplace, and a bookcase and writing-table should be constructed, to fill up the corresponding space on the other side.

Next to the office is the *library*. This should have no connection with the office, because the latter should be comparatively private. Indeed, when the drawing-room, as in this house, is so large as not to render it needful to connect it with adjoining apartments, we would close up the door indicated between it and the library. The library then would be a retired and secluded room—more, perhaps, in keeping with its uses. But this matter of connection or privacy of the different apartments is a matter of personal preference. The continental taste is for suites of rooms, all connected— like Design XXXII.; while the English, on the contrary, prefer that privacy and seclusion in most of the principal rooms, which may be had in this residence.

Of the *drawing-room*, we need say little. A large apartment like this, 19 by 28 feet, looking on the lawn upon two sides, connected by a glass door with the arcade at one end and the corridor at the other, so well disposed as regards light, prospect, and connection with the rest of the house, could not fail, if well treated, to produce a very satisfactory and beautiful effect.

Besides this spacious drawing-room, the ladies of this residence would have a more cosy reception-room in the *boudoir* at the end of the corridor. This little apartment being the ladies' own room, may be treated with a fancifulness and delicacy of decoration that the more spacious drawing-room would forbid, and, in the hands of a lady of taste, may be made the most charmingly feminine and attractive apartment in the house.

The eye of the domestic economist will not overlook the wing, in Fig. 169, extending in the rear of the dining-hall, which contains the kitchen offices. Here are the back stairs, the butler's pantry, the store-room, and the passage to the kitchen. We have not indicated the kitchen itself, because, as we have before mentioned, in a Southern house this would be *detached*. But, if built in the Middle States, the kitchen, laundry, scullery, etc., would extend this wing of the house some 25 or 30 feet beyond what is shown in the plan, adding exteriorly, at the same time, to the good effect of the whole composition.

The plan of the second floor, Fig. 170, will be easily understood. It contains 7 bed-rooms and 2 large dressing-rooms, that might occasionally be used as bed-rooms. The apartments for servants are supposed to be placed over the kitchen wing, and there may also be two or more good servants' bed-rooms over the drawing-room.

In the large dressing-room, 13 by 13 feet, there is a light and pretty staircase, rising to the apartment in the upper part of the tower. This latter apartment, a charming prospect gallery

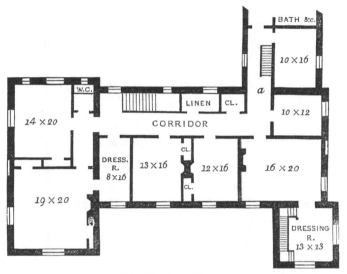

[Fig. 170. Second Floor.]

or belvedere in a country of varied scenery, would be a very agreeable feature; hence, the bed-room, 16 by 20, connected with the dressing-room below, might be the "state bed-room," with both dressing-room and belvedere attached to it.

At the end of the long corridor is a water-closet (W. C.), and at the opposite extremity, beyond the back stairs, a, is a large bath-room, etc.

CONSTRUCTION. Of course, this villa would require solid materials, to give the proper effect to the style adopted. Walls of light-colored free-stone would, perhaps, be the most satisfactory, but brick and stucco would be far cheaper for the Middle or Southern states, and the effect nearly as good. We, however, would prefer to build the whole of brick,* as we have

---

* Of course, colored externally, of an agreeable hue.

already suggested, with the details of windows, doors, and arcades, ornamented with moulded bricks, and enriched with terra-cotta decorations, built into the solid walls.   In this way, a rich and striking effect would be produced for a reasonable sum ; while brown stone would add a third more to the cost.— even if used, as it now is, chiefly as *facings* to the walls.

It is needless to give details for a building of this kind, as any person desiring to adopt the plan would of course consult a competent architect for the working drawings.   We may remark, however, that it would not be difficult, in a style like this, to give a distinctly American or local expression to all the architectural decoration, so that the whole villa would be felt to

have a national character about it.   To take the arcade, for example : the capitals of the columns might be formed of the foliage and ear of Indian corn, for which our sketch here given, Fig. 171, may serve as a hint.   Capitals of columns, like this design, might be cast in terra-cotta, at a very trifling expense, and produce a very pleasing effect.   By the introduction, in an artistic manner, of the cotton, the tobacco, the magnolia, and other characteristic forms of

[Fig. 171. Design for a new Capital.]   foliage and flowers in the decorative parts of such a building, a novel and beautiful character would be given to the architecture, which every American would feel to have more meaning here than the zig-zag or billet-moulding of the Northern, or the more classical ornaments of the Southern Romanesque style, as it is seen in Europe.

Nothing can exceed the richness of some of the window-dressings of the Romanesque edifices of the south of Europe.

Merely to copy these for villa architecture would, of course, be out of keeping, since they were originally designed for edifices of a public character, where the most elaborate decoration was called for. But new compositions, in the more simple mode, adapted to private residences, and with forms and materials taken from the nature and life around us, could be made by an architect of genius, in a manner that would unite the beauty of the old and the significance of the new, so as to produce the happiest effects.

Estimate. It is difficult to say, precisely, what would be the cost of this villa, without going into greater detail than our limits allow respecting the execution of both the interior and exterior. Neither do we know enough of the cost of building at the South to say what the average expense of construction would be there. In this part of the Middle States where we write, however, assuming the walls to be built of good hard brick (worth $6 per 1000), treated in the manner we have suggested, and the interior finished in a consistent and complete manner—the first story 14 feet, and the second 11 feet high—the cost of the whole would not vary much from $14,000.

SECTION XI.

INTERIOR FINISHING OF COUNTRY HOUSES.

EVERY tasteful dwelling-house which may be considered architectural, exhibits, in the composition of its exterior, certain predominant forms or lines, which give it architectural character—and which constitute what is called the style—as Grecian, Gothic, etc. This we have, in some degree, made familiar to our readers, by the exhibition of views of the exteriors of country residences of different classes, and it now remains for us to consider briefly the subject of *interiors*.

It is almost needless to remark here, that a certain manner of treating a subject architecturally, which we call style, and which is nothing more than making the same general spirit of composition pervade all the lines and forms, may be exhibited in the smallest details, as well as the boldest outlines of a building; that it governs the form and proportion of the least moulding upon a table, as well as the strongest lines of tower or roof.

Granting this fact, and coupling with it the circumstance that a long series of years has accumulated, in all the well-defined styles of architecture, a wealth of decorative forms ready for use, it will readily be seen that the province of the architect does not cease with designing the general plan and exterior of any building, but that he should carry out the same spirit or style in all parts of the edifice. A building in which this is done throughout, has a great advantage over one where the style is only manifested on the outside; that advantage, in short, which every thing in art or nature has, where we find unity and harmony pervading every portion of the entire work, and where we see that there is clearly no surface delusion, but an intelligent unity reigning over the whole.

Now this complete expression of style in all parts of a building may be manifested, in a greater or less degree, in proportion to the character of the building, and the number and elaborateness of the details.

Hence, that elaborate exhibition of style, which is befitting many public buildings, is out of keeping with domestic architecture; hence, much of the intricate ornamentation which is bestowed on town residences, is not called for in country houses; and hence, much of the decoration which would be in good taste 'in a villa or country house of the first class, would be unsuitable and out of keeping in a cottage or plain farm-house. *Fitness* and *truthfulness*, if one will only listen to the judgment as well as the feelings, will speedily bring us back to sound principles on this head.

Still, even in very modest cottages, there are certain simple lines and forms, indicative of particular styles of building, which may be introduced, with no more cost—provided the workmen who execute the plans are familiar with them—than any other simple lines and forms. A degree of cultivation is necessary, perhaps, to enable us to appreciate all the enjoyment which grows out of this attention to details; but, as it is a large and enduring source of pleasure, it should receive attention in all country houses of considerable importance. We shall therefore offer a few hints, under two separate heads, for the interior finishing of country houses.

I. COTTAGE INTERIORS.   Of course, in most of the small cottages in this country, every thing like *decoration* in the interiors would be uncalled for.   Still, the forms of the windows and doors, the lines in the cornice (if there is one), and the mouldings of the wainscot or wood-work, will give an agreeable impression, if they show that the style indicated on the outside is consistently carried out within.

The manner of finishing the window and door casings, internally, gives as much character to the interior of a simple cottage as any other feature.   It does not follow that windows need be pointed, to be Gothic, and round to be Italian, though such are highly characteristic forms of windows in these styles; but mouldings comparatively flat and broad always indicate the finish of the classical styles, and mouldings rather thick and projecting, the pointed styles.   In all cottage interiors, the casings or architraves of the windows and doors should be very simple; but they may be made correct as cheaply as incorrect. It is well, therefore, for the proprietor to know, that while a cottage in the Italian or bracketed style may have architraves or casings six inches wide, with a plain back moulding on the outer edge, a cottage in the Gothic style should not have architraves more than half that width—indeed, the effect is better, generally, in the latter style, when the architrave is no wider than the moulding which covers it.

Every carpenter and joiner in the country who undertakes to build cottages, should provide himself with *planes*, to form mouldings of different styles, since it is as easy to finish the wood-work of a cottage correctly as incorrectly. There are few persons about building cheap cottages, who go to an architect for working drawings of the interior—hence, the greater necessity of some knowledge and attention on the part of those mechanics actually constructing such cottages.

The most satisfactory wood-work or wainscot for the interior of a cottage is that composed of the native wood of the district where the house is built—such as maple, birch, ash, black-walnut, or oak. This requires no painting, simply a coat or two of varnish, and the effect is excellent. But, in most cases, the extra cost of working hard wood will render its employment rare in economical cottages. As a substitute, however, we would strongly recommend that the wood-work be either grained, in imitation of these woods, or, in the cheapest cottages, *stained*, to have the same effect (see page 184).

The great advantage which grained wood-work has over that which is simply painted white or any plain neutral tint is, that it is so easily kept clean. The surface of painted wood is always somewhat rough, and catches dirt readily, and white-lead (or other light shades of which it is the base) always oxidizes or changes color, more or less. The grained surface, on the contrary, being made smooth by varnishing, does not readily become soiled, and when it does, a moment's application of a damp cloth will make all clean and bright:—while, if the same surface were painted only, it would require frequent and most vigorous scrubbing by the house-maid, to restore it to its original condition. Every one who has made a trial of grained or stained and varnished wood-work, will agree with us that it is great economy of time and labor in housekeeping, while the addition to the cost of plain painting is very trifling.

Ash, maple, birch, and oak are the best woods to imitate in graining a cottage. Black-walnut, if not too dark, has an excellent effect. But both that peculiarly yellow oak, which many painters like (and which, as frequently seen, is a better imitation of molasses-candy than of the wood of a tree), as well as a very sombre hue, should be avoided in the wood-work of cottages—where the general effect should be lively and cheerful.

We have said nothing of the great assistance of grained wood-work in making a room look *furnished*—with but little furniture—a point, sometimes, of no trifling importance.

The *interior walls* of a cottage have much to do with the impression that the rooms make upon the eye. There are several modes of treating them, but the most common are whitewashing and papering.

Whitewashing. The majority of cheap cottages have the walls of all the rooms finished with two or three coats of lime and sand, and afterwards whitewashed. This has the advantage of cheapness, and in cottages that are severely used, an annual whitewashing is the readiest and most complete mode of putting all in order, and making every thing " sweet and clean."

Where a better effect than that of a mere white wall is desired, it is easily obtained by coloring the ceiling white, and the side walls of a delicate neutral tint—such as fawn, or drab, or gray. The addition of a little blue-black (or very finely powdered charcoal) to the whitewash will produce a gray ; add to this a little raw umber, and the result is a drab ; or mix a little blue-black, Indian red, and yellow ochre, and you have a fawn color. The extra cost of these tints for a room 14 feet square will, perhaps, be 15 cents—and the superiority of effect, to those who are not fond of the intolerable glare of white, is incalculable.

All whitewash is improved and rendered much more fixed or permanent for interior walls by the addition of a little *size* just before using it—say two quarts of thin size to nearly a pailful of whitewash. The best size for this purpose is made of shreds of glove-leather, but any clean size of good quality will do for common use.

Papering. We confess a strong partiality for the use of paper-hangings for covering the walls of all cottages. In some countries—England, for example—papered walls are objectionable, on account of their retaining dampness in a moist climate. But in the United States, there is no complaint of this kind.

The great advantage of papering the walls, lies chiefly in the beauty of effect, and cheerful, cottage-like expression, which may be produced at very little cost; in its lasting from half a dozen to a dozen years (depending on the treatment it receives), when it is easily renewed—not requiring annual attention, like whitewashed walls; and lastly, but mainly, in the enhanced architectural effect which may be given to a plain room, by covering the walls with paper of a suitable style.

And this leads us to remark, that within a couple of years, cheap patterns of paper have been introduced, exactly suited to the walls of cottages, in various styles of architecture—such as Gothic, Italian, Grecian, etc. Some of these are plain, with only panels and cornices printed on them—giving the room in which they are placed a simple and elegant effect; others present the appearance of the graining of oak wainscot, and are particularly well suited to the entry or living-room of a cottage, or to whole interiors of cottages in the Gothic style; and others, again, are tastefully enriched by panelling and chaste artistic decoration.*

If these papers are varnished after they are thoroughly dry, they may be washed like a painted wall, without injury, so that they will last twenty years or more without renewal. And some papers are now made with a surface ready varnished, to answer this purpose.

The mode of treating cottage walls now most in favor, is that of papering the principal rooms and best bed-rooms, and whitewashing the kitchen, inferior passages, and bed-rooms.

A *cornice* adds very considerably to the architectural character of any room, though it is seldom or never introduced in cheap cottages, except, perhaps, in a parlor or best rooms. When the walls are papered, its place is in a good degree supplied by the border, representing a cornice on the paper itself.

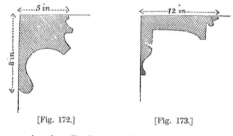

[Fig. 172.]   [Fig. 173.]

Fig. 172 is a section (scale $\frac{1}{2}$ inch to a foot) of a simple cornice of plaster for cottages in any modified Grecian or Italian forms; Fig. 173 is suitable for cottages in the Gothic style.

The walls of cottages are seldom *painted in oil*, because, in

---

* In selecting papers for cottages and for small dwellings, good taste will lead us to reject all showy and striking patterns, however beautiful in themselves—because they are out of keeping with the modest character of the cottage. Simple patterns —and those, if possible, which have some architectural expression accordant with that of the cottage—are most satisfactory.

order to do this, they should be "hard-finished," that is, the last coat should be laid on with plaster of Paris—common lime and sand walls absorbing oil colors rapidly. As it costs less to paper a room with tasteful architectural paper than to hard-finish it, and as the effect of the paper is much more cheerful and agreeable in a small room, we greatly prefer to use paper. When, however, hard walls are introduced, they should always be accompanied with a cornice—both to heighten the character of the room architecturally, and to lessen the baldness of plain walls.

The *floors* of the better cottages in this country—at least, in the Northern States—are universally covered with carpet or matting. A very good effect is produced, especially in the entry and living-room, by using narrow matched floor-plank, of good quality, and *staining* every other plank of a dark color, like black-walnut. This may be done with diluted sulphuric acid, or with the stain mentioned in page 184.

Afterwards, give the floor a coat of linseed oil, and it will have a good appearance, and save the cost of oil-cloths or carpets.

It will be seen that an agreeable effect in cottage interiors is to be produced chiefly by arrangement of colors and the selection of furniture. Still, as we have before remarked that a few simple lines may indicate a certain style of architecture, it is plain that the most satisfactory cottage interior will be that in which there is an obvious reason as well as beauty in the preference given to certain lines and forms, which appear there. It not only shows that select forms and lines have been chosen, but also forms and lines expressive of certain acknowledged modes of beautiful composition.

We may add another word as to the arrangement of colors.

The best effect in rooms of small size (or, indeed, of any size) is produced by having the ceiling lightest, the side walls a little darker, the wood-work a shade darker still, and the carpet darkest of all.

There are few persons living in cottages who can afford to indulge a taste for pictures. But there are, nevertheless, many in this country, who can afford engravings or plaster casts, to decorate at least one room in the house. Nothing gives an air of greater refinement to a cottage than good prints or engravings hung upon its parlor walls. In selecting these, avoid the trashy, colored show-prints of the ordinary kind, and choose engravings or lithographs, after pictures of celebrity by ancient or modern masters.* The former please but for a day, but the latter will demand our admiration forever. Next to prints of this kind, medallion casts, in plaster, of celebrated antique subjects—one or two feet in diameter—are fine objects to hang upon the walls, and may now be had in the cities for a small sum. It is no mean or trifling part of our worship of the Deity to cultivate a daily love for those beautiful forms in art which human genius has revealed and made permanent for us, the study of which will, next to a higher worship, most tend to purify our hearts and lives.

As regards the furniture of cottages, it can scarcely be too simple, too chaste, too unpretending in its character. It has been the crying sin of all cottage interiors, until very lately, that they were filled with cockney furniture—fine mahogany chairs and sofas—the same patterns which the city cabinet-

---

* Messrs. Goupel, Vibert & Co., Broadway, New York, offer the largest collection of fine prints in the country.

makers supplied their town customers with. It is too fine and too town-bred for amiable association with country lives and habits. We congratulate the cabinet-makers on the new light which has dawned upon them in the matter of "cottage furniture"—which is now afforded in all our principal cities, of pretty forms and at moderate prices—so that one can furnish a cottage in the country, at short notice, without having it look as if it had been stuffed with chairs and tables sent up from a town house five times its size.

There is still another feature in the interior of cottages which has a great deal to do with bestowing an air of taste and refinement on its best apartments. We mean *window-curtains*.

Next to carpets, which are universal in all but the dwellings of the very poor in America, nothing "furnishes" a room so much as curtains to the windows; and this, not merely because they take away from the bareness of plain casings and subdue the glare of light, but because there are always pleasing and graceful lines in the folds of hanging drapery—even of the plainest materials. Although the drapery of cottage windows comes more especially within the province of feminine taste than within that of the architect, we shall nevertheless venture a hint or two on the subject, if only to lead them to believe that it is not all a matter of fancy. The French, among all people, have the best taste in the management of curtains, because they have both a natural and a cultivated taste for dress and the arrangement of drapery. And we notice a growing development in the same direction in our countrywomen.

In the first place, we may remark, that as all country houses are furnished with shutter-blinds, either fixed to the outside or the inside of the windows, and as coolness and airiness are the

most desirable things from May to November, curtains are little
used or to be desired in summer.   On the other hand, the
coldness of the air, and bright sun of winter, render curtains
particularly grateful for protection from currents of air and
from glare of light.   For the plainest cottages, therefore, one
would use chintz, which may be had for a few cents a yard,
and which, if selected with regard to harmonizing in color
with the carpet and walls, will always produce a pretty effect,
at very little cost.   Printed cottons are also manufactured for
this purpose, with separate borders, that may be sewed on, to
heighten the effect.   For a better kind of curtain, moreens, of
single colors—browns, drabs, crimsons, or blues—may be used,
which, though more expensive, are more durable than cotton.

The simplest and most architectural mode of arranging
cottage curtains is, to hang them from a projecting cornice of
wood, fixed to the top of the window.   This should project a
few inches from the wall, so as to allow the drapery or valance
which forms the upper part of the curtain to be tacked to its
inner side—or, which is better, to a narrow strip of wood,
which is itself tacked to the inside of the cornice.   This
cornice should be formed of a moulding similar to that of the
room, or, in other words, it should have a Gothic moulding
for a Gothic cottage, or a Grecian moulding for a dwelling in
any classical style.   If the wood-work of the cottage is stained
or grained, in imitation of oak, black-walnut, or any other
wood, then the cornice of the curtain should correspond to it,
or, otherwise, to the color of the wood-work of the room.
The sketch, Fig. 174, shows a Gothic window-curtain, in
which *a* is the cornice, *b* the drapery or valance, *c* the
curtains.   In order to change the style to Italian, it will only

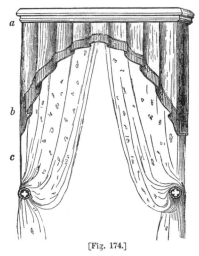

[Fig. 174.]

be necessary to use a carved or classical moulding for the wooden cornice, and cut the lower part of the drapery, *b*, in a round arch, instead of a pointed one; or, if the cottage is Grecian, then the cornice should show Grecian mouldings, and the lower edge of the drapery should extend two-thirds or all the way across in a horizontal line.

The cornice itself may be fastened to the head of the window-casing with screws, so as to be taken down at pleasure, and the curtains, *c*, may either be fastened to the inner side of it with tacks, or, which is better, they may run on a small rod by brass rings, all concealed by the cornice.

Inside *roller-blinds* are very useful in many situations, to soften the light in apartments, when the windows are much exposed to the sun. The best blinds of this description are made of plain brown or drab linen. Nothing can be more vulgar and tawdry for a country house than most of the transparencies and painted curtains which we sometimes see used in this way. If they are badly painted, as is generally the case, they are only an offence to cultivated taste; if they are well painted, with copies of landscapes, etc., they are not good, in the sense of pictures, while they only hide, nine times in ten, a more interesting view of the real landscape without. Such specimens of the arts as these may be tolerated in towns, as they awaken a sentiment of nature in the midst of brick walls, but are unworthy of the least toleration in a country house.

II. VILLA INTERIORS. Country houses are often built in a plain and simple manner, which, without showing a strongly marked architectural style, either upon the exterior or interior, yet produce a very pleasing effect, through a general prevalence of pleasing lines and harmonious colors. This is more especially the case, if there is manifested throughout an essentially rural and home-like character.

Of course, the larger number of our country houses will come under this denomination—because it is rarely the case in any country, that rural buildings exhibit elaborate architectural style. It requires the hand of the artist to produce and carry out, in all the details of an edifice, that peculiar treatment of lines and forms throughout all the principal features of a building which is called style; and, of course, the larger number of country houses are built without the aid of an architect, and, while they may be tasteful, expressive, and picturesque, they are rarely faultless specimens of style.

It cannot be denied, however, that there is a certain charm in style, whether it is applied to the composition of a book or a house. The same facts or materials shall be so treated by one author or architect as to be confused and unsatisfactory, or tame and insipid, while they shall come from the hands of another endowed with a freshness, beauty, power, and completeness, that render them capable of awakening emotions of continual delight. And as there are, among writers, the dramatic, the serious, the narrative, and the didactic styles, each peculiarly adapted to the expression of certain modes of thought and life, so there are the Grecian, the Italian, the

Gothic, the Romanesque, and other styles—each peculiarly capable of manifesting certain mental temperaments or organizations, or of harmonizing with certain tastes in the life of the individual.

When one builds a simple and plain country house, in which there is no attempt at architectural style, good sense and good taste are at least never violated. But, unfortunately, nothing is more common than the love of imitation; and when either persons of uncultivated tastes, or ignorant architects, attempt to decorate dwellings after certain styles which they have somewhere seen, and, perhaps, make a jumble of two or three styles in the same building, a result is produced as incongruous as that of hearing a friend read alternate pages of Shakspeare, Prescott, and Jonathan Slick. The great charm which we find in a house where beauty and convenience are combined with that kind of artistic treatment which is called style, is, that the whole has a certain *unity of design*, which shows that, from the smallest to the greatest feature, all has been the result of one harmonious plan; that it has been produced by a mind working consistently throughout, adjusting and arranging all with a purpose, both of beauty and utility—not by a mind full of odd caprices and whimsical fancies—sometimes producing good effects, and sometimes detestable combinations.

The difference between architectural style, and a *fashion* of finishing and fitting up apartments, cannot, perhaps, be better or more briefly pointed out than it has already been done by a clever French artist*—who has, in the following words, indicated clearly that style is that decoration of a subject, based upon its internal spirit or organization; fashion, on the other

---

* Quatremère de Quincy.

hand, transferring into its fancy for the hour, whatever falls in its way, without regard to its internal character.

" Construction is to buildings what bones are to the human body ; it ought to be embellished, without being entirely concealed. *It is the construction which,* according to the climate, the country, the sort of edifice, *gives the motive* for the ornaments ; and, if this connection does not appear, the whole is vicious. The execution of the work, whatever may be its extent and importance, will have no effect on the mind [judgment], if the construction has not dictated the embellishment ; if the first form does not seem in accordance with its accessories ; and if, in short, it is perceived that two wills, without harmonizing together, have operated in the execution of the work."

Hence the folly of adopting, internally, the ornaments which belong to a perpendicular style, as the Gothic, in finishing the rooms of a villa which is built in a horizontal style, like the Grecian. Reason teaches us that the construction and the decoration are at variance, and that the treatment is false.

Out of this perception of the unity of purpose in the builder or designer, grows also the pleasure we often experience, even in comparatively simple cottages, where we find every line and form, however plain and unpretending, has been selected with that nice sense of adaptation and fitness to each other which makes a complete and harmonious whole.

Considering this branch of the subject as one of importance, we therefore propose to offer a few suggestions—sufficient to give the novice some general ideas of the treatment of interiors in different styles. Pursued into detail, this part of our subject is an almost endless one in itself. But we do not intend to

PLAIN INTERIOR, GRECIAN STYLE.

Fig. 175.

DINING ROOM—ITALIAN STYLE.

Fig. 176.

dwell minutely upon it, partly because, to carry out a style in an elaborate manner, requires more study than the amateur or proprietor, for whom this work is chiefly written, can give it; and, partly, because we think those simple modifications of the different styles which are easily understood, are the most suitable for the interiors of country houses.

The Grecian Style. This style is almost too familiar to the eyes of our readers to need any explanation. Fig. 175 is the interior of a large parlor in a country house in this style— finished in a very plain but characteristic manner. The unbroken horizontal cornice, and the prevalence of straight lines, with a few bold classical mouldings, are what chiefly mark the style here. The ceiling is often left wholly plain, or ornamented with a centre-piece of foliage; but throwing it into panels, indicative of the construction, in the way shown in the figure, relieves the bare expanse in a large room very happily. To go a step further, the ceiling may be intersected at right angles, to throw the few long panels into numerous square ones, and a still higher step would be to decorate the borders of the panels with Grecian mouldings.

The arrangement of the pictures, with reference to the doors and windows, in this apartment, is indicative of the style. A very simple and expressive effect is produced, where there are no pictures, by dividing the wall in panels (precisely in the forms indicated by the frames of the pictures), either by forming the panels in the plaster, or painting panels in the walls themselves. As the latter is a very simple, effective, and cheap mode, it is that usually adopted in country houses. In particular rooms, where a lighter or more elegant decoration is wanted, the centre of each panel may be filled with a bas-relief, a classical device, or a group of flowers painted on the wall.

When, however, decoration is carried to this length upon the walls, the architraves of the doors must also be correspond ingly enriched, so that all portions shall be in keeping.

The Grecian moulding—such as the ovolo, cyma, covetto, torus, astragal, etc.—are familiar to all builders, and need not be further noticed here. The peculiar characteristic of the Grecian mouldings is, that they are formed of portions of the *ellipsis*. Some of the Grecian ornaments, as the egg and dart moulding, and the classic honeysuckle, stand alone for artistic beauty, though their indefinite multiplication at the present day, in all manner of buildings, has somewhat deadened the eye to their fine proportions.

The Italian Style. The new element of beauty introduced into the style called Italian is the use of the circle, subordinate to, and contrasting with, the horizontal or straight line. This is seen, chiefly, in the round arch, which appears in the doors and windows. There is also far greater latitude and variety in the ornaments of the different modes of the Italian architecture— including the Florentine, Venetian, and French under this head—than in the purely classical style. It addresses itself more to the feelings and the senses, and less to the reason or judgment, than the Grecian style, and it is also capable of a variety of expression quite unknown to the architecture of the five orders. Hence, we think it far better suited to sym bolize the variety of refined culture and accomplishment which belongs to modern civilization than almost any other style.

A room in the Italian style, see Fig. 176, may be compara- tively simple, or it may permit the utmost luxury of decoration, as in some of the modern French examples, known as the Louis XV. or Louis XIV. styles. In our example, the style is recognized in the large arched opening of the bay-window, in the secondary treatment of the arch in the doors, in the mouldings, and in the coved ceiling. The interlacing or trellis stucco-work on the ceiling gives richness to that part of the wall, but it is more frequently omitted, and the ceiling only diversified by a central group of foliage.

A beautiful feature, and a strictly appropriate one in the decoration of Italian columns, is the introduction of works of art. Among these, bas-reliefs and vases may be considered as strictly architectural. Circular bas-reliefs, well cast in plaster, and inserted in the walls (like that over the sideboard, Fig. 176), afford a fine mode of giving interest and beauty to bare walls at little cost; and where more means are used, a very noble species of decoration is obtained, by extending a continuous bas-relief, as a frieze, 18 inches or 2 feet wide, just below the cornice, and quite round the room.*

Vases supported on brackets against the wall have also a rich effect, and many beautiful forms in Italian, Etruscan, or Roman taste may be had now at moderate cost, either in metal, porcelain, or terra-cotta. Many forms of these may now be had of terra-cotta—a material not only cheap, but especially suitable for country houses, in design and execution. Among these we may notice hanging flower-baskets, as shown in the large window of Fig. 176, and a larger view of which is

---

* A complete set of the cast of Thorwaldsen's famous " Triumph of Alexander," one of the finest things in modern art, forming the entablature to a room 18 by 20 feet, may be had at the present time in New York for about $150.

[Fig. 177.   Hanging Terra-Cotta Basket.]

given in Fig. 177. For bay-windows, these are admirably adapted, and their effect, when filled with flowers, is extremely pretty.

Of the modern French style, now so much admired and so much adopted in our town houses, we do not offer any specimens, because, except, perhaps, for a lady's boudoir or a drawing-room, we are not greatly in favor of any considerable use of it in country houses. It is a modification of the Italian, distinguished by curved and flowing lines, and a profusion of delicate ornaments in relief, producing a very ornate and elegant effect, but rather too ornate to be strictly in keeping with rural architecture. When French furniture is introduced, the apartments should be sufficiently enriched to correspond with it in character.

The mouldings used in interior finishing of the Italian style are sections of the circle, and, having more relief than the flatter mouldings of the Grecian style, are capable of bolder effect, even when used in plain and simple forms.

The Gothic Style. The distinguishing characteristics of this style in interior finish are the prevalence of perpendicular lines, and the introduction, in all important openings, of the pointed arch, together with the use of the bold and deep mouldings that belong to its ornamental portions.

There are several modifications of the pointed or Gothic

style. The ecclesiastical Gothic, for example, with its high, pointed arch, the Tudor Gothic, with a low, flat arch, and later modifications, in which most of the window and door openings are square-headed, either with the low spandril of the Tudor arch, placed beneath it, or the style only indicated by the

[Fig. 178. Interior in a simple Gothic Style.]

mouldings. In Fig. 178, the bay-window opening at the end of the parlor, in this style, shows the Tudor arch, and the side window, a square-headed window, with the style recognized by the introduction of the arch in the wood-work of the architrave. To our own feeling, there is more *domesticity* in the square-headed window, and we would therefore only introduce the arch, in the doors and windows of private houses, in particular cases, when the stronger indication of style is needed to give spirit to the composition.

The ceilings of rooms in the Gothic style are not treated as if supported on horizontal beams, as in the classical styles, because the principle of support is supposed to be perpendicular. Hence, the ceiling is traversed by *ribs*, running down and resting on brackets, so as to convey the idea of vertical support. The cornice itself is not deep and heavy, as in the Italian or Grecian style, but similar to the ribs—being formed, in fact, by a continuation of the same or corresponding mouldings round the angles of the ceiling. Figs. 178 and 179 are both examples of the usual treatment of Gothic rooms in this style. The former is only a sketch, for illustration, of a neat and simple style of finishing the parlor of a substantial house. Fig. 179 represents the interior of the drawing-room at Kenwood, the seat of J. Rathbone, Esq., near Albany, New York.

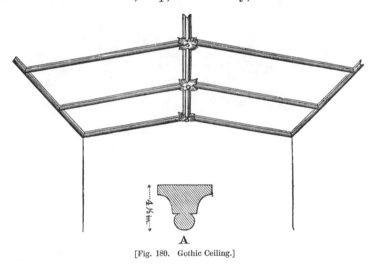

A.

[Fig. 180. Gothic Ceiling.]

A very characteristic and excellent mode of treating ceilings in this style is shown in Fig. 180, which is a sketch from the rooms on the principal floor of the residence of the author. The ceiling, instead of being flat, is formed here by two inclined planes, rising 10 inches from the sides to the centre—

DRAWING ROOM AT KENWOOD—GOTHIC STYLE.

Fig. 179.

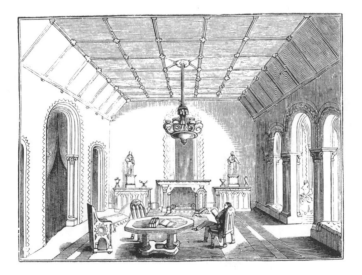

INTERIOR IN THE NORMAN STYLE.

Fig. 182.

a form easily and cheaply produced, by *firring-down* from the beams above by pieces of plank, sawn in the form of a wedge. On these the laths are nailed, and the ribs run in plaster in the usual way. The form of the rib is shown at A. The cost of a ceiling in this way does not exceed that with a common heavy Grecian cornice.

The superior effect of this ceiling arises, partly, from its carrying the eye upwards, and thus recognizing the principle of perpendicular rather than horizontal support, as well as causing it to appear higher than it really is; and, also, from a certain airy lightness, found in a ceiling in which the lines rise, however slightly, but never in one entirely flat.

The ceilings of bed-rooms in country houses in this style are, for the most part, flat, and only relieved by a simple Gothic cornice.

[Fig. 181. Interior of Bed-room ir the Gothic Style.]

In Fig. 181 (from a sketch by Mr. Davis), a more characteristic mode of finishing bed-rooms in the upper story of country houses is shown. In this, the four ribs shown are the rafters of the roof, planed, and stained and varnished. Between these rafters the space (in fact, the under side of the roof) is lathed and plastered like the side walls. Over the highest part of the ceiling, a space in the peak of the garret is cut off by horizontal pieces of timber, matching the rafters—between which, the lath and plaster ceiling is formed in the usual way.

This gives a lofty bed-room, combining spaciousness and good effect with a fine circulation of air. In order to make such a room thoroughly cool, it is only necessary that a void space should be left between the ceiling and the sheathing of the roof. There is also the void space in the peak of the roof, above the ceiling, communicating with the open air by a small round opening or window, just under the apex of the projecting eaves. In building the house, carry up in the walls, from the cellar to this hollow space in the peak (at the end opposite to the opening under the eaves), an air-flue, 8 or 10 inches in diameter, and the ventilation which will constantly go on, will maintain, in such a bed-room, a cool and agreeable temperature at all times—provided, also, there is a register or valve in the side wall, near the ceiling, to allow the heated air of the room to pass into the space in the peak of the garret.

Good examples of this mode of treating bed-rooms may be seen in the very complete villa of Mr. Harold, at Bridgeport, Ct., built from the designs of Mr. Davis.

A most satisfactory and picturesque mode of treating the ceilings of the entrance-hall, dining-room, and, indeed, any of the plainer portions of a country house in the Gothic style, is that of boldly showing the beams which support the floor above—rendering them somewhat ornamental by planing, champfering, and beading them on the under side, and supporting them, where they join the side walls, by suitable and characteristic brackets. The beams themselves, if not of oak, should be stained and varnished, to resemble this or some other native wood. The space between the beams may be either wrought, so as to show the floor above, also stained and varnished, or it may be lathed and plastered, and painted of some pleasing neutral tone, to contrast with the beams; or the plaster surface may be grained in oil, so as to resemble oak boards. This kind of treatment, which shows the construction in a bold and massive manner, is not only peculiarly picturesque and rustic in character, and, therefore, in far better keeping with many country houses than highly elaborate ceilings of stucco, but it is also, if judiciously treated by a builder who understands how to use his materials, by far the cheapest of all modes of finishing interiors, and one which only a picturesque style, like the Gothic, or some of its rustic variations, will readily permit.

Perhaps the error into which interior decorators are most apt to fall, in the treatment of apartments in this style, is to render them too elaborately Gothic. In some houses, we see every thing tending to the *high-pointed arch* (only fit for churches), and bristling with crockets. A more subdued and quiet manifestation is in better keeping with domestic architecture, and, especially, with rural dwellings.

A great beauty of this style, when properly treated, is the home-like expression which it is capable of, in the hands of a person of taste. This arises, mainly, from the chaste and quiet colors of the dark wood-work, the grave, though rich hue of the carpets, walls, etc., and the essentially fireside character which the apartments receive from this kind of treatment. The prevailing character of the Grecian and Italian styles partakes of the gay spirit of the drawing-room and social life; that of the Gothic, of the quiet, domestic feeling of the library and the family circle. Those who love shadow, and the sentiment of antiquity and repose, will find most pleasure in the quiet tone which prevails in the Gothic style; as those who love sunshine, and the enjoyment of the present moment, will prefer the classical or modern styles.

The mouldings of the Gothic style are thick and massive, and composed of many members, affording great variety and force of shadow. Trefoils and quatrefoils are the simplest and most familiar forms of tracery for decorating all spaces formed by the intersection of right lines or angles; and "roses," "Tudor flowers," and a great variety of foliage and flower forms, richly and picturesquely treated, are among the predomi nant decorations of this style of architecture.

The Romanesque Style. Under this head we include the Lombard or early Italian, the round-arch style of the Rhine, and the Norman style of the North of Europe. They are all variations of revived Roman architecture, and all bear the impress of the Roman arch as their type form. This style preceded the Gothic in its date, and undoubtedly owed its origin to the use of the materials of ancient classical art, culled by a late generation from the splendid remains of decayed Rome. The main difference between the Lombard or South of Europe Romanesque, and the Norman or Romanesque of the North of Europe, is, that the former is purer—being almost wholly based on the Roman type of the round-arch and horizontal development, while the latter is a more mixed style, and is continually running into the Gothic—so that pointed and round arches frequently occur, not only in the same building, but sometimes intermingled side by side or above each other.

The truth is, the Romanesque style was never perfected. Before it crystallized into a refined and complete form, the Gothic sprang into existence, and overshadowed and extinguished it.

As a domestic style, there are no examples of Romanesque that are satisfactory as authorities for works adapted to the present age. There is a rudeness and clumsiness about some specimens, and a barbarous incongruity about others, that renders them useless, except as studies for this purpose. But whoever will study carefully the Romanesque architecture of Southern Europe, will find it full of instructive details, from which the most valuable suggestions for interior, as well as exterior decoration, may be derived. The use of terra-cotta ornaments, externally, the introduction of diaper or mosaic patterns impressed on the walls while the plaster is wet, so as to have the effect of ornamental sculpture, and the repetition of bold and striking mouldings, so as to form rich borders to the doors and windows, are all particularly worthy of the attention of the artist of genius, who wishes, out of good materials in the past, to glean something towards forming a style suited to the present time.

In Fig. 182—a sketch for an interior in the Norman taste, by Mr. Lamb, an English architect—we have some approximation to an adaptation of the style to modern domestic purposes. Fig. 183 is a chimney-piece, from the same hand. For the

[Fig. 183.   Norman Chimney-Piece.]

clumsy column, and rather barbarous, zigzag moulding of the
Norman style, we would, however, substitute the twisted
pillar and the more elegant foliage decoration of the true
Romanesque school.   At the same time, while we would avoid
the heavy proportions of many of the Norman details, we would
preserve, as a distinguishing feature between the Romanesque
and the Italian styles, that somewhat ruder form and more
picturesque and rustic treatment of details and ornaments,
which would render the Romanesque especially adapted for
country architecture.

The Elizabethan, or Renaissance Style. We follow most
English writers in calling this style Elizabethan, because it
came into use in England during the reign of Elizabeth, though
it really originated in Italy, at the revival of the arts in the
fifteenth century, and thence spread all over Europe.   It is
known as the *Cinque Cento,* or Fifteenth Century style, in
Italy; as the *Renaissance* or revived Roman style in France;
and the former is undoubtedly the correct term to be applied to it.

Looking at the Elizabethan or Fifteenth Century style

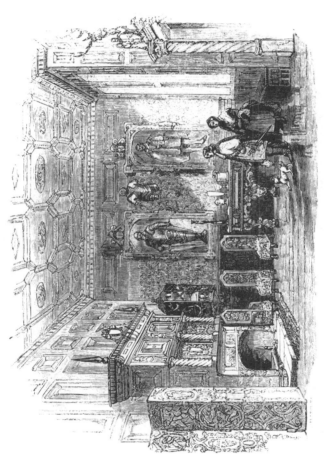

ANTIQUE APARTMENT—ELIZABETHAN STYLE

Fig. 184

critically, or in a philosophical point of view, we cannot deny that it often violates all rules of art, and indulges in all manner of caprices. Mere architects and pedantic judges have accordingly condemned it in all ages. Viewed, however, as a style addressed to the feelings, and capable of wonderfully varied expression, from the most grotesque and whimsical to the boldly picturesque and curiously beautiful, we see much in that style to admire—especially for domestic architecture. Still, as we think it a most dangerous style for any but an architect of great taste and judgment to handle, and one rarely in keeping with character or circumstances in this country, we have not presented any strictly Elizabethan designs for exteriors.

The best reason which can be given for the introduction of Elizabethan architecture here, is, as we have already remarked, the natural preference which Europeans, becoming naturalized citizens among us, have for indulging the charm of old associations, by surrounding themselves by an antique style that has been familiar to their eyes, and formed part of their homes from childhood. In such cases, the whole house may, very properly, be designed in this style, or certain apartments fitted up in accordance with it.

There are, also, many among us who have a taste for *antiquities*, and find the greatest pleasure in collecting about them the furniture and forms of a past age. Such persons may incline to fit up a library, or some one or two rooms in their house, in this style, and will find more pleasure in hunting for old Elizabethan chairs than in the possession of the finest and most faultless productions of any modern school of art.

A very good general idea of the Elizabethan style, as seen in the interiors of the great English country houses of the fifteenth century, may be gathered from a glance at the interior, Fig. 184 (which we take from the Abbotsford novels).* The walls and ceiling were heavily wainscoted in oak, and the former portion often hung with tapestry. The mouldings and decorations were in a mixed taste, mainly Italian, but often intermingled with Gothic. Twisted columns, scroll-work, and heavy and quaint carving in wood—the figures often grotesque, and almost always comparatively rude—such were the principal characteristics of this style. The effect is often grand and sombre, always massive, rich, and highly picturesque—as well as essentially manorial and country-like.

The *Cinque Cento* affords, in its best examples, evidences that the Italian artists had a fine feeling for beauty of form; and their decorations are always purer in design and superior in execution to those of the Flemish or Elizabethan school.

The French, in their Renaissance style, which is at the present moment in high favor on the Continent, offer the best examples, and are the best masters of it, as applied to modern uses. Their works, especially in interiors and furniture, retain all the picturesqueness and antique beauty of the works of the fifteenth century, with more artistic execution and a more select and chaste arrangement of the details.

As there is an affinity between the more domestic forms of Gothic architecture and this style of the fifteenth century— which is much strengthened by the ancient custom of fitting up even the finest Gothic houses with Elizabethan furniture—

---

* Still better studies will be found in that picturesque folio—*Nash's Mansions of England in the Olden Time.*

there is no reason why a room or two in any of our Gothic villas should not be finished and fitted up in a chaste Elizabethan or Renaissance taste. There are already some examples in this country, where the effect of this is striking and agreeable, whether regarded as illustrating a past age, or as gratifying a love of antiquity in the possessor.

Of course, with our feelings of the significance of the present time in this country, we would not desire to see the growth of an affected taste for a by-gone style, like that of the fifteenth century. But there is little fear of this. Both the costliness of an elaborately carved and decorated style like this, and the natural preference of most minds for forms strictly adapted to modern wants, will always prevent it from becoming more than an occasional example of the taste of wealthy and curious amateurs in the United States.

The Elizabethan is, by the soberness and gravity of tone given by the introduction of so much dark wood or wainscot work, particularly agreeable for the interior of a library. In Fig. 185, which is a sketch of a library in a modified and comparatively simple Elizabethan style, is shown the treatment that is often given it by modern English architects.

The Bracketed Style. Here is certainly a mode, without the demerit of being old, for even the name, as applied to any style of building, is unknown on the other side of the Atlantic. We apply it to the mode of construction with projecting roofs, neither so high pitched as those of the Gothic, nor so low as the classical styles—roofs always supported on brackets, and always decidedly rustic or country-like in expression. If it is not the best and highest style of architecture which will be developed in this country, it has the merit of being the first that has taken a distinct shape and meaning in the hands of our countrymen. If it has features similar in origin and use with the Swiss and Venetian styles, it is also essentially distinct. Its elements are simple and useful, but this simplicity and utility both spring from our circumstances and climate. It is needless for us to detail the external features of what we call the Bracketed style, for any one may find them by turning over the designs of cottages and farm-houses in many of the preceding pages. They are simple and plain enough, as all first efforts must be, but a few years more will undoubtedly raise this style to a more dignified and artistic character.

In the interior, the Bracketed partakes, in some measure, of the Italian character—that is to say, the prevailing lines are horizontal—but the principle of strength or support, instead of being the post or pillar, as in the Grecian, or the arch, as in the Italian, is that of the *bracket*. This feature is not only used where it is absolutely required, as under the eaves of the roof, and where a beam rests upon a wall, but, like the round and pointed arch, it is made a characteristic and ornamental, where it is not absolutely a necessary, feature in decoration.

The Bracketed may be the plainest of all styles, showing itself externally only by the ends of the rafters supporting the extended roof, and internally, by a bracket placed in the angles where two pieces of timber or wall meet, to bear part of the weight, or it may be a very rich and highly ornamental style, employing brackets and beams of beautiful forms, perforated, carved, and highly decorated.

In Fig. 186, we give a sketch of an interior, in the Bracketed style, of a comparatively plain and simple kind, but showing its application to the ceiling, the windows, and the leading features of the apartment.

The ribs and brackets should be rather bolder than they are here represented, and are usually formed of wood, though they may easily be formed of plaster, in the usual way. As the bracketed style is one essentially derived from wood, it should always aim at picturesqueness, rather than elegance and symmetry; and as strength and power, and a certain want of finish, are as necessary to the Picturesque as delicate contour and perfect execution are to the Beautiful, it will be better to treat wood picturesquely than to attempt to finish it so as to give it the opposite character.

A still bolder and more characteristic interior for a country house, than Fig. 186, is obtained by showing about half the depth of the real beams of the ceiling, plastering as usual between, and placing bold brackets underneath them along the cornice of the room. The whole of the wood-work may be real oak, or so finished as to resemble it.

Having thus briefly designated the leading features of the Bracketed style, we leave it in the hands of our American architects. It is certainly capable of great variety, force, and picturesqueness. There is scarcely any limit to the variety of bracket ornamentation, that may be devised; and if the capacities of the style are rightly understood, and the fact borne in mind, that it is essentially rural and picturesque in character, it can scarcely fail to be developed into admirable forms for country houses.

DETAILS IN GENERAL. No architect has, to our knowledge, laid down fixed rules for the proportion of rooms in modern domestic architecture. The rules of Palladio and others are intended for palaces and private mansions, on a scale wholly unknown in our republic.* Economy, which obliges us, in most cases, to have all the rooms on a floor of the same height, while the rooms themselves are necessarily of different sizes, prevents us from adhering to any absolutely fixed rules of proportion. We may remark, however, that from 12 to 14 feet is the general range for the height of the principal story in our best country houses. Occasionally, a large room, especially if it is detached, is from 16 to 20 feet high. The width varies from 16 to 20 feet—and the effect is always better, with the height of ceiling we have named, if apartments are considerably increased in *length*, when large dimensions are required, rather than extended much beyond 20 feet in width.

As general principles, we may, however, remark, that height always gives an expression of dignity, width and height bestow grandeur, and width, height, and length, nicely adjusted, produce elegance. On the contrary, while rooms that are rather broad and low have an ill effect in a modern classical villa, they give a farm-house that homely and rustic expression which is in better keeping with its character and use, than rooms with lofty ceilings.

An ingenious architect will, therefore, proportion the height of the stories to the style he has chosen. Thus, the Gothic or pointed styles should, strictly, have the highest ceilings; the

---

* The proportions laid down by Sir Wm. Chambers, an English authority, were as follows :—"If the plan of the room be a square, the height should not exceed five-sixths of the length of the side, nor be less than four-fifths; and when it is an oblong, the height may be equal to the width." This applies to classical architecture, and the architect who feels and understands *proportion* will be better able to express the idea of the style he has adopted, than by following rules like these, which are only of very limited application.

Italian, next; and the Elizabethan and bracketed may be high or low, according to the simplicity or dignity of the building to be erected.

Chimney-pieces are among the essentially architectural features of rooms, and they should therefore always strictly correspond in style with the rest of the house or apartment in which they are fixed.

Chimney-pieces, of excellent design and workmanship, in Italian, Gothic, and the other more important styles, may now be found in our principal cities, at very moderate prices. Those of the more simple forms are preferable to very elaborate patterns, the latter belonging, more properly, to highly enriched town houses. A very fine effect is always produced, when the drawing-room is one of considerable importance, by placing a large mirror over its chimney-piece, with its frame designed so that the former and the latter form one composition.

The walls of all the best apartments in villas are usually finished in three coats of plaster, the last coat being laid on with "hard-finish," i. e. plaster of Paris, so as to form a perfectly hard and smooth surface. This may either be left white, or it may be colored in distemper, or painted in oil. It is usual, in either case, to allow the walls to remain untouched for a year before painting them, in order that they may become perfectly dry and seasoned.

Since we look upon bare white walls, in the principal apartments of a country house, as, in point of taste, a complete nullity, destructive of all tone, and harsh and glaring in effect, we would, in all cases, either paint the walls in oil, color them in distemper, or cover them with paper.

Paper-hangings offer so easy, economical, and agreeable a means of decorating or finishing the walls of an apartment, that we strongly recommend them for use in the majority of country houses of moderate cost. Where they are to be used, the expense of applying the stucco or hard-finish to the side walls may be saved, for common plastered walls, well sized, are equally well adapted to receive paper.

A good deal of taste is requisite in the choice of paper-hangings, in a house where there are rooms of importance. All flashy and gaudy patterns should be avoided, all imitations of church windows, magnificent carved work, pinnacles, etc. Those papers which are in the best taste are either flock-papers, made to imitate woven stuffs—such as silk or worsted hangings—or fresco-papers, which give the same effect as if the walls were formed into compartments or panels, with suitable cornices and mouldings. If the fresco-papers (which may now be had in New York, well designed, of chaste and suitable patterns for any style of architecture) are chosen, they will produce a tasteful, satisfactory, and agreeable effect, in almost any situation.* The great point consists in judicious selection, and the best guiding principle that we can lay down, is to choose a paper of the same style as the room, and a modification of that style in keeping with the furniture, etc., to be placed in it. We make this latter remark, because one often sees fresco-paper which in style and details is exactly suitable to a palace, placed upon the walls of

---

* A very artistic and excellent effect is produced, by employing paper of a single plain color for the whole ground of the wall, and forming lines, panels, and compartments, by portions and strips of other plain colors. See page 336.

LIBRARY IN THE ELIZABETHAN STYLE.

Fig. 185.

INTERIOR IN THE BRACKETED STYLE.

Fig. 186.

a country house, where the furniture and all else is modest and simple, and therefore wholly out of keeping with it.

When the walls of an apartment are papered, the ceiling is generally all left white, or painted or colored some delicate neutral tint, nearly white, and harmonizing with the prevailing colors of the paper.

Painting in Distemper. This is nothing more than a water-color wash, the color being mixed with clean, thin *sizing*, instead of oil. The body of the paint or wash is either whiting or kalsomine—the latter a very fine kind of earth (burned in a peculiar manner), pure white in color, and producing a more mellow. and softer effect than whiting. The wash is laid on warm, so that the sizing will flow freely: and it may be used upon common plastered walls, though the effect is, of course, better upon a stucco or hard-finished wall.

The advantages of distemper over oil-colors are, 1st, the short time necessary to perform it—two coats only being necessary, so ,that a room or a number of rooms may be finished in a day; 2d, the absence of all smell, so disagreeable and unwholesome, during two or three weeks, when oil paint is used; 3d, economy, the expense of coloring a room in kalsomine being only about a third of that in oil paint. We may add to this, that there is no glare in kalsomine, but a softness and delicacy of tint, rarely or never seen in oil-colors.

The disadvantages are, that it will not bear washing, and is more easily stained than a surface painted in oil. For all rooms liable to "hard usage," distemper colors should never be resorted to; but we have had them for six or eight years upon the walls of parlors, where they are still quite satis-factory.

The tints used for coloring walls in distemper are generally
French gray, drab, fawn, stone color, and other delicate neutral tints. To produce these, the following colors are added
in small quantities to the basis of whiting or kalsomine : Chrome
yellow, yellow ochre, Venetian red, burnt umber, patent black,
French blue, etc. As the tints dry lighter than they appear, it
is necessary to paint strips of paper or bits of board, and allow
them to dry, in order to judge if the required shade is obtained.

Painting in Oil. There is, undoubtedly, no mode of
finishing the walls of an apartment so entirely satisfactory, in
many respects, as painting them in oil. It is very durable,
and as such walls can be cleaned at any time without injury,
by washing them, it is also, in the end, the most economical
mode—though troublesome, tedious, and expensive at first. As
there are several ways of performing the operation, we give
the following as the best yet known. It is the practice of Hay,
the famous Edinburgh painter.

It should be premised that the wall to be painted is hard-
finished.

"The process of painting plaster-work is as follows :—White-
lead and linseed oil, with a little litharge, to facilitate drying,
are mixed together, to about the consistence of thin cream : a
coating of this being applied, the oil from it is sucked into the
plaster in the course of a few hours, leaving the white-lead
apparently dry upon the surface. In the course of a day or
two, when this coat has sufficiently hardened, another is given,
a few degrees thicker, the oil from which is partially absorbed,
according to the nature of the plaster. In the course of a few
days more, a third coat is applied. This coat is made pretty
thick; and, if the absorption of the oil from the second coat

has not been great, about one-fourth of spirits of turpentine is
added; but when the absorption has been great, a less proportion of the spirits of turpentine is employed. Into this coat are
put the *coloring* ingredients, to bring it near the shade intended
for the finishing coat. Should the plaster now be thoroughly
saturated, the *flatting* or finishing coat is applied; before this
is done, however, a fourth coat, thinned with equal portions of
oil and spirits of turpentine, is generally given, particularly
when the work is intended to be of the most durable kind.
The flatting or finishing coat is composed entirely of paint;
that is, of white paint and the coloring ingredients, mixed
together, and ground in oil to an impalpable paste. This
mixture is of a very thick consistency, and must be thinned
with spirits of turpentine, until it will flow easily from the
brush. The spirits of turpentine, being very volatile, evaporate
entirely, leaving the surface of the paint of a very compact and
hard nature. By this process, the plaster is rendered incapable
of absorption; and the surface of it, entirely free from gloss,
is hardened by the oil which it has sucked in from the first
and second coats, and is thereby rendered less liable to breakage,
with the great advantage of being washable."

A great deal of taste may be evinced in the manner of coloring the different apartments in a country house of considerable
size. An apartment may be richly painted, decorated, and
filled with fine furniture, and yet the effect will be discordant
and unpleasing, if forms and colors are badly arranged. How
to produce harmony of style we have already indicated. The
most powerful source of pleasure in all interiors, next to style,
is color, and to the majority of persons who have little knowledge of architecture, it is even a larger and more easily

recognized element of satisfaction. The principal masses of color in a room are in the carpet and the walls, and these, therefore, should always harmonize with each other—that is to say, if they do not agree in color, they should be selected so as to contrast harmoniously. The same rule applies to window-curtains, drapery, and stuffs with which chairs are covered. And though there may be contrasts in the furniture of a room, there must be a predominance of some leading color, to give a *tone* to the whole.*

---

* " The first and most obvious defect in the coloring of rooms is, when there is no particular tone fixed on for an apartment; that is, when one part of the furniture is chosen without any reference to the rest, and the painting done without any reference to the furniture. This generally produces an incongruous mixture; and is, in comparison to a tastefully decorated apartment, as far as regards coloring, what a child produces with its first box of paints, to the work of a great master. A second and more common fault is, the predominance of some bright and intense color, either upon the walls or floor. It is evident that such a predominance of an overpowering color upon so large a space as the floor or wall of a room, must injure the effect of the finest furniture. This great error often arises from the difficulty of choosing a paper-hanging or carpet, and our liability to be bewildered amongst the multitude of patterns which are produced, the most attractive of which, on a small scale, are often, from this very circumstance, the more objectionable, in regard to their forming a large mass in an apartment; particularly as the artists who design them are often regulated by no fixed principle, but in many cases seem to give themselves up to the pursuit of novelty alone. A third error is, introducing pale and deep colors together, which may have been well enough chosen with regard to their tints, but whose particular degrees of strength have not been well attended to. There is a fourth defect, and rather a common one, and that is, a want of the media which unite and harmonize an assemblage of bright colors, which may, in other respects, be perfectly well arranged, for it is a rule in the higher branches of the art, that a confusion of parts of equal strength (of color) should always be avoided. A room of this description resembles a Chinese landscape, where foreground and distance are jumbled together."—*Hay's Harmonious Coloring.*

The tone or style of coloring should depend upon the use of the apartment, and a great deal of interest and variety may be conferred on a country house, by thus making the interior, in color and decoration, express the character of the apartment itself. In a small cottage, one does not expect these refinements; but in a country house of the first class, nothing is so insipid as to find all the principal apartments of one color, and finished and furnished in the same manner, without any regard to their uses.

The *hall*, and all entries, staircases, and passages should be of a cool and sober tone of color—gray, stone color, or drab. They also should be simple in decoration. The effect of the richer and livelier hues of the other apartments will then be enhanced by the color of the hall, while every one will feel that the prevailing tone of the latter is strictly in keeping with its uses. For the floors of halls, we greatly prefer tiles of marble or pottery* to carpet or oil-cloth—as far more durable and characteristic, and, in the end, much more economical.

The *drawing-room* should always exhibit more beauty and elegance than any apartment in the house. In color, it should be lighter, more cheerful and gay, than any other room. The furniture should be richer and more delicate in design, and the colors of the walls decidedly light, so that brilliancy of effect is not lost in the evening. In town houses, white, relieved by gold, is preferred; but in country houses, gilding should be very sparingly used—and very delicate tints, such as ashes of rose,

---

* Beautiful patterns of *encaustic tiles*, which have a good effect, are now manufactured at very moderate cost. The colors are chiefly browns, enriched with patterns and figures of fawn or blue.

pearl-gray, pale apple-green, etc., have a more chaste and satisfactory effect for the side walls—relieved by darker shades, for contrast.

The *dining-room* should be rich and warm in its coloring, and more of contrast and stronger colors may be introduced here than in the drawing-room. The furniture should be substantial, without being clumsy, but much simpler in decoration than that of the drawing-room.

The *library* should be quiet, and comparatively grave in color. Some shade of fawn or neutral tint for the walls, the furniture of dark oak, or wood like the bookcases, and the carpet selected so as to accord with the severe and quiet tone of the walls and furniture. Leather or morocco makes the best and most appropriate covers for the seats of chairs and other furniture for a library.

The *boudoir*, which is essentially the ladies' apartment, may be colored and fitted up with any variation of coloring that their fancy may dictate—always supposing that it will be essentially delicate and feminine in its general effect.

Bed-rooms may vary from the greatest simplicity and chasteness of color to any light and cheerful style of decoration. Paper-hangings are largely used for the walls in most of our country houses, and should always agree in general tone with that of the furniture used in the apartment.

The interior *wood-work* of villas or country houses should be painted so as to harmonize with the prevailing tone of the room. It may be lighter or darker than the walls, and generally of a quiet, neutral tint, but never the same color, and never white, except in those drawing-rooms where white is relieved by gilding. In all libraries, and in other apartments, the wood should either be oak or other dark wood, varnished, or it should be painted and grained, to resemble it. Indeed, the use of varnished wood-work has much to recommend it for most apartments of country houses, both on the ground of adaptation and economy of labor.

With these general principles in his mind, any country gentleman, of moderate taste, may succeed in painting and finishing his apartments in a correct and pleasing manner. When the ladies of a family have some cultivation in the arts, they may do much more.* When a villa is designed by an architect, he generally superintends and directs the finishing of the interior; and in villas of considerable importance, *interior decorators*, who devote themselves to this branch of the pro fession, are called in to complete the whole, as the builder leaves it. Some of these, like Mr. Geo. Platt, of New York (who is at present the most popular interior decorator in the country), possess talent enough to take an apartment or a suite of apartments, design and execute the decorations, and color, and furnish them throughout in any style.

---

* We remember a beautiful effect produced in a simple country house, whose apartments were decorated in a chaste and artistic manner by mere charcoal drawings, done by a lady—one of the inmates. The subjects were Flaxman's outlines, enlarged to life size, in panels, on the walls.

SECTION XII.

FURNITURE.

IF it is true that the general character of a room depends on the architectural forms and lines which compose its walls, ceiling, doors, and windows, it is no less true that the expression of the same room largely depends on the manner in which it is *furnished*. To satisfy one's self on this point, it is only necessary to look at the same apartment, or suite of apartments, with and without furniture. In the one case, it has, to be sure, the intrinsic elements of proportion, symmetry, and suitable architectural decoration; but it wants all that variety, intricacy, and significance of meaning which the same room has, when filled with furniture in keeping with its uses, and the social life of those who inhabit it. As a smile or a glance, in familiar conversation, often reveals to us more of the real character of a professional man than a long study of him at the pulpit or the bar, so a table or a chair will sometimes give us the key to the intimate tastes of those who might be inscrutable in the hieroglyphics of white walls and plain ceilings. How often does the interior of the same house convey to us a totally different impression, when inhabited and furnished by different families. In the one case, all is as cold, hard, and formal, as solid mahogany and marble-top centre-tables, *alias*, bare convention-alities and frigid social feeling, can make it; in the other, all is as easy and agreeable as low couches, soft light chintzes and cushions—*alias*, cordiality, and genuine, frank hospitality can render it.

More than this, if it so happens that one is forced to inhabit a house meagre and poor in its interior, its baldness and poverty may be, in a great degree, concealed or overcome, by furnishing the rooms in a tasteful and becoming manner.

It is, therefore, by no means irrelevant that we should devote some little space to the subject of the furniture of country houses. Our fair readers will doubtless pardon us for the seeming intrusion on their province, when we say that our object is mainly to furnish them with reasons for the natural good taste which they usually show in this department, and point out the shoals on which those few who fail from want of native perception are wrecked, so that they may, if possible, be avoided.

And here we may be allowed to prose a little, at the outset, by an allusion to the blunders committed by many persons in furnishing a house. We mean the blunder of confounding *fashion* with *taste;* of supposing that whatever the cabinet-makers and upholsterers turn out as the latest fashion must necessarily be the only things worth having; and of a total ignorance of the fact, that the most fashionable furniture *may* be in the worst taste, while furniture in the most correct taste is not always such as is easily obtained in the cabinet ware-houses.

Tasteful furniture is, simply, furniture remarkable for agree-able and harmonious lines and forms, well adapted to the purpose in view.   Furniture in *correct taste* is characterized by its being designed in accordance with certain recognized styles, and intended to accord with apartments in the same style. Furniture in "good keeping" adds to correctness in point of taste, a propriety of color, character, form and material, which befits the uses for which it and the apartment in which it is placed are intended.   Thus, the furniture of the hall, however correct, would not be in good keeping with the dining-room, nor the furniture of the dining-room in keeping with the library.

The great advantage which furniture in correct taste has over merely fashionable furniture is, that the latter is no sooner out of fashion—which may happen in a twelvemonth—than lo! its whole charm and power of pleasing is lost to its possessor. It must, therefore, be sent to auction, or consigned to the upper story, and more, of the latest mode, put in its place—while furniture in correct taste, depending on its excellence and the adaptation of its forms and lines to the apartments of whose architecture it is an echo, never loses its power of pleasing, but only grows dearer to us by age and association.

Again, the power which furniture of correct taste has, of affording us pleasure, does not depend on rich materials or elaborate execution—though it may, in many cases, be heightened by them.   It arises rather from the *mind* which it evinces—the evidence it conveys at a glance that it is part of the same plan, idea, or conception which is shown in every other part of the house, or enters into the very room where it is placed.   We are thus made to feel that the furniture belongs in a certain house or room, because it was specially designed for that house or room, or for one in the same architectural style and character, and for no other. It is for this reason—because beauty and significance both unite to make furniture in correct taste permanently satisfactory—that it often happens that some modest cottage, with its furniture of oak or walnut, all chaste, simple, and expressive, but in strictly correct taste and good keeping, awakens in our minds a far higher pleasure than the most costly saloon, bright with gilding, and rich with satin and velvet, where we only discover magnificence and expense, without taste or propriety. We feel that there is some living spark of genius in the former, however simple and unpretending its manifestation, but in the latter—only unlimited credit at the banker's.

The most unfortunate circumstance for the progress of good taste in furnishing our country houses is that, hitherto, the fashions of town houses have been implicitly followed everywhere in the country. To be able to show a parlor in a country house as nearly as possible a fac-simile of one in the Fifth Avenue, Beacon, or Chestnut street, according as New York, Boston, or Philadelphia is the meridian of calculation, has, for the most part, been the highest ambition of most persons furnishing a first-class house in the country. And the result is, that the room so furnished, instead of inspiring us with the feeling of appropriateness, comfort, and good taste, rather wearies us with the recollection of the extra expense, inappropriateness, and over-elegance of so many things made for display, rather than convenience and beauty.

The first step towards escaping from this, is the recognition of the fact, that a country house (even when the same wealth and style are supposed) should always be furnished with more chasteness and simplicity than a town house; because, it is in the country, if anywhere, that we should find essential ease and convenience always preferred to that love of effect and desire to dazzle, which is begotten, for the most part, by rivalry of mere wealth in town life. As a country gentleman rejoices in the fact that he is in happy ignorance of the routine of daily dress-coats and white gloves, so he prefers a comfortable couch or easy-chair, covered with substantial stuffs, and not so fine or so frail as to forbid his enjoying it remorselessly at all times, to gilt fauteuils, covered with white satin, which are objects of no more real utility in the country than a *chasseur*.

The great desideratum in the furniture of country houses is, that it should be essentially *country-like*—which, we think, is attained only when it unites taste, comfort, and durability in the greatest degree. It should be in correct taste, so as to harmonize with the house in which it is placed; it should be convenient and comfortable in the highest degree; and it should be substantially made, so as to unite durability with the capacity of being used without the fear of being spoiled by fulfilling its true purpose.

Of course, it is as yet difficult to find such furniture —because most of our patterns are of Parisian taste, designed for town houses. But there are evidences of better things in the future. Hennessey, of Boston, has already made a successful attempt in the manufacture of cheap, light furniture for cottages, and more solid and substantial designs, in the different styles suited to large country houses, will soon follow.

There is, at the present moment, almost a mania in the cities for expensive French furniture and decorations. The style of royal palaces abroad is imitated in town houses of 50 feet front, and we could name examples where from $5000 to $10,000 have been expended in the decoration and furniture of a single apartment in New York. It is not our province to read a philippic against this species of extravagance in cities. "God made the country, but man made the town," and a little more indulgence may be made for the latter, considering how the tastes and passions of men are excited in rich cities. But in the country, we protest against such display (whatever the ability to pay for it), as not only in bad taste, but out of keeping with the comparative simplicity and ease of manners which ought to characterize rural life. Even Lord Chesterfield would have been ill at ease if he had been obliged to live the life of a country gentleman in purple and fine linen, every day.

But there is a readier and more powerful argument why persons of good taste should not indulge in this extraordinary display of gilding, mirrors, and decoration in the interior of their houses in this country. We mean, because such showy wares are likely to become too "base, common, and popular" to gratify them by possession. When the proprietors of our great steamers and hotels can afford, as they now do, from motives of policy, to lavish far more in the furniture, gilding, and decoration of their saloons, than our best private fortunes will allow, and when, instead of this species of decoration being confined to the palaces of royalty or the nobility, as abroad, it is here made the common property of the sovereign people, to enjoy whenever they travel, it is clear that the taste for private display of the same kind must take some other channel, or it will soon become "vulgar." Hence, the only resort for a gentleman who wishes his house to be distinguished by good taste, is to choose the opposite course, viz. to make its interior remarkable for chaste beauty, and elegant simplicity, rather than for elaborate and profuse decoration.

In presenting the designs of furniture which follow, we are far from giving them as perfect specimens of what we should desire the furniture of country houses to be. To achieve this, the assistance of some genius who especially understands and has carefully studied the nature of the desideratum in country furniture, would be required. No such artist has yet arisen, and in the mean time we give a selection from furniture, in various styles now in use, and to be had of the cabinet-makers in our principal cities.* The representations given will at least familiarize our readers with the different styles of design, and enable them to understand more clearly what they really want.

We may add, that the furniture dealers in most repute in Boston are Hennessey, for cottage furniture, and Paul, for French and Elizabethan furniture. In New York, the rarest and most elaborate designs, especially for drawing-room and library use, are to be found at the warehouse of Roux, in Broadway. Platt, who designs and executes furniture in all styles, we have already referred to.

I.—*Furniture in the Grecian or Modern Style.*

The furniture most generally used in private houses is some

---

* A few of these designs are original ones, furnished for this work by Mr. Hennessey, of Boston, and Mr. Platt, of New York. We are also indebted to M. A. Roux, 479 Broadway, New York, for permission to copy patterns in his extensive collection. For a portion of the remainder we are indebted to Webster's Encyclopædia of Domestic Economy, and Loudon's Encyclopædia of Architecture.

modification of the classical style, and usually in what is called Grecian or French taste—the former being characterized by lines and forms found in the antique classical compositions, and the latter being variations of the same, with the addition of some modern embellishment of detail and decoration.

Modern Grecian furniture has the merit of being simple, easily made, and very moderate in cost. Its universality is partly owing to the latter circumstance, and partly to the fact that by far the largest number of dwellings are built in the same style, and therefore are most appropriately furnished with it.

The simplest and cheapest kind of furniture by which an air of taste may be given to a cottage, consists of a plain box or bench, made of boards, by the hands of the master of the dwelling, stuffed with hay, corn-husks, moss, or hair, held in place by a covering of coarse canvas, and covered with chintz by the mistress of the cottage. Seats of all kinds are made at very trifling cost in this way, so that, with a little ingenuity, a room may, by the aid of a few boards, nailed together, a little stuffing and canvas, and a few yards of shilling chintz, be made to produce nearly the same effect as one where the furniture is worth ten times as much. The

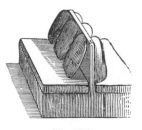

[Fig. 187.]

next step is to add square pillows or cushions to all the benches, seats, or couches, in order that any person sitting upon them may have a support for his back without touching the wall. Fig. 187 represents an ottoman made in this manner, intended for the middle of a room. Formed with the seat on only one side of the upright back, it is called a divan; or, if broad, the back omitted, and pillows placed at one or both ends, it is called a couch.

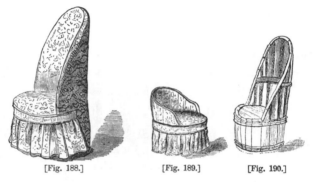

[Fig. 188.]   [Fig. 189.]   [Fig. 190.]

Another of the cheapest and simplest seats for a cottage is the *barrel-chair*. Fig. 188 is a large one, stuffed in the seat and back. Fig. 189 is a low one, for the chimney corner. These chairs are easily made by sawing off a portion of the barrel—nailing on a few boards, to form the seat, and leaving part of the staves a little higher than the others, to form the back or arms. To make the high-backed chair, the staves must be *pieced out* a little, as in Fig. 190, the outside or rim of the back being confined in its place by a piece of hoop neatly

[Fig. 191.]

applied. The seat and back are stuffed with any cheap material, covered with strong coarse canvas, and covered with chintz.

Fig. 191 is a cottage couch, of a somewhat superior style, but made in the same manner, and easily produced, when there is a little mechanical ingenuity in the family.

[Fig. 192.]   [Fig. 193.]

Figs. 192 and 193 are cottage sofas, from the cabinet-shop, in simple and pretty forms.

As successful attempts at cottage furniture now made in this country, we may call attention to the complete sets of *chamber* or *bed-room furniture*, got up at the manufactory of Edward Hennessey, 49 and 51 Brattle street, Boston. Mr. H.'s prices are so moderate, and the design and finish of the articles so good, that his reputation is an extended one, and he supplies orders from various parts of the Union and the West Indies. This furniture is remarkable for its combination of lightness and strength, and its essentially cottage-like character. It is very highly finished, and is usually painted drab, white, gray, a delicate lilac, or a fine blue—the surface polished and hard, like enamel. Some of the better sets have groups of flowers or other designs painted upon them with artistic skill. When it is remembered that the whole set for a cottage bed-room may be had for the price of a single wardrobe in mahogany, it will be seen how comparatively cheap it is. There are now various imitators of this cottage furniture in other cities, but we have seen none so excellent or cheap as that made at Hennessey's warehouse.

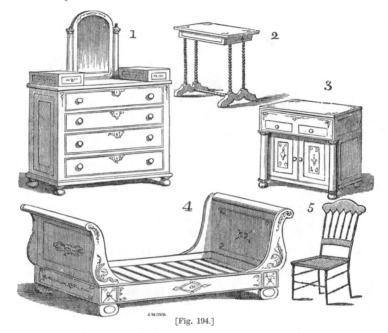

[Fig. 194.]

Fig. 194 shows one of these sets. It consists of

1. A Dressing Bureau.   2. A small Table.

3. A Wash Sink.   4. A French Bedstead.

5. Four Cottage Chairs.

This set, painted white, drab, or blue, is sold for $37.

Another more complete set, in the same style, but intended for a larger bed-room, is shown in Fig. 195. This consists of

1. A Commode, or Wash-stand.   2. A Bureau.

3. A Zomno, or Night-stand.   4. A Bedstead.

5. A Towel-stand.   6. A small Table.

7. Four Cottage Chairs.

The price of this set, without marble tops, but highly

[Fig. 195.]

finished, " china white, peach-blossom, or blue ground, single gilt lines, ornamented," is $68. The same, with marble tops to several of the articles, $80. The wardrobe shown with the set costs $18 more.

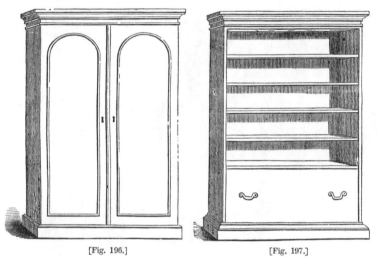

[Fig. 196.]   [Fig. 197.]

Fig. 196 shows a simple form of wardrobe in the Italian style—which may be made by any cabinet-maker—of pine, and either stained, painted drab, or grained in imitation of oak or black-walnut. The interior of this wardrobe is shown in Fig. 197, being adapted for a clothes-press or linen-closet. Fig. 270, on a succeeding page, shows a wardrobe proper, as usually made—one side provided with hooks, for hanging up dresses, and the other with shelves, for laying linen, etc., upon.

Iron bedsteads are to be had now in New York, of a great variety of patterns—some of beautiful designs. The latter, however, are as dear, and not so satisfactory as those of wood. But the simple forms are offered at low prices, and for cleanliness

[Fig. 198.]

J. W. ORR

a

and durability, are the best of all bedsteads for servants' bed-rooms.

A neat and satisfactory *dining-room set* for a cottage, made at Hennessey's warehouse, is shown in Fig. 198. This set consists of an extension-top dining-table, which, when closed, measures four feet, and when extended (as shown in the cut), measures 12 feet, and will seat 12 persons; a side table, 3 feet long and 2 feet 4 inches wide, with drawers; and 8 arm-chairs, with cane seats. The whole is furnished at $50, made of oak, maple, or birch, as may be preferred. This set is in a mixed style—rather Flemish or Elizabethan than Grecian, but will not be out of keeping with a cottage or plain country house. The chairs are strongly braced, and not so slender as they appear in the engraving.

A plain pine sideboard, in the Grecian style, for a cottage, which may be made by any carpenter, and grained or painted, to correspond with the rest of the furniture, is shown in Fig. 199. Fig. 200 is another design in a simple Italian taste.

Pedestal sideboards, like the latter, are

[Fig. 199.]

[Fig. 200.]

made in a great variety of forms, and are not only the most characteristic of all furniture for the dining-room, but also the most useful. Under the top may be placed drawers for tablecloths, napkins, etc., and the side doors may inclose shelves and drawers for holding plate, wines, etc., while the open space between the pedestals is a suitable place for a wine-cooler, or for tea-trays, when not in use. Where there is not an abundance

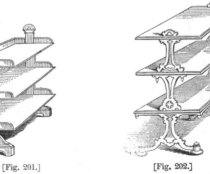

[Fig. 201.]   [Fig. 202.]

of closet or pantry space attached to the dining-room, a large sideboard is indispensable.

The *moving sideboard*, Figs. 201 and 202, is a very convenient piece of dining-room furniture for receiving dishes, holding dessert, etc., when there is not room for a large sideboard, and is frequently used, even where there is one— as, being light, and upon castors, they may be wheeled from one part of the room to the other, and may even perform, in part, the duties of a servant, in time of need. These designs, which are in the French taste, may easily be simplified in detail, without impairing their good effect.

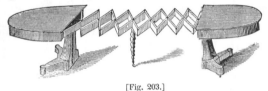

[Fig. 203.]

Briggs's newly invented extension dining-table, Fig. 203, is more easily managed and cheaper than the common form. It closes with the aid of a small windlass; there is a leg in the centre which supports the additional leaves when extended, and is received in a hollow space in the solid column of the table; the whole appears like an ordinary circular centre-table, when shut up.

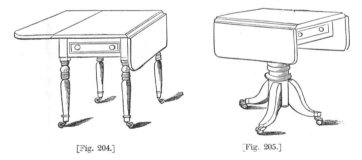

[Fig. 204.]   [Fig. 205.]

Small *breakfast* or *tea tables*, Figs. 204 and 205, are useful and indispensable articles of furniture in a cottage.

[Fig. 206.]

Ladies' work-tables, Fig. 206, are popular English furniture for the sitting-room, and are usually made of mahogany or walnut, and fitted up with a silk bag with a fringe, attached to a frame that draws out. This bag is a very convenient receptacle of various articles of needle-work, which otherwise would, perhaps, lie about upon chairs or sofas, to the discomfort of all parties, and the detriment of the work itself. The lower one is a small circular work-table for fancy work, that may have a place in the parlor.

A prettier and more convenient article for this purpose, and one more suitable to the parlor, is the *basket-stand*, Figs. 207 and 208, being easily lifted and carried about from one part of the room to another—wherever it may be most agreeable to sit. These are made in various modes, either very tastefully and fancifully of rosewood or mahogany, curiously carved, for the villa; or of rustic work, varnished, in the Swiss manner; or of

[Fig. 207.]　　　[Fig. 208.]

bamboo, after the Chinese fashion, for the cottage.

A very useful piece of furniture for the cottage parlor, is one made in a great variety of forms—Fig. 209 being one of the

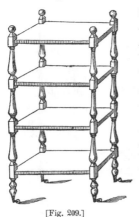

simplest. It is called a *what-not* by the English, and an *étagère* by the French. It usually stands in the corner of the room, and is employed as a stand for little articles, curiosities, books, or whatever trifles of useful or ornamental character may accumulate, with no other special place devoted to them.

Though few cottages of moderate size have a room specially set apart for

[Fig. 209.]

a library, no cottage in America need be without books. If no better means of placing them is within reach, the simple

hanging book-shelves, Fig. 210, which may be made by any one, with a few pieces of board and some strong cord, will suffice ; and the walls of an humble cottage sitting-room, decorated in this way, have a higher meaning there than those of the most superb

[Fig. 210.]

picture-gallery in a villa — since we know that it signifies intellectual taste in the former case, while it *may*, perhaps, be only a love of display in the other. A better mode of forming book-shelves, is that of substituting sides of the same material as the shelves, for the cords, as shown in page 454.

The *secretary*, or writing-desk, is an exceedingly useful piece of furniture, and may be found, at the cabinet-maker's, in a great variety of forms. Fig. 211 is one in the French classical taste—the flap of which falls down to form the writing-table,

[Fig. 211.]

and when shut up, forms part of the panelled front. The shelf on the top may hold books or vases for flowers, etc.

Library tables are generally more massive than any other tables, and are usually inlaid upon the top with morocco or cloth, to afford a smooth surface for writing upon. Figs. 212 and 213 are good specimens of the ordinary treatment of this piece of furniture in the classical style.

A more complete, modern library table, suitable for the

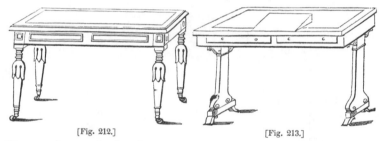

[Fig. 212.]   [Fig. 213.]

library of a professional or literary man, is shown in Fig. 214. It is called a *pedestal library table*. It may have drawers on both sides, or doors and cupboards on one side and drawers on the other. " There is a rising flap on the top, which may be raised to any height, to write or read upon; and when not required, it can be let down flush with the top of the table. The ends are hinged at the bottom, and fold outward; remaining open, in consequence of being supported by a stay-joint near the bottom. This forms a very convenient place for portfolios or large drawings. The depth of the recess may be varied, according to the width of the pilasters. The top is covered with embossed Russia leather."

[Fig. 214.]

Bookcases for a library in the Grecian or modern style are too familiar to need illustration, being usually little more than glazed cases, with Grecian architraves and mouldings.

Library chairs should be rather heavy and solid, compared with those of the drawing-room or dining-room. We prefer those made of oak or black-walnut, and covered with leather. The sort lately come into use, and known as *almond leather*, is excellent for this purpose. It may be had of all colors,

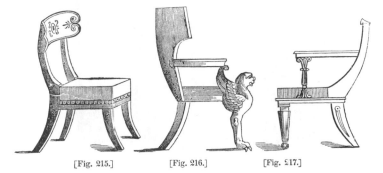

[Fig. 215.]   [Fig. 216.]   [Fig. 217.]

including bronzed or embossed patterns. Figs. 215, 216, and 217, are examples of library chairs in a pure classical style.

Forms much simpler may be easily obtained. The great desideratum in a chair of this description, is a well-stuffed seat, and an easy curve to the back, united to pleasing outline and proportions. Our American cabinet-makers have lately made some improvements in these respects, in cheap furniture, even upon the best European models.

[Fig. 218.]

Fig. 218 is a reading-chair of a simple and good form, a very useful piece of furniture, having a desk for a book on one arm, and a stand for a candle on the other — both being movable—and easily lifted out and put away, when not in use. A still better form now to be had, contains the book-stand and candlestick on the same side, and has also a movable foot-board attached to the chair, and the back so contrived as to be easily adjusted in any position which comfort dictates.

A *drawing-room sofa*, in the purest classical taste, is shown

[Fig. 219.]

in Fig. 219. The contrast of horizontal and curved lines, the proportion, and the details of this sofa, are nearly perfect, as a combination of graceful outline and excellent adaptation. Even the footstool which accompanies it (always a rather difficult subject) is designed with the same purity of form and detail.

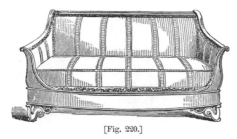

[Fig. 220.]

A classical sofa, in the French taste, is shown in Fig. 220.

Though tasteful and pleasing, it will not bear comparison with the preceding one.

A *boudoir sofa*, in the same style, exceedingly pretty in outline and detail, is seen in Fig. 221. This would also be appropriate, when a pair of sofas were needed in the same room, and the room only of moderate size. These sofas are usually covered with figured damask, either worsted or silk, but the stuff should always be chosen to harmonize, both in material and color, with the room in which it is to be placed. For country houses of moderate cost, the covering of all furniture should be rather heavy and serviceable than fanciful and showy—constant utility being more important than occasional elegance.

[Fig. 221.]

The *ottoman* is a piece of furniture which we borrow from oriental countries, and which has become quite popular among us of late. It is in excellent keeping with buildings in the classical or Venetian style, and in hot climates, affords a more agreeable lounge than any other seat whatever—while, if made of a good breadth, it will also serve as a bed, should occasion require.   Ottomans are made in various forms, from

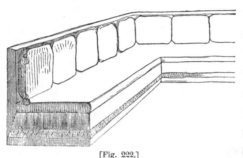

the simple continuous seat, extending round the wall, Fig. 222, to the octagonal stuffed seat.   Perhaps the most pleasing form is the octagonal ottoman (see Fig. 242), placed

[Fig. 222.]

in the middle of a large room.   Ottomans, generally, being wholly covered with stuffs, and not showing any costly wood, are much cheaper than sofas—and, unless the latter are of beautiful forms, are therefore preferable.

Sofa-beds, which may now be found in a variety of forms, at most of the modern upholsterers, are pieces of furniture, having externally the exact appearance of a sofa, ottoman, or divan, but which are so contrived, that the seat draws out, so as to form a comfortable bed in a moment, and with very little trouble.   They are particularly convenient in a house where the number of bed-rooms is limited—or as seats for dressing-rooms,

enabling the mistress of the house, when her hospitality is severely taxed, to turn a dressing-room into a bedroom at a moment's notice.

Centre-tables,   Fig. 223, have long been

[Fig. 223.]

popular pieces of parlor furniture.   In towns, they have given place to sofa-tables—as the latter, scattered here and there in a room, afford various gathering-places for little conversation parties—while the centre-table draws all talkers to a single focus.

As the centre-table is to us the emblem of the family circle, and the sofa-table that of the evening party, we think the

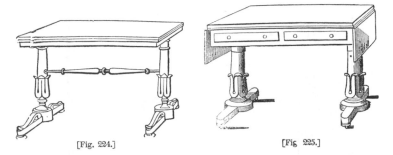

[Fig. 224.]　　　　　[Fig. 225.]

former should hold its place in the country, *par excellence.* Figs. 224 and 225 are plain Grecian forms of the sofa-table— more elaborate and fanciful ones being easily obtained. Both sofa and centre tables depend for their good effect mainly on the drapery or *cover* of handsome cloth or stuff usually spread upon their tops, and concealing all but the lower part of the legs.

The *piano-forte* is the universal accompaniment of the drawing-room or parlor in America. Even in simple cottages, where such a thing would excite astonishment in Europe, the piano will be found. It by no means follows that a knowledge of music is equally universal—but the desire for it certainly is; and if, as we suspect, music demands more age and higher culture than our young nation has yet attained, we will have faith that, by-and-by, we may be as musical a people as the Germans. We do not give here any designs for piano-fortes, because they are usually made in better taste than any other article of furniture in this country—perhaps, because more expensive than any other. They may be had of the best makers, in all the principal styles of design.

Music-stools, *music-stands*, and *music canterburies*, are all indispensable pieces of furniture for the drawing-room of the country house, when there is decided musical taste in the family.

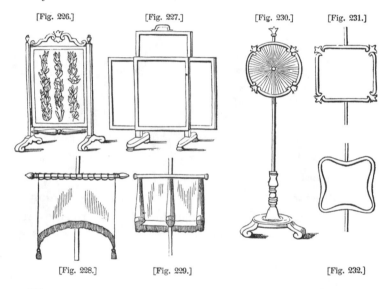

[Fig. 226.]   [Fig. 227.]   [Fig. 230.]   [Fig. 231.]

[Fig. 228.]   [Fig. 229.]   [Fig. 232.]

Fire-screens are more necessary in country than town houses, because open fires are more universal in the former. Fig. 227 is an extension fire-screen, the sides and top drawing out when required. It is chiefly used in the dining-room to screen the dining-table from the fire. Fig. 226 is a *cheval screen* for a parlor; the frame of mahogany, and the panel filled with ornamental embroidery or tapestry. Figs. 228 and 229 are drawing-room fire-screens, easily made by suspending a piece of silk on a wooden or brass rod, with a base like that in

Fig. 230. Fig. 230 is another, the screen formed of fluted silk; and Figs. 231 and 232 have the screen formed by a single piece of plate-glass. The latter are both curious and ornamental, as they enable one to see the fire without feeling it— since, though the solar light and heat readily pass through glass, yet the radiated rays producing the heat of a fire are almost wholly cut off by it.

For the bed-rooms of villas in this style, in this country, the simple French furniture, in the same plain, modern, classical taste, is almost universally preferred. The high four-post bedstead, with curtains, still common in England, is almost entirely laid aside in the United States for the French bedstead, low, and without curtains, as in Fig. 194. Indeed, for the majority of country houses, of the first class, we prefer Hennessey's painted cottage furniture to the more elaborate and expensive, but less appropriate and useful, designs carved in expensive woods. A very good specimen of a modern bedstead with canopy and drapery complete, in the English taste, is

[Fig. 233.]   [Fig. 234.]

represented in Fig. 233, and another in the French taste in Fig. 234.

Modern French furniture, and especially that in the style of *Louis Quatorze*, stands much higher in general estimation in this country than any other. Its union of lightness, elegance, and grace renders it especially the favorite of ladies. For country houses we would confine its use, chiefly, to the drawing-room or boudoir, using the more simple and massive classical forms for the library, dining-room, and other apartments.

"The style of Louis XIV. is known by its abundance of light, ornamental scroll-work, and foliage. Its elegance of form, though not of the first order, together with its admission of every species of enrichment, as carving, gilding, painting, inlaying, with coverings of the richest silks, velvets, and the choicest stuffs, admirably adapt it for the modern drawing-room. Certainly no kind of furniture equals it in general splendor of appearance."—(*Ency. of Dom. Econ.*) The style of Louis XIV. is characterized by greater delicacy of foliage ornamentation, and greater intricacy of detail. We may add to this, that besides the greater elegance of most French drawing-room furniture, its superior workmanship, and the luxurious ease of its admirably constructed seats, strongly commend it to popular favor.*

Figs. 235, 236, and 237, are specimens of light drawing-room chairs in the modern French style. There is just at the

---

* At the warehouse of M. A. Roux, Broadway, may be found a large collection of furniture for the drawing-room, library, etc.—the most tasteful designs of Louis Quatorze, Renaissance, Gothic, etc., to be found in the country—many of which we should gladly have copied for our pages had we seen them earlier. The chairs and sofas are particularly elegant.

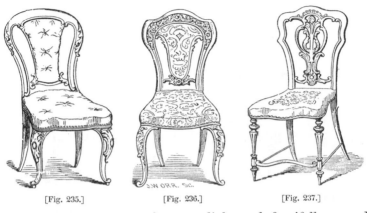

[Fig. 235.]   [Fig. 236.]   [Fig. 237.]

present moment, a rage for very light and fancifully carved chairs for drawing-rooms, far more elaborate than these; and they are certainly remarkable for their great combination of lightness and strength. Fig. 238 is a drawing-room sofa in the Louis Quatorze style. An otto-man for the centre of a drawing-room is shown at Fig. 239.

[Fig. 238.]

This has a central piece, stuffed, against which the cushions or pillows rest. The effect is graceful and pretty. We cannot say as much for Fig. 240—a couch in the same style. If the reader will turn back for a moment and com-pare the two, he will see how awkward and destitute of grace is the outline of this

[Fig. 239.]

[Fig. 240.]

couch as compared with the sofa.

A far more successful example (from M. Roux's) is Fig. 241, a sofa which unites graceful form and good ornamentation, with luxurious ease in the seat.

Fig. 242 is a group of furniture from the warehouse of Platt, 60 Broadway, New York. It consists of a chair, fire-screen, and ottoman, in the Louis XIV. style.

[Fig. 241.]

The ottoman is remarkable for its elegance and an expressive dignity, arising from its large size and good proportions. It is octagonal in shape,

[Fig. 242.]

and in the centre of a large square, octagonal, or circular

saloon, would have a fine effect. There are, of course, several pillows, though only two are shown in the engraving.

Fig. 243 is a *bracket-shelf*, Fig. 244 a *side-table*, and Fig. 245 an *encoigneur*, also from original designs of Mr. Platt. The bracket, which is 4 feet long, is intended to be fixed against the wall—in some blank space, where

[Fig. 243.]

it serves the purpose of a table, as a place for books, vases of flowers, and rare articles of *virtu*. Fig. 245, devoted to the same purpose, is intended to be fixed in the corner of a room.

These are made in black-

[Fig. 244.]

walnut or rosewood, carved, or in wood and composition—in imitation of dark oak—or relieved by gilding.

Nothing so much adds to the splendor and gayety of an apartment as *mirrors*. Although we would introduce them nowhere else in a country house, we think one or two large ones are indispensable in the drawing-room

[Fig. 245. Encoigneur.—Louis XV.] of a first-rate villa. The two most effective positions for mirrors are as chimney mantel-glasses and pier-glasses. A mantel-glass, designed to form a whole

with the chimney, and reaching nearly to the height of the
ceiling, always has a more architectural effect than in any

[Fig. 246.]   [Fig. 247.]

other place.   Fig. 246 is a mantel-glass in the Louis XV.
style, of pleasing design.   Fig. 247 shows a portion of a pier-
glass, with the pier-table below it, in the Louis XIV. style.

[Fig. 248.]   [Fig. 249.]

Figs. 248 and 249 are from the manufactory of Roux.   The

former is a handsome carved *étagère* for the drawing-room; the latter, a pretty and tasteful lady's *escritoire*, or writing-

[Fig. 250.]

desk. It is represented as it appears when closed. When the door which forms the front opens, it turns down,

and forms a neat and steady writing-table, with all the appurtenances of correspond-ence at hand. It is more delicately carved than is here shown, and is altogether a very pretty and useful piece of furniture.

Fig. 250 is a settee, hand-

[Fig. 251.]

somely carved in oak, suit-able for a hall or billiard-room. This, as well as Fig. 251, a rich toilet-table, in the Louis Qua-torze style, is from the designs of Mr. Platt, and may be seen executed at his show-rooms. A ward-robe, in a simple French style, is seen at Fig. 252. A great variety of light and fanciful tables is pro-duced by the French furni-

[Fig. 252.]

ture makers. They are not only useful in the drawing-room for books, ladies' work, flower-baskets, etc., but they give an air of feminine taste and occupation to an apartment, without

[Fig. 253.]   [Fig. 254.]

which it is apt to look stiff and solemn.   Fig. 253 is a very use-

[Fig. 255.]   [Fig. 256.]

ful species of light table, for tea, or an occasional side-table; as, when the leaves are shut down, it occupies less space than any other table, and may be set against the wall in the library or sitting-room. Fig. 254 (drawn on too large a scale) is an-other light table in rosewood, by Roux.

Small stands, for vases of flowers, candlesticks, etc., are among the prettiest and most

[Fig. 257.]

elegant pieces of furniture for the drawing-room, and may be

[Fig. 258.]

[Fig. 259.]

found of very tasteful designs, either at Platt's or Roux's, in New York.

French Furniture, in the style of Francis I., is shown in Figs. 255 to 260. This furniture, as will be seen by a glance at the figures, owes its character chiefly to antique details rather more delicately treated than the Elizabethan. Being of mixed character, it may be used with propriety either in Italian, Bracketed, or Gothic houses—but only for the drawing-rooms—as it is too ornate for any other apart-

[Fig. 260.]

ment. It has neither the quaintness and boldness of the true Renaissance, nor the graceful curved lines of the Louis XIV. furniture—and though rich, has rather a frippery character in its details. The idea embodied in the small octagonal ottoman, Fig. 256, of holding a basket bouquet of flowers, fixed in wet sand, in a tray, supported by the centre, is very good, and would have a pretty and agreeable effect in such an ottoman, carried out in this or any other style. Fig. 260 is a showy pier-table and glass—inferior, however, in point of taste, to Fig. 247.

II.—*Furniture in the Gothic Style.*

WELL-DESIGNED furniture in this style is rarely seen in this country, and is far from common on the other side of the Atlantic. The radical objection to Gothic furniture, as generally seen, is, that it is too elaborately Gothic—with the same high-pointed arches, crockets, and carving usually seen in the front of some cathedral. Elaborate exhibition of style gives it too ostentatious and stately a character. Hence, in many of the finest Gothic mansions abroad, Elizabethan or Flemish furniture has long been used in preference to Gothic furniture, as combining the picturesque and the domestic far more successfully than the latter.

There has been little attempt made at adapting furniture in this style to the more simple Gothic of our villas and country houses in America. Yet we are confident this may be done in such a manner as to unite a simple and chaste Gothic style with forms adapted to and expressive of our modern domestic life.

In the mean time, we give a few examples of Gothic furniture, such as it is now seen in the warehouses of our principal cabinet-makers—chiefly to familiarize the eye of the reader with this, as contrasted with other styles—hoping for something better in the way of design at no distant time.*

---

* The most correct Gothic furniture that we have yet seen executed in this country is by Burns and Tranque, Broadway, New York. Some excellent specimens may also be seen at Roux's.

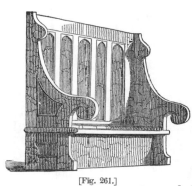

[Fig. 261.]

Fig. 261 is an antique settle, suitable for a large hall in a country house in the *Gothic* style. It is made of oak or walnut, with a leather cushion.

A *hat and cloak stand*, in a very simple modification of the Gothic style, for the entrance-hall, is shown in Fig. 262. This may be made by any carpenter. For simple cottages, it would answer made of pine, stained; but for a superior house, it should be made of oak or walnut. At the bottom is a place for umbrellas, which should have a movable tin tray placed in it, to catch the water.

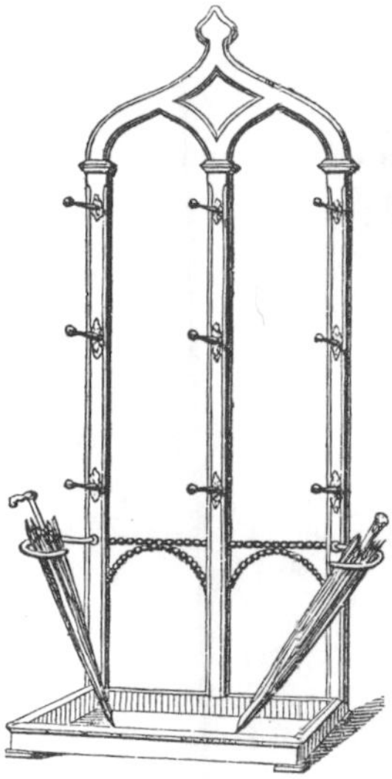

Cottage chairs, of a simple pattern, very suitable for the ordinary rooms of plain country houses in this style, are shown in Figs. 263 to 265. Fig. 264 is a chair more strictly in the Norman or Romanesque style. Cane and rush-bottomed chairs are particularly useful in country houses, because one is not afraid of spoiling them; and the same simple forms may be rendered much more elegant, by stuffing the seats, and covering them with hair-cloth, or various colored worsted stuffs.

[Fig. 262.]

Arm-chairs, Figs. 266 and 267, are suitable for the hall or common sitting-room.

Elaborate bed-room furniture in the Gothic style is seldom seen in country houses in the United States. More simple

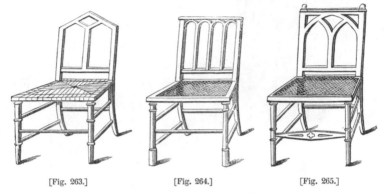

[Fig. 263.]   [Fig. 264.]   [Fig. 265.]

sets of cottage furniture, in an Elizabethan or mixed style, are preferred, as cheaper and more appropriate. Fig. 268 represents one of Hennessey's sets, which may be had in dark wood, or tastefully painted, the ground of drab, enriched with well-executed vignettes in the panels, and marble tops to the principal articles, at from $70 to $100 the set, including four chairs.

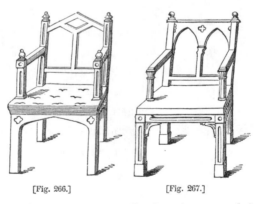

[Fig. 266.]   [Fig. 267.]

A Gothic character may easily be given to plain chamber furniture by any joiner or cabinet-maker who has tools to make the necessary mouldings. A hint for the treatment of such

[Fig. 268.]

furniture may be taken from the plain Gothic wardrobe, Fig.

[Fig. 269.] [Fig. 270.]

269. Fig. 270 shows the interior of the same. Let this ward-

robe be made of handsome black-walnut, and the panels in front filled with a single plate of looking-glass (which would

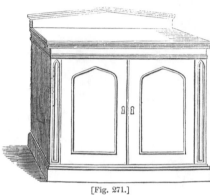

[Fig. 271.]

thus have a double use in a bed-room), and this plain design would be at once chaste and rich enough for any country house.

A very simple, small sideboard for a Gothic cottage is seen in the accompanying Fig., 271, which may be made by any carpenter.

A *corner bookcase*, in the sim-

[Fig. 272.]

[Fig. 273.]

plest Gothic style, is shown in Fig. 272. It would answer well, if necessary, as a china-closet, in the sitting-room of such a cottage.

Hanging book-shelves, like Fig. 273, exceedingly well adapted
for a small house where there is no regular library, or for
bed-rooms, even where there is one, are easily made, and are
both useful and agreeable to the eye in a country cottage.

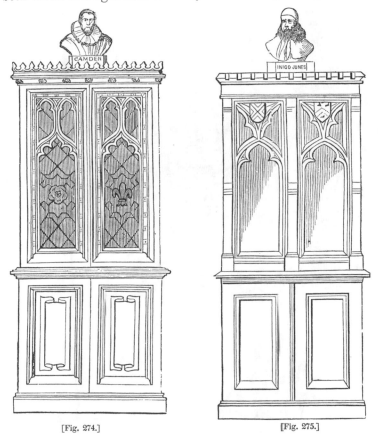

[Fig. 274.]   [Fig. 275.]

Figs. 274 and 275 are two very correct and satisfactory
designs, from Loudon's Encyclopædia, for bookcases in a
Gothic villa. When there is a large collection of books to be
provided for, either of these designs may be adopted, and

extended along both sides or all round the library. The spaces below afford excellent closets for pamphlets and manuscripts, and the busts of distinguished men, in different departments of letters, may be so placed along the top as to designate to what particular class of books the space directly below is allotted.

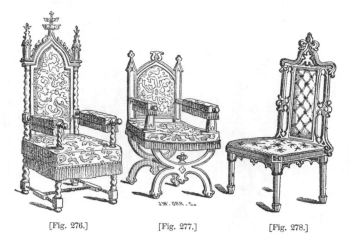

[Fig. 276.]   [Fig. 277.]   [Fig. 278.]

Drawing-room and library chairs in the Gothic style are generally expensive and elaborate, being covered with rich

[Fig. 279.]

stuffs, and highly carved. Fig. 276 is an arm-chair in the English taste, partly Elizabethan and partly Gothic. Fig. 277

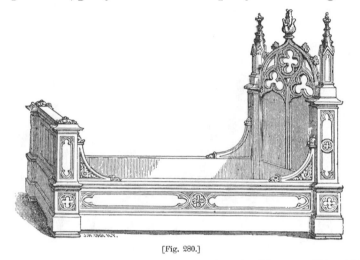

[Fig. 280.]

is a quaint arm-chair, very suitable for the library. Fig. 278 is the most chaste and refined design of the three, and, if made rather smaller than here shown, would be a very suitable drawing-room chair for a villa in this style. The top of Fig. 276 is too elaborate and ecclesiastical in character for most private houses—or, at least, only one or two such chairs, at the most, are all that should ever be introduced there. We much

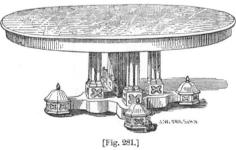

[Fig. 281.]

prefer, when richness is requisite, to get it, in Gothic furniture, by covering rather plain and simple designs with rich stuffs, rather than by the exhibition of elaborate

Gothic carving, the effect of which is usually rather severe and angular, when applied to furniture.

The preceding Fig., 281, is a dining-table (which extends

[Fig. 282.]   [Fig. 283.]

so as to dine 16 persons); Fig. 282 an étagère sideboard; and Fig. 283 a dining-room chair, all in excellent taste. They are copied from furniture in the ware-rooms of Mr. Roux, New York, where they may be seen, admirably made of oak, and, like all furniture, appearing much better in reality than in our representations.

III.—*Furniture in the Elizabethan and Romanesque Styles.*

WE have already explained the characteristic features of these styles in the preceding Section. The basis of the style is Roman and Italian art, but the treatment of details is far more picturesque than in the strictly classical or even the Roman style—sometimes being rather rude, and even grotesque in character, but always quaint, and often, in the more elaborately carved specimens, very rich and magnificent.

It has been for a long time the custom of architects to decry all furniture in this style, as debased and unworthy of the notice of a critic of just taste—and this, simply, because it abounds in caprices, and, in its principal licenses, transgresses the strict rules of classical art.

It is not a little remarkable, however, that notwithstanding this constant tirade of the professors against Elizabethan or Renaissance furniture, it has maintained its popularity, more or less, for nearly three hundred years; and, at the present moment, among lovers of highly characteristic and expressive design, it is still more admired than that in any other taste. Artists have always, even down to this day, and at a time when Louis Quatorze and Grecian furniture is most in vogue, significantly borne testimony to the picturesque beauty of Elizabethan or Flemish furniture, by introducing the antique chair or table, with its twisted legs, quaint carving, and rich fringes, into their pictures.

The *picturesque* charm of this kind of furniture being conceded, to what, then, is it owing? We think, to the *domestic feeling* which pervades it. We have already (page 346) given our reasons for the peculiarly domestic expression of the twisted column, which, modified, is a largely used feature of Elizabethan furniture; and we may here add, that in the quaint forms of Elizabethan furniture, there is a certain rustic freedom of design and quaint manner of execution, which seem to us admirably adapted to country houses in certain styles. It has a homely strength and sober richness—like the traits of a rude yet fine nature but moderately subdued, as compared with the measured and chaste development of the more regularly classical features of the opposite style. Let us add to this the dark, mellow tone of the wood, the rich stuffs, brocades, velvets, fringes, etc., with which the furniture is covered, and we have additional reasons for the good effect it produces when tastefully introduced. But, above all, it is undeniable that, to the present age, the charm of this antique furniture is in its *romance*—in its long association with times, events, and names that have an historical interest, and that move our feelings deeply by means of such powerful associations.

Economically considered, Elizabethan furniture has hitherto been more expensive than any other—from the boldness and variety of the carving it exhibits. But it is likely soon to be greatly lowered in price by an ingenious mode of carving by machinery, lately introduced on both sides of the Atlantic.

We may here remark, that the French are by far the most successful in their manufacture of this furniture, styled in France, *Renaissance*. Their designs preserve the quaintness of the antique, united with modern comfort and luxury—while many of the English and Flemish designs are quaint and grotesque, but are of much less value, except as specimens of the unluxurious habits of a past age. The antiquarian may often obtain, in foreign cities, genuine old specimens of furniture in this style, of great richness and beauty, and at very moderate cost; and there are many fine specimens of Elizabethan chairs, tables, etc., brought out by the Puritans from England and Flanders to this country, still to be seen in fine preservation, adorning the houses of their descendants in Boston and other parts of New England.

The best specimens of Elizabethan and Renaissance furniture to be seen for sale in this country, are at the warehouses of Roux, in New York, and Paul, in Boston.

We may here repeat what we said in the preceding chapter, that Elizabethan furniture is very generally employed in certain rooms of houses in the Gothic style—and though not strictly in keeping with that style, yet its intrinsic picturesqueness and constant use in this way, in the finest Gothic mansions abroad, have given it a kind of right there which it has not intrinsically, by its origin. It is so much richer and more domestic than strictly Gothic furniture, that it will always be preferred to the latter by most persons.

For residences like Design XXXII., Design XXI., and even for Design XXXIII., Elizabethan furniture would be especially well suited; and for certain rooms, as the library, in Design XXIX., it would be equally well adapted.

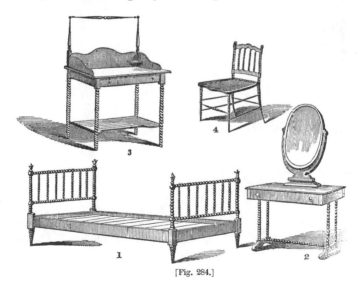

[Fig. 284.]

Elizabethan furniture is too expensive for cottages, but a very simple and cheap modification of it—which is of Swiss origin—has now become common in the cabinet-shops, is afforded at very low prices, and is particularly well suited to cheap cottages and farm-houses in the *Bracketed* style. We allude to sets like Fig. 268, page 443, and the one shown in Fig. 284. This, one of Hennessey's cheapest cottage sets, is very suitable for the bed-rooms of the simple bracketed cottage, as Fig. 268 is for a cottage more expensively finished.*

Chairs, tables, and all kinds of furniture, may be had in the same cheap style for bracketed country houses. Fig. 285 is a shaving-stand for a gentleman's dressing-room—equally simple, but the legs turned in a more strictly Elizabethan style.

A very useful tea or side-table, which folds down so as to occupy very little room when not in use, is shown in Fig. 286. This is now common in the cabinet-shops, and

[Fig. 286.]

[Fig. 285.]   may be had with twisted legs, or turned in the cheaper knotted manner shown in Fig. 284.

Fig. 287 is an easy-chair, or lounge, better adapted for the siesta, than to promote the grace or dignity of the figure.

Antique forms of Flemish or Elizabethan chairs are shown

---

* The price of this set, at the ware-room in Brattle street, is $36—made of black-walnut, maple, or birch. It consists of 4 pieces, viz. No. 1, a bedstead; 2, dressing-table with oval glass; 3, wash-stand with towel-rack on the back; and 4, set of bed-room chairs.

in Figs. 288, 289, 290. Such chairs are seldom manufactured
for sale now, but as they are comparatively simple, especially
Figs. 288 and 290 (which might be made by any ingenious

[Fig. 287.] [Fig. 288.]

country cabinet-maker familiar with the use of the turning-
lathe), we give them, as affording hints for suitable chairs for
the sitting-rooms of substantial farm-houses. There is a

[Fig. 289.] [Fig. 290.]

strong, honest, rustic character about Figs. 288 and 290, that
would render them well adapted for each side of the fireplace
of a first-rate farm-house. The chairs should be of oak or
black-walnut—if possible, the growth of the farm—and the

seats stuffed with hair and covered with leather or strong worsted-work.

Elizabethan chairs of modern designs, suited to the library

[Fig. 291.]   [Fig. 292.]   [Fig. 293.]

or drawing-room, are shown in Figs. 291, 292, and 293. The seats are covered with velvet or other rich stuffs, and bordered

[Fig. 294.]   [Fig. 295.]   [Fig. 296.]

with fringe. Chairs in this style, but of a great variety of designs and highly elaborate carving, may now be found in the principal warehouses in our largest cities.

Three *drawing-room chairs* in this style, with high backs, are shown in the succeeding figures. They are usually made of rosewood or ebony, sometimes relieved by gilding.

A *tête-à-tête*, or conversation chair, is shown in Fig. 297. It holds but two persons, who are so seated, however, as, though side by side, to face each other in conversation. A chair of this kind is an agreeable piece of library furniture in the winter evening, placed between the table on which the lamp stands and the fire—as the wife

[Fig. 297.]

can sit towards the light, sewing, while her husband sits towards the fire with his book to the light, in the best position for reading.

The *flower-stand*, or *jardinière*, is made in a great many

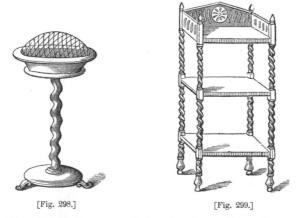

[Fig. 298.]   [Fig. 299.]

forms, Fig. 298 being one of the simplest. Into the top of the stand is fitted a tin or Japanned tray, containing wet sand, and the flowers are arranged upon the wire trellis-work above it.

A *what-not*, or *étagère*, in this style, suitable for the corner of a cottage parlor, is shown in Fig. 299. It is a very useful repository for books and other little articles.

[Fig. 300.]

Fig. 300 is a large and handsome *étagère*, of French design, suitable for the drawing-room of a villa. In the centre is a handsome mirror, on either side of which are shelves for articles of *virtu*—bouquets of flowers, scientific curiosities, or whatever else of this kind the owner may indulge his taste in.

An *Elizabethan sideboard*, of beautiful form and proportions, copied from one designed and executed by Platt, of New York, is shown in Fig. 301. This is in the best Renaissance taste, and, while it has none of the defects of the ruder and more mixed Flemish designs, it has more elegance and more domestic beauty than any design in a strictly classical or Gothic style.

[Fig. 301.]

The fine group of Elizabethan furniture, Fig. 302, showing a richly-carved bookcase, sofa, and table, executed in dark oak, is taken from the library at Wodenethe, the residence of our neighbor, H. W. Sargent, Esq. The whole furniture of this library is in the same style, and the effect is very rich and striking.

The handsome bedstead, with canopy, Fig. 303, is from Wood's designs, and is a successful combination of the antique beauty of the Elizabethan, with strictly modern requirements as regards comfort and elegance.

[Fig. 302.]

[Fig. 303.]   [Fig. 304.]

[Fig. 305.]   [Fig. 306.]

Fig. 304 is a toilet-table in this style. To show how chaste and beautiful even this style becomes when treated by artists of taste, we give the three accompanying designs, which are excellent specimens of the modern Renaissance school of design. The first (Fig. 305) is a dressing-table, the second (Fig. 306) a wardrobe, and the third (Fig. 307) a bedstead.

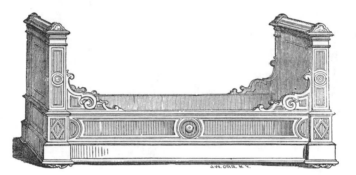

[Fig. 307.]

These would be highly characteristic and appropriate for the guest chambers of such a house as Design XXXIII., as they are essentially Romanesque in their whole composition.

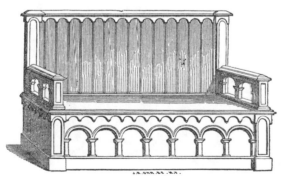

[Fig. 308.]

Furniture for a hall, in a strictly Romanesque or Norman style (like Designs XXI. and XXXIII.), is shown in Fig. 308 and Fig. 309. Further ideas of drawing-room furniture, in this style, may be gathered from a glance at Fig. 182; we may remark, however, that as most of the furniture designed in this antique Romanesque or Norman manner is too clumsy and heavy for modern use, it should be confined to the entrance-hall and passages of residences in this style, and the more domestic furniture of the Elizabethan or Renaissance taste used for the drawing-rooms or parlors.

[Fig. 309.]

SECTION XIII.

WARMING AND VENTILATING.

THERE is no subject directly connected with domestic life on which there is so large an amount of popular ignorance as ventilation. When a man is hungry, nature compels him to cry out for food and drink; and as necessity makes such the most immediate and pressing of all wants, he undertakes to supply them before all others. Yet, men have been known to live without food for five weeks, though any person wholly deprived of air will die in three minutes.

The want of attention to ventilation arises from the fact that the poison of breathing bad air is a slow one, and though its effects are as certain as those which follow from taking doses of prussic acid, yet they are only observed remotely, and little by little. Nature does not immediately protest against slightly impure air as against want of food and water, and, therefore, we go on from day to day, suffering the accumulated evils resulting from our ignorance, and only wondering at our want of physical health and spirits.

Let us glance very briefly at the process of respiration and its results.

A healthy man takes in about a pint of air (40 cubic inches) at every breath or inspiration. As the amount of respirations in an hour is 1080, it follows that *every twenty-four hours he takes into the lungs fifty-seven hogsheads of air.*

What is the use of this enormous amount of fresh air, which he must, sleeping or waking, continually have, to sustain life?

The answer is very simple—to vitalize and purify the blood. The human lungs are the apparatus by which this process is effected, and the atmospheric air the agent that performs the work. In each of our two lungs there are one hundred and seventy millions of air-cells, and every time breath is drawn in, the air passes down and fills these little air-cells. On the other hand, the blood is always going and returning to and from these air-cells which compose the lungs; and in the short space of time that it remains there—only a moment—it is entirely changed in its appearance and character. That is, it comes into these air-cells of the lungs, impure and of a *purple* color, from the veins, and after having been submitted to the action of the air, goes out of the lungs red, pure, and bright, through the arteries. The arteries immediately distribute again, to all parts of the system, the purified blood, which, as it goes through the system, imparts warmth, strength, and life; and by the time it is poured into the veins, on its return course, it becomes quite dark and impure again. And this process, continually repeated, is what is called the circulation of the blood. "When the web of a frog's foot is placed under the microscope, the blood can be seen going from the artery into the veins, changing its color, and becoming impure, just as it does when it goes through the arms, legs, head, and body of a man. When it has become bad, it goes to the lungs to be made pure and bright red again: for this reason the lungs ought to be in a very good state, as they have important work to do; and if they cannot do their work well, bad health must follow."

After this concise explanation of the use of the lungs, and the vital necessity of air, we must add that the air is not a simple but a compound gas. It is made up of oxygen or vital air; and nitrogen, a gas which will not support life. It is the oxygen which vitalizes the blood and removes all its impurities by contact with it in the lungs. The use of the nitrogen is mainly to dilute it; as, if oxygen alone were breathed, the vital force would be so much accelerated that the system would speedily give way, and death would soon follow.

The substance which makes the blood dark and impure, and which it is the business of the oxygen to remove, is *carbon*, known in a more familiar form as charcoal. The process of breathing or respiration is then nothing more, in simple language, than exposing this carbon to the oxygen and *burning* it, as we burn charcoal in a furnace; and Professor Liebig has estimated that in the process of respiration, carbon, equivalent to 14 ounces of charcoal, is burned within a man daily, which is the source of animal life. Now, it must be remembered that when we burn charcoal, the gas thrown off in its combustion is carbonic acid gas, a very deleterious one; and this is precisely the gas which, produced in a like manner, is thrown off from the lungs.

The atmosphere which we breathe is healthy, then, because it is composed of oxygen, or vital air, diluted with a sufficiency of nitrogen, or unwholesome air, to render it salutary. But as the oxygen, after having been through the lungs, has been taken up and combined with the carbon of the blood, what remains must be nitrogen and carbonic acid gas. And such, actually, is the air thrown off continually from the lungs—a mixture of two unwholesome and poisonous gases.*

---

* "The fresh air, before it is taken into the lungs, is composed of 23·2 per cent. of

We are quite unconscious of the presence of this bad air, because it is *invisible* to the eye—though the oppression at the lungs, in crowded or close rooms, should warn us plainly that we are transgressing a law of health. But a very simple experiment will convince any one of the difference between wholesome atmospheric air, and the impure gas that is expired from the lungs. To prove that air which has once been breathed is bad, take two bottles and fill them with clear lime-water. With a straw or tube, blow into one of these bottles, so that the air from the lungs may pass through it. After continuing the experiment a few minutes, the lime-water will become quite white and milky, showing the action of the impure gas. Now, take a pair of bellows and blow common pure air through the same water in the other bottle, and it will be found that it is not in the least changed by it, but will remain quite clear.

It has been well remarked, that if the air as it comes from the lungs, impure, and robbed of its vital principle, were thrown off colored, so that it would not mix with the common air of a room, but remain visible to the eye, the impression which would be made upon the mind, by the presence of the large

---

oxygen, 75·5 of nitrogen, and about 1½ per cent. of carbonic acid, and a variable quantity of vapor of water. After it has been expired from the lungs, in which it remains from 10 to 12 seconds, it contains a larger quantity of vapor, the same quantity of nitrogen, from 11 to 12 per cent. only of oxygen, and between 8 and 9 per cent. of carbonic acid; so that nearly one-half of the oxygen or vital element of the air has been changed into carbonic acid. If atmospheric air contains 3·5 per cent. only of this latter gas, it is unfit to support animal life. Air, therefore, which has been expired from the lungs contains 2·4 times this quantity; so that a person who inhales 600 cubic inches a minute, renders 1440 cubic inches unfit to be breathed again."—*Bernan*.

source of disease, would be so strong that the first of all invariably acknowledged duties for the preservation of health, not excepting cleanliness, would be ventilation. The sickly aspect of children confined to the nursery, or to the close air of towns and cities, as compared with those who have the free range of country air, is, perhaps, the most familiar illustration of the effect of want of fresh air, and it is only the more apparent in their cases because they are more delicate thermometers to measure the effect by than older persons—not that the latter are less injured by it, but that they show it less. We are forced also to attribute the general want of health of women in America, and the paleness, delicacy, and want of color and bloom upon the cheek after the first few years of youth are past, to their voluntary in-door life, and sedentary habits, in rooms always close, and always badly ventilated, for at least five months of the year.

Having pointed out the ignorance regarding a supply of fresh air in our living-rooms, and the necessity of providing for it, let us investigate the simplest and best modes of producing a sufficient supply of fresh air at all times.

In order to ventilate a room, there must be something to cause a movement in the air within it. The simplest and most common means of effecting this is by means of the chimney with an open fireplace. Every one is familiar with that law in nature which causes heated air to rise. Now, when a fire is made in an open fireplace, a column of air of the size of the chimney-flue is continually carried upwards, taking just that amount, continually, from the air of the room. To supply the vacancy thus made, the fresh air, of course, is constantly coming in through crevices of windows and door, by which means, in the case of a large fireplace for burning wood, **a** pretty effectual supply of fresh air is maintained. When the opening is made much smaller, for grates, and the windows tighter, as in most modern houses, the ventilation is far less perfect; and when close stoves are used, and the chimney-flue closed up, there is almost no ventilation at all. This explains one reason for the undeniable fact that the inmates of houses in forest countries where the houses are not very well built, and wood fires are made in large open fireplaces, are so much more healthy than the inmates of modern-built houses—especially as regards consumption, and all those diseases that grow out of derangement of the respiratory organs.

Let us look for a moment at a room in a modern house, Fig.

310, warmed in winter by a common grate. The only means of escape for the bad air thrown off from the lungs in this room is through the throat of the grate *a*; the principal means of entrance for fresh air through the

[Fig. 310. Room without ventilation.]

crevices of the window *b*. Now it will be remembered that, as the impure air expired from the lungs is of considerably higher temperature than the air of the room, it will naturally rise to the ceiling. The upper part of the room, therefore, after persons have been breathing it for a few hours, will be mainly filled by bad air—while the imperfect ventilation is chiefly confined to the lower part—say bounded by a line from the top of the window to the grate. Hence, the heads of persons in such a room as this, in a winter's day, are almost always in a stratum of bad air.

Take the case of a room like this warmed by a close stove, and it is vastly worse. There is now no escape of impure air up the chimney, because the fireplace is closed up; and modern stoves being constructed as nearly as possible on the air-tight principle, take up scarcely air enough to cause any appreciable influx of fresh air to supply the vacuum. Consequently, the persons in such a room are mostly in a kind of poisonous air-bath, where they are continually breathing, over and over again, the impure air thrown out from the lungs, from which the vital principle has already been abstracted, and which is, therefore, as certain, sooner or later, to affect the health of those breathing it, as an anodyne is to produce sleep; and, finally, to bring about confirmed ill-health, paleness, and often consumption.

The simplest and readiest mode of ventilating a room is that of introducing a *chimney-valve*, or register, in the flue, near the

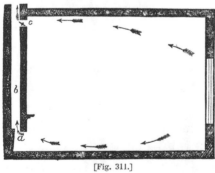

[Fig. 311.]

ceiling. In the accompanying diagram of a room, *a* is the fireplace, *b* the flue, *c* the chimney-valve. Now the impure air, rising as it does to the upper part of the room, would have a tendency to pass off slowly through any opening near the ceiling. But whenever there is a fire in the flue, as is usually the case in winter, when ventilation is most needed, a strong *upward* current is created in the flue by the rising of the heated air of the fire, and the bad **air** which pours into the chimney-valve is therefore carried off rapidly. It is only necessary to hold a candle to the mouth of the valve, and observe how the flame is immediately drawn **in,** to become fully aware of the action of the valve.

A chimney *register* is also manufactured for this purpose, which is inserted into the flue, and acts in the same manner as the valve, and may be opened and shut at pleasure. This answers very well in most cases; but in some chimneys it does not, like a chimney-valve, always prevent the escape of the smoke into the room.

Dr. ARNOTT, of London, well known both for his science and philanthropy, has invented a chimney-valve for this purpose, which bears his name, and which is admirably adapted for ventilating rooms, where only a moderate supply of fresh air is necessary.

Arnott's chimney-valve is a very simple box of cast-iron, with an iron valve, so simply and nicely contrived that it remains open while there is the slightest pressure of impure air from within, but closes against any passage of smoke from the chimney into the room. By a neat thumb-screw, the valve may be adjusted to suit the draught in any chimney, or to remain

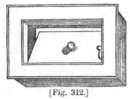

[Fig. 312.]

more or less open. Fig. 312 shows the general appearance of the exterior. It is made of cast-iron, and the front, which is even with the wall, may be painted or whitewashed of the same color as the wall, so as to be inconspicuous. It is easily built into the chimney-breast when the dwelling is erected; or put up by any bricklayer, in half an hour, in a house already built. Two or three biicks are cut out to make a hole in the flue, and the chimney-valve put in with a little mortar to make it tight; and as the face or outside border is wider than the iron box or body of the valve, the latter can be set without visibly breaking or defacing even the hard-finished wall of a parlor. The valve is usually inserted on the *side* of the chimney-breast, near the ceiling; but it may, if necessary, be put in front, with a corner door, and concealed by a picture or engraving hanging *forward*, so as not to stop the current of air.*

The sanitary effect of Arnott's chimney-valve has been well tested in England. Not only have thousands been benefited by having the air rendered pure and elastic, giving a fresh and healthful sensation to the lungs in rooms of private dwellings previously close and oppressive, but also in several hospitals and other public institutions crowded with sick patients. The mortality has been surprisingly lessened by the mere introduction of this valve, thus carrying off the bad air which, but too often, loads the wards and stories of such buildings, and puts an end to the lives of many who, in a pure atmosphere, would speedily recover health.

To make the ventilation of a room perfect, there should be some means provided for the *ingress of fresh air* from without, as well as for carrying off the bad air from within. This is especially necessary if the house is new and well built—for, in many old houses, the windows are loose enough to permit a

---

* We sent out to London for one of these valves when first brought into notice and have been so satisfied with its great value that we have induced Chilson, Allen, Walker & Co. to keep a supply constantly on hand at their warming and ventilating warehouses in New York and Boston.

considerable supply of fresh air to come in to supply the vacuum caused by the outward passage of the bad air through the chimney-valve. But the room is more comfortable if the air is not forced to enter in this way; and, instead, some provision is made for introducing it otherwise. The most perfect way of doing this is to form a hollow space in the chimney-breast behind the bricks or lining of the grate or fireplace. This hollow space should communicate with the room by a register, or plain slide, about equal, in the opening, to the chimney-valve above, and with the open air by a pipe or box leading under the floor to the outer wall, or some place where there is a supply of fresh and pure air. In a room arranged in this way,

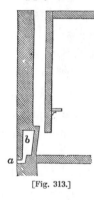

[Fig. 313.]

the fresh air would enter from the outside— Fig. 313, *a*—become slightly warmed in the brick air-chamber, at the side or back of the fireplace, *b*, and pass into the room through the opening at the side. On the other hand, the air, rendered impure by respiration, the exhalations from the skin, etc., would rise and pass out of the chimney-valve at the top. It would be best for the circulation, in this arrangement, to have the opening for the admission of fresh air, and the valve for the escape of bad air, on opposite sides of the chimney-breast, instead of on the same side.

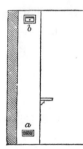

[Fig. 314.]

Fig. 314 shows the outside of the same chimney-breast, of which Fig. 313 is a section. In this, *a* is the register, admitting the fresh warm air, *b* the chimney-valve for carrying off the impure air.

Unquestionably, the introduction of Arnott's chimney-valve will greatly lessen the unwholesomeness of rooms heated by close stoves, since it will carry off a good deal of bad air; though not all, because unless the cracks and crevices of the room are very open there cannot be a perfect and continual circulation. The only stove, therefore, really fit for the living-room of an intelligent family—(we mean intelligent respecting the poison of bad air)—is one which provides for the ingress of a current of fresh air, combined with a genial warmth. Any thing like a heating surface of iron, liable to become red-hot, which destroys the vital air rapidly, should be shunned like a pestilence, and a fire-brick lining, therefore, demanded as an absolute necessity.*

---

* Perhaps the best close coal-stove yet invented, is Clark's Patent Ventilating Stove, now adopted in most of the common schools about Boston. This stove is composed of two cylinders: the inner one lined with fire-brick, in which the fire is made; and the outer one of sheet-iron, with a perforated top, and a regulator upon it, rising and falling at pleasure The lower part of the outer chamber stands over an air-box or pipe, connected directly with the open air, while the upper part admits the air into the room through the perforated openings. In this way the space between the two cylinders becomes an air-chamber, drawing a constant supply of fresh, cold air from out of doors, and distributing it in a genial current in the room. Fig. 315, *a*, shows the interior chamber with upward current of warm air; and

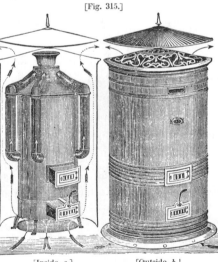

[Fig. 315.]

[Inside, *a*.]   [Outside, *b*.]

The open fireplace is the most agreeable and healthful mode
of warming an apartment, and next to this, the grate with air-
chamber behind or along side of it, to admit a warm supply of
pure air. Whoever can afford these means of warming and
ventilating an apartment (in connection with the chimney-valve)
should never be persuaded to introduce a stove, of any kind,
into his room. Next to this we rank the open chimney-grate;
and nearly as good, and more economical, is the *stove-grate*,
with air-chamber within it, connected with the open air by a
pipe, and with the room by small openings near the top.

These are made in several forms, but Fig. 316
will give a good idea of the general appearance. Connected with Arnott's chimney-valve,
such a stove-grate will warm a room nearly as
pleasantly as an open fire.

[Fig. 316.]

It should be remembered, in adopting any
grates or stoves of this kind, that their efficacy in ventilating a
room depends mainly on the introduction at the same time of a
chimney-valve, register, or other opening, at the top of the room,
in order to carry off a stream of bad air, and to afford a space
for the entrance of an equivalent stream of pure, warm air.
For a room full of air may be likened to a bottle or jar full of
water: you cannot pour more fresh water in unless you provide
also an escape, somewhere, for a part of that which already

Fig. 315, *b*, the outside of the stove with the regulator open. For a hall or passage,
this stove is nearly perfect. It may be had at Chilson's, in New York and Boston.

We know that there are few "notions" of which our people are fonder than
stoves—of all descriptions—but we protest against them boldly and unceasingly.
Close stoves are not agreeable, for they imprison all the cheerfulness of the fireside;
and they are not economical, for though they save fuel they make large doctor's bills

occupies it. And with such an arrangement as we have here suggested, viz. the fresh air brought in warm at the bottom of the room through the fireplace, grate, or stove, and the bad air carried off at the top of the room through a chimney-valve, an insensible but complete ventilation is kept up, in any room of moderate size, without any trouble, and which will secure the constant purity and salubrity of the air to be breathed. Lamentable indeed must be the perverseness of those cognizant of these facts, who will still neglect so simple and cheap a means of securing a constant supply of fresh and wholesome air for the lungs.

EMERSON'S VENTILATORS. The simple means of ventilation already described, by means of the chimney and fireplace is, of course, one calculated to be used solely in connection with chimney-flues, and at seasons of the year when fires are needed. It is true, for the most part, that it is at such seasons that ventilation is most important, because in the United States, for the rest of the year, the 'Venetian blind, with the open window, is the active ventilator of most of our apartments. A difficulty, however, is often experienced in upper rooms in summer, in keeping them sufficiently cool.

This, however, is largely obviated by the use of Emerson's ventilator, which we have already explained in page 191.

The operation of this ventilator depends neither upon fires nor the chimney-flues, but solely upon the action of currents of air on the *ejector* upon the top of the roof. It consequently ventilates by exhausting the bad air at all times, and its action is increased by the difference in the temperature of the air without and within the house. Hence, it ventilates equally well in summer and winter, and helps to cool an apartment ın a warm part of the house in July, as well as to maintain a pure atmosphere in December.

With Emerson's ventilators, an air-duct is carried from any room or closet in the house (which is to be ventilated) to the attic, where it empties itself into one or more ejectors placed on the roof. These air-ducts are square trunks, or boxes, con-cealed in the walls of the room, and opening into it by two apertures or valves, one near the ceiling of the apartment, and the other near the floor. These openings (about 6 by 12 inches) are closed or opened at pleasure by small swivel-blinds connected with cords and tassels. These blinds are small and ornamental; they may be placed in the least conspicuous part of the room, in the corner, or by the side of the chimney-breast, and painted like the wall, or architecturally deco-rated.

By opening the lower valve of the air-duct in a room, the lower stratum of air may be carried off slowly; by opening the valve at the top, the upper current will ascend more quickly, thus affording means of changing the air, more or less rapidly, at will. (See Fig. 318, succeeding page, where G is the ejector on the top of the roof, connected with the air-ducts below, D the blind or valve in the upper part of the room, and E the same in the lower part of the room.)

If only two or three apartments are to be ventilated, it may be sufficiently well done by the means we have already pointea out, viz. a supply of warm air through an air-chamber at the back of the grate or fireplace. But in most cases, when this apparatus is introduced, it is with a view to warming and ventilating the whole house, or a large part of it. It is, there-fore, generally used in connection with some means of warming the house by a single heating apparatus placed in the cellar or basement. The best mode of doing this, yet known, is either by a furnace or by hot water.

Heating by a hot-air furnace.—Hot-air furnaces offer a very complete means of warming a house of any size—since, by means of hot-air pipes and registers, one fire, in the lowest part of a house, may be made to warm a large column of heated air, which, with its natural tendency to rise, may be distributed to every room in the house.

But most of the hot-air furnaces hitherto used are open to the strongest objections, on account of their unwholesomeness. They are so constructed as to heat the air by means of a surface of heated iron, raised to a very high temperature—often quite red-hot. Dr. Ure has correctly remarked that as " cast-iron contains, besides the metal itself, more or less carbon, sulphur, phosphorus, and even arsenic, it is possible that the smell of air passed over it in an incandescent state, may be owing to some of these imperfections; for a quantity of noxious effluvia, inappreciably small, is capable of affecting not only the olfactory nerves, but the pulmonary organs."*

Let us suppose a house heated by one of these red-hot furnaces, on a cold winter's day, and, as is usually the case, a great quantity of deleterious hot air constantly pouring into the rooms, and no means of ventilation provided for its escape. It is easy to see that only good constitutions can withstand, even for a time, the injurious effects of the atmosphere of such a house.

---

* Many persons suppose that the objections to a furnace may be wholly obviated by evaporating water in the air-chamber. But though this lessens the dryness of the air it is a great mistake to suppose that it restores its purity.

Hot, stifling, and close, its atmosphere produces languor, debility, headache, and, sooner or later, pulmonary diseases.

No furnace is fit for warming a dwelling-house which delivers the air warmer than 120°—because air may be heated to that temperature by passing over iron, without in the least impairing its salubrity; while, if raised to 150° or 180°, as is frequently the case, it is sure to become gaseous and impure. Now a furnace, to perform its work properly, and deliver *warm* air instead of hot air, must be so constructed that, in the first place, the fire is burned in a grate lined or surrounded by fire-brick; and, in the second place, that the iron-heater is so far above the fire that it can never become red-hot, or in other words, raised to so high a temperature as to vitiate the air.* Besides this, an air-chamber of large size, connected with the open air by an air-duct or passage of twice the usual dimensions, should be provided, in order that such a volume of fresh air is constantly introduced that it can never become raised to a high temperature before it passes into the room above.

The best hot-air furnace yet invented in this country, so far as our knowledge extends, is one invented by Mr. Chilson, of Boston. We have carefully examined several of the best patents, and found them all objectionable, from heating the air too hot, while this (which we have satisfactorily proved in our own residence) will deliver a large supply of warm air, heated

---

* Some of the modern furnaces are constructed in direct violation of this principle—with the heater extending *horizontally*—exposing a part of the iron directly over and very near the fire, as if contrived purposely to make that part red-hot. It is clear that the higher above the furnace the heater is, the less it will become heated

to that temperature which warms the rooms agreeably, without deteriorating it in quality.

Chilson's furnace has the following merits :—First, the grate, or fireplace, is lined with fire-brick, so that the sides can never be made red-hot: second, the heater, or iron-surface which warms the air, is placed high *above* the fire, and the surface which takes the heat is so extended (by causing the draught to pass through a series of pipes before going into the chimney) that no part of it becomes violently heated. Third, from the arrangement of the grate, a very small quantity of coals may be burned in it, rendering it economical.

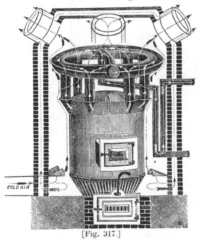

[Fig. 317.]

Fig. 317 shows a section of Chilson's furnace, but the air-chamber formed by the brick-wall which surrounds it, is represented much smaller than it is usually built—about 8 feet square being required for a furnace of moderate size. Cold air is represented as entering on the side—though it is frequently brought in beneath the furnace, and, passing round and over the furnace, goes out in the direction of the *black arrows* through warm-air pipes leading to the different rooms of the house. The draught of the furnace itself, on the other hand, is shown by the course of the *white arrows* rising from the fire, passing through the various arms of the heater, and, finally, moving off through the smoke-pipe into the chimney.

After a trial of this furnace for five months, we can safely commend it as remarkable for the purity, freshness, and mild-ness of the warm air it delivers, as compared with half a dozen other kinds now in repute, and as capable, in connection with suitable means of ventilation (*i. e.* provision for the escape of the air from the rooms, after it has been breathed), of perfectly warming an entire house or building of any kind, in a whole-some and agreeable manner.*

Heating by hot water. This is the most healthful and perfect mode of heating buildings yet invented; but, as it is an expen-sive mode, costing about five times as much as heating by hot air, it has, as yet, been confined to town houses of the first class, in our cities. There are several modes of heating by hot water, but that to which preference is as yet universally given, in New York and Boston, is very simple. In a spacious air-chamber, in the lower story or cellar, is arranged a large coil of pipes connected with a boiler in a separate furnace. These pipes heat the first air which flows into the air-chamber from the outside of the house, and which, after being heated, is distributed through the house exactly as in the case of the hot-air furnace.

---

* The scarcity of good servants is proverbial in America, and among the instances of the want of judgment we may state that of always overloading the fires (*except* on very cold days!) The most valuable hint, therefore, that we can give any house-keeper having a furnace of any kind is this:—when you provide a winter stock of coal, buy also a few loads of anthracite *coal dust.* Use this as a *moderator* of the furnace, in connection with the damper; that is, when the fire is thoroughly lighted in the furnace, have it completely covered over with a coat of the coal dust. All servants will attend to this, because it saves them trouble, and we find that the coal only burns out half as fast, while the possibility of heating the air too much is almost entirely lessened by its use. In other words, the use of coal dust will **not** only save half the amount of coal but give a much pleasanter temperature.

The superiority of this mode consists in the fact, that the air which comes from a hot-water chamber is always of a mild and gentle heat, since it can never be raised to a high temperature, robbed of moisture, or injured in quality. Consequently, it is never either hot, or loaded with the *flavor* of cast-iron, both of which in many hot-air furnaces so largely destroy and vitiate the air. For this reason we hope to see more attention paid to heating by hot water, so that, if possible, it may be rendered simple and cheap enough to come within the reach of persons in moderate circumstances.*

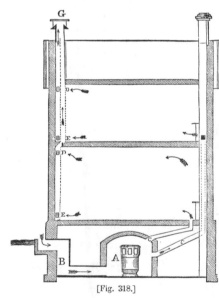

[Fig. 318.]

By connecting Emerson's ventilators and ventiducts with Chilson's air-warming furnace, or the hot-water apparatus we have just described, a house may be warmed and ventilated in a very complete manner, so as to combine health, comfort, and economy in a high degree.

A glance at Fig. 318, the section of a house thus warmed and ventilated, will make the whole plain in a moment. In this figure, A is the air-chamber, with air-warming furnace or water-pipes in the centre. B is the cold-air pipe, leading from the open air to

---

* Perkins's hot-water system, and various other modes, have been tried in this country, but have met with little approbation.

the bottom of the air-chamber, A.   C, C, are air-warming pipes, conveying a constant supply of fresh warm air to every room in the house, or by shutting the register in any room, to all but that room.   On the side of the room opposite where the warm air enters, are two ventiducts, square boxes concealed in the wall or partition, and running up and terminating in the ejector on the roof, G.   These ventiducts have two valves or openings in the room, D and E—the former near the ceiling, and the latter near the floor.   By means of these, the whole air of the room can be equally ventilated, or the lower and upper part separately.   When the temperature of the room is low, and it is desirable to ventilate and yet raise the temperature, the lower valve or blind in the ventiduct is opened.   When the room is warm and it is desirable both to ventilate and cool it, open the upper valve also.*

It is in these particulars—that the warm air is introduced on the side of the room *opposite* to the ventiduct, that there are openings for regulating the temperature as well as the salubrity of the air, and that the process goes on quite independently of the action of the fire in a flue—that Emerson's Ventilator, combined with a proper heating apparatus, is superior to the more simple, though highly useful, fireplace and chimney-valve.   The greater satisfaction of having the whole house warmed and ventilated by one combined apparatus, instead of being at the trouble and exposure of many fires, will undoubtedly bring the system into general use.†

---

* We advise those of our readers interested in this subject to call at the Warming and Ventilating Warehouse of Messrs. Chilson, Allen, Walker & Co., 351 Broadway, New York, where they may see Emerson's and other apparatus in operation.

† We have a great love of the cheerful, open fireplace, with the genial expression

The difference between a house warmed and ventilated in this manner, and one warmed in the ordinary way, is not a trifling one,—whether we consider it in respect to permanent healthfulness, or the mere pleasure of sensation at the moment. The lassitude, the debility, the blanched complexions, which invariably result from the pernicious habit of heating a house by furnaces or stoves, with the fireplaces all closed (as they generally are), and no means of ventilation, would cease, and persons, living in the same houses after the introduction of proper ventilating apparatus, would be surprised at the elasticity, freshness, and purity of the air, always changing, and yet always of an agreeable temperature. There are many persons, who have been at great pains and cost to warm their houses, and after having done every thing " to make the house comfortable," in the way of heating it, find that there is something oppressive and distressing about the very " comfort" they have achieved. This is wholly owing to the want of fresh air, arising from the total neglect of all means of ventilation. If they would but consider for a moment, that the house itself must *breathe*, by means of its current of fresh air coming in, and its current of bad air going out, or *they* cannot breathe easily and

---

of *soul* in its ruddy blaze, and the wealth of home associations that surround its time-honored hearth. All the perfection of the best system of heating and ventilating does not, therefore, banish from our minds the desire for an open fire in the living-room. However perfect the active *mutes*, hot water or hot air, may be in the other apartments, we must have a little of the living soul—the glow of the hearth—there. The perfection of modern comfort, therefore, we consider this : that the whole house be well warmed and ventilated by the apparatus we have described, with the exception of a wood fire in the sitting-room. The genial temperature of the rest of the house will make it necessary only to burn an October fire there ; but that will give a look of life to a house that would seem cheerless without it.

comfortably, the matter would speedily be righted. Many persons in delicate health, who fear to sleep with the windows raised, even in summer, and rest uneasily, therefore, breathing the bad air of the bed-rooms over and over again the whole year round, would find their slumbers far sounder and more refreshing, without the least danger of taking cold by draughts, if the rooms were provided with a chimney-valve, or Emerson's Ventilator. The former may be fixed in any room for a few shillings, and the latter can be made to ventilate the whole house for a less sum than the cost of some piece of furniture, made, perhaps, rather for show than for use.

There is, perhaps, but one objection which can be raised to Emerson's Ventilators; and that is one merely relating to a matter of taste, and not to its utility. We mean the appearance of the ejector, or exhausting cap which is placed on the roof of the house. This is decidedly unarchitectural and stove-pipe like, if in connection with the outlines of a handsome country house, though the best-looking yet invented.

We have, however, conceived a very simple means of overcoming this objection, and submitted it to Mr. Emerson, who has approved of it. It is nothing more than making the ejector or ventilator-top architectural, by placing it in an open cupola, corresponding to the style of the house. In this way, the cupola (of any moderate size, so as not to have the pretentious

look of the cupola of a public building) may be made as significant and characteristic an ornament of a dwelling-house as a chimney-top, for it will soon come to be recognized as the sign of pure air provided for the inmates of the house. Fig. 319 shows the external appear-

[Fig. 319.]

ance of such a ventilator inclosed in a cupola, in the classical style, and Fig. 320, in the Gothic style. The effect of such a feature upon the roof of a house may be seen by turning back to Design XXX., page 329. In many cases, a lantern-

cupola of this kind, may be introduced in such a manner as to add very much to the good effect of the exterior, or aid the architect materially in composing an agreeable outline; since it may be made to balance a stack of chimneys, and restore the symmetry of an otherwise unsymmetrical elevation. In some cases, two ventilator-tops may be required, but all the different air-ducts from the various rooms below may usually be led, in the garret, to one large ejector placed in the open cupola.

[Fig. 320.]

The following extract from Mr. Emerson, in reply to our inquiries, should have a place here:—

"There is no objection to placing an ejecting ventilator in a cupola, as you propose, provided there is sufficient space above and below the cap or opening of the ventilator. The base of

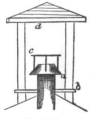

the conic frustum of the ventilator, Fig. 321, a, should be as many inches above the deck, or floor b, of the cupola, as equals *once and a half* the diameter of the tube of the ventilator; and it *must* be placed as high above a, as equals once the diameter of the tube; while the space between the disk or top of the ventilator c, and the ceiling of the cupola d, should not be less than

[Fig. 321.]

twice the diameter of the tube—and no matter how much more.

"I do not mean to be understood, that the ventilator will

operate *quite* as well in a cupola as in the open space; but I mean, that its operation will be satisfactory; its exhausting force on the air-ducts being diminished more or less, in proportion as the wind is more or less obstructed by the pillars that support the canopy.

"In all cases where ventilation is to be carried on through the cupola, there should be but one ejector or ventilator-top, and that placed in the centre of a cupola. If several rooms are to be drawn from, then that one ejector at the top should have its tube partitioned off into several flues, each flue being apportioned to a separate room."

Boston, Feb. 12, 1850.

We will only repeat, in conclusion, that, fond as our people are of improvement, the greatest possible improvement in a dwelling-house—ventilation—is as yet a thing almost unknown in this country; though we predict, that in a few years, the man who warms his room by a close stove, with no ventilator, will be looked upon as little better than he who should more openly undertake to poison his family and friends with a brazier of charcoal.

THE END.